By Sidney Alexander

. .
.

Novels
THE HAND OF MICHELANGELO
MICHELANGELO THE FLORENTINE
THE CELLULOID ASYLUM

.

Poetry
THE MARINE CEMETERY:
Variation on Valéry
TIGHTROPE IN THE DARK
THE MAN ON THE QUEUE

.

Plays
SALEM STORY
THE THIRD GREAT FOOL

.

Translations
THE BERENSON COLLECTION
(*with Frances Alexander*)
THE HOUSE IN MILAN

THE HISTORY

OF ITALY

PORTRAIT OF FRANCESCO GUICCIARDINI

*According to Vasari, this portrait was painted by Giuliano Bugiardini when
". . . messer Francesco Guicciardini . . . was in his villa at Montici writing
his History . . ." This would date the portrait toward the end of 1538 or the
beginning of 1539 when the historian, then in his middle fifties, was beginning
his masterwork, the* incipit *of which indeed may be read on the page.*

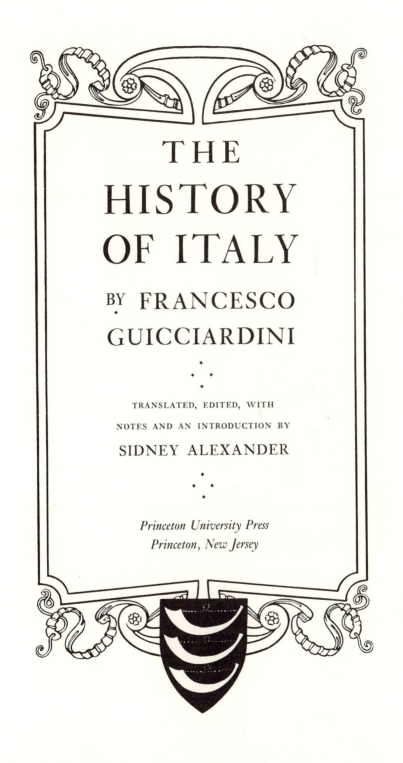

THE
HISTORY
OF ITALY

BY FRANCESCO
GUICCIARDINI

TRANSLATED, EDITED, WITH
NOTES AND AN INTRODUCTION BY
SIDNEY ALEXANDER

Princeton University Press
Princeton, New Jersey

Published by Princeton University Press, 41 William Street,
Princeton, New Jersey 08540

Copyright © 1969 by Sidney Alexander

ALL RIGHTS RESERVED

First Macmillan hardcover edition, 1969
First Collier Books Edition, 1972

First Princeton Paperback printing, 1984
LCC 83-43221
ISBN 05417-7   ISBN 00800-0 pbk.

Printed in the United States of America by Princeton University Press
Princeton, New Jersey

CONTENTS

· **BOOK THIRTEEN** ·
(1517–1520)

· **BOOK FOURTEEN** ·
(1521–1522)

· **BOOK FIFTEEN** ·
(1522–1525)

THE present translation is based on the exhaustive critical edition of the text of the *Storia d'Italia* by Alessandro Gherardi, published in Florence, 1919, in four volumes. Gherardi offers frequent variants on discussable readings of the original manuscripts; I have followed his conclusive interpretation in most cases. In others I have collated Gherardi's reading against the texts of three Cinquecento copies of the *Storia d'Italia* in my possession: the first edition published by Torrentino in Florence, 1561—the famous *editio princeps*; and two Venetian editions: Bonelli, 1562, with marginal notations by Remigio Fiorentino; and Polo, 1599, containing Remigio's life of Francesco Guicciardini, and Thomaso Porcacchi's commentary and collation of the text against other sixteenth-century historians.

Bibliography does not fall within the purview of this book. The critical literature on Guicciardini is enormous, and the reader who does not possess Italian is cut off from some of the best writing in this field. The fundamental archival studies are those of Roberto Ridolfi whose definitive biography has now been translated into English—*The Life of Francesco Guicciardini*, London, 1967. Vittorio de Caprariis, *Francesco Guicciardini dalla politica alla storia*, Bari, 1950, contains a basic bibliography. De Sanctis' celebrated essay, *L'Uomo del Guicciardini*, may be found in *Nuovi Saggi Critici*, Naples, 1879. Readers limited to English may consult: Francesco de Sanctis' chapter on Guicciardini in his *History of Italian Literature*; Vincenzo Luciani, *Francesco Guicciardini and his European Reputation*, New York, 1936; the extracts from Guicciardini's *History of Italy* and *History of Florence*, translated by Cecil Grayson with an introduction by John R. Hale, New York, 1964; and *Maxims and Reflections of a Renaissance Statesman*, translated by Mario Domandi with an introduction by Nicolai Rubenstein, New York, 1965. On the general subject of Renaissance historiography, see: Wallace K. Ferguson,

The Renaissance in Historical Thought, Cambridge, 1948; Federico Chabod, *Machiavelli and the Renaissance*, New York, 1958; Myron P. Gilmore, *The World of Humanism, 1453–1517*, New York, 1952; Felix Gilbert, *Machiavelli and Guicciardini*, Princeton, 1965—all of which contain concise analytical bibliographies.

For assistance in gathering the illustrations and permission to reprint, grateful acknowledgment is made to: the staff of Harvard University Center for Italian Renaissance Studies at the Villa I Tatti; Ulrich Middeldorf, director of the Kunsthistorisches Institut; Fratelli Alinari; Biblioteca Nazionale—all located in Florence; as well as the Gabinetto Nazionale delle Stampe in Rome.

Count Francesco Guicciardini was good enough to allow me to make use of the family archives in which propitious setting, presided over by the shade of his illustrious namesake and ancestor, some of the first drafts of this translation were attempted. Gino Corti provided paleographic wizardry. Dean Frank Piskor kindly made available a Syracuse University faculty research grant to help me complete this work and also provided bibliographical assistance. The late Professor Garrett Mattingly was originally responsible for recommending me to The Macmillan Company as the most likely translator of the *Storia*. Mr. Peter V. Ritner, Editor-in-Chief of The Macmillan Company, encouraged me in gloomy times when I was lost in the Guicciardinian labyrinth, and his keen historical eye saved me from several errors. My wife, as always, participated in this book far beyond the call of conjugal obligation: the original draft was dictated to her; she typed and retyped the numerous revisions of the huge manuscript; she scrutinized every word and made many suggestions that were embodied in the text. Most of all I was sustained by her conviction that a translation of this scope was not a deflection from, but another kind of creative literary labor.

"IF we consider intellectual power [the *Storia d'Italia*] is the most important work that has issued from an Italian mind." The judgment is that of Francesco de Sanctis, surely himself one of the foremost Italian minds. But like a great many classics, Guicciardini's *History of Italy* (published for the first time in 1561, twenty-one years after the author's death) is more honored in the breach than in the observance. Which is a pity, for if not every word need be read, surely a great many of them should be read, not only for the light they cast on a dark time in Italian (and European) history but for the light they cast on the processes of history. For most readers (I do not speak of professional historians) the chief interest here resides not in the details of treaties long since crumbled into dust, or the shed blood of dynasties, but rather in the perennial mystery of human behavior.

Francesco Guicciardini might be called a psychological historian— for him the motive power of the huge clockwork of events may be traced down to the mainspring of individual behavior. Not any individual, be it noted, but those in positions of command: emperors, princes and popes who may be counted on to act always in terms of their self-interest— the famous Guicciardinian *particolare*.

Guicciardini's style is Jamesian, Proustian—that is to say, his basic meanings reside in his qualifications. His mind portrays itself in its *sfumatura*: the conditions, the exceptions, the modifications, the qualifications with which the author weighs every human act and motivation. He had not read, of course, but he was a fellow Florentine of Leonardo da Vinci who wrote (in mirror-writing in his arcane notebooks) that slashing attack on the *abbreviatori*—those impatient abbreviators of anatomy who do not realize that "impatience, mother of folly, praises brevity," and that "certainty is born of the integral cognition of all the parts. . . ."

So Leonardo over his cadavers and messer Francesco over the bleeding body of Italy—there is indeed a similarity in the stance of both men: a distrust of systems, a scorn for theory, a reliance upon experience, a surgical dispassion, a moon over a battlefield. So with lunar indifference the vegetarian da Vinci designs war chariots for the Sforza and serves Cesare Borgia, the enemy of his country. And so Francesco Guicciardini, who favors a republic, is for many years the faithful servant of Medici tyrants. The scientific temperament can lead to schizophrenia: makers of atomic bombs can work for one side or the other. There is the public mask and the private face; what decides is self-interest:

"I know no man who dislikes more than I do the ambition, the avarice, and the lasciviousness of the priesthood: not only because each of these vices is odious in itself, but also because each of them separately, and all of them together, are quite unsuitable in men who make profession of a life dedicated to God. . . . And yet the position I have served under several popes has obliged me to desire their greatness for my own self-interest; and were it not for this, I would have loved Martin Luther as myself. . . ."*

Truth resides therefore in the specific instance, in the *particolare*, in the clash of egotisms as these work themselves out in great events. And yet, his cold surgical eye fixed on this cause, cautious Francesco Guicciardini does not conclude that he has isolated *the* cause. No historian was ever less monomaniacal. Even though he would seem to have tracked the motive power down to its source in individual behavior—more especially individual ambition—ultimately all is mystery, for all rests in the hands of Fortuna. And the lady has aged; she is more implacable than the goddess of Fortune whom Machiavelli felt could still be taken by assault, the lady who yielded at least 50 percent of the time to man's intervention. Guicciardini's Fortuna is more impersonal, distant; no one can ever predict how she will act, whether favorably or unfavorably; the world has become very bleak indeed. Man acts, always in terms of self-interest; he attempts, if he is wise, to weigh all possibilities with reason and a clinical knowledge of human behavior; he will preserve his dignity, his honor (the sole quality which the fickle goddess cannot sully); but what ultimately ensues is beyond all calculation.

. .

* The entire quotation from the *Ricordi,* second series, No. 28, reads:

Io non so a chi dispiaccia più che a me la ambizione, la avarizia e le mollizie de' preti: sì perché ognuno di questi vizi in sé è odioso, sì perché ciascuno e tutti insieme si convengono poco a chi fa professione di vita dependente da Dio; ed ancora perché sono vizi sì contrari che non possono stare insieme se non in un subietto molto strano. Nondimeno el grado che ho avuto con più pontefici, m'ha necessitato a amare per el particulare mio la grandezza loro; e se non fussi questo rispetto, arei amato Martino Luther quanto me medesimo, non per liberarmi dalle legge indotte dalla religione cristiana nel modo che è interpretata ed intesa communemente, ma per vedere ridurre questa caterva di scelerati a' termini debiti, cioè a restare o sanza vizi o sanza autorità.

"If you had seen messer Francesco in the Romagna . . . with his house full of tapestries, silver, servants thronged from the entire province where—since everything was completely referred to him—no one, from the Pope down, recognized anyone as his superior; surrounded by a guard of more than a hundred landsknechts, with halberdiers and other cavalry in attendance . . . never riding out with less than one hundred or one hundred and fifty horse; immersed in governing bodies, titles, 'Most illustrious lords,' you would not have recognized him as your fellow citizen . . . but considering the importance of his affairs, his boundless authority, the very great domain and government under him, his court and his pomp, he would have seemed on a par with any duke rather than lesser princes. . . ."

Thus Francesco Guicciardini depicts himself, to the life, as he appeared and behaved at the time when he was governor of the central Italian province of the Romagna. Like his contemporary and fellow Florentine Niccolò Machiavelli—but on a much more exalted level—he had always been an active participant in the politics he wrote about; and all his writings, like Machiavelli's, are the fruits of enforced idleness. Guicciardini's *History*, his last and greatest work, was the compensation of a man of action removed against his desire from the scene. Like Niccolò after 1512, a brain-truster out of work, messer Francesco after 1537, no longer *persona grata* to the Medici back in power after the siege, retires to his villa in the green hills of Santa Margherita in Montici above his native Florence and commences for the third time to write a history of his epoch.

But now his vision has broadened. He is fifty-five years old; he has seen much, experienced much, been confidant and adviser to three popes; now the great spider must cast his web much wider than in his earlier attempts at writing the traditional humanistic history of his city-state. Now the youthful *Florentine History* must become the *History of Italy* (a title itself never applied by Guicciardini), and since Italy has become the cockpit where Hapsburg Charles V struggles with Valois Francis I, Holy Roman Emperor versus Most Christian King, Guicciardini's *Storia d'Italia* becomes perforce the history of Europe. Since Thucydides no vision had ranged so far. As in a Greek tragedy, after the prologue of Laurentian peace and prosperity, the fates begin to spin out the tragic succession of events from the French invasion of Charles VIII in 1494 to the death of Pope Clement VII in 1534, years dense with dramatic happenings and calamities which seem to confirm Guicciardini's disenchanted convictions.

On the surface he seems to be following the conventions of the chroniclers; patiently telling his story year by year; draping, like any good Renaissance humanist, his actors in togas; imitating—like Biondo, like Machiavelli—the classical historians, especially Livy and Tacitus;

inventing stage speeches uttered by his captains on the eve of every battle; intending to deal exclusively with what was considered the true business of the historian: politics and war.

Intending, I say, for the greatness of the *Storia* is where it deviates from its set models, as a novel is successful only when the characters talk back to their creator and go their own ways against the author's will. Imitation of the ancients is first supplemented and then superseded by meticulous documentation from municipal archives (many of which Guicciardini had simply taken home to his villa from the Palazzo dei Signori); the text is rewritten more than seven times and not for stylistic concerns alone.

And as Guicciardini examines his world, the tumultuous world of the end of the fifteenth and the first three decades of the sixteenth century, his history, almost against the author's will, begins to comprehend far more than mere dynastic politics and wars. The discovery of the new lands misnamed America; the invention of those terrifying weapons called cannon; the first appearance of syphilis; the threat of the Turks and the greater threat of Martin Luther whose Christ-centered theology reduces the Church as Copernicus' heliocentric astronomy had reduced the earth; the history and huckstering of the Swiss, most dreaded mercenary soldiery of Europe; battle pieces full of gallantry and butchery; the incredible corruption of the Borgia and the martyrdom of Savonarola; the origins of Church claims to secular power; a brilliant picture gallery of Renaissance popes; the sack of Rome; the siege of Florence; the amatory complications of Henry VIII—all this and more we find in a richly orchestrated narrative wherein are embedded many of the famous maxims or *Ricordi* which the historian had been secretly writing all his life for his own edification. But now, confined to instances rather than abstracted in the void, how much more resonant are these scathing pessimistic opportunistic observations!

He is the master of the fillip; in the solemn Ciceronian periods of his rhetoric, how his irony flickers: a dragon's tail. "So that as a result of reverence for their way of life, the holy precepts which our religion contains in itself, and the readiness with which mankind follows—either out of ambition (most of the time) or fear—the example of their prince, the name of Christian began to spread marvelously everywhere, and at the same time the poverty of the clerics began to diminish."

Vanity vanity, Guicciardini seems always to be saying; and yet his art offers the comfort of a true discovery, a light placed in focus, a scientific examination carried to its limits. His capacity to reveal the psychology of single personages by relating them to the logic of events is truly extraordinary. His profiles are constructed from within, just as are his plots, crimes, wars, treaties, grave and dramatic moments in Italian history. The master builder always, he never loses command of his grand design.

But with all his fine discriminating political sense, his absence of dogmatism, his openness to the lessons of experience, his extraordinary sensitivity to the play of interests, there is something inhuman about the ice palace of this greatest of Italian historians. The irony is that Guicciardini, who abjures all system building, has fallen victim to a reductive fallacy that equally distorts the range and variety of human behavior. Although (unlike Machiavelli) he believes that man is essentially good, in practice he depicts him as almost invariably bad. Hence his psychological portraiture is all nuance and monochrome. Here are his comments on Piero de' Medici in exile asking advice of the Venetian senate:

"Nothing certainly is more necessary in arduous deliberations, and nothing on the other hand more dangerous, than to ask advice. Nor is there any question that advice is less necessary to wise men than to unwise; and yet wise men derive much more benefit from taking counsel. For, whose judgment is so perfect that he can always evaluate and know everything by himself and always be able to discern the better part of contradictory points of view? But how can he who is asking for counsel be certain that he will be counseled in good faith? For, whoever gives advice (unless he is bound by close fidelity or ties of affection to the one seeking advice) not only is moved largely by self-interest, but also by his own small advantages, and by every slight satisfaction, and often aims his counsel toward that end which turns more to his advantage or is more suitable for his purposes; and since these ends are usually unknown to the person seeking advice, he is not aware, unless he is wise, of the faithlessness of the counsel."

An almost mathematical exposition of ethical relations, an algebra of behavior. Who has ever put it so neatly? But isn't the very precision, almost predictability, of this world without ideals itself an intellectual construction, cleaving to experience and yet remote from it? Throughout the *Storia* such Guicciardinian structures glimmer, subtle spider webs of psychological analysis on the rich green field of sheer storytelling.

. .

Francesco Guicciardini was born in Florence on 6 March 1483, third of a numerous family. The Guicciardinis were among the *ottimati* of the city of the red lily, a patrician line high in city councils and traditionally supporters of the Medici who controlled the government at that time. Even in his youth Guicciardini displayed signs of his boundless ambition (unlike Machiavelli, Guicciardini did not consider ambition a vice provided it was exercised by the right people) and his desire to be first in everything, as a consequence of which his schoolmates dubbed him with the nickname "Alcibiades."

Early dedicated by his father for the law, Francesco probably had a political career always in mind; thus when on the death of his uncle, Archdeacon of Florence and Bishop of Cortona, an ecclesiastical career seemed open, the twenty-one-year-old Guicciardini was disposed to embark upon it for the chance of "achieving greatness in the Church and hopefully becoming a cardinal some day." His father Piero, however, an ardent follower of Savonarola, apparently considered worldly ambition insufficient substitute for a true religious calling, and Guicciardini continued his law studies, at Florence, Prato and later at Ferrara and Padova.

His ambition must have made him a rather solemn young man. In his *Ricordi* he writes that he is proud to be able to say that in his earlier years "there were no corruption, no frivolity of any sort, no waste of time." However he regrets that he never learned to dance and to be a man of the world, not because he regrets lost pleasures but because such social graces are useful to the political man.

After receiving his degree in *ragione civile* from the University of Pisa in 1505, Guicciardini was immediately successful as a lawyer, securing engagements from some of the patrician Florentine houses (with whom his family had connections), from the merchants' guild, the commune of Santa Croce and various monastic orders. Undoubtedly the young advocate already displayed those qualities found in his earliest writings: a cool judicial temperament and analytical skill. In 1508 he married the daughter of Alammano Salviati, one of the leading *ottimati* families; in his *Ricordanze* Guicciardini confesses that he was set upon this marriage even against his father's will, and even though there were available girls of noble houses with greater dowries. Love, even money, took second place to politics: Maria Salviati's father was the head of that minority aristocratic faction to which Francesco adhered.

In October 1511 the Florentine republic elected the young advocate ambassador to Ferdinand the Catholic, King of Spain. It was a great honor to be offered so high a position when he had not yet arrived at the legal age of thirty; and although it meant interrupting a prosperous legal career, Guicciardini after some hesitation took the post. The two years in Spain at the court of the most cunning politician in Europe were Guicciardini's introduction to the world of politics—a world which he could now observe first hand at one of the centers of power. His habit of examining events in their formation, of learning from life rather than from the books of the ancients, must have been set at this time; and if Guicciardini's history soars beyond his city walls to take in all of Europe, this too must have been initiated by his Spanish experience.

While Guicciardini was in Spain, the Florentine republic fell and the Medici came back to power after eighteen years in exile. The already seasoned diplomat immediately proceeded to make himself available to the new regime, and returned to his native city in January 1514. Shrewdly playing the cards of his family, his wife's family, and his new-won prestige, Guicciardini swiftly entered into the good graces of the new ruler of Florence, the young Lorenzo de' Medici, who offered him posts and offices, one of which was to go to Cortona to receive Pope Leo X, Lorenzo's uncle. Already from these first experiences one of Guicciardini's outstanding traits is revealed: his spirit of adjustment to any given political situation, a chameleonic power later condemned as opportunism in de Sanctis' celebrated essay on the "Guicciardinian man" as the curse of Italy.

In 1516 Pope Leo X nominated Guicciardini as governor of Modena and commissary of the district, a post which proved to be the beginning of almost twenty years of continuous activity in the service of the Church. In 1517 his commissariate was extended over Reggio, and from 1521 over Parma. In these difficult posts in a region noted for its unruly population, Guicciardini proved himself a severe but honest administrator, skilled in diplomatic maneuvering, ruthless in dealing with opposition and crime; and when later war broke out in the region, messer Francesco displayed military talents as well, organizing a successful defense of Parma in the winter of 1521 against the French, determinedly adopting a scorched-earth policy in the suburbs despite popular opposition.

His reputation as administrator and military captain was so well established that after Leo's death (1521) the succeeding Pope Adrian VI confirmed Guicciardini's governorships; and after that unhappy Fleming—last of the non-Italian popes—had passed to his reward (to the great rejoicing of the Italians), the new Medici pope, Clement VII, nominated Guicciardini in 1524 as president of the Romagna, with full powers over the entire region, excluding Bologna. Postwar problems of plague, famine and rebellion confronted the new president; and he was on the verge of bringing some order into the region when, in January 1526, Guicciardini was summoned to Rome by Pope Clement, who, already displaying those qualities of indecision and vacillation that were to make his pontificate a tragedy, wanted counsel on the question of whether to ally himself with Francis I or Charles V.

Guicciardini was a Florentine and the Florentines were traditionally pro-French in their policy, if only for the fact that the bulk of their profitable cloth trade had always been in that realm. Perhaps nothing had been so decisive in turning the Florentine merchants against Savonarola as the fact that by darting *banderillas* at the Borgia bull, the Dominican had brought down a papal excommunication against their city, which meant a loss of trade, especially with France, thus pinching Florentines in their most sensitive organ, their purse.

At any rate in this instance, Guicciardini firmly advised the French alliance. Some critics believe Guicciardini saw imperial domination in

Lombardy as a threat to Italian liberty, but if so he was surely not motivated by Machiavellian dreams of a united Italy. Italian liberty, as Guicciardini saw it, was predicated simply on the power of the various Italian city-states to maneuver in the interstices of a subtle and ever-changing balance of power among the great states: France and the Hapsburg Empire. Whatever his reason, Guicciardini took an active part in preparing for the anti-imperial League of Cognac (May 22, 1526); and no sooner were the agreements arrived at than he directed military operations as lieutenant-general of the pontifical armies.

But the campaign of resistance soon collapsed. In November the Paduan plain was invaded by 11,000 landsknechts—the dreaded "Lutheran" mercenaries—and shortly afterward there died Giovanni de' Medici (of the Black Bands), whom Guicciardini esteemed as the only true soldier of the League.

Charles' troops, united with the German hordes of landsknechts, now marched on Rome, and in May 1527 that city was captured by the imperials and suffered the worst sack since Attila the Hun. The horrors of the sack represented not only the most tragic hour for Italy in its time of troubles; it also represented the complete collapse of Francesco Guicciardini's pro-French policy. Pope, Florentines, everyone turned against him, and when he returned to his native city he was made the target of accusations from all sides, and retired as soon as possible to lick his wounds at his villa at Finocchieto in the Mugello, where he remained until 1529.

Several years earlier his friend Machiavelli had examined the villa at Francesco's request and thus described it: "Three miles around one sees nothing pleasing: the Arabian desert is no different." Probably the erstwhile secretary of the Ten—*Nicolaus Machiavellus quondam secretarius in villa*—was remembering his own exile at Sant' Andrea in Percussina after 1512 when the bitter fruit of his *Prince* and *Decades* had been born. Anywhere away from the center of power was the Arabian desert. So now like Machiavelli (whose death in 1527 terminated the political dialogue between passion and patience), Francesco Guicciardini *in villa* sets his hand to a second Florentine history, drawing this time even more elaborately than in his first youthful history from documents in his possession or available to him.

But when the government in Florence fell into the hands of the *Arrabiati*, the extreme anti-Medicean and republican party, Francesco, threatened with arrest, abandoned Tuscany and went to Rimini, then to Bologna where Pope Clement had come for a conference with the Emperor. At Lucca, Guicciardini learned of the decree of the 17th of March 1530, whereby the Florentine republic had declared him a rebel and ordered the confiscation of his property.

When after nine months of heroic resistance under siege, Florence, threatened with starvation, finally capitulated to the combined forces of Pope and Emperor (the recent captive and captor now allies), the anti-Medicean party under Carducci lost power, and Guicciardini could re-enter his native city, sent there by the Pope to prepare a new government. There is considerable debate about the degree of responsibility Guicciardini shares for the cruel punishments—death and exile—that were meted out to the leaders of the ousted *Arrabiati* party. Federigo Chabod believes that Guicciardini sought to salvage a certain amount of democracy and avoid the out-and-out Medicean tyranny demanded by the Medici Pope, and this, therefore, was the cause of an inevitable break between Clement and Guicciardini.

In 1531 he was practically exiled for a second time as pontifical vice-legate to Bologna, where he faced a violently hostile population; the death of Pope Clement (1534) relieved him of this unwanted post, and Guicciardini returned to Florence. His defense of Duke Alessandro de' Medici against the Florentine exiles who had petitioned the Emperor to adjudicate their quarrel with the Medici and his consequent intervention in favor of the election of Duke Cosimo I after Alessandro's assassination by his cousin Lorenzino in 1537 were both motivated by his anti-imperial policy; and both actions earned him the detestation of the popular party. When, however, Cosimo I came to an agreement with Charles, yielding Florence, Pisa, and Livorno to the Emperor, Guicciardini—his counsels ignored by the duke whom he had helped elect—retired to his villa in Santa Margherita in Montici near Arcetri, where from 1537 until his death on the 22nd of May 1540, he labored on his last and major work, the *Storia d'Italia*.

. .
.

Santa Margherita in Montici is surely not the "Arabian desert" of his first retreat. Here, writing his history amidst silvergreen olive groves and the blackpointed exclamations of cypresses, Guicciardini could look down on Brunelleschi's rosy dome and Giotto's chromatic campanile and see the tall grim tower of the Palazzo Signoria where his brother Luigi had been gonfaloniere, and wherein he and so many other Guicciardinis had illustriously served. Close by on the hill of San Miniato, he could also have seen the new earthworks which a fellow citizen, Michelangelo Buonarroti, governor of fortifications, had thrown up during the siege; but he probably would not have known or taken any comfort in the fact that, like himself, the artist had also been subject to a ban as traitor to his country. It is doubtful that Guicciardini was aware of Buonarroti. In a city burgeoning with art, the wellspring of the Renaissance, Francesco Guicciardini seems never to have looked at a picture or hearkened to a lute. He wasn't interested in art; he was interested in power. The more impulsive Machiavelli had also been obsessed with the problem of power and had also seemed disinterested in art; but he wrote political science like a poet, contrived the funniest play of the Renaissance, and complained of Ariosto that he had omitted him from the list of Italian bards. None of this for our Francesco; he had none of the Secretary of the Ten's literary itch; the curial robes he donned were not those of the ancients but of his own day. Although he might follow the lead of the humanists in their imitation of classic models, in a true sense he is not a humanist at all; and surely he is not very humane.

A man difficult to like but equally difficult not to admire. For never under the guise of rhetoric was there a more honest and rigorous and thoroughgoing anti-rhetorician, never did a surgeon look upon the wounded body of his country with more dispassion, with almost frightening phlegm, with the objectivity of absolute zero. Such unrelenting pessimism is not without its nobility, and cynicism is not the right term to be applied to one who held personal honor, incorruptibility in such esteem. But given Guicciardini's personality and his acceptance of the cleavage between private and public morality in the interests of no broader ideal than one's personal self, it is no wonder that the heralds of the more generous Risorgimento, like de Sanctis, while recognizing Guicciardini's undoubted magistral gifts as a historian, could not help but detest him as a man.

It has been said that no one ever saw Francesco Guicciardini smile, but surely there are smiles to spare in the letters to Machiavelli; there is laughter when he speaks in the person of his villa; irony—sometimes ponderous, sometimes whiplash—when he delineates the fall of princes; he is even capable of indignation in his slashing, blood-drawing attacks on the corruption of the clergy and the Church. He wasn't quite the monster of immorality John Addington Symonds saw; the unscientific rhetorician Ranke attacked for uncritically making use of previous histories; the dehumanized political zoologist de Sanctis portrays. The true Guicciardini was not entirely "the Guicciardinian man."

．　．
．

None of Guicciardini's writings were issued during his lifetime. Only in 1561 were the first sixteen books of the *Storia* (out of twenty) published in Florence, and three years later the last four appeared separately in Venice. Many others followed this first edition, all of them, however, based not directly on the manuscripts but on the expurgated Torrentino text of 1561 which had appeared while the Council of Trent, the general staff of the Counter-Reformation, was in full session. Hence, in all these editions certain passages considered injurious to the Roman pontiffs were truncated, especially in Book Four, wherein Guicciardini traces the origin of Church claims to temporal power. Finally in a magnificent edition dated from Freiburg,* Guicciardini's *History* was published in its entirety according to the manuscript conserved in Florence, the final version which had been revised and corrected by the author himself, containing the mutilated passages. The *Ricordi* had various partial editions between 1576 and 1585; his other writings were extracted from the family archives and published in the second half of the nineteenth century.

Within the very sixteenth century that saw its first publication, the *History of Italy* was swiftly translated into French, Latin, Spanish, German, Flemish, as well as the first English "translation" by Geffray Fenton of which I will speak later. According to Roberto Ridolfi, whose brilliant biography and Guicciardini studies have done more than anything else to set the record straight, in the same Cinquecento Italian editions alone, both integral and partial, counted almost one hundred. Obviously poor messer Francesco is another of those not infrequent cases of posthumous literary success.

The English version by Sir Geffray Fenton, an Elizabethan literatus, first published in London in 1579, is most curious. Fenton knew no Italian and his "translation"—considered his major work and greatly successful in his time—was derived not from Guicciardini's original text but from the foreign language Fenton knew—namely French. Fenton based his work on the 1568 French version of Chomedey; what we have therefore is a translation of a translation! As Paolo Guicciardini has pointed out in his *Le Traduzioni Inglesi della Storia Guicciardiniana* (Olschki, Firenze, 1951) Fenton's dependence on the French version is proved by the fact that he maintained in his English text the spellings of proper names used by Chomedey instead of adopting, which would have been more logical, the Italian spellings. Thus we have Petillane for Pitigliano, Triuulce for Trivulzio, Francisquin Cibo for Franceschetto Cibo, Ceruetre for Cerveteri, etc.

Furthermore I have discovered that Fenton indulges throughout his text (which is remarkably faithful considering that it is second hand) in numerous excisions, paraphrases, omissions, ellipses, and revisions, frequently in the interest of courtly bows to the English ruling house. In any case, to render it available to the modern reader, Fenton's knotted Elizabethan English would require a translation, in which case we would have a translation of a translation of a translation!

---

* This edition, dated 1774–76, was actually published in Florence; the fiction of its having been printed in "Friburgo" was obviously intended to deceive the censor. This is the first edition, after the *editio princeps,* to be based on the Codex Mediceo Palatino, and the first to restore almost all the passages Bartolomeo Concino, the Secretary of Duke Cosimo I, had expurgated in the original edition which Agnolo Guicciardini, the historian's nephew, had dedicated to the Duke (*see* Alessandro Gherardi, ed. *La Storia d'Italia,* Firenze, 1919, I, p. clxxviii).

The only other integral English version of the *History of Italy* is that by Austin Parke Goddard, published in ten volumes in London over the years 1753 to 1756. Goddard was expert in Italian, had studied and resided in Italy for many years at the invitation of Cosimo III, the Grand Duke of Tuscany, who was a friend of his family. Furthermore, aside from his expertise in the language, Goddard's intentions were scrupulously to adhere to Guicciardini's phraseology rather than redo it "in a very elegant Style."

But unfortunately the road to paraphrase is paved with good intentions. Goddard extracts wholesome lessons from Guicciardini and then puts them into courtly periwigged English. What he has accomplished for the most part is a good, sometimes sparkling paraphrase of the *Storia d'Italia*, clothing it in the opulent Gibbonsonian style of eighteenth-century historical rhetoric. Much more serious are Goddard's frequent variations of meaning, reinterpretations, polite omissions, invented gallantries—a general transformation of Guicciardini's feeling-tone from solemn Latinate obliquity and acerbity to a very English mixture of manners and morals.

Hence we have the unusual situation that since Guicciardini's classic was first published more than four hundred years ago, the only two integral versions in English of his work are both disqualified as true translations—one because it was not based on the original Italian text, the other because it is a paraphrase.*

. .

There is a theory and practice of translation in our day which, in an effort to avoid the archaicism and "no-language" of translatese, leaps

* More serious is the fact that both Fenton and Goddard omit practically all of the famous forbidden passages—the sections in Book III concerning the incestuous loves of the House of Borgia; Book IV on the effect of the new discoveries of Columbus and the Portuguese on interpretations of Sacred Scripture; Book X on Cardinal Pompeo Colonna inciting the people of Rome to rebel against the papacy; as well as numerous Guicciardinian anticlerical ironies such as his remark that the Holy Ghost must have inspired the cardinals in the election of Adrian VI, etc.

Neither Fenton nor Goddard, of course, could make use of most of these omissions since they were restored only in the "Friburgo" edition which appeared *after* their works. Available to them in print were two suppressed sections of the *Storia* published in a Protestant pamphlet in Basel (Pietro Perna, 1569). The 1618 Fenton in my possession declares on the title page: "The third Edition, diligently revised, with restitution of a Digression towards the end of the fourth Booke, which had bene formerly effaced out of the Italian and Latine copies in all the late Editions." None of the other cuts, however, are restored. Goddard prints two of the scandalous passages from Books III and IV in an appendix but flatly declares them spurious (Paolo Guicciardini, *Le Traduzioni Inglesi della Storia Guicciardiniana*, pp. 12-15, 24, Olschki, Florence, 1951; and Vincent Luciani, *Francesco Guicciardini and His European Reputation*, pp. 35 ff., K. Otto, New York, 1936).

to the other extreme and gives us Romans of antiquity who talk pure Hemingwayese.

But I should say that a true translation, while rendering available to the modern reader the speech of another time and culture, will also preserve the savor of that speech, the flavor of that time. A pinch of antiquity must be added. A good translation of a sixteenth-century text should be redolent of its period. It should bring us back there; we should not only understand it, we should be permeated by it in a kind of historical osmosis, research through the pores. To render Guicciardini in clear modern English available to the modern reader may be admirable pedagogy but it is not the art of translation.

I have called Guicciardini a Proustian historian—that is, a vision and a logic manifested in a certain kind of language. The stylistic challenge I set myself therefore was more than searching for English equivalents that would avoid archaicism on the one hand and clear modern English (which is archaicism in reverse) on the other. I have tried instead to re-create an English that would be faithful to the literal meanings of the text, and yet convey Guicciardinian involutions, his Ciceronian periods, his Proustian *longueurs*—an English that would convey in the twentieth century the flavor of a personalized Latinate Italian style of the sixteenth century.*

Enmeshed in this web, one found that one was searching the processes of Guicciardini's thought. Sometimes one had to cut the interminable sentences, balanced like some incredible trapeze act, clause upon (and within) clause, often a page high. Sometimes one had to clarify Guicciardini's casual way with antecedents and pronouns, substitute proper names for his strings of ambiguous he's and him's. (Those scholars who claim that Guicciardini never writes other than crystal-clear merely betray thereby their ignorance of the text.) Great monuments are not marred by scratches, even Homer nods (or makes us), and Guicciardini's marvelous rhetoric is not without its faults of overelaboration, density, impenetrable thickets.

The true translator must only clear up as much of this Sargasso Sea as is absolutely necessary to make for passage. But to clarify what was ambiguous in the original is not translation but explication. The job of the translator is not to make clear that which was not clear, but to render in another tongue (and sometimes another century) the same degree and kind of ambiguity wherever this occurs.

Guicciardini's chief literary fault is his prolixity—the inevitable outcome of his obsessive search for detail, his quest for truth by amassing

---

* Luciani, *op. cit.*, p. 35: "A gifted translator would attempt to render in the foreign tongue the serious majestic level of the Italian." This follows an acute and detailed analysis of the various inadequacies—both scholarly and artistic —of Fenton and Goddard.

all particulars—which gave rise to the legend of the Laconian (condemned because he had used three words where two would do) who was offered his freedom if he read entirely through Guicciardini's interminable account of the siege of Pisa, but who pleaded—after attempting a few pages—that he be sent instead to row in the galleys.

I hope the reader will be able to savor in these pages (from which most of the siege of Pisa has been cut) something of Guicciardini's extraordinary qualities as a historian. Scholars debate whether Francesco is more *res* than *verba*, but I should say that if there is a discrepancy between his hard skeletal thinking and the rhetorical artifices in which it is shrouded, this literature is very important. To transform it into simple modern English is to destroy those obliquities which are the very mark of the man: his intellectual clarity, his astuteness, his diplomatic visor glinting at all times.

The present version consists of more than half of the original enormous text and, in view of what I have indicated with regard to Fenton and Goddard, may justly claim to be the first extended English translation that is not a paraphrase or derived from a secondary source. Selections have been made from all twenty books, so organized as to present a running and coherent narrative from first to last, tied with bridge passages wherever necessary. In the light of Thoreau's "If you are acquainted with the principle, what do you care for a myriad instances and applications?" I have excised only repetitious episodes—thus a few battles serve as the models for Guicciardini's descriptions of many battles; a few examples suffice for his thirty or so invented set speeches.

Guicciardini's *History of Italy* has been pillaged for the past four hundred years as the chief source of Renaissance history and politics. Now the modern reader will be enabled for the first time in English to go to the source itself, and experience immersion in a world remote perhaps in time but discouragingly up-to-date so far as man's political behavior is concerned.

SIDNEY ALEXANDER

LA HISTORIA

DI ITALIA

DI M FRANCESCO GVICCIARDINI

GENTIL' HVOMO FIORENTINO

Con i Privilegi di Pio IIII Sommo Pont. Di Ferdinando I. Imp.
Del Re Cattolico: & di Cosimo Medici II
Duca di Firenza & di Siena

IN FIORENZA
Appresso Lorenzo Torrentino Impressor Ducale
M D L X I.

Title page of a first edition (Florence, 1561) of Guicciardini's The History of Italy in the possession of the translator. Although the text is precisely the same as that in all other first editions, the slight variations in the colophon and woodcut portrait of the historian, as well as the name "Mesere Loren" handwritten at the back of the book, indicate that this was the personal copy of the printer, Lorenzo Torrentino. (Reduced by approximately one-half.)

Original manuscript of the first page of Guicciardini's Storia d'Italia (COURTESY OF THE GUICCIARDINI ARCHIVE, FLORENCE)

BOOK

I

Prologue: Peace and Prosperity of Italy Around 1490.
Praise of Lorenzo de' Medici, the "Balance of Italy."
Alliance Among Florence, Naples and Milan to
Curb the Venetians

I HAVE DETERMINED TO WRITE ABOUT THOSE EVENTS
WHICH HAVE OCCURRED IN ITALY WITHIN OUR MEM-
ORY, EVER SINCE FRENCH TROOPS, SUMMONED BY OUR
own princes, began to stir up very great dissensions here: a most memorable
subject in view of its scope and variety, and full of the most terrible happenings; since for so many years Italy suffered all those calamities with
which miserable mortals are usually afflicted, sometimes because of the just
anger of God, and sometimes because of the impiety and wickedness of
other men. From a knowledge of such occurrences, so varied and so grave,
everyone may derive many precedents salutary both for himself and for
the public weal. Thus numerous examples will make it plainly evident how
mutable are human affairs, not unlike a sea whipped by winds; and how
pernicious, almost always to themselves but always to the people, are those
ill-advised measures of rulers who act solely in terms of what is in front of
their eyes: either foolish errors or shortsighted greed. Thus by failing to
take account of the frequent shifts of fortune, and misusing, to the harm
of others, the power conceded to them for the common welfare, such
rulers become the cause of new perturbations either through lack of
prudence or excess of ambition.

But the misfortunes of Italy (to take account of what its condition
was like then, as well as the causes of so many troubles) tended to stir up
men's minds with all the more displeasure and dread inasmuch as things
in general were at that time most favorable and felicitous. It is obvious
that ever since the Roman Empire, more than a thousand years ago,
weakened mainly by the corruption of ancient customs, began to decline

[3]

from that peak which it had achieved as a result of marvelous skill* and fortune, Italy had never enjoyed such prosperity, or known so favorable a situation as that in which it found itself so securely at rest in the year of our Christian salvation, 1490, and the years immediately before and after. The greatest peace and tranquility reigned everywhere; the land under cultivation no less in the most mountainous and arid regions than in the most fertile plains and areas; dominated by no power other than her own, not only did Italy abound in inhabitants, merchandise and riches, but she was also highly renowned for the magnificence of many princes, for the splendor of so many most noble and beautiful cities, as the seat and majesty of religion, and flourishing with men most skillful in the administration of public affairs and most nobly talented in all disciplines and distinguished and industrious in all the arts. Nor was Italy lacking in military glory according to the standards of that time, and adorned with so many gifts that she deservedly held a celebrated name and reputation among all the nations.

. . .

Many factors kept her in that state of felicity which was the consequence of various causes. But it was most commonly agreed that, among these, no small praise should be attributed to the industry and skill of Lorenzo de' Medici, so eminent amongst the ordinary rank of citizens in the city of Florence that the affairs of that republic were governed according to his counsels. Indeed, the power of the Florentine Republic resulted more from its advantageous location, the abilities of its citizens and the availability of its money than from the extent of its domain. And having recently become related by marriage to the Roman Pontiff, Innocent VIII, who was thus induced to lend no little faith in his advice, Lorenzo's name was held in great esteem all over Italy, and his authority influential in deliberations on joint affairs. Realizing that it would be most perilous to the Florentine Republic and to himself if any of the major powers should extend their area of dominion, he carefully saw to it that

---

* *Virtù:* In Renaissance literature *virtù* is frequently contrasted with *fortuna—virtù* being those qualities of force, action, power, courage, resourcefulness, intelligence, virtue, capacity, steadfastness, etc., whereby the will of man (*vir*) is opposed to the vagaries of fortune (an intervention which is successful 50 percent of the time, according to Machiavelli, but far less frequently, according to the more pessimistic Guicciardini). Out of this shuttle between universal and individual will, the stuff of history is woven.

The fact that in current Italian *virtù* is opposed to *vizio* (vice) rather than to *fortuna* indicates the contrast between the amoral Renaissance, which judged by success and style, and the moral judgment, basically verbal, imposed by the Council of Trent.

I have translated *virtù* variously, according to the context.

LORENZO DE' MEDICI CALLED THE MAGNIFICENT

In this portrait, by an unknown painter of the period, the city of Florence and the river Arno may be seen in the background (COURTESY OF FRATELLI ALINARI)

House of Sforza

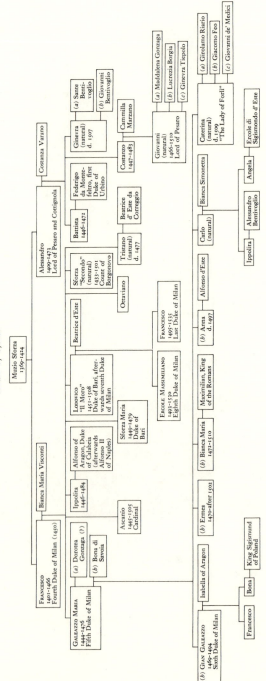

the Italian situation should be maintained in a state of balance, not leaning more toward one side than the other. This could not be achieved without preserving the peace and without being diligently on the watch against every incident, even the slightest.

Sharing the same desire for the common peace was the King of Naples, Ferdinand of Aragon,* undoubtedly a most prudent and highly esteemed prince, despite the fact that quite often in the past he had revealed ambitions not conducive toward maintaining the peace, and at this time he was being greatly instigated by his eldest son Alfonso, Duke of Calabria. For the Duke tolerated with ill grace the fact that his son-in-law, Giovan Galeazzo Sforza, Duke of Milan, already past twenty, although of very limited intellectual capacity, kept his dukedom in name only, having been suppressed and supplanted by Lodovico Sforza, his uncle. More than ten years before, as a result of the reckless and dissolute behavior of Donna Bona, the young prince's mother, Lodovico Sforza had taken tutelage over his nephew and, using that as an excuse, had little by little gathered into his own hands all the fortresses, men-at-arms, treasury and foundations of the state, and now continued to govern, not as guardian or regent but, except for the title of Duke of Milan, with all the outward trappings and actions of a prince.

Nevertheless, Ferdinand, more immediately concerned with present benefits than former ambitions, or his son's grievances, however justified, desired that Italy should not change. Perhaps he feared that troubles in Italy would offer the French a chance to assail the kingdom of Naples, since he himself, a few years earlier, had experienced amidst the gravest perils the hatred of his barons and his people, and he knew the affection which many of his subjects held toward the name of the house of France in remembrance of things past. Or perhaps he realized that it was necessary for him to unite with the others, and especially with the states of Milan and Florence, in order to create a counterbalance against the power of the Venetians, who were then formidable in all of Italy.

Lodovico Sforza, despite the fact that he was restless and ambitious, could not help but incline toward the same policy, since the danger of the Venetian Senate hung over those who ruled Milan as well as over the others, and because it was easier for him to maintain his usurped authority in the tranquility of peace rather than in the perturbations of war. And although he always suspected the intentions of Ferdinand and Alfonso of Aragon, nevertheless, since he was aware of Lorenzo de' Medici's disposition toward peace, as well as the fear that Lorenzo also had of their grandeur, Sforza persuaded himself that, in view of the diversity of spirit and ancient hatred between Ferdinand and the Venetians, it would be

---

* This Italian prince should not be mistaken for his contemporary, Ferdinand V, the Catholic, 1452–1516, King of Aragon and husband of Isabella I, Queen of Castille and Leon.

foolish to fear that they might set up an alliance between them, and decided that it was most certain that the Aragonese would not be accompanied by others in attempting against him what they could not achieve by themselves.

Therefore, since the same desire for peace existed among Ferdinand, Lodovico and Lorenzo, in part for the same reasons and in part for different reasons, it was easy to maintain an alliance contracted in the names of Ferdinand, King of Naples, Giovan Galeazzo, Duke of Milan, and the Republic of Florence, in defense of their states. This alliance, which had been agreed upon many years before and then interrupted as a result of various occurrences, had been adhered to in the year 1480 by practically all the minor Italian powers and renewed for twenty-five years. The principal aim of the pact was to prevent the Venetians from becoming any more powerful since they were undoubtedly stronger than any of the allies alone, but much weaker than all of them together. The Venetians continued to follow their own policies apart from common counsels, and while waiting for the growth of disunion and conflicts among the others, remained on the alert, prepared to take advantage of every mishap that might open the way for them toward ruling all of Italy. The fact that they aspired toward Italian hegemony had been very clearly shown at various times; especially, when taking advantage of the death of Filippo Maria Visconti, Duke of Milan, they had tried to become lords of that state, under the pretext of defending the liberty of the Milanese; and more recently when, in open war, they attempted to occupy the duchy of Ferrara.

This alliance easily curbed the cupidity of the Venetian Senate, but it did not unite the allies in sincere and faithful friendship, insofar as, full of emulation and jealousy among themselves, they did not cease to assiduously observe what the others were doing, each of them reciprocally aborting all the plans whereby any of the others might become more powerful or renowned. This did not result in rendering the peace less stable; on the contrary, it aroused greater vigilance in all of them to carefully stamp out any sparks which might be the cause of a new conflagration.

Death of Lorenzo the Magnificent and Innocent VIII.
Election of Alexander VI as Pope

Such, therefore, was the state of affairs, such were the foundations of the tranquility of Italy, disposed and counterposed in such a way that not only was there no fear of any present change, but neither could anyone easily conceive of any policies or situations or wars that might disrupt such peace.

But then in April of the year 1492, there unexpectedly occurred the death of Lorenzo de' Medici: a death bitter for him in view of his age, inasmuch as he had not yet completed his forty-fourth year, and bitter for his country which had flourished marvelously in riches and all those benefits and arts in human affairs which are the usual concomitants of a long-lasting peace, all resulting from Lorenzo's reputation and wisdom and talent for all manner of honorable and excellent undertakings. His death was indeed most untimely for the rest of Italy, not only because efforts toward the continuation of the common security were carried on by hands other than his, but also because he had been the means of moderating, and practically a bridle, in the disagreements and suspicions which very often developed for diverse reasons between Ferdinand and Lodovico Sforza, princes of almost equal power and ambition.

Lorenzo's death was followed after a few months by the death of Pope Innocent VIII: thus every day prepared more occasions for future calamities. Aside from the fact that this Pope had been useless so far as public welfare was concerned, in one regard at least his life had served a purpose: namely, that he had quickly abandoned the war which, at the beginning of his pontificate, he had unfortunately launched against Ferdinand at the instigation of many barons in the kingdom of Naples. Thereafter, the Pope devoted his entire mind to indolent pleasures and was no longer interested, either for himself or for his friends, in matters which might disturb the felicity of Italy.

Innocent was succeeded by Rodrigo Borgia of Valencia, one of the royal cities in Spain. He had been a cardinal for a long while and was one of the most important figures in the Roman court; his election to the papacy resulted from the conflict between the Cardinals Ascanio Sforza and Giuliano of San Pietro in Vincoli.* But primarily his election was due to the fact that he had openly bought many of the cardinals' votes in a manner unheard of in those times, partly with money and partly with promises of offices and benefices of his own which were considerable. The cardinals, without any regard for the precepts of the Gospel, were not ashamed to sell their influence and make a traffic of the sacred treasures, under the name of divine authority, in the most eminent part of the temple.

Cardinal Ascanio induced many of them to engage in such abominable merchandising, as much by his own example as by persuasion and appeals; for, corrupted by his boundless appetite for riches, he struck a bargain to be rewarded for his iniquity with the Vice Chancellery, the most

---

* Giuliano della Rovere, later Pope Julius II; his office as cardinal-priest of San Pietro in Vincoli was only one of the many favors he received from his uncle, Pope Sixtus IV. Rival of Pope Alexander VI, he went to France in 1494.

important office of the Roman Curia, as well as church benefices, the castle and chancellery palace in Rome, full of the most valuable furnishings. But despite all this, he could not flee divine justice or the infamy and just hatred of mankind, who were horrified by this frightful election which had been carried on with such crude devices; especially since the nature and behavior of the person chosen were notorious everywhere. For example, it is known that the King of Naples, although he dissembled his grief in public, told the Queen, his wife (shedding tears which he usually could control even at the death of his children), that a pope had now been created who would prove most pernicious for Italy and all Christendom. A prognosis truly not unworthy of Ferdinand's wisdom! For Alexander VI (as the new Pontiff wished to be called) possessed singular cunning and sagacity, excellent judgment, a marvelous efficacy in persuading, and an incredible dexterity and attentiveness in dealing with weighty matters. But all these qualities were far outweighed by his vices: the most obscene behavior, insincerity, shamelessness, lying, faithlessness, impiety, insatiable avarice, immoderate ambition, a cruelty more than barbaric and a most ardent cupidity to exalt his numerous children; and among these there were several (in order that depraved instruments might not be lacking to carry out his depraved designs) no less detestable than the father.

Thus the death of Innocent VIII brought about a great change in the affairs of the Church. But a change of no less importance resulted from the death of Lorenzo de' Medici so far as Florence was concerned; where Piero de' Medici succeeded without any opposition to his father's grandeur. Piero was the eldest of Lorenzo's three sons, still very young, and not qualified either by age or understanding to carry so heavy a burden, nor capable of governing with that moderation with which his father had proceeded both in domestic and foreign affairs. For Lorenzo had known how to temporize wisely among his allies and thus had improved both public and private affairs during his lifetime, and, dying, had left Italy in a condition of peace, the conservation of which was, everyone agreed, primarily due to his efforts.

No sooner had Piero entered into the administration of the Republic than he took a course diametrically opposed to his father's policy, without consulting the principal citizens as is usual in serious deliberations. Piero was persuaded by Virginio Orsini,* his kinsman (Piero's mother and wife were Orsinis), to ally himself so closely with Ferdinand and Alfonso, on whom Virginio depended, that Lodovico Sforza had very good reason to fear that whenever the Aragonese wanted to harm him they would be assisted by the force of the Florentine Republic through the authority of

---

* G. spells it Verginio Orsino. Renaissance Italians are as footloose in their orthography as the Elizabethan English. I have adopted the present spelling.

POPE ALEXANDER VI

Pinturicchio depicts the Pope in a detail of the lunette on the resurrection of Christ, in the Appartamento Borgia of the Vatican (COURTESY OF FRATELLI ALINARI)

House of Medici

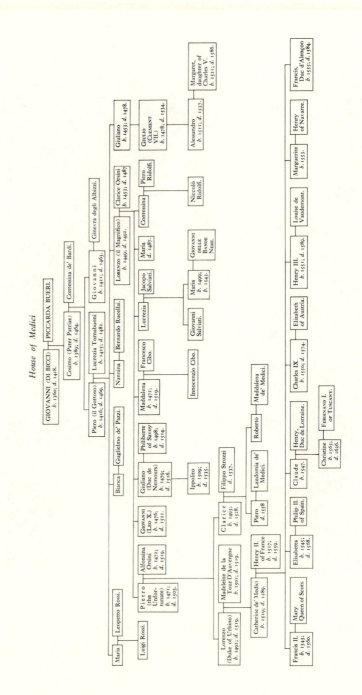

House of Medici

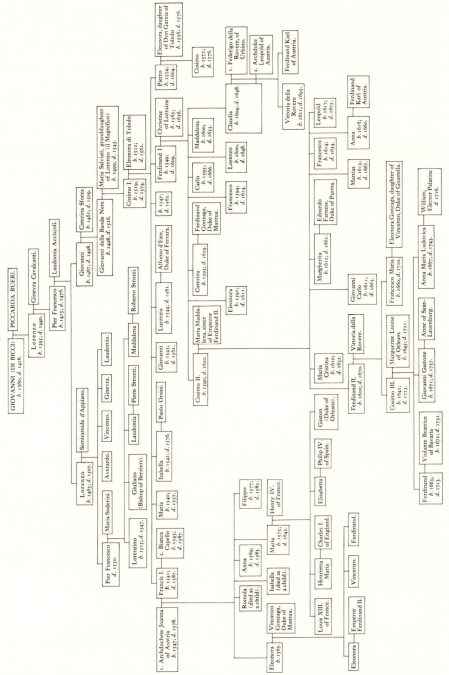

Piero de' Medici. This alliance, which was the seed and source of all the misfortunes to come, although at first it had been compacted and stabilized most secretly, began almost inevitably, although through obscure hints, to arouse suspicions in Lodovico, a most vigilant and sharp-witted prince.

According to long-established practice, princes all over Christendom had to send ambassadors to pay homage to the new Pontiff and declare their obeisance to him as Vicar of Christ on earth. Lodovico Sforza (who was always seeking ways to appear, by means of hitherto unthought-of devices, wiser than anybody else) had proposed that all the ambassadors of the League should enter Rome on the same day and that one of them should speak in the name of all. In this way they would demonstrate to all of Italy that not only was there an alliance and friendship among them, but even more, they were so united that they seemed almost a single body under one head, and this would increase the reputation of the entire League. Reason, as well as a recent example, demonstrated the usefulness of such a procedure; for it was believed that the Pope who had recently died had been more disposed to attack the kingdom of Naples, finding a pretext in the disunion among the allies who had sent separate legations at various times to lend him obedience.

Ferdinand readily approved Lodovico's scheme, as did the Florentines; nor did Piero de' Medici oppose the plan in a public meeting, although privately he was much annoyed by it. Having been chosen as one of the ambassadors elected in the name of the Republic, and having decided to make his legation illustrious with a very proud and almost royal ostentation, Piero was aware that in entering Rome and presenting himself to the Pope together with the other ambassadors of the League, all his splendor and pomp would not make much display in such a multitude. This juvenile vanity of Piero's was supported by the ambitious counsel of Gentile, Bishop of Arezzo, who was also one of the elected ambassadors. The Bishop of Arezzo had been chosen to speak in the name of the Florentines in view of his episcopal dignity and the reputation which he had in those studies called humanistic; the Bishop was vexed at losing the opportunity of displaying his eloquence in so honored and solemn a setting, as a result of Sforza's unusual and unexpected scheme. Therefore Piero, goaded partly by his own frivolity and partly by the Bishop's ambition (but not wanting Sforza to know that he was impugning his plan), requested the King of Naples to declare that he did not consider it possible to carry out these ceremonies communally without a great deal of confusion, and therefore supported the idea that each of the allies, according to ancient custom, should proceed independently. The King, desirous of pleasing him, but not so much as to totally displease Lodovico, satisfied Piero's demand more in show than in substance; nor did he hide the fact that he had shifted from his previous support of Sforza's plan only as a result of Piero de' Medici's insistence. Lodovico reacted with more irritation to this sudden change than such a matter really deserved, and complained bitterly that since his first proposal was already known to the Pontiff and the entire Roman court, as well as the fact that he had been the author of it, now they were deliberately changing their minds in order to damage his reputation. But he was all the more displeased because this slight and almost trivial incident made him realize that Piero de' Medici had a secret understanding with Ferdinand, which emerged more clearly every day as a result of the events that ensued.

.   .
.

Franceschetto Cibo of Genoa, the natural son of Pope Innocent VIII, possessed Anguillara, Cerveteri, and several other castles near Rome. After the death of his father, he went to live in Florence under the protection of Piero de' Medici, who was the brother of Maddalena, his wife. No sooner had he arrived in Florence when, under Piero's instigation, he sold those castles to Virginio Orsini for forty thousand ducats: Ferdinand had been the main adviser in this matter and had secretly lent Orsini most of the money, convinced that it would turn out to his advantage the more Virginio, who was an officer in his army as well as his kinsman, extended his power around Rome. For the King considered pontifical power to be the most likely instrument for stirring up dissensions in the kingdom of Naples, which was an ancient fief of the Roman church and whose confines extended for a great distance alongside the ecclesiastical domain. He also remembered the troubles he and his father had often had with the popes, and he was aware that there were always grounds for new contentions in the jurisdiction of boundary lines, census, collation of benefices, appeals of the barons, and many other differences which often arise between neighboring states, and just as frequently between a vassal and his feudal lord. Thus, Ferdinand always held it as one of the fundamental bases of his security that either all or part of the most powerful barons of the Roman domain should depend on him. Ferdinand at that time especially followed such a policy, because he believed that Lodovico—through his brother, Cardinal Ascanio—had very great influence over the Pope. Many believed that Ferdinand was perhaps no less motivated by the fear that Alexander might have inherited the covetousness and capacity for hatred of his uncle, Pope Calixtus III. Had not death interrupted his plans, Calixtus, out of an immoderate desire to aggrandize his nephew, Pietro Borgia, would have gone to war as soon as Alfonso (father of this Ferdinand) was dead, in order to despoil him of the kingdom of Naples which the Pope asserted had reverted to the Church. The Pope forgot (so briefly do men recall the benefits they have received) that it was through Alfonso's efforts (in whose kingdom he had been born and whose counselor he had been for a long time) that he had obtained his other ecclesiastical dignities, and that the same King had helped him considerably to gain the pontificate.

But it is certainly most true that wise men do not always discern or pass perfect judgments; often it is necessary that they show signs of the weakness of human understanding. Although reputed to be a very wise prince, King Ferdinand did not sufficiently consider how important it was to reject this decision which in any case could only prove of very slight benefit, and on the other hand might result in the most serious troubles. The sale of these little castles stirred up new schemes in the minds of those who, either out of responsibility or interest, would have otherwise attended to the preservation of a common agreement. The Pope claimed that since the sale had been carried out without his knowledge, therefore, according to the law, the castles devolved to the Apostolic See, and considering this as a serious offense against pontifical authority and being, furthermore, suspicious of Ferdinand's ultimate aim, the Pontiff stirred up all of Italy with charges against the King of Naples, against Piero de' Medici and against Virginio, affirming that so far as it lay within his power, he would not neglect any opportunity to maintain the dignity and claims of the Holy See. Lodovico Sforza was equally disturbed; he had always been suspicious of Ferdinand's actions; and since he had foolishly convinced himself that the Pope would rule according to the counsels of Ascanio and himself, he felt that any diminution in Alexander's power was a diminution of his own. But he was especially worried by a growing conviction that one could no longer doubt that the Aragonese and Piero de' Medici had joined in the closest alliance, since they were proceeding jointly in such an enterprise. In order to disrupt their plans, which he considered harmful to his own interests, and, by taking advantage of this occasion to draw the Pope all the more closely into his camp, Sforza incited the Pontiff as much as he could to protect his own dignity. Lodovico Sforza reminded the Pope that he should be aware not only of what was happening at present, but also what the future consequences might be, if in the very first days of his pontificate his vassals should act so scornfully and so openly against his Papal Majesty. The Pope should not believe that Virginio's cupidity or the importance of the castles had been the real reason behind Ferdinand's action, but rather a desire to try the Pope's patience and offend him in what seemed, at first, small matters: after which, if these were tolerated, he would in time dare to attempt greater affronts. His ambition was no different than that of the other Neapolitan kings, perpetual enemies of the Roman church, who had many times persecuted the Popes with wars and often occupied Rome. Had not this same king twice attacked two popes with armies sent under his son's command up to the very walls of Rome? Had he not always manifested the open hatred of his predecessors? And now spurring him on against the

Pope was not only the example of the other kings, not only his natural greediness to rule, but even more so, a desire for revenge stirred up in him by the memory of injuries which he had received from Alexander's uncle, Calixtus. Sforza urged the Pope to take careful consideration of these things and be aware that if he tolerated these first offenses patiently, honored only with ceremonies and vain titles, in effect everyone would scorn him, and he would lend encouragement to even more dangerous schemes. But if he showed offense now over this matter of the castles, he would easily maintain his untarnished majesty and the grandeur and true veneration which all the world owed to the Roman pontiffs.

To these persuasions, Sforza added most efficacious promises but even more efficacious facts, because he soon lent the Pope forty thousand ducats and dispatched three hundred men-at-arms,* at joint expense, but completely at the Pontiff's disposal. Nevertheless, desirous of avoiding the necessity of entering into new travails, he urged Ferdinand to see to it that Virginio, in some honorable way, might appease the Pontiff's anger, hinting at the serious consequences that might otherwise result from this trivial beginning. But more freely and with more effectiveness, he more than once admonished Piero de' Medici to consider how skillfully his father, Lorenzo, had maintained peace in Italy, always acting as an intermediary and common friend between Ferdinand and himself, and that Piero should seek rather to follow this paternal example (particularly since he should model himself after so distinguished a personage) instead of hearkening to new counsels, giving someone else the pretext, nay the necessity, of making decisions which in the long run would be harmful for everyone. Furthermore, he should remember how the long-enduring friendship between the Sforza and Medici had served for their joint security and reputation, and how many affronts and injuries the house of Aragon had committed against his father and his forefathers and the Florentine Republic, and how many times Ferdinand (and before him, Alfonso his father) had tried to occupy the domain of Tuscany, sometimes by war and sometimes by intrigue.

But these admonitions and counsels did more harm than good. For Ferdinand felt that it was beneath his dignity to yield to Lodovico and Ascanio, who were said to be the agents stirring up the Pope's anger; and spurred by his son Alfonso, the King of Naples secretly advised Virginio that he should not delay in taking possession of the castles by virtue of the contract, promising to defend him from whatever opposition might

---

* These mounted men-at-arms, iron-clad from top to toe and carrying enormous lances for the initial shock and swords and daggers for close combat, were the core of every army until the end of the fifteenth century. In Italy the term "*lancia*" or "lance" was applied to each group consisting of the man-at-arms, his page and his groom, also mounted. (See p. 50 for Guicciardini's definition of the terms according to French usage.)

arise. At the same time, operating in his usual crafty manner, he proposed to the Pope various plans of settlement while secretly advising Virginio not to agree to any other terms except keeping possession of the castles, satisfying the Pope with some sums of money. Wherefore, Virginio took so much courage that many times afterward, he refused to accept those conditions which Ferdinand, in order not to irritate the Pope too much, urged him to accept.

When Lodovico Sforza observed that Piero de' Medici continued to support the King and that it was vain to hope that he could be deflected from such a course, and considering how much Florence, on which he used to base his security, was now leaning toward his enemies, and therefore feeling that he was threatened with many perils, he determined on what new remedies he might provide for his own safety. Sforza was well aware that the Aragonese were ardently desirous that he be removed as his nephew's regent; Ferdinand also desired this although, full of the most incredible simulation and dissimulation in all his actions, he forced himself to remain silent; but Alfonso, a man who was naturally much more open, never ceased to complain about the persecution of his son-in-law, crying out insults and threats with more freedom than prudence. Besides, Lodovico knew that Isabella, Giovan Galeazzo's wife, a young woman of intrepid spirit, was continually soliciting her father and grandfather that if they did not revenge the infamy of all the indignities suffered by her husband and herself, they should at least take precautions against the dangers to which their own lives, as well as their children's, were exposed.

But what disturbed Lodovico most was the realization of how much he was hated by all the people in the duchy of Milan, both because of the unusual taxes which he had levied, and out of the compassion which everyone felt for Giovan Galeazzo, legitimate lord of the city. And although he tried to arouse suspicions that the Aragonese longed to take possession of the state of Milan, which they claimed belonged to them on the basis of an ancient will left by Filippo Maria Visconti, who had declared Alfonso, father of Ferdinand, as his heir; and that in order to facilitate this plan they were seeking to deprive the nephew of his rule; nevertheless, despite all these efforts, Lodovico could not lessen the hatred felt against him, nor prevent the whole world from realizing how much wickedness a pestiferous thirst for domination usually induces in men.

Therefore, after he had reflected for a long while on the situation and the imminent dangers, to the exclusion of everything else, he directed his entire mind and soul to seek for new support and alliances. With this purpose in view, Lodovico felt that the Pope's anger against Ferdinand offered a great opportunity, and since it was believed that the Venetian Senate was eager to dissolve the League which had for so many years acted in opposition to their designs, he proposed to both parties to set up a new league in the common interest.

But even more than by anger and any other passion, the Pope was moved by his unbridled greed to exalt his children whom he loved ardently. He was the first of all the popes (who usually concealed their infamy to some degree by calling their children nephews) to declare and present them openly to all the world as his children. And as at the moment no other opportunity presented itself to gratify his intentions, he sought to obtain Alfonso's natural daughter as wife to one of his sons, with a dowry of some rich portion of the kingdom of Naples. So long as this hope was not entirely ruled out, he lent his ears rather than his soul to Lodovico's offer of an alliance; and if this proposal had been accepted, perhaps the peace of Italy would not have been so soon disturbed. But although Ferdinand was not averse to such a marriage, Alfonso, who abhorred the Pope's ambition and pomp, would never consent to it. Thus, not by openly showing that they were opposed to the marriage but simply setting up difficulties with regard to the dowry, they would not give Alexander any satisfaction. Consequently, the Pope became so provoked that he resolved to follow Lodovico's advice, spurred by his ambition and rage, and also to some degree by his fear. For Ferdinand had under his protection not only Virginio Orsini (who was then very powerful in the entire ecclesiastical state as a result of the great favor in which he was held by the Florentines and the King, and because of his following in the Guelph faction), but also Prospero and Fabrizio, the heads of the Colonna family. The Cardinal of San Pietro in Vincoli, a most highly regarded prelate who had withdrawn to his fortress at Ostia where he was Bishop, out of suspicion that the Pope had designs against his life, had also declared himself openly for Ferdinand, although previously he had been the King's greatest enemy (against whom he had instigated first Pope Sixtus, his uncle, and then Innocent). But the Venetian Senate was not quite as ready for this alliance as had been believed, because although they were very pleased at the disunion of the others they were suspicious of the lack of good faith of the Pope, whom everybody distrusted more each day. Furthermore, they recalled the alliances which they had entered into with Sixtus and Innocent, his immediate predecessors. From Innocent they had received injuries without any benefits at all. As for Sixtus—he had fanned the war against the Duke of Ferrara, pressing the Venetians to undertake it; then he had changed his mind and took up not only his spiritual but also temporal arms against them in conjunction with the rest of the Italians. But by his industry and diligence, and by privately conferring with many of the senators, Lodovico finally managed to overcome all the difficulties in the Senate; and in April 1493, a new confederation was formed among the Pope, the Venetian Senate and Giovan Galeazzo, Duke of Milan (whose name was used in all public transactions of that state), for their common defense, and particularly for the support of Lodovico's rule. The pact stipulated that the Venetians and the Duke of Milan were each obliged to send two hundred men-at-arms immediately to Rome for the security of the Ecclesiastical State and the Pope's person, helping him with these and, if need be, greater forces to seize the castles occupied by Virginio.

All of Italy was no little stirred up by these new counsels, since the Duke of Milan now remained isolated from that League which for more than twelve years had maintained the common security. For according to the League, it had been explicitly forbidden for any of its members to enter into a new alliance without the consent of the others. Therefore, seeing this union on which everyone's security depended now sundered into unequal parts, the princes were suspicious and full of resentments, for how could they fail to foresee that out of such seeds must grow fruits detrimental to everyone? Therefore the Duke of Calabria [Alfonso] and Piero de' Medici, deeming it safer for their interests to forestall rather than to be forestalled, hearkened very favorably to Prospero and Fabrizio Colonna, who at the secret instigation of the Cardinal of San Pietro in Vincoli, offered to suddenly seize Rome with men-at-arms of their own companies and with men of the Ghibelline faction, provided the Orsini forces would follow them, and the Duke of Calabria would first take up a position, within three days of their entrance into the city, from which he might be able to march to their help. But Ferdinand, who wished not to irritate but rather to mitigate the Pope, and to correct what had been rather imprudently done up to that time, totally rejected these counsels which he felt would engender not security but rather much greater dangers and evils. Ferdinand, therefore, bethought himself to do everything possible, no longer deceitfully but with all his heart, to compose his difference of opinion with regard to the castles, convinced that if only this cause of so much trouble were removed, Italy would be able to return with little difficulty, indeed almost automatically, to its previous state.

But the elimination of causes does not always eliminate the effects which have had their origin in those causes. Because, as often happens, resolutions taken out of fear appear to the fearful as inadequate to their peril.* Thus Lodovico was not certain that he had found sufficient security for the dangers besetting him. In view of their diversity of aims, he doubted that he would be able to depend very long on the alliance which he had made with the Pope and the Venetian Senate, and his interests might, for various reasons, fall into many difficulties. Therefore, he applied all his efforts to find a fundamental cure for the disease that now presented itself, rather than for those that might subsequently result from it; not considering how dangerous it is to use medicine which is stronger than

---

* A sample of the *ricordi* which Guicciardini had been noting down all his life—crystallizations of his practical experience—now scattered throughout the *Storia*.

the nature of the disease, or the constitution of the patient can tolerate. But, as if entering into greater dangers was the only remedy for present perils, he decided to seek protection from foreign armies, since he placed no faith in his own forces and in Italian friendships. Hence he resolved to attempt in every way possible to provoke Charles VIII, King of France, to invade the kingdom of Naples, to which the house of Anjou had long-standing claims.

[*The claims of the house of Anjou to the kingdom of Naples are discussed by Guicciardini. In 1262, Pope Urban IV conceded it in fee, together with Sicily, under the title of the Two Sicilies, to Charles, Count of Provence and Anjou. In 1414 the crown passed to Giovanna II, who "placed the government of her realm into the hands of those to whom she shamelessly gave her body." Eventually, harassed by the third Louis of Anjou and Pope Martin V, Giovanna was forced to make Alfonso, King of Aragon and Sicily, her son by adoption, although she later annulled this act. Thereby the basis was laid for subsequent wars between Aragonese and Angevins, both of whom claimed title to the kingdom of Naples. On the death of Louis XI, King of France, the Angevins' rights to the kingdom of Naples reverted to his son, Charles VIII. Thus "Ferdinand, King of Naples, began to have a most mighty foe. . . ."*]

At that time, the kingdom of France was more populous, had more military power and glory, was wealthier and more influential than any other kingdom perhaps since the time of Charlemagne. It had recently expanded each of those three parts into which, since ancient times, all Gaul was divided. Not more than forty years before, under Charles VII (a king called the Fortunate as a result of many victories obtained amidst the gravest perils), it had reduced Normandy and the duchy of Guyenne under its sovereignty, provinces which had earlier been possessed by the English; during the latter years of Louis XI the county of Provence, the duchy of Burgundy, and most of Picardy; and then by marriage, Charles VIII had added the duchy of Brittany to the French crown.

Nor was Charles lacking in desire to conquer the kingdom of Naples, which he believed justly belonged to him—a belief instilled in him from childhood almost by a kind of natural instinct, and then nourished by the counsels of several very close advisers. These people also filled his mind with vain thoughts to the effect that this would prove an opportunity for him to surpass the glory of his predecessors, for once having acquired the kingdom of Naples, it would be easy for him to conquer the Turkish Empire. Since Charles' ambitions were widely known, Lodovico Sforza was hopeful that he could easily persuade the King to carry out his desire; furthermore, Lodovico was very confident in the renown of the Sforzas at the French court, because he, and before him his brother

Galeazzo, had always maintained by many outward indications and good services the friendship begun by their father, Francesco Sforza, thirty years before. . . .

. .
.

However, Lodovico felt it would be dangerous to be solely responsible for setting so great an undertaking in motion; and in order to deal with the French more authoritatively and with more credit, he first sought to persuade the Pope to the same idea, spurring on his ambitions as well as playing on his resentments, showing him that he could not depend in any way on Italian princes or their armies to help him take revenge against Ferdinand or secure preferments for his children. He found Alexander readily disposed, either because he was avid for new undertakings or thought to obtain, by frightening the Aragonese, what they had refused voluntarily to concede to him. Then Sforza and the Pope secretly dispatched agents to France to sound out the King's mind and his closest counselors. Lodovico, devoting all his efforts to this scheme, openly dispatched (although under another pretext) Carlo da Barbiano, Count of Belgioioso, as his ambassador. After several days of private audiences with Charles and separately with his ministers, during which he diligently sought to persuade them, Barbiano was finally introduced into the royal council, where, in the presence of the King, his ministers, all his lords and many prelates and nobles of the court, he delivered a speech on the matter.

[*This is the first of a series of set speeches (several examples will follow) composed by Guicciardini on the classical model. The burden of the speech rests on the righteousness of French claims to Naples, the weakness of the enemy, and the glorious strategic opportunity that would result in the conquest of Naples, affording a launching platform for a crusade against the Turks, striking through Greece at Constantinople.*]

This incitation was not favorably received by the great lords of France, especially by those who exercised greatest authority because of their nobility or reputation for wisdom. They judged that such a war would inevitably prove very difficult and dangerous inasmuch as the armies had to be brought to a foreign country very far from the kingdom of France to fight an enemy who was considered very powerful. Ferdinand was highly reputed everywhere for his sagacity, and no less so was his son Alfonso for his skill in military science; and it was believed that since Ferdinand had ruled for thirty years, and at various times despoiled and destroyed so many barons, he must have accumulated a great deal of money.

The French nobles estimated that King Charles would hardly be capable of supporting so heavy a burden by himself, and that his counselors were weak in managing wars or affairs of state, and his closest advisers inexperienced since the King's confidence in them rested more on favor than reason. Added to this there was the lack of money, of which it was considered a great deal would be necessary; and the importance of keeping in mind Italian capacity for intrigue and scheming. Also, they ought to be aware of the fact that putting the kingdom of Naples under the power of a French king was not likely to please any of the Italians, not even Lodovico Sforza who was known all over Italy for his treachery. Whence, victory would be difficult, and maintaining the fruits thereof even more so. For that reason, Charles' father, Louis, a prince who had always been more attentive to the substance than the appearance of things, had never been beguiled by Italian affairs, nor had taken any account of his claims to the kingdom of Naples, always affirming that sending armies beyond the mountains was simply looking for trouble and buying danger at the cost of boundless treasure and French blood. . . .

[*Other counselors point out that before engaging in a dangerous war in Italy, the French should come to agreements with their neighbors: Ferdinand, King of Spain; Maximilian, King of the Romans, and his son Philip, Archduke of Austria; nor could they count on the benevolence of Henry VII, King of England, because "the natural hatred of the English for the French" would prove stronger than the peace made between them a few months earlier.*]

But Charles, a youth of twenty-two years, not very intelligent by nature with regard to worldly affairs, and carried away by an ardent desire to rule and a thirst for glory based more on levity and a kind of impulse rather than mature counsels, listened most reluctantly to these arguments. Either of his own inclination or following his father's example

CHARLES VIII

This medal, showing the French King wearing the pendant of Saint Michael over his robe, is dated about 1494-95 and attributed to Niccolò Fiorentino. The inscription reads "KAROLVS OCTAVVS FRANCORVM IERV-SALEN ET CICILIE REX." (COURTESY OF THE NATIONAL GALLERY OF ART, WASHINGTON, D.C., SAMUEL H. KRESS COLLECTION)

and precepts, Charles lent little faith to the lords and nobles of his kingdom; once he was no longer under the guardianship of his sister Anne, Duchess of Bourbon, he paid no further heed to the Admiral's [Iacopo Gravilla] counsels or to any of the others who had played a great role in that government. Instead, Charles ruled according to the advice of a number of men of low condition, almost all of whom had been trained in his own personal service. These closest in the King's favor warmly agreed with him, some of them being venal (as ministers of princes frequently are), corrupted by money and promises put forward by Lodovico's ambassador, who left no stone unturned to win over those sympathetic to this proposition; and some stirred by hopes either of acquiring property in the kingdom of Naples or obtaining certain ecclesiastical preferments and revenues from the Pope.

· ·
·

Thus, amidst these diverse opinions, the decision remained suspended for several days. Not only were the ministers undecided, but also Charles was uncertain and inconstant, now spurred on by greed for glory and empire, now bridled by fear; sometimes he was resolute and at other times he swung around to the contrary of what he had previously determined. Finally, however, his original desire and the unhappy fate of Italy prevailed; rejecting all peaceful counsels, and unknown to anyone except the Bishop of San Malò and the Seneschal of Beaucaire, Charles signed a convention with Lodovico's ambassador.

The terms of this agreement were kept secret for several months, but the upshot was that once Charles had marched in person into Italy or dispatched his army there for the conquest of Naples, the Duke of Milan would be obligated to grant him passage through his domain, to supply him with five hundred paid men-at-arms, to permit him to arm as many vessels as he wanted at Genoa, and to lend him 200,000 ducats before he left France. On the other hand, the King obliged himself to defend the duchy of Milan against anyone (with particular mention of maintaining Lodovico's authority) so long as the war lasted, and to keep two hundred lances* posted at Asti, a city belonging to the Duke of Orleans, in readiness for such defense. Furthermore, Charles promised that once he had taken possession of the kingdom of Naples, or soon after, he would confer upon Lodovico, according to a written statement signed by the King's own hand, the principality of Taranto.

· ·
·

---

* By Guicciardini's definition, p. 50, this figure must be multiplied by six to arrive at the actual number of men!

Now men's opinions change but perhaps the underlying causes of things do not. Lodovico was inviting the French to cross the mountains, not fearing from a most powerful King of France in possession of the kingdom of Naples, that danger which Lodovico's father, most valorous in arms, had feared from the possibilities of a similar conquest on the part of a little count of Provence; and Charles was eager to make war in Italy, preferring the rash counsels of inexperienced and vulgar men over the example of his father, a prudent king of long-proven experience. Undoubtedly, Lodovico's idea was also encouraged by his father-in-law Ercole d'Este, Duke of Ferrara, who was very eager to recover the Polesine of Rovigo, a territory contiguous to and very important for the security of Ferrara.

. . .

But now that rumors of what was being planned beyond the mountains were beginning to resound all over Italy (although based on uncertain evidence), a variety of ideas and discussions were aroused in men's minds. Some considered it a matter of the gravest import in view of the power of the kingdom of France, the readiness of that nation to embark on new enterprises and the discord among the Italians; while others, in view of the King's youth and capacities, and the indolence which is typical of the French, as well as the various impediments that so great an enterprise would encounter, judged that this was rather a case of youthful impulse than well-considered counsel, and it would therefore quickly evaporate, although it was somewhat boiling up at the moment.

Nor did Ferdinand, against whom all these preparations were being set in motion, show very much concern, saying it would prove a most difficult undertaking. For, if the French should think of attacking him by sea, they would find his fleet sufficiently armed to enter into combat with them on the high seas; his ports well fortified and completely under his command. Nor would there be any barons in the realm able to welcome the French, as the Prince of Rosanno and other grandees had welcomed Jean d'Anjou. As for an expedition by land—that would prove very difficult, arouse widespread suspicions, and have to cover too great a distance. For the French armies would first have to pass through the whole length of Italy, with the result that each of the other states would have particular cause for alarm, and perhaps Lodovico Sforza most of all (although he might pretend to the contrary, wishing to show that the common peril referred only to the others) because, in view of the closeness of the duchy of Milan to France, the King had the easiest possibility and actually the greatest desire to take possession of it.

And since the Duke of Milan was closely related by blood to the

King of France, how could Lodovico be so certain that the King did not have in mind the idea of liberating the Duke from his oppression, especially since he had openly affirmed, a few years before, that he would not tolerate having his cousin Giovan Galeazzo so grossly mistreated.

Nor were the French justified in hoping that the Aragonese were weak in Naples, and therefore that they might boldly attack that kingdom. In fact, Ferdinand was well-provided with many valorous men-at-arms, an abundance of fighting horse, munitions, artillery and all provisions needed for war, as well as plenty of money which he could augment without any difficulty whenever necessary. And besides the many highly experienced captains trained in leading his armies and handling his weapons, he had his oldest son, the Duke of Calabria, a captain whose valor was as great as his fame, with many years of experience in all the wars in Italy. In addition to his own forces, he could count on the prompt aid of his relatives, for there was no doubt that the King of Spain, his cousin and his wife's brother, would surely rally to his side, not only because of the double chain of relationship, but also because he would suspect any approach of the French toward Sicily.

This, at any rate, is how Ferdinand spoke in public, magnifying his own power and minimizing as much as possible the forces and possibilities of his adversaries. But as he was a king of singular prudence and broad experience, he was actually very disturbed, since he vividly remembered the troubles the French had given him at the beginning of his reign. He realized full well that he would have to go to war with a most powerful and warlike enemy, greatly superior in cavalry, infantry, sea forces, artillery, money, and men most ardent to confront every peril for the glory and grandeur of their king. On the other hand, his every action was suspect; almost all his subjects either detested the Aragonese, or were quite inclined to rebel. Besides, most of them were usually eager for a new regime, readier to follow fortune than fidelity. He knew that his reputation was greater than his actual strength: that the money which he had accumulated would not suffice for his defense, and that once the war started, everything would burst into rebellion and tumult which would annihilate all of his income in one moment. He knew that he had many enemies in Italy and no stable and trustworthy friend: for who had not been offended at some time or another either by his arms or by his intrigue? Nor, judging by past examples and the situation in that kingdom, could he count on Spain for any help against his peril, other than the broadest promises, and a great noise about preparations which in effect would be minimal and much too late.

Furthermore, his premonitions grew as a result of many unhappy predictions about his house which had come to his notice at various times, partly from ancient writings which had been rediscovered, and partly by men, who, although often uncertain about the present, did not hesitate to arrogate to themselves certain prognostications about the future: predictions which in times of prosperity are taken little heed of, but are too much believed once matters tend toward adversity.

Troubled by these considerations, and his fears and perils appearing incomparably greater than his hopes, Ferdinand knew no other remedy than either deflecting the French King from these ideas as quickly as possible by coming to some agreement, or else eliminating some of the reasons which were inciting him to war.

Therefore, since Ferdinand's ambassadors were already in France, having been sent there in connection with the marriage of Charlotte, daughter of Don Federigo, his second son, with the King of Scotland; and inasmuch as the bride's mother had been King Charles' aunt, and Charlotte had been brought up in the French court, Ferdinand took this opportunity to add a new commission to those for which the ambassadors had been sent. Therefore, he dispatched Cammillo Pandone, who had served as his French agent at other times, to join the ambassadors for the purpose of secretly attempting to bribe the King's ministers with money and promises; and if they could not change the King's mind in any other way, to offer him conditions of tribute and other acts of submission, and thus attempt to obtain peace.

Besides this, not only did Ferdinand apply all his diligence and authority to compose the conflict stirred up as a result of Virginio Orsini's purchase of the castles, blaming Virginio's stubbornness as the cause of all these disorders; but he also renewed negotiations with the Pope regarding a treaty of marriage between their families which they had previously discussed. But his chief concern and effort was directed toward appeasing and making sure of Lodovico Sforza, author and promoter of all these evils, for Ferdinand was convinced that fear more than any other reason had impelled Sforza to so dangerous a resolution.

Therefore, placing his own security above the interests of his granddaughter and the safety of her child, he made various offers to yield entirely to Lodovico Sforza's wishes with regard to the duchy of Milan and the question of Giovan Galeazzo without any regard for his son Alfonso's opinion. Alfonso judged that the best way of forcing Sforza to withdraw from his new resolutions was by treating him harshly, threatening and terrorizing him. Alfonso took courage from Lodovico's natural timidity, failing to remember that desperation will lead a frightened man into precipitous actions as easily as lack of judgment will a rash man.

Finally the question of the castles was settled, after numerous difficulties raised more by Virginio than by the Pope; Don Federigo intervened in this settlement, having been sent for that purpose by his father. The agreement stipulated that Virginio should retain the castles, but should pay the Pope as much money as he had previously paid Franceschetto Cibo for them. At the same time, a match was concluded between

Donna Sancia, Alfonso's natural daughter, and Don Goffredo,* the Pope's youngest son, although both of them were as yet too young for the consummation of the marriage.

Conditions were that Don Goffredo should leave within a few months to go and stay at Naples where he would receive the principality of Squillace as his dowry with an income of ten thousand ducats a year, and have one hundred men-at-arms under his command at Ferdinand's expense. This confirmed the widespread opinion that what the Pontiff had negotiated in France had been primarily for the purpose of frightening the Aragonese into agreeing to this match. Once again Ferdinand attempted to form an alliance with the Pope for their common defense; but since the Pontiff raised so many difficulties, he did not obtain anything other than a very secret promise, in the form of a brief, to help defend the kingdom of Naples on the condition that Ferdinand promise to do the same with regard to the states of the Church. An agreement having been reached, the Pope dismissed the men-at-arms which the Venetians and the Duke of Milan had sent to his aid. Ferdinand was hopeful that he would have equal success in the negotiations which he was undertaking with Lodovico Sforza. But Lodovico parried in the most artful manner: now seeming displeased at Charles' Italian claims as perilous for all the Italians, now justifying his actions as necessitated by his ancient alliance with the French ruling house, and his obligations to Genoa, which he held in fief, obliging him to take heed of the request which the King (it was said) had made to him; and now promising, sometimes to Ferdinand and sometimes to the Pope and to Piero de' Medici, to do all he could to cool Charles' ardor. Then he thought it would be possible to lull them all asleep, in the hope that no moves would be made against him before the French were well prepared and organized; and he was all the more readily believed because the decision to invite the King of France into Italy was judged so risky even for Sforza, that it didn't seem possible that ultimately, considering the danger, he would not have to withdraw from it.

All summer was consumed in these negotiations. Lodovico proceeded without arousing Charles' suspicions, while Ferdinand, the Pope and the Florentines neither distrusted nor totally confided in his promises. At the same time, in France, they were carefully laying the basis for the new expedition for which the King was becoming more eager every day, despite the counsels of almost all the ministers. And in order to expedite these matters, Charles settled his differences with Ferdinand and Isabella, King and Queen of Spain, sovereigns very celebrated in those days, highly reputed for their wisdom and for having brought great tranquility and order into their realms which had formerly been most turbulent; and for

---

* Jofré in Spanish.

having waged a war for ten years which resulted in their recuperating, in the name of Christ, the kingdom of Granada which had been held by the African Moors almost eight hundred years; a victory for which the Pope had conferred upon them, to the great applause of all Christians, the title of Catholic kings.* . . . For the same reasons, Charles made peace with Maximilian, King of the Romans, and his son Philip, Archduke of Austria. . . .

. .
.

Having thus established peace between the kingdom of France and all its neighbors, the Neapolitan war was decided upon for the following year; meanwhile all necessary provisions were to be prepared, as Lodovico Sforza was continually urging. And as men's thoughts range farther and farther, Lodovico Sforza was no longer thinking only about being secure in his government, but was now also aspiring to loftier goals; he intended, by taking advantage of the difficulties of the Aragonese, to confer the duchy of Milan entirely upon himself, and in order to lend some color of justice to such an act of injustice and to build his affairs on a firmer foundation against any possibilities that might intervene, he married off his niece, Bianca Maria, sister of Giovan Galeazzo, to Maximilian, who had recently succeeded to the Roman Empire after the death of his father, Frederick. Lodovico promised her a dowry consisting of 400,000 ducats in ready money to be paid in allotments, and forty thousand ducats in jewels and other effects. On his part, Maximilian, who had acceded to this marriage more for the money than for ties of affinity, obligated himself, in prejudice of Giovan Galeazzo, his new brother-in-law, to grant the investiture of the duchy of Milan upon Lodovico himself, his children and his descendents, as if that state had never had a legitimate duke after the death of Filippo Maria Visconti, Maximilian promising to consign Lodovico with the privileges of the dukedom, drawn up in the broadest terms, at the time of the last payment. . . . Thus Lodovico, acting at the same time wickedly against his living nephew and injuriously against the memory of his deceased father and brothers, affirmed that none of them had been legitimate dukes of Milan; that the duchy had devolved upon the Empire and that he had received his investiture from Maximilian, therefore entitling himself, not the seventh, but the fourth Duke of Milan. However, so long as the nephew lived, very few people knew about these matters. . . .

. .
.

* Goddard omits this entirely, either because he was working from an imperfect text or because he was loath to celebrate the Spanish sovereigns. (*History of Italy*, Austin Parke Goddard, tr., London, 1753–56, Vol. I, p. 67.)

Ferdinand was more confident now that the marriage which Lodovico had arranged would create dissension between Sforza and the King of France. He judged that differences would inevitably arise between them, since Sforza was pledging so much money to Charles' rival and, on many occasions, his enemy. He was certain that Lodovico would take courage from this new family alliance and would now boldly withdraw from his French enterprise. This hope Lodovico nourished with the greatest cunning; nevertheless (such was his skill and manipulative power), he was capable of giving pledges at the same time to Ferdinand and the other Italians while simultaneously entering into deals with the King of the Romans and the King of France. Similarly, Ferdinand hoped that the Venetian Senate, to whom he had sent ambassadors, would be bound to consider themselves threatened by the entrance of a prince, so much stronger than themselves, into Italy, where they held first place so far as power and authority were concerned; nor was he lacking in assurances and encouragement from the King and Queen of Spain, who promised to help him on a large scale in case their persuasions and authority proved inefficacious to thwart this invasion.

On the other hand, the King of France, having removed all impediments on his side of the mountains, now took steps to eliminate whatever difficulties and obstacles might arise from the other side. Therefore, he sent Peron de Baschi, a man not lacking in skill with regard to the affairs of Italy (where he had served under Jean d'Anjou), to notify the Pope, the Venetian Senate and the Florentines of his King's decision to recover the kingdom of Naples, and urged all of them to join in this undertaking with him. But he did not secure anything other than general hopes and replies, because everybody hesitated to reveal their intentions so soon, when the war was not scheduled until the following year. Similarly, the King requested the Florentine ambassadors, who with Ferdinand's approval had been sent to him earlier, to clear themselves of the imputation of being partial to the Aragonese, by promising him safe passage and provisions for his army through their territory, together with a proper payment, and that they should also send one hundred men-at-arms to him as a token that the Florentine Republic would continue in its friendship.

And although the ambassadors pointed out to him that such a declaration could not be made without grave danger until his army had first entered Italy, affirming that he could always, in any event, count on the friendship and devotion which the city of Florence had always borne toward the French crown; nevertheless, Charles, with French impetuosity, constrained them to make such promises, otherwise threatening to cut off the trade which so many Florentine merchants were carrying on in his kingdom. Subsequently it was discovered that these recommendations were instigated by Lodovico Sforza, who was then the guide and director of all the French dealings with the Italians.

Piero de' Medici attempted to persuade Ferdinand that these demands were so unimportant compared with the possibility of war that it would be better for the Republic and himself to keep in Charles' good faith; indeed, they might perhaps serve as an opportunity to come to some agreement, whereas by refusing such small demands, the Florentines would become open enemies of the French, which was no advantage to the King of Naples. Besides this, he pointed out how great was his responsibility, and how much hatred would be stirred up against him in Florence if Florentine merchants were expelled from France; and that it was a mark of good faith, a fundamental principle of alliances, that each ally should patiently put up with some inconveniences in order that the other might not run into much greater dangers.

But Ferdinand, who was aware of how much his reputation and security would diminish if the Florentines should break with him, did not accept this reasoning but complained bitterly that Piero's constancy and loyalty should have so soon begun not to correspond with what he had promised him. Whence Piero, determined above all to maintain his friendship with the Aragonese, dragged out by devious means his reply, which the French demanded immediately, declaring at last that the final decision of the Republic would be made known by new ambassadors.

At the end of this year, the alliance between the Pope and Ferdinand began to waver: either because the Pontiff aspired by raising new difficulties to obtain major advantages from the King of Naples, or because he thought in this way to induce him to bring the Cardinal of San Pietro in Vincoli under his obedience. The Pope was very anxious for this Cardinal to come to Rome, offering for his security the pledges of the College of Cardinals, of Ferdinand and the Venetians. The Cardinal's absence made Alexander feel very uneasy because of the importance of the fortress of Ostia (as well as Ronciglione and Grottoferrata which he held near Rome), the Cardinal's great authority and many followers in the court, and finally, because he was by nature ambitious for new undertakings, pertinacious, and ready to run any risk rather than deviate from his plans to the slightest degree.

Ferdinand effectively excused himself, stating that he could not force the Cardinal of San Pietro in Vincoli to comply, since he was so suspicious that any surety whatever seemed less sure than his danger. Ferdinand complained of his hard fate with the Pope, who always attributed to him what really derived from others: thus the Pope had believed that Virginio had bought the castles with Ferdinand's money and on his counsels, whereas the purchase had really been carried out without any participation on his part; in fact, he had been the one to induce Virginio to an agreement, and for this reason had advanced money to be paid in compensation for the castles. But since the Pontiff did not accept any of these excuses, reproaching Ferdinand instead with bitter and almost menacing words, it seemed that no firm foundation could be laid on their reconciliation.

The Beginning of the Years of Misfortune

IN such a state of mind and in such confusion of affairs, likely to lead to new disturbances, began the year 1494 (I date according to the Roman usage)—a most unhappy year for Italy, and in truth the beginning of those years of misfortune, because it opened the door to innumerable horrible calamities, in which, one could say, for various reasons, a great part of the world was subsequently involved.

At the beginning of this year, Charles, utterly opposed to any agreement with Ferdinand, ordered his ambassadors to immediately take their departure from the kingdom of France as if they were ambassadors of an enemy king.

And almost the very same day, Ferdinand, oppressed more by grief than age, died of a sudden pneumonia.* He was a king renowned for his industry and wisdom, by means of which, together with the help of good fortune, he maintained his rule over the kingdom newly acquired by his father, in spite of the many difficulties which manifested themselves at the beginning of his reign, and rose to greater glory than perhaps any king had ever possessed for many years. A good king, if he had continued to govern as skillfully as he had begun; but in the course of time (having either acquired new habits because, like almost all princes, he knew not how to resist a lust for domination, or because, as almost everyone believed, his natural proclivities which he had earlier disguised with great adroitness, now revealed themselves), he became known as a man of little faith, and so cruel that his own followers felt that it would be suitable to call him inhuman.

It was held certain that Ferdinand's death would prove harmful to the common cause. For, aside from the fact that he would have attempted anything likely to prevent a passage of the French, no one doubted that inducing Lodovico Sforza to ally himself with Alfonso's haughty and immoderate personality would prove more difficult than it would have been to get him to renew friendship with Ferdinand, who in the past had often been inclined to yield to Sforza's will in order to have no cause for conflict with the state of Milan. Among other things, it is clear that when

---

* . . . *catarro repentino* . . . (Gherardi, op. cit., I, p. 36). Fenton translates this as "apoplexy"! (*The Historie of*   *Guicciardin* . . ., tr., Gefray Fenton, London, 1618, p. 21).

Alfonso's daughter Isabella went to join her husband, Lodovico fell in love with her at first sight and wanted her for his own wife; and in order to obtain his ends (as everyone in Italy believed at that time), Lodovico saw to it by means of sorcery and enchantments that Giovan Galeazzo was impotent for many months after his marriage. Ferdinand would have consented to Lodovico's suit, but Alfonso rejected it; whence Lodovico, all hope lost, took another wife and had children by her, and turned all his thoughts to transferring the duchy of Milan to them. . . .

. .

   As soon as his father was dead, Alfonso sent four ambassadors to the Pope . . . with whom a mutual defense alliance was openly concluded, each party allotting a fixed number of men toward the other's assistance. The Pope also would confer the investiture of the kingdom upon Alfonso with the same diminution of tribute which Ferdinand had obtained (but only for his lifetime) from other pontiffs, and send an apostolic legate to crown him; and he would create a cardinal of Lodovico, son of Don Enrico, Alfonso's bastard brother, who was subsequently called the Cardinal of Aragon. On his part, the King would immediately pay thirty thousand ducats to the Pope; provide the Duke of Gandia* with estates in the kingdom yielding an income of twelve thousand ducats a year, and also bestow upon him the first of the seven main offices that became vacant; promised that during the Pontiff's lifetime, he, Alfonso, would commission at his own expense the Duke with three hundred men-at-arms, obliged to serve both of them equally; that he would bestow upon Don Goffredo (who almost as a hostage of his father's pledge, would go to live with his father-in-law) the post of Prothonotary (one of the seven offices), in addition to the appointments promised at the earlier agreement. The King would also bestow the revenues of benefices in his realm upon Cesare Borgia, the Pope's son, who had recently been raised by his father to the cardinalate, the impediment of being a bastard (who were not usually granted the purple) removed by means of false witnesses to prove that he was someone else's legitimate son.
   Furthermore, Virginio Orsini, who was also present with a royal mandate at this agreement, promised that the King would help the Pope recover the fortress of Ostia in the event that the Cardinal of San Pietro in Vincoli refused to return to Rome. The King, however, claimed that this promise had been made without his consent or knowledge; Alfonso felt that it was very harmful at such a dangerous time to alienate that Cardinal, so powerful in Genoa, on which, at the Cardinal's instigation, the King planned to make an attempt. And lest amidst such great broils, a Council

* Pope Alexander VI's youngest son, Don Goffredo.

might possibly be called, or other actions taken which would be prejudicial to the Apostolic See, Alfonso sought by all means to reconcile the Cardinal of San Pietro in Vincoli with the Pope.

But Alexander would not come to any agreement unless Vincoli returned to Rome, and since the Cardinal was stubbornly determined never to entrust his life to the good faith of Catalans (such were his words), Alfonso's efforts and desires in this respect were in vain.

For after feigning that he would almost certainly accept the agreement being negotiated, the Cardinal suddenly departed one night aboard an armed brigantine from Ostia, leaving that fortress well guarded; and after resting a few days at Savona and then at Avignon, where he was legate, he finally arrived at Lyons, where Charles had come just a little time before, in order more conveniently and more publicly to make provisions for the war which he was already openly proclaiming he intended to conduct in person. There the Cardinal was received by the King with the greatest honor and ceremony and joined with the others who were making ready to loose troubles upon Italy.

. .

At Lodovico's advice, Charles dispatched four ambassadors to the Pope with the commission that while passing through Florentine domain, they should request a declaration of policy from that Republic. . . . Following the instructions which had been mainly laid out for them in Milan, these delegates made speeches in various Italian localities with regard to the reasons whereby the King of France, as successor to the house of Anjou and for want of a direct descendent of Charles I, was laying claim to the kingdom of Naples, and had determined to enter Italy in person that very year, not in order to take possession of anything belonging to others but only to obtain that which justly belonged to him; although his ultimate aim was not so much the kingdom of Naples as the possibility of subsequently turning his forces against the Turks, for the exaltation and propagation of Christianity.

At Florence these ambassadors* pointed out how much confidence the King placed in that city, which had been rebuilt by Charlemagne and had always been favored by the French kings, Charles' ancestors, most recently by his father, Louis XI, in the war which had so unjustly been waged against them by Pope Sixtus, by Ferdinand who had recently died, and by the present King Alfonso. The ambassadors also reminded the Florentines of the very great profits and goods which ensued to them from their trade in France, where Florentine merchants were well received and encouraged just as if they were of French blood. With that as an

* Beraud Aubigny, a Scottish captain; the General of France; the President of the Parliament; and Peron de Baschi.

example, they might look forward to similar advantages and benefits in the kingdom of Naples when Charles took possession of it. Thus, as the Florentines had never received anything but harm and injuries from the Aragonese, the ambassadors asked if they would not wish to give some indication of joining the King in his undertaking; and if for some just cause they were unable to participate, they might at least concede the French troops passage through their domain and provisions, to be paid for by the French army.

In this manner, the ambassadors negotiated with the Republic. But with Piero de' Medici, they dealt privately—reminding him of the many favors and honors conferred by Louis XI on his father and his family; and how, in troublesome times, the King had openly on many occasions supported the reputation of Florence, honoring in sign of amity their escutcheons with the very escutcheons of the house of France. Whereas, on the contrary, Ferdinand had not been content to wage war openly against the Florentines, but had also wickedly enmeshed himself in civic plots, in which Piero's uncle Giuliano had been murdered and his father Lorenzo seriously wounded.

Not receiving any definite satisfaction from the Florentines, the ambassadors went on to Rome; there they reminded the Pope of the traditional interest and continuous devotion of the French crown to the Apostolic See (ancient and modern history being full of examples), as contrasted with the contumacy and frequent disobedience of the Aragonese. They then demanded the investiture of the kingdom of Naples for Charles as his juridical right, alluring the Pope with many hopes, and putting forward many offers, if he should be propitious to this enterprise, which after all had been set in motion as much because of the Holy Father's persuasions and authority as for any other reason. . . .

. .

In Florence there was a great deal of sympathy toward France, partly because so many Florentines engaged in commerce in that kingdom; partly because of the inveterate, although false, belief that Charlemagne had rebuilt their city after its destruction by Totila,* King of the Goths; partly because of the very close alliance which their Guelph ancestors had long maintained with Charles, first King of Naples, and many of his descendants who were partisans of the Guelphs in Italy; partly because of the memory of the war which first old Alfonso, and later, in the year 1478, Ferdinand had waged against their city, sending his son Alfonso in person against them.

---

* Florence was, toward the middle of the sixth century, utterly destroyed by Totila, one of the later kings of the Os- trogoths. The chronicler Giovanni Villani mistakes Totila for the much earlier Attila, King of the Huns.

For these various reasons, all the commonality were in favor of grant-ing free passage to the French. But even the wiser and more authoritative citizens of the Republic were equally in favor, deeming it most imprudent to drag so dangerous a war (arising out of other people's controversies) into Florentine territory, setting themselves up against so powerful an army and against the person of the King of France, whose entrance into Italy was favored by the state of Milan and, if not consented to, at least not opposed by the Venetian senate. Their judgment was confirmed by the authoritative precedent of Cosimo de' Medici, considered in his time one of the wisest men in Italy; who in the war between Jean d'Anjou and Ferdinand (although the Pope and the Duke of Milan supported Fer-dinand) had always recommended that Florence should not oppose Jean. They also recalled the example of Lorenzo, Piero's father, who was always of the same opinion at every rumor of the return of the Angevins. Indeed, terrified at French power after their king had taken Brittany, Lorenzo often used to say that the greatest calamities were in store for the Italians once the King of France became aware of his own strength.

But Piero de' Medici, weighing the situation more by will than by wisdom, and too self-confident, and convinced that the French enterprise would more likely end up in noise rather than effects, and confirmed in these opinions by several of his advisers (bribed, it was said, by Alfonso), stubbornly persisted in maintaining friendship with the Aragonese; and so great was Piero's strength that all the other citizens finally had to submit to his will. I have it on reliable authority that Piero, not content with the power which his father had obtained in the Republic (although that was already so great that even the magistrates were nominated as he wished, and nothing of real importance was decided without his opinion), never-theless was aspiring to more absolute power and the title of Prince; unwisely failing to realize that a city which was then very powerful and rich, and had drawn its strength for many centuries from its outward aspects as a republic, whose most important citizens were accustomed to play a role in the government as equals rather than as subjects, would not be likely to tolerate so great and sudden a change without violence. Hence Piero, knowing that the most extraordinary foundations were necessary to bolster his greed for power, had immoderately tied himself up with the Aragonese and was determined to run all their risks, in order to have a powerful prop to support his new princedom. . . .

. .
.

The Florentines answered the King's ambassadors with most ornate and respectful words, but without the conclusion which they desired: pointing out, on the one hand, the natural devotion which the Florentines

had toward the French crown and their immense desire to satisfy so
glorious a king; and on the other, the various obstacles. For surely nothing
was more unworthy of princes and republics than not observing one's
pledged word, and they could not satisfy his demands without openly
dishonoring their previous promise. For the alliance was still in effect
which King Charles' father Louis had drawn up with Ferdinand, with a
stipulation that after his death it was to extend to Alfonso; wherein the
Florentines were not only explicitly bound to come to the defense of the
kingdom of Naples, but also to prohibit passage through their domain
against anyone who might be marching to attack it. They were extremely
sorry to be unable to reach any other decision, but they hoped that the
most wise and just King, aware of their good intentions, would attribute
their refusal to these legitimate impediments. The King was infuriated by
this reply, and immediately ordered the Florentine ambassadors to leave
France, and he also followed Lodovico Sforza's advice by expelling from
Lyons, not the other Florentine merchants but only the representatives
of Piero de' Medici's bank, which the Florentines would interpret to mean
that the King considered himself offended not by the citizens in general,
but by Piero in particular.

Thus all the other Italian powers were divided: some in favor of the
King of France, some opposed. Only the Venetians determined to remain
neutral and idly await the outcome of this affair; either because it was
not to their disadvantage that Italy should be in turmoil, in hopes that
protracted wars of others would give them an opportunity to expand their
empire; or because, being so powerful, they were not afraid of easily falling
prey to the conqueror; and that it was therefore unwise, with no evident
necessity, to become involved in other people's wars.

[*Rejecting the appeals of both Ferdinand and the King of France to
support their respective causes, the Venetian senate declares its
friendship for the French crown but claims that all their forces were
involved in guarding their empire against the Turks.*]

[*Charles prepares by land and sea for his expedition against Naples.
He sends his grand equerry to Genoa to prepare heavy ships and light
galleys, and fits out other vessels in Villefranche and Marseilles.*]

Many people in France believed that ultimately all these bellicose
preparations and mobilizations would prove in vain because of the King's
incapacity, the base quality of his advisers, and the lack of funds. Nevertheless, Charles' ardor was unquenched. At the advice of some of his
favorites, he had recently assumed the title of King of Jerusalem and the
Two Sicilies (the title, at that time, of the Neapolitan kings), and was
fervently making provisions for war, collecting money, organizing his

men-at-arms, and keeping close counsel with Galeazzo da San Severino who was privy to all of Lodovico Sforza's secrets and decisions.

On the other hand, Alfonso had never ceased preparations by land and by sea, judging that there was no more time to permit himself to be deceived by Lodovico's promises, and that it would be more expedient to frighten and molest him than wear oneself out trying to assure and mollify him. He therefore ordered the Milanese ambassador to leave Naples and recalled his from Milan, and took possession of the duchy of Bari. . . .

He also determined to personally lead a strong army into Romagna, and thence proceed immediately into the territory of Parma where, by proclaiming the name of Giovan Galeazzo and raising his banners, he hoped that the people of the duchy of Milan would rise against Lodovico. And even if this scheme should run into difficulties, he still judged it useful that the war should begin in a place far from his own realm; most important, in his opinion, was that the French should arrive in Lombardy in winter, so that, as usually happens in the Italian wars, their armies could not take to the field before the end of April because of insufficient pasturage for the horses. Thus he presupposed that, in order to avoid the bitterness of that season, they would be obliged to remain in their ally's country until spring; and he hoped that, in the meanwhile, something useful for his cause might occur. He also sent ambassadors to Constantinople asking help from Bajazet Ottoman, Prince of the Turks, as one facing a common danger, since it was well known that Charles intended to move on into Greece once he had conquered Alfonso. He knew that Bajazet did not underestimate this peril, because the Turks had no small fear of French arms, remembering as they did the expeditions which the French had carried out in past epochs against the infidels in Asia.

[*Supported by Alfonso, the Pope captures the fortress of Ostia held by the Cardinal della Rovere. Lodovico induces the King of France to send Swiss troops to Genoa, and plays his usual double game with the Pope and Piero de' Medici to hinder their attempt on Genoa. King Alfonso musters his army in the Abruzzi, but after a meeting with the Pope, decides to halt his march, leaving part of his army to defend the States of the Church and his own, while his eldest son Ferrando, Duke of Calabria,* would proceed to the Romagna, accompanied by Gianiacopo da Trivulzio,** governor of the royal troops.*]

* The title given to the eldest sons of the kings of Naples. Guicciardini calls him Ferdinando, but this would introduce the third Ferdinand just when the reader has managed to sort out Ferdinand the Catholic, King of Aragon, from Ferdinand of Aragon, King of Naples!

** Guicciardini performs numerous vagaries on this name: Giovaniacopo Triulzi, Trivulzi, etc. Trivulzio (1448–1518) was a Milanese noble who later shifted over to the French side, became one of the best generals of Louis XII, and was created a marshal of France.

Meanwhile the fleet sailed from Naples under the command of the Admiral Don Federigo.]

Don Federigo's expedition to Genoa finally unleashed the Italian war. This commander undoubtedly possessed the biggest and best-provided fleet that had sailed the Tyrrhenian Sea for many years; he had thirty-five light galleys, eighteen ships and a great many smaller vessels, much artillery and three thousand infantrymen to be set on land. As a result of these preparations, and also because the Genoese exiles sailed with him, he set forth from Naples in great hopes of victory. But the tardiness of his departure, caused by difficulties which usually beset great undertakings, and to some degree by the artificial hopes aroused by Lodovico Sforza, and then having dallied at the ports belonging to the Sienese in order to enlist five thousand footsoldiers—all of this had created difficulties in what would have been very easy had they attempted it a month earlier. For their adversaries, having had time to make formidable preparations, the Bailli of Dijon [Antoine de Baissey] had already entered Genoa with two thousand Swiss troops, levied and paid by the King of France, and many of the ships and galleys in that port were already rigged and armed. At the same time, several vessels arrived which had been armed at Marseilles.

Lodovico also, sparing no expense, had sent many footsoldiers there under the command of Gasparo da San Severino, surnamed Il Fracassa,* together with his brother, Antonio Maria; and in order to be as certain of Genoese good will as of foreign forces, he offered gifts, provisions, money, promises and various rewards, to win over Giovan Luigi dal Fiesco, brother of Obietto, the Adorni,** and many other gentlemen and leaders of the popular faction of Genoa who were vital in holding that city firmly to his cause. On the other hand, he summoned many followers of the exiles to Milan from Genoa and towns along the Riviera.

The presence of Louis, Duke of Orleans, was an added source of great reputation and strength during all these preparations, powerful in themselves. On the same day the Aragonese fleet sailed into Genoese waters, Louis marched into that city by order of the King of France, having first conferred with Lodovico Sforza in Alexandria concerning their common undertaking. At that meeting, Lodovico had welcomed him happily and with great honors (so full of dark shadows are the doings of mortals), treating him as an equal, little realizing how soon his domain and his very life would be in Louis' power.

This was why the Aragonese, who previously had planned to sail with their fleet into the port of Genoa, hoping that this would set off an upris-

---

* Il Fracassa means "the swaggerer," "the blusterer."
** The "adorned ones," the "ornate ones."

ing on the part of the exiles, changed their minds and decided to attack the coasts of the Riviera; and after some discussion as to whether it was better to begin the action against the Riviera of the east or of the west, Obietto's opinion was accepted, based upon finding many supporters along the Riviera di Levante.*

Hence the fleet sailed to Porto Venere, only to discover that the Genoese had already sent four hundred infantrymen there, and the inhabitants were rallied behind Gianluigi dal Fiesco, who had arrived at La Spezia. After fighting in vain for several hours and losing hope of conquering the city, they withdrew to the port of Livorno** to refurnish their victuals and increase their soldiers, because they decided that greater forces would be necessary to conquer the well-fortified towns along the Riviera.

At Livorno, Don Federigo learned that the French fleet, which was inferior to his in galleys but superior in ships, was preparing to leave the port of Genoa. Don Federigo, therefore, sent his ships back to Naples, in order to be able more expeditiously to escape from the enemy with the swifter galleys, should the French ships and galleys combined come to attack him. Nevertheless, he still retained hope of victory if, by chance or plan, the enemy's galleys should be separated from their ships.

. .
.

At the same time, Ferrando, Duke of Calabria, was marching with a land army toward Romagna with the intention of continuing, according to his original plans, into Lombardy; but in order to have free transit and leave no impediments or perils behind his back, he had to come to an agreement with the state of Bologna and the cities of Imola and Forlì; for Cesena, a city directly subject to the Pope, and the city of Faenza, which was subject to Astorre Manfredi, a young boy who was supported by and ruled under the protection of the Florentines, were already disposed to willingly provide all necessities to the Aragonese army.

. .
.

These difficulties were resolved at a meeting which Ferrando, leading his army into Romagna, had with Piero de' Medici at Borgo San Sepolcro. At their very first encounter the Duke, in his father Alfonso's name, offered Piero his personal assistance and his army, to be used as Piero pleased in matters relating to Florence, Siena and Faenza. Whence Piero's

---

* The Riviera di Levante refers to the coast southeast of Genoa; the Riviera di Ponente southwest of Genoa.

** Leghorn is the absurd Anglicization.

former fervor was rekindled; and, returning to Florence, he insisted that this agreement, which Ferrando had strongly pressed for, be ratified, although the wisest citizens advised him against it.

Having ratified this policy, to be carried out at the joint expense of the Pope, Alfonso, and the Florentines, the city of Bologna joined the pact a few days later, induced thereto by Giovanni Bentivoglio under whose arbitrary authority the city was governed. For Bentivoglio had received a promise from the Pope, guaranteed by the King and Piero de' Medici, that his son, Antonio Galeazzo, then Apostolic Prothonotary, would be created cardinal.

. .
.

Piero de' Medici's rashness was not curbed in the least by the difficulties which Ferrando had encountered in his attempt at Genoa nor the obstacles which had occurred in Romagna. By a secret agreement which Piero, unknown to the Republic, had made with the Pontiff and with Alfonso, he was obliged to openly oppose the King of France. Not only had he agreed that the Neapolitan fleet should be permitted to anchor and gather provisions in the port of Livorno and levy infantrymen throughout the Florentine domain, but unable to contain himself within any bounds whatever, Piero also saw to it that Annibale Bentivoglio, son of Giovanni, a captain in the service of the Florentines, together with the company under the command of Astorre Manfredi, should join Ferrando's army as soon as it entered the environs of Forlì. Besides this, Piero sent a thousand men-at-arms and artillery to Forlì.

The Pope continually manifested a similar point of view. Besides provisions for war, and not satisfied with having earlier entreated Charles, by a brief, not to invade Italy and to act according to justice rather than force, he now, by another brief, pronounced similar commands under pain of ecclesiastical censure. And through the efforts of the Bishop of Calagora, his nuncio at Venice (where Alfonso's ambassadors were working toward similar ends, and also the Florentines, although their demands were more deviously presented), the Pope strongly petitioned the Venetian senate to offer armed resistance against the King of France for the common benefit of Italy; or at least to make Lodovico Sforza roundly understand that they would consider themselves threatened by a French incursion.

However, the Doge, speaking in the name of the senate, replied that it was not the office of a wise government* to attract war into its own

---

* Guicciardini says *principe*. A literal translation here would give a mistaken notion of the nature of the Serenissima which was not ruled by a prince but by an oligarchy.

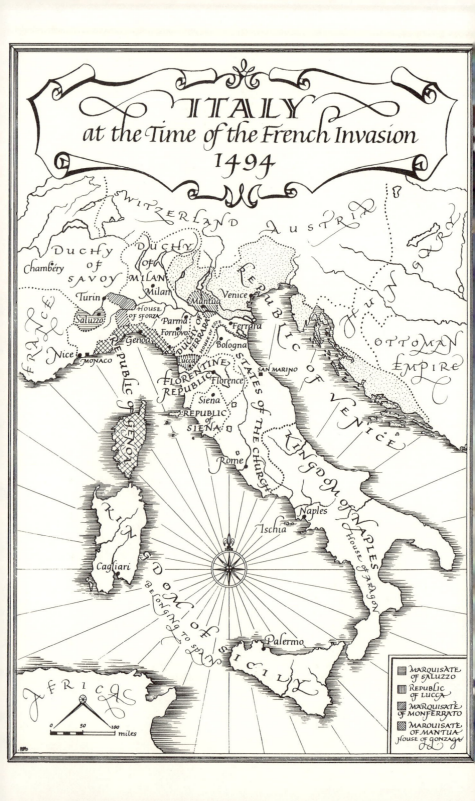

house in order to remove it from the house of another; and therefore they would not agree to undertake, either by demonstrations or deeds, anything which might displease any of the parties.

The King of Spain, strongly solicited by the Pope and Alfonso, promised to send his fleet, together with a great many troops, to Sicily in order to support the kingdom of Naples whenever necessary, but he apologized for not being able to do this immediately because of a lack of money. Hence Alfonso lent him certain sums; besides which the Pope gave consent that the King of Spain might make use, for this purpose, of the money which had been gathered in Spain under the authority of the Apostolic See for a crusade: funds which were not supposed to be used except against enemies of the Christian faith.

Meanwhile, having met with no success either on land or sea, Alfonso and Piero de' Medici now sought to beguile Lodovico Sforza, using his own craft and cunning; but their wiliness had no better outcome than their force.

Many people were of the opinion that Lodovico, out of concern for his own peril, would have taken it amiss should Charles acquire the kingdom of Naples, but that his plan was, once he had made himself Duke of Milan and brought the French army into Tuscany, to then interpose and bring about some agreement, whereby Alfonso would acknowledge himself tributary to the crown of France with suitable guarantees to the King, and after having dismembered perhaps the lands which the Florentines held in Lumigiana, the King would then return to France. Thus the Florentines would have been beaten; the King of Naples weakened in force and authority; and he, Lodovico, having become Duke of Milan, would have achieved just as much as was necessary to maintain his security without incurring the impending danger of a French victory. He also hoped that, overcome by the depths of winter, Charles would find himself in difficulties which would restrain his victorious course; and he expected the natural impatience of the French, the King's lack of money, and the opposition of many of his courtiers to this undertaking, would make it easily possible to find some means of agreement.

The French Invasion

AND now, not only were preparations being made on land and sea, but the very heavens and mankind concurred in predicting the future woes of Italy. For those whose profession it is to foretell the future by means of science or divine inspiration unanimously affirmed that more frequent and greater changes were in store, and stranger and more horrible events were about to occur than had been seen in any part of the world for many centuries. With no less terror did rumors spread everywhere that in various parts of Italy there had appeared things alien to the natural course of nature and the heavens. In Puglia one night, three suns appeared in the sky, surrounded by clouds, and with frightful thunder and lightning. In the territory of Arezzo an infinite number of armed men on enormous horses were seen for many days passing through the air with a terrible clamor of drums and trumpets. In many places in Italy the sacred images and statues had openly sweated. Everywhere monsters of men and other animals were being born. Many other things beyond the usual course of nature had happened in various sections: whence the people were filled with unbelievable dread, frightened as they already were by the fame of French power, and by the ferocity of that nation which (as history abundantly tells us) had already marched across all of Italy, plundering as they went, sacked the city of Rome and laid it waste with fire and

Typical of Renaissance mentality—as exemplified in Guicciardini's text—was the coexistence of scientific observation and medieval fancy. Thus in Sebastian Münster's Cosmographia Universale *new-drawn maps of the expanding knowledge of the world are published together with illustrations of "monsters" indifferently assigned to Africa or India.*

sword, and subjugated many provinces in Asia; nor was there any part of the world which at one time or another had not felt the weight of their arms. People were only surprised that amidst so many prodigies there did not appear a comet which the ancients reputed to be an unfailing messenger of the mutation of kingdoms and states.

But with all these celestial signs, predictions, prognostications and prodigies, people became more and more convinced every day that soon they must confront the dire effects. For Charles, persisting in his plans, had now arrived at Vienne, a city of the Dauphiné, since neither the entreaties of his entire kingdom nor a lack of money could dissuade him from personally moving into Italy. At that time, his shortage of money was such that he had no way of covering his current needs other than by pawning (and not for a great amount of money) certain jewels lent to him by the Duke of Savoy, by the Marchioness of Monferrat and other lords of the court. The money which he had gathered previously from French sources and that which had been lent to him by Lodovico had been spent partly in provisioning the ships (on which he based his greatest hope for victory), and the rest had been inconsiderately squandered on various people before leaving Lyons. And since at that time rulers were not readily disposed to extort money from the people (as later, avarice and boundless greed taught them to do, in violation of respect for God and men), it was not easy, therefore, to accumulate it again. So petty were the events and causes for unleashing so grave a war, the King being influenced more by rashness and impulse than by prudence and wise counsels. But as often happens when one begins the execution of a new, great and difficult enterprise, no matter how carefully planned, reasons which might be considered in opposition present themselves to men's minds.

So now, as the King was on the brink of departure, his troops in fact already marching toward the mountains, there arose serious murmurings and complaints throughout the court, stressing the difficulties inevitable in such an enterprise, some pointing out the dangers of Italian faithlessness, and above all, the untrustworthiness of Lodovico Sforza; others recalling the Florentine warning with regard to Sforza's deceitfulness (by chance, certain monies expected from him were late in arriving). The result was that not only did those who had always damned this invasion audaciously speak out against it (as happens when it seems that one's advice has been confirmed by events), but also those who had originally been in favor of it, among others the Bishop of San Malò, now began to vacillate to no small degree.

And finally when the King heard of these murmurings, they were already causing such dissension throughout the court, and in his own mind as well, and such a widespread inclination not to proceed further, that he suddenly gave orders for the army to halt. Therefore, many courtiers who were already on the march, having heard it publicly stated that it had been decided to no longer move into Italy, returned to the court.

And, it is believed, this changed decision would easily have taken effect if the Cardinal of San Pietro in Vincoli (then and formerly and subsequently the fatal instrument of the misfortunes of Italy), had not rekindled, by means of his prestige and vehemence, those whose spirits were almost frozen; and redirected the King's mind toward his former decision, reminding him not only of the reasons which had goaded him toward so glorious an expedition, but also sharply and solemnly pointing out that he keep before his eyes how much infamy would result for him throughout the world should he so lightly be deflected from so noble a design.

For what purpose (said the Cardinal) had he therefore weakened the frontiers of his kingdom by yielding up the towns in the province of Artois? For what reasons had he opened one of the gateways of France to the King of Spain by giving him the county of Roussillon, to the great displeasure not only of the nobility but of the common people? Similar concessions had been made by other kings only to free themselves of imminent perils, or to gain thereby very great advantages. But what necessity, what danger had impelled him? What reward did he expect from it? What fruit would result except that of having purchased at a very great price a shame that was even greater? What mishaps have occurred, what difficulties have intervened, what dangers have been disclosed, after he had announced his enterprise to the entire world? On the contrary, are not hopes of victory obviously increasing every moment, since the foundations on which the enemy based all his hopes of defense have proved vain? For the Aragonese fleet, having shamefully fled to Livorno after its fruitless attack on Porto Venere, was unable to make any headway whatever against Genoa, defended by numerous troops and a fleet more powerful than theirs; on land, their army, checked in Romagna by the resistance of a small number of Frenchmen, lacked courage to march ahead. Then how would they act when the news spread all over Italy that the King had crossed the mountains with a mighty army? What tumults would break out everywhere? How panic-stricken would be the Pope when, from his own palace, he saw the armies of the Colonna at the gates of Rome? How terrified would be Piero de' Medici having his very own blood as his enemy, knowing that the city of Florence has always been most loyal to the French crown, and is eager to recover its liberties which Piero has repressed? There was no obstacle that could check the King's impetuous course to the frontiers of the kingdom of Naples, where no sooner did he approach, than there would be the same uprisings and panic, and nothing but flight or rebellion everywhere. Was he perhaps apprehensive because of a lack of money? But no sooner would the tramp of his troops be heard,

GIULIANO DELLA ROVERE

The Cardinal of San Pietro in Vincoli (the future Pope Julius II) in the fresco by Melozzo da Forlì of Sixtus IV (Della Rovere) receiving Platina. Pinacoteca Vatican. (COURTESY OF FRATELLI ALINARI)

no sooner would his mighty artillery sound their terrible thunder, than all the Italians would compete to shower him with money. And even if some of them might chance to offer resistance, the spoils, the booty, the riches of the vanquished would suffice to nourish his army: for Italy, accustomed for many years rather to the images of wars than real wars, lacked spine to sustain the fury of the French. Therefore, what fear, what confusion, what dreams, what vain shadows had entered his breast? Wherefore had he so quickly lost his magnanimity? Where was that ferocity with which, four days earlier, he had boasted that he could conquer all the Italian powers combined? He should realize that his decisions were no longer in his own hands; things had already gone too far, too many dominions had already been alienated, ambassadors given audience, dispatched, banished; too many expenses already incurred; too many elaborate preparations, all the open and public announcements, and the fact that he had already come in person almost to the Alps. No matter how dangerous the enterprise might be, necessity constrained him to attempt it; since between glory and infamy, between dishonor and triumph, between being either the most esteemed or the most despised king in the entire world, no middle course whatever remained. Why therefore should he hesitate to gain the victory and celebrate the triumph already waiting for him and manifest?

This speech (in substance)* which the Cardinal, according to his nature, delivered more by means of efficacious argument and fiery gestures than ornate words, so moved the King's soul that, no longer listening to anyone except those favoring the invasion, he left the same day from Vienne accompanied by all the lords and captains of the kingdom of France, except the Duke of Bourbon, to whom in his absence he committed the administration of the entire realm, and the Admiral together with a few others appointed to govern and guard some of the most important provinces.

The King passed into Italy through the mountains of Montgenèvre, a much easier pass than Mont Cenis, through which Hannibal, the Carthaginian, had marched in ancient times, although with incredible difficulty. Charles entered Asti on the ninth day of September of the year 1494, bringing with him into Italy the seeds of innumerable calamities, of most horrible events and changes in almost the entire state of affairs. For his passage into Italy not only gave rise to changes of dominions, subversion of kingdoms, desolation of countries, destruction of cities and the cruelest massacres, but also new fashions, new customs, new and bloody ways of waging warfare, and diseases which had been unknown up to that time. Furthermore, his incursion introduced so much disorder

---

* *Dette in sostanza:* a conscientious admission by the author that he himself made up the speech (Gherardi, *op. cit.,* Vol. I, p. 55).

into Italian ways of governing and maintaining harmony, that we have never since been able to re-establish order, thus opening the possibility to other foreign nations and barbarous armies to trample upon our institutions and miserably oppress us. And what is all the more disgraceful, we cannot mitigate our shame because of the valor of the victor, since he whose coming caused so many misfortunes was, although well endowed in wealth and fortune, almost completely devoid of any natural or mental gifts.

For it is certain that Charles, from boyhood on, was of very feeble constitution and unhealthy body, short in stature, very ugly (aside from the vigor and dignity of his eyes), and his limbs so ill-proportioned that he seemed more like a monster than a man. Not only was he without any learning and skill but he hardly knew the letters of the alphabet; a mind yearning greedily to rule but capable of doing anything but that, since he was always surrounded by courtiers over whom he maintained neither majesty nor authority. He was neglectful of almost all effort and enterprise, and those affairs which he did take care of, he managed with very little judgment or wisdom. Indeed, if anything in him seemed worthy of praise, if one looked at it more closely, it proved to be further from virtue than from vice. Desirous of glory but more open to impulse than advice, generous but inconsiderate and acting without measure or distinction, sometimes immutable in his decisions but often on the basis of a poorly founded stubbornness rather than constancy; and that quality in him which many called goodness deserved more aptly to be called coldness and lack of spirit.

The Formidable French Artillery and Troops Compared with the Italian Forces

Lodovico Sforza and Beatrice, his wife, had immediately come to visit Charles at Asti with great pomp and a most honorable company of many noble and beauteous ladies from the duchy of Milan, together with Ercole d'Este, Duke of Ferrara. Conferring about their joint enterprise, it was decided that the army should march as soon as possible. And in order that this might be most expeditiously accomplished, Lodovico advanced more money to the King, who was in great need of it. For Lodovico feared not a little that should the bitter weather come during the campaign, the French army would halt all winter in the lands of the duchy of Milan. But the King, discovering that he had that illness which we call smallpox, remained in Asti for about a month, billeting his army in that city and the surrounding countryside. The number of these troops (as well as I can gather from various sources) besides the two hundred gentlemen of the King's guard (and counting the Swiss who had gone first to Genoa with the Bailli of Dijon, and those who fought under Aubigny* in Romagna) consisted of sixteen hundred men-at-arms, each of whom has, according to French usage, two archers, with the result that each lancer (as men-at-arms are called) has six horsemen under him. Also six thousand Swiss infantry and six thousand infantry of his own kingdom, of whom half were from the province of Gascony, which was, according to the French, better endowed with warlike infantrymen than any other part of France. Furthermore, the army was to be provisioned by a great quantity of artillery for battering down walls and for use during the campaign, but of a sort never before seen in Italy. This artillery had already been transported by sea to Genoa, from which it would join the army.

This new plague of artillery, developed many years before in Germany, had been brought to Italy for the first time by the Venetians during their war against the Genoese in the year of Salvation 1380, when the Venetians were defeated at sea and so afflicted over the loss of Chioggia that they would have accepted whatever conditions the victors imposed, had not moderate counsels prevailed on that famous occasion. The biggest of these artillery pieces were called bombards, which were subsequently employed throughout Italy since this new invention could be adapted for attacking towns. Some of them were made of iron, some of bronze, but they were so big that the large pieces could be dragged only very slowly and with the greatest difficulty; furthermore, men were unskilled in handling them, and the grappling irons were unwieldy. For the same reasons, it was difficult to plant them in position against cities; once placed, there was such an interval between one shot and another compared to later developments, that a great deal of time was consumed with very little reward. Consequently, the defenders of the place under attack had time to calmly make the necessary repairs and fortifications.

Nevertheless, the explosion of the powder mixed with saltpeter was so violent, the balls flew through the air with such stupendous speed and with such horrible thunder that even before they had been perfected, this kind of artillery rendered ridiculous all former weapons of attack which had been used by the ancients, to the great renown of Archimedes and other inventors. But the French developed many infantry pieces which were even more maneuverable, constructed only of bronze. These were called cannons and they used iron cannonballs instead of stone as before, and this new shot was incomparably larger and heavier than that which had been previously employed. Furthermore, they were hauled on carriages drawn not by oxen as was the custom in Italy, but by horses, with such agility of manpower and tools assigned for this purpose that they almost always marched right along with the armies and were led

---

* Robert Stuart d'Aubigny (d. 1544), marshal of France, cousin of the King of Scotland.

THE CANNON

Engraving by Albrecht Dürer, dated 1518 (COURTESY OF GABINETTO NAZIONALE
DELLE STAMPE, ROME)

right up to the walls and set into position there with incredible speed; and
so little time elapsed between one shot and another and the shots were so
frequent and so violent was their battering that in a few hours they could
accomplish what previously in Italy used to require many days. They
used this diabolical rather than human weapon not only in besieging cities
but also in the field, together with similar cannon and other smaller pieces,
but all of them constructed and maneuvered, according to their size, with
the same dexterity and speed.

This artillery made Charles' army all the more formidable throughout
Italy; formidable, besides, not so much because of the number as for the
valor of his troops. For, his men-at-arms were almost all the King's subjects
and not plebians but gentlemen whom the captains could not enlist or
dismiss simply at their will; nor were they paid by their officers but by
the royal ministers. Furthermore, their companies were at full muster, the
men in prime condition, their horses and arms in good order, since they
were not constrained by poverty in providing for themselves. Each one
competed with his fellow to serve more honorably, impelled by the thirst
for glory which noble birth nourishes in men's breasts; and also because
they could hope that their valor would be rewarded, both outside the

army and within the army, which was so organized that one could rise by promotions up to the rank of commander.

The captains of companies, almost all of whom were barons and lords, or at least of very noble blood and almost all subjects of the kingdom of France, had the same incentives. When the company's rolls were complete (because according to the custom in that kingdom no one was given command of more than a hundred lancers), they had no other goal than to win praise from their King. Consequently, among them there was no reason for instability of changing leadership, either because of ambition or avarice, nor was there any competition with the other leaders to rise to a higher command.

All these things were different in the Italian army, where many of the men-at-arms were either peasants or plebians subject to some other prince and completely dependent on the captains with whom they contracted for their salaries, and who had the power of paying them or dismissing them. Wherefore they lacked, either by nature or circumstance, any exceptional incentive to serve well. The captains were very rarely subjects of those whom they served; besides, they often had different interests and ends, and were filled with emulation and hatred among themselves, nor was there any fixed termination of their services. The result was that they were complete masters of their own companies; they did not keep at full muster the number of soldiers for which they were being paid, nor were they satisfied with the honest conditions to which they were bound and took every possible occasion to make covetous demands on their employers; unstable, they frequently passed from one service to another, sometimes tempted by ambition or greed or other interests to be not only unstable but faithless.

No less apparent was the difference between the Italian infantry and Charles', because the Italians did not fight in firm, well-ordered squadrons, but scattered throughout the countryside, retreating most of the time to the security of river banks and ditches. But the Swiss, a most bellicose nation whose long military experience and many outstanding victories had resurrected their ancient reputation for ferocity, went into battle in square ranks, organized and clear according to a certain number of soldiers per file. And they would face the enemy like a wall without ever breaking ranks, stable and almost invincible, when they fought in a place wide enough to be able to extend their squadron. The French and Gascon infantry fought with similar discipline and order, although not with the same skill.

· ·
·

While the King lay ill at Asti, new disturbances arose in the towns around Rome. For, although Alfonso had accepted all the immoderate demands which the family of the Colonna had put forth, no sooner had Aubigny entered into Romagna with French troops than the Colonna cast aside their disguise, openly declared themselves soldiers of the French King, and seized the fortress at Ostia by coming to an agreement with several of the Spanish infantry who were there on guard. This seizure of Ostia caused the Pope to complain about the French to all the Christian rulers, especially to the King of Spain and the Venetian senate, from whom he demanded help, although in vain, under the obligation of the alliance which they had drawn up the previous year. The Pope also seriously set about preparing for war, summoned Prospero and Fabrizio Colonna to Rome, and then ordered their palaces there to be razed, and combined his troops and part of Alfonso's under Virginio at the Teverone near Tivoli, and sent them to invade the lands of the Colonna who had no more than two hundred men-at-arms and one thousand footsoldiers.

[*The Aragonese army fails to make headway in the Romagna. King Alfonso, believing the enemy's advance will be delayed until the winter, orders his son, the Duke of Calabria, and Gianiacopo da Trivulzio not to risk the kingdom of Naples to the fortunes of war.*]

But all King Alfonso's precautions for his safety proved insufficient, for neither seasons nor any other difficulties could restrain Charles' fiery temperament. Hence, as soon as he had recovered his health, he ordered his army on the march again. When he passed through Pavia he lodged at the castle, paying a friendly visit to Giovan Galeazzo, Duke of Milan, his first cousin (their mothers had been sisters, daughters of Louis II, Duke of Savoy), who was lying there seriously ill. Since Lodovico Sforza was present, the conversation remained on general terms, the King expressing his grief at his cousin's illness, and urging him to be hopeful for a speedy recovery. But Charles and all his company felt great compassion, since they were all convinced that the life of that unhappy young man must prove very brief as a result of his uncle's machinations. And their compassion was all the more stirred up by the presence of Isabella, the Duke's wife who, not only anxious for her husband's health and for their little son, but in addition, afflicted by the danger facing her father and family, cast herself down unhappily at the King's feet, in full view of everyone, and weeping bitterly, begged him not to harm her father and the house of Aragon. Although the King was moved by her youth and beauty and gave outward signs of his pity, nevertheless he replied that he could not halt so great an undertaking for so trivial a reason, and that since the enterprise had been already carried so far, it was necessary to continue.

From Pavia the King went to Piacenza; during his stay news came of Giovan Galeazzo's death, as a result of which Lodovico, who had accompanied the King, now returned posthaste to Milan. There the leading members of the Ducal Council, suborned by Lodovico, proposed that it would be a most harmful thing for the prestige of that state, especially in terms of the difficult period which Italy was entering, if Giovan Galeazzo's son, who was five years old, should succeed his father; but that it was requisite to have a duke who would act with wisdom and authority. Therefore, in the interest of public safety and necessity, they were obliged to dispense with the legal regulations (as those very laws themselves permitted), and urge Lodovico to consent that the honors of the dukedom, a heavy responsibility at such a time, be transferred to him for the benefit of all.

Under this pretext—honesty yielding to ambition—although he feigned somewhat to resist, the following morning Lodovico assumed the title and seal of Duke of Milan, having secretly insisted before that he received them as due him by virtue of the investiture of the King of the Romans.

The rumor was widespread that Giovan Galeazzo's death had been provoked by immoderate coitus; nevertheless, it was widely believed throughout Italy that he had died not through natural illness nor as a result of incontinence, but had been poisoned; and Teodoro da Pavia, one of the royal physicians who had been present when Charles visited him, asserted that he had seen manifest signs of it. Nor was there anyone who doubted that if it had been poison, it had been administered through his uncle's machinations, who, not satisfied with possessing absolute governmental authority in the duchy of Milan, was avid and ambitious, as is commonly the case with men in high position, to make himself more illustrious with titles and honors; and especially because he felt that the legitimate prince's death was necessary for his own security and for the succession of his children, Lodovico wanted the power and title of duke to be transferred and endowed upon himself. Such was the greed which forced his nature, ordinarily mild and abhorring blood, to so nefarious a deed.

Almost everyone believed that this had been his intention ever since he had begun dealing with the French to invite them into Italy, thinking that the most opportune occasion to perform this deed would be when the King of France had marched into his duchy with a mighty army, and therefore everyone would lack courage to express their objections to such wickedness.

Others believed that this was an entirely new idea, born out of fear that the King (so sudden are French decisions) might precipitously proceed to liberate Giovan Galeazzo from such subjection, moved to do so either because of their relationship and pity for his youth, or because Charles would feel more secure should the dukedom be in his cousin's power rather than in Lodovico's. Furthermore, a number of important people high in the King's counsels were continually filling him with suspicions of Lodovico's fidelity. But since Lodovico had procured the investiture the previous year, and had anxiously solicited that his imperial privileges be sent to him just a little before his nephew's death, would seem to argue more likely for a premeditated and entirely voluntary deliberation on his part, rather than a sudden decision, almost forced by present danger.

Charles remained several days in Piacenza, not without some thoughts of returning beyond the mountains, for the shortage of money and the failure of any new signs in his favor to manifest themselves in Italy, cast doubt on his success. Charles was also no little suspicious of the new Duke of Milan, about whom the rumor was that although he had promised to return when he left, he would no more return. And it is also likely that since the wicked custom of poisoning men (a common practice in many parts of Italy) was practically unknown in those nations beyond the mountains, Charles and all his court, besides suspecting Sforza's fidelity, held his name in horror; in fact, the King considered his honor outraged that Lodovico should have inveigled him into Italy in order to be able to perpetrate with impunity so abominable a deed. Finally, however, he decided to continue his campaign, as Lodovico was continually urging him to do, promising to return to the King within a few days; for whether the King remained in Lombardy or suddenly returned to France were equally contrary to Lodovico's desires.

．　．
．

The very day King Charles left Piacenza, Lorenzo and Giovanni de' Medici* had come to see him: they had secretly stolen forth from their villas, and now petitioned him to come to Florence, assuring him that the Florentines bore as much good will toward the house of France as hatred toward Piero de' Medici. The King's anger against Piero had considerably increased as a result of new reasons. For when Charles had sent an ambassador to Florence from Asti, offering many advantages to the Florentines if they granted passage and abstained in the future from helping Alfonso; and in case they persisted in their original intentions, threatening them direly, and in order to frighten them even more had instructed his ambassador to leave, if they did not immediately agree; the Florentines had sought excuses for postponing their reply, answering that since the leading citizens of the government were in their country villas, as was the custom among Florentines during that season, they could not give him a definite answer so quickly but would soon inform the King of their decision via one of their own ambassadors.

* Of the collateral branch of the Medici; sons of Pier Francesco. Giovanni subsequently married Caterina Sforza; their son was the famous condottiere, Giovanni delle Bande Nere (of the Black Bands).

[The French decide to march into Tuscany across the Apennines of Parma; the vanguard crosses at Pietroemoli on the River Magra which divides ancient Liguria from Tuscany. At Lunigiana they are joined by the Swiss who had participated in the defense of Genoa, and the artillery which had been shipped by sea to La Spezia; the combined forces then took the town of Fivizzano, a Florentine stronghold.]

by assault and sacked it, killing the entire foreign garrison and many of the inhabitants: a thing unheard of and very frightening in Italy, which for a long time had been used to seeing wars staged with beautiful pomp and display, not unlike spectacles, rather than waged with bloodshed and dangers.

The Florentines decided to make their principal resistance at Serezana, a little city which they had strongly fortified . . . It was not considered easy to capture this citadel . . . nor could the French army remain very long in that region: the country being barren and narrow, pent up between the sea and the mountains . . . The King might have bypassed Serezana and attacked Pisa, but he felt that if he did not vanquish the first city which offered resistance, his reputation would be so diminished that all the other towns would quickly take heart and try to act in the same manner.

But it was ordained, either by good fortune or at the orders of some higher power (if men's imprudence and faults deserve such excuses), that a sudden remedy would intervene to remove this obstacle, since Piero de' Medici proved no more courageous or constant in adversity than he had been moderate or prudent in prosperity.

The harm resulting to the city of Florence from their opposition to the King had continually increased from the very beginning, not only because of the new edicts banning Florentine merchants from the entire kingdom of France, but also because of apprehensions of French power. These fears had grown excessively as soon as it was learned that Charles' army had begun to cross the Appenines, and later, when news came of the cruelty shown in taking Fivizzano.

Therefore, everyone in the city openly expressed opposition against Piero de' Medici's rash policy; since he had unnecessarily and thoughtlessly provoked the armies of a most powerful French king, aided by the Duke of Milan, by placing more faith in himself and in the advice of counselors who were bold and arrogant in times of peace and useless in times of peril, rather than in citizens, friends or relatives who had given him wise counsels. Worst of all, Piero was unskilled in matters of warfare and had failed to fortify their city, leaving it poorly garrisoned with soldiers and munitions; similarly, all the rest of Florentine domain was ill-prepared to defend itself against so great a threat.

Nor did it appear as if any of the Aragonese, for whom they were exposing themselves to such danger, were engaged against the enemy (except for the Duke of Calabria whose forces were fighting only a small part of the French army). Thus, as a result of all these actions and omissions of Piero, their city and domain, abandoned on every side, remained an object of boundless hatred and a likely prey of one who had sought so painstakingly not to be constrained to harm them.

Almost the entire city was already in this state of mind, fanned to greater heat by many noble citizens who highly disapproved of the present government, and the fact that a single family should have arrogated the power of the entire Republic to itself. Thus, the fears of those already fearful were augmented, and those who wanted a new government were emboldened. The nobles, indeed, had bolstered the people's spirit to such an extent that already many were beginning to fear that there was likely to be an uprising in the city. Furthermore, Piero's outrageous behavior and arrogance incited the Florentines all the more: in many ways, his mode of acting had deviated from the mild and civilized behavior of his ancestors; whence, almost from his youth on, he had always been hated by all the citizens; and to such a degree, indeed, that his father, Lorenzo, aware of Piero's nature, had often lamented to his most intimate friends that his son's recklessness and arrogance would bring about the ruin of the house of the Medici.

Piero, therefore, frightened by the peril which he had first boldly scoffed at, and now finding himself lacking the aid promised by the Pope and by Alfonso (who were deeply involved, what with the loss of Ostia, the attack against Nettuno, and fear of the French army), now suddenly decided to search among his foes for that safety which he no longer hoped to find among his friends. Piero thought that he was thereby following his father's example, who in 1479, reduced to gravest peril during the war waged against the Florentines by Pope Sixtus and Ferdinand, King of Naples, had gone to Naples to parlay with Ferdinand, and returned to Florence, bringing public peace and private security. But governing oneself by examples is undoubtedly very dangerous if similar circumstances do not correspond, not only in general but in all particulars, and if things are not managed with similar judgment, and if, aside from all other fundamentals, one does not have similar good fortune on one's side.*

Having left Florence with this purpose in mind, Piero learned that

---

* Also found in somewhat different terms in the *Ricordi*, second series, number 117: "*E fallacissimo el giudicare per gli esempli; perché se non sono simili in tutto e per tutto non servono, conciosiaché ogni minima varietà nel caso può essere causa di grandissima variazione nello effetto, ed el discernere queste va-* rietà, *quando sono piccole, vuole buono e perspicace occhio.*" The role of *fortuna* is omitted. By the time he came to write the *Storia*, the historian had grown even more dubious about the power of reason without luck. (Guicciardini, *Ricordi*, ed. Janni, Milan, 1951, p. 97.)

before the King's arrival, Paolo Orsini's cavalry and three hundred foot-soldiers sent by the Florentines to support the Serezana garrison had been routed by some French cavalry who had ridden there from the Magra, most of the Florentine forces either slain or taken prisoner. At Pietrasanta, Piero waited for his royal safe conduct, until the Bishop of San Malò and several other courtiers came to lead him safely to the King. Accompanied by the Bishop and these lords, Piero arrived at the camp the same day that the King, together with the rest of his army, had joined the advance-guard which was storming the fortress of Serezanello, but making so little headway that they had no hope of conquering it.

Brought before the King, who received him kindly (more in appear-ance than actuality), Piero mitigated the King's ire to no small extent by capitulating to all his numerous and excessive demands: namely, that the fortresses of Pietrasanta, Serezana, and Serezanello, key points in the Florentine domain, and the fortresses of Pisa and the port of Livorno, most important members of their state, should be rendered up to the King. On his part, the King promised in an agreement signed by his own hand to restore them as soon as he had conquered the kingdom of Naples. Piero would also see to it that the Florentines would lend Charles 200,000 ducats, in exchange for which the King would accept them as allies under his protection. Some of these matters, promised with simple words, might be deferred until the written agreement had been sent to Florence, through which city the King intended to march. But the handing over of the fortresses was not deferred; Piero immediately turned over the castles of Serezana, Pietrasanta and Serezanello to the King, and a few days later, ordered a similar consignment of the fortresses at Pisa and Livorno. All the French themselves were greatly amazed that Piero had so lightly com-plied with such important demands; for the King undoubtedly would have been satisfied with much easier terms.

. .
.

Piero's acquiescence not only secured Tuscany to the King, but also removed all his obstacles in Romagna where Aragonese fortunes were already declining very much. For one who is scarcely able to defend himself against imminent dangers finds it very difficult to provide for the security of another at the same time.

. .
.

When news of Piero de' Medici's concessions reached Florence, tre-mendous indignation flared up all over the city at the realization of how greatly their domain had been diminished, and how grave and ignominious a blow had been dealt to their Republic. Aside from the magnitude of the losses, others were furious because Piero had given away such important parts of Florentine domain without any council of the citizens, without any decree by the magistrates—a thing unheard of and never practiced by his forefathers. Consequently there were the most bitter complaints about him, and all over the city could be heard voices of citizens inciting each other to rise and recover their liberty; and even those who, of their own free will, were Piero's adherents, did not dare openly to express their opposition, either by words or force, against all this agitation.

But although the Florentines had no means of defending Pisa and Livorno, and no prospect whatever of dissuading the King from his desire to possess those fortresses, nevertheless they immediately dispatched many ambassadors to Charles from amongst those persons dissatisfied with the power of the Medici. For it was felt that a line should be drawn between the decisions of the Republic and the decisions of Piero; at least matters pertaining to public interest should not be recognized as private affairs.

Piero realized that these were the first stirrings of rebellion; hence he departed from the King, under pretext of leaving to implement what he had promised, but actually in order to see to his own affairs before greater disorders should break out.

The Florentine Revolution

Piero de' Medici returned to Florence to find a majority of the magistrates opposed to him, and his more important friends indecisive, because he had unwisely made all these decisions against their advice. And the people were so incensed that, when on the following day, the ninth of November, Piero sought to enter the palace where the Signoria, the supreme magistracy of the Republic, was residing, several armed magistrates guarding the door, led by Iacopo de' Nerli, a noble rich youth, prohibited him from entering. As soon as this news spread through the city, the people immediately, and in great tumult, seized arms, all the more agitated because Paolo Orsini, whom Piero had summoned, was approaching with his men-at-arms.

Piero had already returned to his house, bereft of courage and counsel; when he learned that the Signoria had declared him a rebel, he fled precipitously from Florence to Bologna, followed by his brothers Giovanni, Cardinal of the Roman Church,* and Giuliano (against whom were similarly imposed the usual penalties against rebels).

At Bologna, Giovanni Bentivoglio, who demanded from others that resolution of spirit which subsequently he himself failed to demonstrate

* Subsequently, Pope Leo X.

in time of adversity, bitterly criticized Piero at their first meeting for having so cowardly, and without the death of even a single man, abandoned such an exalted position; thereby jeopardizing not only himself, but setting a bad example for all those who were oppressing the liberties of their countries.

Thus, through the rashness of a young man, the family of the Medici was overthrown from that power, which under most legal aspects and title it had maintained in Florence for sixty years in succession, beginning with Cosimo, Piero's great-grandfather, a citizen of rare wisdom and inestimable riches, and therefore most celebrated all over Europe; especially because he had spent over 400,000 ducats in building churches, monasteries and other sumptuous edifices not only in his own country but in many other parts of the world, doing all this with admirable magnificence and truly regal spirit, since he had been more concerned with immortalizing his name than providing for his descendants. His grandson Lorenzo, a man of great ability and excellent counsels and no less generous than his grandfather, exercised even more absolute authority in governing the Republic, although he was much less rich and lived much fewer years. Lorenzo was highly esteemed all over Italy, as well as by many foreign rulers; and after his death, his reputation turned into a most clear memory, for it seemed that the concord and felicity of Italy had disappeared with him.

The very day in which the uprising occurred in Florence, Charles being at that time in the city of Pisa, the Pisans flocked to him en masse demanding their liberty, and complaining bitterly of the harm which they said the Florentines had done them; several of the King's courtiers who were present, affirmed this to be a just demand, for the Florentines ruled them harshly. The King, failing to consider what such a request implied, and how contrary it was to the agreement made at Serezana, replied immediately that he was well disposed: at this response the Pisan people took up arms, and tearing down the insignia of the Florentines from public places, casting them to the ground, they eagerly reasserted their freedom. Nevertheless, the King contradicting himself, and not realizing what he had conceded, wanted the Florentine officials to remain there to exercise their usual jurisdiction; at the same time, he left the old citadel in the hands of the Pisans, keeping the new one, which was much more important, for himself. These events at Pisa and at Florence might seem to confirm the common proverb that when misfortunes approach, men mainly lose that wisdom with which they would have been able to impede their ill-fate; for the Florentines, always most suspicious of Pisan fidelity, and always expecting war from so great a peril, failed to summon the leading citizens of Pisa to Florence for security, as they usually did in great numbers on every slight occasion; nor did Piero de' Medici, confronting such difficulties, man the Piazza and Public Palace* with foreign footsoldiers as had often been done on much less provocation. Such precautions would have greatly hindered this uprising. But as far as Pisa was concerned, it is obvious that although the Pisans were most inimical by nature against Florentine control, the moving spirit behind this rebellion was the authority of Lodovico Sforza who had previously held secret meetings for this purpose with several Pisan citizens exiled for private offenses. . . .

It is equally manifest that the night before, several Pisans had communicated their intentions to the Cardinal of San Pietro in Vincoli, who perhaps before that day had never been the author of pacific counsels. But in this instance, the Cardinal gravely advised them to consider not only the superficial aspects and beginnings of things, but more deeply weigh the consequences that might eventually ensue.

. .
.

Amidst all this confusion, Charles left Pisa for Florence, not entirely decided how he wished to settle the Pisan affair; he halted at Signa, a place seven miles from Florence, in order, before entering the city, to wait at last until the tumult of the Florentines had ceased, inasmuch as the people had not laid down the weapons which they had seized the day Piero de' Medici was expelled; and to give time to Aubigny to join him in order that the King's entrance into Florence might evoke more terror . . .

And by many indications it was understood that the King's idea was to frighten the Florentines, by his military strength, into yielding absolute rule of the city over to him; nor was he able to conceal this plan from the ambassadors who had come to him several times at Signa to decide upon the mode of his entry into Florence, and complete the agreement under negotiation. The King undoubtedly had been greatly provoked and conceived a hatred against Florentines, because of the efforts which the ambassadors had made to block him; and furthermore, although it was plain that their resistance was in no way indicative of the will of the Republic, and that the city had behaved toward him with the utmost correctness, nevertheless this had not allayed his irritation. It was commonly believed that he had been stirred up by many of his counselors, who felt that he must not neglect the opportunity to become master of Florence, or, moved by avarice, did not wish to lose a chance to sack so rich a city; and it was bruited throughout the army that the Florentines would have to be punished to set an example for the others, since they had presumed to be the first Italians to oppose French power.

* Piazza Signoria and Palazzo della Signoria, later called Palazzo Vecchio.

Nor, among his leading counselors were there lacking those who urged him to put Piero de' Medici back into power, especially Philippe, Lord of Brescia, brother of the Duke of Savoy, induced by private friendships and promises. Either because these counsels prevailed (although the Bishop of San Malò was opposed), or because Charles hoped to bend the Florentines to his will by terror, or to have, when need be, a more pliant justification for taking whatever decision he pleased, the King wrote a letter to Piero and had one written by Monsieur Philippe, urging him to come near Florence, since the King had decided to restore him to his former power on the basis of the friendship which had existed between their fathers and because of the good intentions which Piero had shown in consigning the fortresses.

But these letters did not reach him (as the King thought) in Bologna. For Piero, displeased at Giovanni Bentivoglio's harsh words, and fearful of being pursued by the Duke of Milan and perhaps by the King of France, had to his own misfortune proceeded to Venice, where the letters were forwarded by his brother, the Cardinal, who had remained in Bologna.

In Florence there were many suspicions about the King's intentions; not seeing any hope of resistance either by force or any other way, they had decided (as the least dangerous course) to receive him into the city, even hoping to find some way of placating him. Nevertheless, to be provided against every possibility, they had ordered many citizens to secretly garrison their houses with men of the Florentine domain, and commanded the captains serving in the pay of the Republic to enter Florence, concealing the reason, with many of their troops, and instructed everyone in the city and surrounding towns to be ready to seize arms at the tolling of the great bell of the Public Palace.

The King made his entry with his army, in the greatest pomp and display, all magnificently and carefully prepared both by his court as well as the city of Florence; and as a sign of victory, he entered, both himself and his horse in armor, and with his lance on his thigh. Negotiations for an agreement were immediately embarked upon, but with great difficulties. For, aside from the excessive favor which several of the King's party manifested for Piero de' Medici, and the inordinate demands for money which were put forward, Charles openly claimed rule of Florence, alleging that, by having entered armed in that manner, he had, according to the military rules of the realm of France, legitimately gained dominion. Ultimately, however, he withdrew that demand; yet he wanted to leave in Florence certain Ambassadors of the Long Robe (as doctors and persons wearing gowns are called in France) with such authority that, according to French institutions, he would have been able to claim considerable jurisdiction for himself in perpetuity. The Florentines, on the contrary, were most stubbornly determined to maintain their liberty entirely, notwithstanding any peril. The collision of such diverse points of view at the conferences continually enflamed passions on both sides. Nevertheless, neither party was disposed to settle their differences by arms; for the Florentines, long habituated to business affairs and not military activities, were terribly afraid of having within their own walls a most powerful king with a mighty army manned by ferocious and unknown peoples; and the French were very apprehensive of the great number of inhabitants, who had shown, on the day the government was overthrown, many more signs of audacity than would have been believed before. The French were also aware of the public rumor that at the sound of the great bell, innumerable men from all the surrounding towns would flock into the city. As a result of these common fears, there often arose unsubstantiated alarms, at which each party would tumultuously seize their weapons in self-defense, but neither side would provoke or assault the other.

The King's plans for Piero's return proved in vain, because Piero, suspended between the hope which had been given him and the fear of being taken prey by his adversaries, asked the advice of the Venetian senate with regard to the King's letters. Nothing certainly is more necessary in arduous deliberations, and nothing on the other hand more dangerous, than to ask advice. Nor is there any question that advice is less necessary to wise men than to unwise; and yet, wise men derive much more benefit from taking counsel. For, whose judgment is so perfect that he can always evaluate and know everything by himself, and always be able to discern the better part of contradictory points of view? But how can he who is asking for counsel be certain that he will be counseled in good faith? For, whoever gives advice (unless he is bound by close fidelity or ties of affection to the one seeking advice) not only is moved largely by self-interest, but also by his own small advantages and by every slight satisfaction, and often aims his counsel toward that end which turns more to his advantage or is more suitable for his purposes; and since these ends are usually unknown to the person seeking advice, he is not aware, unless he is wise, of the faithlessness of the counsel.

Thus it happened to Piero de' Medici. For the Venetians, judging that his departure would make it easier for Charles to reduce Florentine affairs to his purposes (which would be the most harmful to their own interests), and therefore counseling themselves rather than Piero, efficaciously advised him not to put himself in the King's power, since Charles considered himself wronged by Piero. And to give him all the more reason to follow their recommendations, they offered to support his cause, and when time permitted, lend him every favor in helping to repatriate him. Nor content with this, in order to make sure that he should not leave Venice at that time, they kept him (if what was later divulged be true) under secret guard.

Charles at Florence

Bᴜᴛ meanwhile, both sides in Florence had reached a stage of exacerbation and had almost arrived at a point of open contention, since the King did not wish to withdraw from his last demands, and the Florentines would not obligate themselves to pay such an intolerable sum of money or agree to any jurisdiction or domination of their state. These difficulties, almost unsolvable except by arms, aroused the spirit of Piero Capponi, one of the four citizens who had been deputized to deal with the King. This Capponi was a man of talent and great courage, held in very high esteem in Florence for these qualities and because he belonged to a most honorable family and descended from persons who had exercised important roles in the Republic. One day, when he and his companions were in the King's presence, and one of the royal secretaries was reading the unreasonable paragraphs of the treaty which had been recently proposed on the King's part, Capponi with an impetuous gesture seized the document from the secretary's hand and tore it up in front of the King's eyes, adding, his voice quivering with agitation: "Since such shameless demands are being made, you sound your trumpets and we will sound our bells!" thus expressedly wishing to infer that their differences would be decided by arms; and in the same burst of anger he immediately left the room followed by his companions.

Undoubtedly the words of this citizen, whom Charles and his entire court had known previously, inasmuch as he had been Florentine ambassador to France only a few months before, so terrified all the French (especially since nobody believed he would have displayed such audacity without good reason) that he was called back, and the demands dropped which he had refused to accept, and the King and the Florentines finally came to an agreement as follows:

That all preceding wrongs should be set aside and the city of Florence be considered a friend, ally and under the perpetual protection of the crown of France; that the city of Pisa, the town of Livorno and all their fortifications should remain in the King's hands for his security; but that he was obliged to restore them at no cost to the Florentines as soon as he had completed his undertaking in the kingdom of Naples, understanding thereby as completed when he had conquered the city of Naples or settled affairs peacefully by a peace treaty or by a truce for at least two years, or when, for whatever reason, he personally had departed from Italy; that the castellans should be sworn now to restore these castles in the aforesaid cases; that, in the meanwhile, the dominion, jurisdiction, government and revenues from the said towns should revert to the Florentines as usual; and that similar agreements should be entered into with regard to

Pietrasanta, Serezana and Serezanello, but as the Genoese claimed these places, the King should be empowered to try to reconcile their differences either by agreement or adjudication; however, if he had not settled them within the aforesaid period, the towns were to be restored to the Florentines. Furthermore, the King might leave two ambassadors in Florence, without whose intervention, during the said Neapolitan campaign, nothing pertaining to the latter should be discussed; nor at the same time, could they elect a captain-general of their troops without his approval; that the King would immediately restore all other towns which had been captured or rebelled against the Florentines, who would have the right to take them by force of arms in case they refused to yield. It was further agreed that to aid the King in his enterprise, the Florentines would give him fifty thousand ducats within fifteen days, forty thousand in the month of March, and thirty thousand the following June; that the Pisans were to be forgiven their crime of rebellion and other crimes subsequently committed; that the penalty of ban and confiscation was to be lifted from Piero de' Medici and his brothers, but Piero could not approach closer than one hundred miles from the borders of Florentine domain (which was done to prevent him from remaining in Rome), nor his brothers within one hundred miles of the city of Florence.

These were the most important articles of the treaty between the King and the Florentines; which, besides being legitimately stipulated, was ceremoniously announced in the cathedral during religious services, where the King in person (at whose request this was done) and the magistrates of the city promised, under most solemn oath made at the high altar, in the presence of the court and all the Florentine people, to observe the articles of the treaty.

Two days later Charles left Florence, where he had remained ten days, and went to Siena: which city, allied with the King of Naples and the Florentines, had followed their leadership until Piero de' Medici's departure for Serezana had forced them to take precautions for their own safety.

After a Stop at Siena, Charles VIII Proceeds Toward Rome. The Pope's Terror as the French Army Approaches. Charles' Entry into the Holy City. His Pact with Alexander VI

THE city of Siena is populous, has a very fertile territory, and has been considered for a long time the most powerful place in Tuscany after Florence. The city was self-governing, but in such a way that it knew the name of liberty much more than the effects thereof, for divided as it was into many factions or groups of citizens, called according to their Orders, it supported whatever party was strongest, according to the accidents of the times and the favor of foreign potentates. At that time, the Order of Monte de' Nove prevailed.

The King tarried a very few days at Siena and left a garrison there because from time immemorial Siena had been inclined toward devotion to the Empire, and was therefore suspect. Charles directed his march toward Rome, every day becoming more insolent as a result of successes much greater than he had ever dared to hope; and since the season was fair and much more serene than is usual for that time of year, he decided to take full advantage of his good fortune, now that he struck terror not only in his avowed enemies but even in those who had been allied with him, or who had never provoked him in any way whatsoever. For, both the Venetian senate and the Duke of Milan, frightened at such success, suspected, especially because of the Florentine fortresses which Charles had retained and the garrison he had left in Siena, that the King's thoughts were not likely to terminate in the acquisition of Naples. Therefore, they began negotiations toward setting up a new alliance in order to obviate their common peril, an alliance which they would have carried into effect sooner had Charles met that resistance at Rome which many hoped for.

[*As the French army marches southward, the Pope vacillates, now thinking to listen to the demands of the French, now to resist them. Charles sends M. Trémouille and Ganay to treat with the Pope; Cardinal Ascanio and Prospero Colonna also come to Rome for the same purpose. The country around Rome is in tumult. Alexander suddenly changes his mind, summons the Duke of Calabria and his army into Rome, arrests Ascanio and Prospero and locks them in the Castel Sant' Angelo, though he sets them free a few days later. The King reaches Nepi.*]

Pope Alexander was in a very ambiguous state of mind; sometimes he resolved to stay in Rome and defend it, and therefore permitted Ferrando and the captains to see to fortifying the weakest positions; at other times the Pontiff felt that defense was difficult because the maritime line of supply had been broken at Ostia, the city thronged with infinite numbers of foreigners, all of diverse mind and will, and the Romans themselves torn into factions.

He therefore began to think of leaving Rome, and wanted all the cardinals in the College to promise in writing, by their own hand, to follow him. Then, alarmed at the difficulties and imminent perils in any of these resolutions, his mind turned to the possibilities of an agreement.

While the Pope was suspended in this state of indecision, the French

SIENA

A sixteenth-century engraving of Siena showing the numerous towers then still characteristic of Renaissance cities, curiously anticipating modern sky-scrapers. In the left foreground the symbol of the she-wolf suckling the twins Romulus and Remus refers to the legend that the city was founded by Senus, son of Remus. The Latin legend above may be translated as "It is not possible to lose sight of a city situated on a mountain," obviously meant to be understood metaphorically. The escutcheon on the upper left indicates that Siena was under the rule of the Medici Dukes when this engraving was made.
(COURTESY OF GABINETTO NAZIONALE DELLE STAMPE, ROME)

overran all the territory on this side of the Tiber,* occupying one town after another, for nowhere did they encounter any resistance, no longer was there anyone who did not capitulate to their attack. Even those who had very good reason to resist followed the example of the others; even Virginio Orsini, tied to the house of Aragon by so many bonds of fidelity, obligation and honor—a captain-general in the royal army, a grand constable of the kingdom of Naples, and very closely related to Alfonso, since his son, Gian Giordano, had married a natural daughter of the dead King Ferdinand, and he had received many favors and states of the realm from the house of Aragon. But forgetting all these things, and forgetting

* Between the west bank and the seacoast.

also that it was in defending his interests that the calamities of the Aragonese had arisen, he agreed, to the astonishment of the French, who were not used to these subtle distinctions of Italian soldiers, that he would himself remain in the pay of the King of Naples, while his sons might come to an agreement with the King of France.

Orsini's sons stipulated to provide passage and victuals to Charles' troops as they marched through the state which their father held under Church domain, and to turn over Campagnano and certain other villages into the hands of the Cardinal of Gurk, who promised to restore them as soon as the army had left Roman territory. The Count of Pitigliano and several others of the Orsini family also joined in the same agreement.

Once the conditions had been signed, Charles left Nepi and went to Bracciano, the main town under Virginio Orsini. The King also dispatched Louis, Lord of Ligny, and Yves, Lord of Allègre, to Ostia with five hundred lancers and two thousand Swiss with orders to cross the Tiber, join the Colonna, and then marching swiftly together, to force their way into Rome. The Colonna hoped somehow to accomplish this plan, with the help of those Romans who were of their faction, although difficulties had now grown as a result of bad weather.

Civitavecchia, Corneto and finally almost all Roman territory had already capitulated to the French; and the entire court and all the Roman people, in the greatest state of terror and rebellion, were already calling for a settlement. Therefore, the Pontiff, reduced to a most precarious position and seeing the foundations for his defense ever weakening, felt himself threatened, if for no other reason than because of the memory that he had been the first to incite the French King to this Neapolitan expedition, and then, without any justification, had employed his authority, council and arms to set up a most stubborn resistance against him; whence he quite justifiably suspected that any pledges he might receive from the King would have the same value as those the King had received from him. And his terror grew all the more in observing that the Cardinal of San Pietro in Vincoli, and many other cardinals who were his enemies, possessed no little authority in the King's councils. Through their influence, and the title of Most Christian borne by the kings of France, and the deep-rooted reputation for religiosity of that nation, and because our most fearful anticipations are always with regard to those whom we know by name only, the Pope feared that the King might set his mind toward a reformation of the Church, as was already being bruited about. To Alexander, this thought of a possible reform was terrible beyond anything else, since he recalled through what infamous means he had risen to the pontificate, and how he had continued to administer it with manners and methods not unlike so foul a beginning.

[*Charles sends three ambassadors to the Pope, who assure him that the King has no intention of interfering with the pontifical power, but is only interested in safe passage for his troops. Although Charles could take Rome by force whenever he would, he forbears to do so out of the reverence which he and his ancestors have always borne toward Roman pontiffs. The Pope finally accepts Charles' hard conditions.*]

Having procured a safe conduct from the King permitting Ferrando and his army to pass safely through the entire Ecclesiastical State, the Pope ordered the Duke of Calabria to leave Rome. But Ferrando contemptuously refused the safe conduct, marching out of Rome through the gate of San Sebastiano on the last day of the year 1494 at the very hour when the French army entered through the gate of Santa Maria del Popolo, headed by the King, armed, with lance on thigh, as he had entered into Florence. And at the same time, the Pope, oppressed by incredible anxiety and dread, took refuge in the Castel Sant' Angelo, accompanied only by the Cardinals Battista Orsini and Ulivieri Carafa, the Neapolitan.

But the Cardinals San Pietro in Vincoli, Ascanio, those of the Colonna and Savello families and many others, did not cease to implore the King to remove from the Pontifical See a pope so full of vices, so abominable in the eyes of the world, in order that a new pope might be elected. They sought to convince the King that liberating the Church of God from the tyranny of a wicked pope would shed no less glory upon his name than had been won by Pepin and Charlemagne, his ancestors, for liberating those pontiffs who led saintly lives from the persecutions of those who were unjustly oppressing them. They recalled to him that this decision was no less necessary for his security than desirable for his glory: for how could he ever trust Alexander's promises, a man by nature extremely fraudulent, insatiably greedy, shameless in all his deeds, and as experience had shown, filled with the most bitter hatred against the very name of the French? And if now he was seeking a reconciliation, it was not spontaneously, but forced by necessity and fear.

Influenced by these arguments, and because the Pope refused to yield up the Castel Sant' Angelo to Charles during the negotiations on the treaty, as assurance against the King's promises, the artillery was twice moved from the palace of San Marco where Charles was lodging, and set into position in front of the castle. But the King had no intention or inclination to offend the Pontiff, and his Privy Council was dominated by those whom Alexander had rendered benevolent by means of gifts and promises. Therefore, it was finally agreed that there should be perpetual friendship and confederation for the common defense between the Pontiff and the King; that the King should receive for his security the fortresses at Civitavecchia, Terracina, and Spoleto to be held until he had acquired the kingdom of Naples (although later, Spoleto was not consigned to him); that the Pope should not harbor any harm or reprisals against any of those cardinals or barons, subjects of the Church, who had followed the King's party; that the Pope should grant Charles the investiture of the kingdom of Naples; that he should deliver up to him Djem, the Ottoman, brother of Bajazet, who after the death of Mohammed, their father, had been persecuted by Bajazet (according to the ferocious customs of the Ottomans, who establish succession in their empire by the blood of their brethren and all those closest to them). For that reason, Djem had taken refuge in Rhodes whence he was brought to France, and finally had been placed under the protection of Pope Innocent. Bajazet (using the avarice of the Vicars of Christ as an instrument to hold his Empire, enemy of Christendom, in peace) paid each year, under pretext of expenses necessary for feeding and keeping his brother Djem, forty thousand ducats to the popes in order that they would be less inclined to set him free or deliver him up to any other princes who might be opposed to Bajazet.

Charles demanded to have Djem in order to facilitate his planned crusade against the Turks. For inflated by the vain adulation of his followers, Charles intended to launch that campaign once he had conquered the Aragonese. And since the last forty thousand ducats sent by the Turks had been seized at Sinigaglia by the prefect of Rome, Charles now insisted that the Pope must leave both the penalty, as well as the restitution of the monies, up to him. An additional article declared that the Cardinal of Valencia* should accompany the King as Apostolic Legate for three months, but in truth was to serve as hostage for his father's promises.

The agreement signed, the Pope returned to the apostolic palace in the Vatican, and afterward, with the pomp and ceremony usual in the reception of great kings, he received the King in the Church of San Pietro; there, according to ancient tradition, Charles genuflected, kissed the Pope's feet, and was then permitted to kiss him on the cheeks. Another day, Charles attended Pontifical Mass, seated first after the first Cardinal Bishop, and according to the ancient rites, during the celebration of the mass, served the water with which the Pope washed his hands. In order that these ceremonies might be preserved in the memory of posterity, the Pope had them painted in a loggia of the Castel Sant' Angelo. Also, at the King's request, he created cardinals of the Bishop of San Malò and the Bishop of Le Mans of the house of Luxembourg, neglecting nothing that might indicate how sincere and faithful was his reconciliation.

. .
.

* Cesare Borgia.

Charles remained in Rome about a month, all the while continuing to send troops to the borders of the kingdom of Naples where commotion was already widespread, with the result that before the King left Rome, Aquila and almost all of Abruzzo had rallied to his standard, and Fabrizio Colonna had occupied the districts of Albi and Tagliacozzo. The rest of the kingdom was no more peaceful, for as soon as Ferrando had left Rome, all the fruits of the hatred which the people bore toward Alfonso began to manifest themselves; besides, they still had bitter memories of the harshness with which old Ferdinand, Alfonso's father, had treated them. Therefore, exclaiming most vehemently against the iniquities of their past governments and Alfonso's cruelty and pride, they openly showed their desire for the coming of the French.

As soon as Alfonso learned of his son's departure from Rome, he fell into such a state of panic that, forgetful of the great fame and glory he had acquired through long experience in many Italian wars, and despairing to weather this fatal storm, he decided to abandon the kingdom of Naples, renouncing his title and royal authority to Ferrando. . . .

There was a rumor (if it be permissible not to entirely scorn such things) that old Ferdinand's ghost appeared three times on sundry nights to Iacopo, chief surgeon of the court, and first with gentle words, and then uttering the most dire threats, commanded him to tell Alfonso, in his name, that he could not hope to offer resistance to the King of France, because it was foredoomed that his progeny, after suffering numberless travails and finally deprived of so illustrious a realm, would be extinguished. For the Aragonese must pay the price for their enormities . . . above all, because Ferdinand, at his son's instigation, had secretly ordered the assassination of many barons of his realm. . . .

Whatever be the truth of this, it is certain that Alfonso decided to flee—tormented by his own conscience, finding no rest for his soul by day or night, the ghosts of those dead lords appearing to him in his sleep, and the people tumultuously in rebellion because of his tortures. But he communicated his intention only to the Queen, his mother-in-law, and did not even, despite her entreaties, tell either his brother or his son, nor did he want to remain even two or three more days in order to complete the full year of his rule.

Alfonso departed from Naples accompanied by four light galleys loaded with treasure; trembling at his departure as if he were already surrounded by the French, starting fearfully at every noise, like one terrified that the very heavens and elements had conspired against him. He fled to Mazari, a town in Sicily, which had been given to him some time before by Ferdinand, King of Spain.

Just as the King of France was leaving Rome, he learned of Alfonso's flight. And when Charles came to Velletri, the Cardinal of Valencia secretly fled from him, and although Borgia's father expressed his grave displeasure, offering to guarantee the King howsoever he wished, it is believed that the flight had taken place at the Pope's orders, as one who wanted to have in his own power the observance or non-observance of the agreement which he had signed with King Charles.

[*The French vanguard bombards the castle at Montefortino, captures it in a few hours, and kills almost all the defenders. The army moves on to attack Monte di San Giovanni, a strongly defended position, and, in the King's presence, takes it by storm after a few hours of furious cannonade and assault.*]

At Monte di San Giovanni, the French committed massacres, induced thereto by their innate fury, and also to warn others by this example not to dare to resist them. After having given vent to every other kind of savage barbarism, they committed the ultimate cruelty of setting the buildings on fire. This method of making war, not used in Italy for many centuries, filled all the kingdom with the greatest terror, because in victory, in whatever way it had been acquired, the farthest point the cruelty of the victors had ever gone was to plunder and then free the conquered soldiers, to sack the towns captured by assault and take the inhabitants prisoners in order that they would have to pay ransom, but always sparing the lives of those men who had not been killed in the heat of the combat.

.   .
.

This was all the resistance and trouble the King of France had in the conquest of so noble and magnificent a realm, in the defense of which was shown neither virtue nor spirit nor wise counsels nor a sense of honor nor power nor fidelity. Meanwhile, the Duke of Calabria (who had retreated, after his departure from Rome, to the borders of the realm) had been called to Naples because of his father's flight, and there had assumed the authority and title of King, with the usual solemnities but without any pomp.

[*Then he assembles his army and prepares for defense at San Germano,* one of the keys of the kingdom of Naples. But at the mere approach of the French, the new King and his troops are seized with confusion, and without putting up a fight, withdraw to Capua.*]

At Capua Ferrando had no better luck or skill. For no sooner had he encamped his army there, much diminished in numbers after the retreat from San Germano, when he learned from letters from the Queen that the loss of San Germano had stirred up such commotion in Naples that unless

---

* Near Monte Cassino, northwest of Naples.

he went there in person, there was danger of an uprising. Ferrando, therefore, rode with a small company to remedy this peril by his personal presence, promising to return to Capua the following day. But Gianiacopo da Trivulzio, to whom he had committed the defense of that city, had already secretly requested the King of France to send a herald so that he might be able to confer safely with him. As soon as this herald arrived, Trivulzio, together with several Capuan gentlemen, went to Calvi, where the King had entered the same day. Trivulzio did this despite the fact that many Capuans, disposed to keep faith with Ferrando, had boldly and haughtily spoken out against it.

At Calvi, Trivulzio was immediately brought before the King, armed as he had come, where he spoke in the name of the Capuans and of the soldiers: namely, that realizing that Ferrando, whom he had served faithfully while there was any hope, now lacked any means of defense, they had decided to follow the King's fortune if they should be accepted with fair conditions; adding that he was confident that he could bring Ferrando himself to the King, provided that he would be recognized as was befitting. To these offers, the King replied with most gracious words, accepting the offers of the Capuans and the soldiers, as well as the arrival of Ferrando, provided that he realized that he was not going to retain any part, no matter how small, of the kingdom of Naples, but would receive due honors and estates in the kingdom of France.

At Capua even before Trivulzio's return there had been a rebellion, Ferrando's quarters and stables had been sacked, and the men-at-arms had begun to disperse in various places.

Not knowing what had happened after his departure, Ferrando returned as he had promised, after having calmed the Neapolitans, for the time being, by giving them hope for the defense of Capua. He was within two miles of the city when, hearing of his return, all the people rose in arms in order not to permit him to enter, and by common agreement sent several of the nobility ahead to meet with him and advise him not to draw nearer, because the city—having now seen itself abandoned by him; the governor of this troops, Trivulzio, gone to the King of France; Ferrando's quarters sacked by his own soldiers; Virginio and the Count of Pitigliano having abandoned him; almost the entire army disbanded—had therefore been obliged for its own safety to yield to the victory. Whence Ferrando (although he had begged, even with tears in his eyes, to be admitted into the city) returned to Naples, certain that the entire kingdom would follow the example of the Capuans. As a result of this episode, the city of Aversa, situated between Capua and Naples, immediately sent ambassadors to Charles offering to surrender. And since the Neapolitans were already openly negotiating with the French, the unhappy King decided not to oppose so unexpected a blow of ill fortune, summoned many of the nobility and people to the piazza of the Castel Nuovo, the royal residence, and delivered a speech [which was heard by many with tears and compassion] . . .

        • •

       •

But so odious among all the people and almost all the nobility* was the reputation of the last two kings, and so much eagerness was there for a French regime, that even Ferrando's declarations [that he was unfortunate not through his own, but his ancestors' misconduct, and now considered himself an exile, and advised his subjects to come to an agreement with the French King] could not placate the disorders in any way. As soon as he had retired into the Castello, the people began to sack his stables on the piazza: an indignity which he could not bear, so that he rushed out with great courage, accompanied by a few men, to put a stop to the plunder; and so potent was the majesty of the royal name in this city already in rebellion that, once the initial impulse had spent itself, everyone abstained from pillaging the stables. Ferrando returned into the castle and, ordering the ships in port to be burned or sunk (there being no other way of depriving the enemy of them), he began to suspect through certain signs that the German infantry constituting the castle guard, to the number of five hundred, were thinking of taking him prisoner; therefore he quickly decided to give them the things which were kept there. While these soldiers were busy dividing up the spoils, and after having first freed from prison all the barons (except the Prince of Rossano and the Count of Popoli) who had managed to survive the cruelty of his father and grandfather, Ferrando left the castle via the Soccorso gate and boarded one of the light galleys waiting for him in the port. He was accompanied by Don Federigo and the old Queen, formerly wife of his grandfather, together with her daughter Giovanna; and followed by very few members of his court, he sailed to the island of Ischia, called Enaria by the ancients, thirty miles from Naples, repeating often, and in a loud voice, while the panorama of Naples lay before his eyes, the verses of the Psalmist: "They watch in vain which keep the city if it be not kept by the Lord."

But meeting now only with difficulties, he was obliged to give proof of his worth at Ischia, and to learn of the ingratitude and faithlessness which reveal themselves against those buffeted by ill fortune. For the governor of the castle refused to admit him, except with a single companion. Ferrando agreed to this, but soon as he had entered, he fell so furiously upon the castellan that his outburst, and the memory of his royal

---

* . . . *quasi in tutta la nobiltà* . . .   this entirely, probably as setting a bad
(Gherardi, *op. cit.,* p. 90). Fenton omits   example (Fenton, *op. cit.,* p. 53).

authority so terrified the occupants that the castle and its governor were immediately yielded up to him.

Ferrando's flight from Naples resulted in general capitulation everywhere; everyone gave way as to a violent flood at the mere rumor of the conquerors. And so cowardly did they yield that two hundred horsemen of the company of Ligny went to Nola where Virginio and the Count of Pitigliano had withdrawn with four hundred men-at-arms, and took them prisoner without meeting the slightest resistance. They surrendered without a blow, partly because of confidence in the safe-conduct which the King, according to their friends, had granted them, and partly swept by the same panic which was sweeping everybody else. Led captives to the castle of Mondragone, all their forces were stripped and plundered.

In the meanwhile, the Neapolitan ambassadors, sent to render up their city, reached Charles at Aversa. After most generously conceding them many privileges and exemptions, the French King entered Naples on the following day, the 21st of February, 1495, received with such general applause and rejoicing that it would be difficult to attempt to express it, since both sexes, people of every condition, every quality, every faction flocked to greet him with incredible exultation, as if he were the father and founder of that city. Nor, among the celebrants, were there lacking those who, either in themselves or in their ancestors, had been raised to high estate and benefited by the house of Aragon. After the King, followed by a great concourse of people, had visited the cathedral, he was then (because Castel Nuovo was held by the enemy) brought to be lodged in the Castel Capuano, formerly the ancient habitation of the French kings. Thus Charles, in a remarkable succession of incredible good fortune, even more than Julius Caesar, conquered before he saw. And with such ease, that in this entire expedition, he never had to pitch camp or even break a lance, and so superfluous were many of his provisions, that his fleet, which had been equipped at very great expense, tossed about by violent seas and driven to the island of Corsica, arrived so late on the shores of the kingdom that Charles had already marched into Naples.

Thus, by domestic dissensions, which had blinded the so-renowned wisdom of our princes, and to the greatest shame and derision of Italian arms, and at the gravest peril and ignominy of all, a renowned and powerful part of Italy fell from Italian rule to the rule of people from beyond the mountains. For, old Ferdinand, although he had been born in Spain, nevertheless, since from his earliest youth he had been (either as king, or the son of a king) continually in Italy and had no principality in any other province, he, together with his children and grandchildren, all born and brought up in Naples, were rightfully considered Italians.

BOOK

2

Debate over the Reorganization of Florence: Popular vs. Aristocratic Government

A T THIS SAME TIME, THE FLORENTINES WERE NO LESS CONCERNED AND INVOLVED IN INTERNAL AF-FAIRS [AS WITH THE LOSS OF PISA]. FOR IMMEDI-ately after the King's departure, they had summoned a Parliament in order to reorganize the government of the Republic. According to their ancient institutions, this Parliament is a congregation of all the citizens assembled in the piazza in front of the Communal Palace, at which time they deliberate in open discussion on proposals put forward by the chief magistracy. The Parliament instituted a kind of policy which under the name of popular government tended in many aspects more toward the power of the few than universal participation.* This offended a great many citizens who had conceived in their minds of a wider extension of power, and suited, at the same time, the private ambition of some of the leading citizens; and it was therefore necessary to reconsider the form of the government anew.

Thus, one day, during a consultation of the principal magistrates and leading Florentines, Paolo Antonio Soderini, a wise and highly esteemed citizen, spoke according to reports as follows:**

"It would certainly be very easy, oh honorable citizens, to demon-strate that although those who have written about civic affairs esteem popular government less than princedoms or aristocracies, nevertheless, since the desire for liberty is ancient and almost innate in this city, and

---

* "*Chi disse parlamento disse guasta-mento*"—"Whoever said parliament said ruination"—an old Florentine proverb. Segni offers a devastating description of how such a seemingly popular institution results in despotism. Savonarola was also opposed to it (cf. John Addington Sym-onds, *Renaissance in Italy*, New York, 1935, p. 116 and footnote).

** This speech, of course (as well as the rebuttal by Vespucci), was composed by Guicciardini in imitation of the style of Livy and Sallust.

PIAZZA DEL DUOMO: FLORENCE

Although this fresco of the school of Vasari dates from the 1560s as indicated by the black Spanish-style costuming, the Piazza is shown substantially as it was in Guicciardini's time: the façade of the Duomo (to the left) still unfaced, flanked by the campanile of Giotto, and the octagonal baptistry facing the cathedral (COURTESY OF FRATELLI ALINARI)

the conditions of our citizens equally proportioned, a most necessary precondition for popular government, one might argue that this form of government should be preferred without any question to all others. But such a dispute would be superfluous, since in all the consultations today, we have unanimously agreed and decided that the city should be governed in the name and authority of the people.

"Our differences of opinion arise from the fact that in the reorganization drawn up by the Parliament, some of us would like to return as closely as possible to that form of government with which this city was ruled before its liberty was oppressed by the family of the Medici: while others, among whose number I must confess myself to be, judging a government so ordered to have in many ways the name rather than the effects of popular government, and frightened by the perturbations which often result from such governments, desire a more perfect form whereby the harmony and security of our citizens would be maintained, a thing which, judging by reason of our experience in the past, can be hoped for, in this city, only under a type of government entirely dependent on the power of the people, so long as it is properly organized and run: which rests primarily on two fundamental things. First is that all the magistrates and officials, whether in the city or in the dominion, be rotated every so often by a universal council of all those who, according to our laws, are qualified to participate in the government; without the approval of such a council, new laws cannot be promulgated. Thus, the distribution of honors and positions of authority not being in the hands of private citizens or of any particular faction or point of view, no one would be excluded by the passion or prejudice of others, but honors would be distributed according to men's virtues and merits. Therefore, everyone would have to strive by virtue of his own capabilities, his good behavior, his usefulness both public and private, to set himself on the road to reputation; and everyone would have to abstain from vices, and harming others, and in short, from all those things which are odious in well-instituted cities: nor would any single person or few persons be enabled to introduce another form of government by means of new laws or through the authority of a magistrate, since they would not be able to alter the government except by the will of the universal council.

"The second fundamental basis is that important deliberations, that is, those referring to war or peace, or to the examination of new laws, and generally all those things necessary to the administration of such a city and dominion, should be dealt with by magistrates especially chosen for this purpose, and by a more select council of experienced and prudent citizens to be delegated by the popular assembly. For, since judgment of such affairs does not fall within the purview of everyone's understanding, it is necessary that they be managed by those who have the capacity to do so; and since swiftness or secrecy are very often required, such exigencies cannot permit of consultation or deliberation with the multitude. Nor for the preservation of liberty is it needful for such matters to be dealt with by a great many people, since freedom remains secure whenever the distribution of magistracies and the deliberation on new laws depend on universal consent.

"Therefore, if we attend to these two matters, a truly popular government will be set up, the liberty of the city will be well founded, and a praiseworthy endurable form of the Republic established. Many other things which tend to make that government of which I am speaking more perfect, it would be useful to defer for another time, in order not to confound men's minds too much, while these principles are being established. For our people still have suspicious memories of the recent tyranny, and since they are not accustomed to deal with free governments, they cannot therefore entirely know what must be done for the maintenance of liberty. But these are matters which, not being too essential, might safely be deferred to a more suitable time and more propitious occasion. The citizens' love for this form of Republic will increase every day, and every day experience will make them more capable of discerning truth; they will desire that the government be continually refined and brought to full perfection; and in this way, it will rest upon the above-stated two foundations. And how easily these might be established, and how much good fruit they would bear, may be proven not only by many reasons, but also be clearly shown by examples.

"For, although the Venetian government is strictly that of an aristocracy, these aristocrats are none other than private citizens, and are in such numbers and of such diverse conditions and qualities, that it cannot be denied that they constitute, to a considerable degree, a popular government, which might well be imitated by us in many ways. And yet it is principally founded on those two pillars whereby that Republic has maintained its liberty, its unity, and its civil harmony for so many centuries and thus risen to such glory and grandeur. Nor is the unity of the Venetians a result of their geographic situation, as many believe, for in that selfsame locality, there might very well be, and there have sometimes been, uprisings and discord. Rather, the form of the government is so well ordered and proportioned in itself that it must, of necessity, produce such admirable and precious results.

"Nor should our own examples move us any less than those of strangers. But we must consider them as contradictory instances. For the fact that our city has never had a form of government similar to that which I propose has been the reason why our affairs have always been subject to such frequent mutations, sometimes trampled upon by violent tyrannies, sometimes lacerated by the ambitious and avaricious discord of a few, and sometimes shattered by the unbridled license of the many. And whereas cities were established to permit of a quiet and happy life for their inhabitants, the fruits of our governments—our felicity, our repose—have been confiscation of our goods, the banishment and decapitation of our unfortunate citizens. The government now proposed to the Parliament is no different from those which existed in this city at other times, governments full of discord and calamity which, after infinite public and private travails, have finally engendered tyrannies.

"For this reason and this reason alone, the Duke of Athens oppressed liberty at the time of our ancestors, and for no other reason, in later times, Cosimo de' Medici did the same. Nor should one marvel at this: for when the distribution of magistrates and the deliberation of laws have no need of universal public census day after day, but depend rather on the will of a small number, then, since the citizens are no longer intent upon public welfare but rather on cupidity and on private ends, factions and particular conspiracies will arise, whereunto are joined the divisions of the whole city: the plague and inevitable death of all Republics and governments. Hence, how much more prudent to eschew those forms of government which, by our own reason and experience, we know to be pernicious, and to try to approximate those forms which, through the reasons and experience of others, we know to be salubrious and happy! Because I would even go so far as to say this, spurred by truth: that in our city a government set up in such a way that a few citizens have excessive authority will always be a government of a few tyrants, which will be so much more pestiferous than a single tyrant alone, as evil is worse and more harmful the more it is multiplied. And this is true for no other reason than that one cannot expect long-lasting agreement because of the difference of opinions, the ambition and the variety of covetousness in mankind. Discord which is most pernicious at any time will be even more pernicious at this moment, when you have sent so powerful a citizen into exile, and when you are deprived of so important a part of your state, and when all of Italy, having foreign armies in its bowels, is in the gravest peril. Very rarely, perhaps never before, has it been entirely within the power of this city as a whole to reorganize itself by its own free will. And since God, out of His goodness, has bestowed this power upon you, do not lose the chance (greatly to your own detriment, and sullying forever the fame of Florentine wisdom) to establish a free regime, so well ordered that so long as it lasts it will not only bring you happiness, but also promise it in perpetuity; thus leaving, as inheritance to our sons and descendants, a treasure and felicity such as neither you nor our ancestors ever possessed or knew."

Such were the words of Paolo Antonio. But in opposition, Guido Antonio Vespucci, a famous lawyer and man of singular ability and capacity, spoke as follows: "If, worthy citizens, the government instituted in the form proposed by Paolo Antonio Soderini would so easily produce the fruits that are desired, as he has so easily set them forth, certainly we would be men of the most corrupt judgment if we should desire any other kind of government in our city. Surely he would be a most dangerous citizen who would not desire to the highest degree a form of Republic in which a man's ability, merits and value were recognized and honored above all other things. But I cannot see how one can hope that a government entirely based upon the power of the people can bring forth so many benefits. I know rather that reason teaches, experience demonstrates, and the authority of worthy men confirms, that in so great a multitude cannot be found such discretion, such experience, such a sense of order as to lead us to believe that they would prefer wise men over ignorant, the good over the bad, the experienced over those who have never managed any public affairs whatever. Just as one cannot expect correct sentences from a judge who is incapable and unskilled, so one cannot expect, except by chance, wise or reasonable decisions or choices from a people full of confusion and ignorance. And can we believe that an inexpert, inexperienced multitude composed of so great a variety of talents, conditions, and ways of doing things, and each one devoted to his own particular affairs, will be able to distinguish and understand that which men who are wise in public affairs, and devoting all their efforts to no other task, can scarcely discern? Besides, the immoderate opinion that each one will have of himself will arouse a greed for honors in everyone. Nor in a popular government will men be satisfied to simply enjoy the honest fruits of liberty, because everyone will aspire to the main positions and want to intervene in the most difficult and important deliberations of affairs; for among us, less than in any other city, reigns that modesty which yields to those who know more and deserve more. And so, persuading ourselves that by right everyone ought to be equal in all things, and placing in the hands of the multitude responsibilities requiring ability, virtue and valor, will result in confusion. Covetousness, widely diffused, will give more power to those who know least and deserve least; for being much more numerous, they will have more strength in a state set up in such a way that opinions are counted rather than weighed.

"Wherefore, what assurance have you that, content with the form which you would now introduce, they would not soon cast into disorder all these methods so prudently thought out, with new regulations and imprudent laws against which wise men will not be able to raise objections? These things are dangerous at any time in such a government, but much more so now, because it is within the nature of men, when they leave one extreme wherein they have been forcibly held, to run willingly to the other without stopping midway. Thus, whoever emerges from a tyranny, if he is not checked, will rush toward unbridled license; which might also more properly be called tyranny, because a people is similar to a tyrant when it gives to those who don't deserve, when it takes from those who do deserve, when it confounds degrees and distinctions among persons: and perhaps the tyranny of the people is even more harmful insofar as ignorance is more dangerous than malignity, which governs by some rule, with some restraint and with some limits, while ignorance has neither weight nor measure nor law. Nor should we be influenced by the example of the Venetians, because in their case, both their geographical situation has some bearing and their long-established form of government is of prime importance, and things there are organized in such a way that important deliberations are much more in the hands of a few than of the many; and their wits and temperament, not being perhaps by nature as sharp as ours, are more easily pacified and contented. Nor does the Venetian government rule only by means of those two foundations which have been discussed; the existence of a permanent Doge and many other institutions have much to do with the perfection and stability of that Republic. And yet, whoever might wish to introduce such institutions into this Republic would run into endless opposition, for our city was not born at this moment, nor have its ordinances been established now for the first time. Therefore, inveterate habits often being strongly opposed to the common good, and men suspicious that, under color of preserving liberty, an attempt is being made to set up a new tyranny, they are not easily going to take advantage of wholesome counsels: just as in a body infected and swarming with malignant humors, medicines are not of as much avail as in a body purged. For which reasons, and because of the nature of human affairs, which normally decline toward the worst, it is more to be feared that that which would be imperfectly set up at this beginning stage would, in the course of time, entirely disintegrate, than to hope that, with time and good occasion, it might be brought to perfection. Do we not have examples of our own without searching for those of others? Have the people ever wielded absolute rule over this city, without it being full of discord, without it being entirely torn assunder, and finally, without the state being quickly overthrown? And even if we wish to look for examples elsewhere, why do we not recall that when Rome instituted an entirely popular government so much tumult resulted that, had it not been for military readiness and skill, the life of that Republic would have been brief indeed? And why do we not remember how Athens, that most flourishing and powerful city, lost its empire and then fell into the servitude of its own citizens and foreigners for no other reason than by referring serious matters to the deliberation of the multitude? But I fail to see how it can be said that in the form of government introduced in the Parliament, liberty is not fully provided for. Every issue is referred to the disposition of the magistrates, who are not perpetual but are changing, nor are they elected by a few; rather, approved by many, they must, according to the ancient usage of the city, be chosen by lot; therefore how can they be distributed according to factions or at the will of particular citizens? We can be much more sure that the most important affairs will be examined and directed by the wisest, most practical and most serious-minded men, who will govern with an altogether different kind of order, reserve and maturity than would the people, who are incapable in these matters: sometimes more lavish in spending when there is least need, sometimes so niggardly at times of greatest need that often they incur the most serious expenses and dangers. And as Paolo Antonio has pointed out, the infirmity of Italy and particularly of our country is very grave. Therefore, what folly it would be, when the most expert and skillful physicians are needed, to put oneself into the hands of those who have the least skill and experience. And finally you should consider that you will keep your people in more tranquility, and lead them more easily to decisions beneficial both for themselves and for the common welfare, by giving them limited participation and authority. For, should you refer everything to their absolute judgment, you run the risk of their becoming insolent, and too difficult and averse to the counsels of your wise and loyal citizens."

Savonarola

INASMUCH as a restricted number of citizens were participating in this Council, the prevailing point of view toward a limited form of government would have triumphed, had not divine authority intervened in the deliberations of men through the mouth of Girolamo Savonarola of Ferrara, a friar of the Order of Preachers.* This man had publicly preached the word of God for several years in Florence, and together with his unusual erudition, had earned very great reputation for holiness, and therefore among most of the people achieved credit and fame as a prophet. For at the time when Italy enjoyed the greatest tranquility, he had often predicted the coming of foreign armies into Italy who would so terrify the people that neither walls nor armies would be able to resist them. And he had furthermore asserted that he was foretelling this and many other things which he was continuously predicting, not by human reasoning or knowledge of the Scriptures, but simply by divine revelation. Several times he had also touched on the question of a change in the government of Florence. And at this time, publicly expressing his detestation of the form of government which the Parliament had decided on, he affirmed that it was the will of God that an absolutely popular government be established, and in such sort that it should not lie within the power of a few citizens to alter either the security or the liberty of others.

The reverence which Savonarola evoked, combined with the desire of many Florentines, swept aside all opposition. Therefore, after this matter had been propounded and debated many times, it was finally decided that a Council of all the citizens should be set up, but that the dregs of the common people should not participate in it (as was reported to be the case in so many parts of Italy), but only those who, according to the ancient laws of the city, were qualified to participate in the

* Dominicans.

HIERONYMI·FERRARIENSIS·ADEO·
MISSI·PROPHETÆ·EFFIGIES·

FRA GIROLAMO SAVONAROLA

Portrait by Fra Bartolommeo in San Marco, Florence. The inscription reads:
"Effigy of Girolamo of Ferrara, prophet sent by God." (COURTESY OF FRATELLI
ALINARI)

government. This Council would be empowered to deal with or dispose of nothing other than the election of all the magistrates of the city and domain, and would approve the provisions of financial outlays, and all legislation which had been previously promulgated by the magistracies and other more limited councils. And in order to eliminate sources of civic discord and offer more assurance, it was publicly decreed (following the example of the Athenians) that crimes and transgressions against the state committed in the past be forgiven. A well-ordered and stable government might perhaps have been constituted on such foundations if, at the same time, there had been introduced all the proposals which the wise citizens had previously taken under consideration. But since such matters could not have been deliberated without the consent of many who were very suspect in memory of things past, it was decided that for the present, the Grand Council be set up as the foundation of their new-won freedom, postponing to remedy what was lacking for a better occasion when those who at present were not capable of knowing, by reason and judgment, what was good for the public welfare, would by experience come to know it.

. .
.

It has been shown above that the desire to usurp the duchy of Milan, and Lodovico Sforza's fear of the Aragonese and of Piero de' Medici, had induced him to summon the French King into Italy. And as a result of this invasion he had obtained his ambitious desire, and the Aragonese were reduced to such straits that only with difficulty could they defend their own personal safety. But now a second fear, much more potent and justified than the first, began to present itself before Lodovico's eyes—namely, the imminent servitude of himself and all the Italians if the kingdom of Naples should be added to the power of the King of France. Therefore, he wanted Charles to encounter as much difficulty as possible in Florentine domain. But when he saw how easily the King had come to an agreement with that Republic, and how he had overcome the Pope's opposition with equal facility and entered the kingdom of Naples without hindrance, his peril seemed more dangerous every day with every new success and facile course of French victories.

The same fear began to preoccupy the minds of the Venetian Senate who, having persevered in their original first intentions of maintaining neutrality, had abstained with much circumspection, not only from any actions, but also from any possible demonstration that might give rise to a suspicion that they inclined more to one side than to the other. Hence, having chosen as their ambassadors to the King of France, Antonio Loredano and Domenico Trevisan (not, however, before it was understood that the King had crossed the mountains), the Senate had delayed so long in sending them, that the King arrived in Florence before they did.

But after seeing the vehement course of French good fortune, and how the King was passing through Italy like a thunderbolt without any resistance, the Venetians began to consider the misfortunes of others as dangers to themselves, and to fear that the ruin of others would inevitably involve their own; especially the fact that Charles had occupied Pisa and the other Florentine fortresses, had left a garrison in Siena, and then done the same thing in the states of the Church, seemed to them to be an indication that the King was thinking somewhat further than merely the kingdom of Naples.

For these reasons, they lent willing ears to Lodovico Sforza's persuasions. For, as soon as the Florentines had yielded to Charles, Lodovico had begun to urge that the Venetians and he should take provisions together against the common danger. And it was believed that if Charles had met with any difficulties, either in Roman territory, or while entering the kingdom of Naples, they would both have taken up arms jointly against him. But his victory succeeded with such speed that it thwarted anything that might have been planned to impede it.

[*The Pope was also terrified of the French; and so was Maximilian,* always displeased at French successes. Ferdinand and Isabella, King and Queen of Spain, had encouraged Charles to fight the infidel rather than Christians, and after the flight of the Aragonese, came out openly against the French.*]

At last, in the month of April, at Venice whither the ambassadors of all these princes had assembled, a confederation** was concluded amongst the Pope, the King of the Romans [Maximilian I],*** the King of Spain, the Venetians and the Duke of Milan. According to the title and public statements, this confederation had been drawn up solely in mutual defense, reserving place to whomever might wish to enter into it under reasonable conditions. But since all of them deemed it necessary to see to it that the King of France should not hold the kingdom of Naples, there were secret articles which stipulated that the Spanish troops who had come to Sicily should assist Ferrando of Aragon (who, entertaining great hope in the good will of the people, was negotiating to enter Calabria) in the recovery of his realm; that the Venetians at the same time should attack the maritime coasts with their fleet; that the Duke of

---

* Guicciardini calls him "Cesare" at this point.
** Sometimes called the League of Venice.

*** After 1508, Emperor-elect. Up to that date Guicciardini sometimes calls him King of the Romans, more frequently Caesar.

Milan, in order to prevent fresh reinforcements from France, should occupy the city of Asti, where the Duke of Orleans had remained with a small force; and that the other confederates should give certain sums of money to the King of the Romans and the King of Spain, in order that each of them might unleash war in the kingdom of France with powerful armies.

Besides these things, the confederates also desired that all of Italy should be united in a common cause, and therefore they urged the Florentines and the Duke of Ferrara (Ercole d'Este) to enter into the same confederation. The Duke, who had been requested to join before the league was made public, refused to take up arms against the King; on the other hand, with Italian caution, he consented to have his eldest son, Alfonso d'Este, enter into the service of the Duke of Milan with one hundred and fifty men-at-arms and the title of lieutenant over his companies.

The situation with the Florentines was different, since they had been invited into the confederacy with great offers, and their reasons for breaking with the French King were most justified. For, when the articles of the league were made known, Lodovico Sforza, in the name of all the confederates, offered the Florentines (in the event they entered the league) all their forces to resist the King, should he attempt to do them harm on his return from Naples, and to help them as soon as possible toward the recovery of Pisa and Livorno. On the other hand, the King, scorning the promises he had made in Florence, had not in the beginning restored the towns which had been in the possession of the Florentines, nor, after he had conquered Naples, had he given them back their fortresses, thus reneging on his own promise and his oath, and yielding to the advice of those who favored the cause of the Pisans and were thereby convinced that the Florentines would unite with the other Italians as soon as they had been given back their towns and fortresses. The Cardinal of San Malò very tepidly opposed these opinions (although he had received a large sum of money from the Florentines) since he wanted to avoid controversy with Charles' other important advisers, on their account.

Not only in this but in many other things, the King had made it manifest that he took no account of his promises, nor was he concerned whether Florentine support might be of some importance to him at such times; with the result that one day, when their ambassadors were complaining about the rebellion at Montepulciano and claiming that he was obliged by treaty to constrain the Sienese to restore this town to the Florentines, the King replied, almost derisively: "What can I do if your subjects rebel because they are badly treated?"

Nevertheless, the Florentines, not permitting their anger to deflect them from their own interests, decided not to hearken to the invitation of the confederates. They did not want to provoke the French army against them anew on the King's return, in order that they might still hope for the restitution of those towns in the King's hands. Furthermore, they placed very little confidence in these promises, knowing that the Venetians hated them for having opposed their undertakings on sundry occasions, and they also clearly realized that Lodovico Sforza aspired to the lordship of Pisa for himself.

At that time, the reputation of the French had already begun to diminish greatly in the kingdom of Naples, because giving themselves over to pleasures and governing by chance, they had neglected to drive the Aragonese out of those few places still loyal to them, which they might easily have done had they pursued their good fortune. But even more had good will toward them declined. For although the King showed himself to be very liberal and benign toward the people, granting so many privileges and exemptions throughout the realm that they rose each year to more than 200,000 ducats, yet other things had not been managed with that order and prudence which they required. The King was indolent, and not inclined to listen to men's complaints and petitions; thus, he entirely left the governing of weighty affairs to his courtiers who, partly as a result of incapacity and partly because of avarice, made a great confusion of all things. The Neapolitan nobility were not received either with humanity or granted rewards; they found it very difficult to gain admittance into the King's chambers or audience; no distinctions were made from man to man; personal merits were not recognized except by chance; the minds of those who were naturally estranged from the house of Aragon were not confirmed; many delays and difficulties were interposed concerning the restitution of the estates and property of the Angevin faction and other barons expelled by old Ferdinand. Favors and emoluments were granted to those who procured them by means of bribes and extraordinary means. From many they took without reason, and to many they gave without reason, distributing almost all the offices and goods among the French. Practically all crown lands (as are called those traditionally and directly obedient to the King) were handed over to the French to the great displeasure of the Neapolitans. And all these things were so much the more displeasurable to them, accustomed as they were to the prudent and well-ordered governments of the Aragonese kings, and counting even more on the new king's promises. Added to this was the natural arrogance of the French, aggravated by their easy victory, as a result of which they held themselves in very great esteem while they had no regard whatever for any of the Italians. Their insolence and violence in seizing lodgings, no less in Naples than in other parts of the kingdom where their men-at-arms

Teracina   Liris R.   L.quila   Troia R.   Mare Adri
Fondi   Gumara R.   aticum
Caieta   Cerana
                  Mola   Aquino   CAMPANIA
          Suessa   Capua Vulturno R.
Ponza   Peschara
        Baia   Saluo R.
Ischla   Neapol   Vesuus   Viguno R.
ænarii   Sureto   Nola   Beneuéto   Trigno R.   Guasto
Crapi   Salerno   Fornou R.
                Aterni   Silez R.   Gargan'
Regnum Neapolita.   Corterio   Gual R.
                                Sipóto
Mare Mediterraneum   Losinto R.   Manfredonia
Felicis
Salmo   Polycastro   Casselle   Barleta
Lipari   Saracina   Potenza APVLIA
                        Bradeno R.   Grauina
Vulcano   S Fumia   Cosenza   CALABRIA   Bari
                                Tarato
Messina   TERRA LABORIS
Regiú   Stil'o   Brendisiú
        Bona   Hydruntú
Siciliæ Pars

The kingdom of Naples under the house of Aragon is shown here in a six-
teenth-century map still basically Ptolemaic (second century A.D.) in its whimsi-
cal geography and admixture of Latin names

were quartered, made them unsupportable; everywhere they treated their hosts badly, so that the warm welcome with which they had been received was now changed into burning hatred. And on the contrary, instead of abhorrence of the Aragonese, there was now stealthily growing a compassion for Ferrando, of whose qualities they had always expected great things; they remembered when he had spoken to the Neapolitans with such gentleness and resolution. Whence that city, and almost the entire kingdom, were now waiting for the chance to call back the Aragonese with no less desire than a few months before they had desired their destruction. Indeed, even the name of Alfonso, so hated, was now beginning to be agreeable, and those acts of severity which they used to call cruelty (while the father was alive and commanding the kingdom's domestic affairs) they now called justice; and those very acts of severity which for many years they had termed arrogance and haughtiness they now called the sincerity of a truthful mind.

Such is the nature of the people, who are inclined to hope more than they ought to, and tolerate less than is necessary, and to be always dissatisfied with the present state of affairs. Especially is this true of the inhabitants of the kingdom of Naples, who among all the peoples of Italy are most noted for their instability and thirst for innovations.

. .

Before this new league was formed, the French King had already made up his mind to return soon to France, impelled thereto more by light fancy and the ardent desire of his court than by sober considerations, for a great many important affairs of principalities and states in the kingdom still remained undecided; nor was his victory complete, since he had not conquered the entire realm. But after he knew that so many princes were leagued against him, he was very much troubled and consulted with his advisers what ought to be done in such a situation. Everyone declared that, indeed, so potent a union among Christians had not been organized for a very long time. Based on these counsels, the French decided to hasten their departure; they feared that the longer they remained the greater would their difficulties grow, because it would give time to the confederates to make greater preparations (and there was a rumor that they had already ordered a large number of Germans to come into Italy and were beginning to spread much talk about the person of the Emperor).

The same council also determined to make every effort, including great offers, to separate the Pope from the other allies and to make him amenable to concede the investiture of the kingdom of Naples to Charles; which (although he had made an absolute promise to that effect at Rome), the Pope had still refused to concede, declaring that such a concession could not be made in prejudice against the rights of others.

[*The affairs of Pisa are also considered; French troops are sent there and pro- and anti-French factions skirmish around Pisa. King Charles distributes his forces: some to remain to defend the kingdom of Naples, some to accompany him back to France. Various French officials are appointed in the kingdom of Naples where the Aragonese cause is reviving. Ferrando, with the help of Spanish forces from Sicily, recaptures Reggio in Calabria.*]

Before the King left Naples, various matters were being negotiated between him and the Pope, and not without hope of an agreement. To facilitate this, the Cardinal of St. Denis was sent by the Pontiff to the King, and then returned to Rome; while as his agent to the Pope, the King dispatched Monsignor Franzi: for Charles desired the investiture of the kingdom of Naples above all; and wanted to be certain that the Pope, even if he should not join with him, at least should not league with his enemies, and be content with receiving him into Rome as a friend.

Although at first the Pontiff lent ear to these proposals, nevertheless, not being of a mind to place confidence in the King and not wishing to break away from his allies, nor to concede the investiture to the King (not deeming it sufficient grounds on which to base a faithful reconciliation), he interposed various objections to the other demands; and with regard to the investiture, he replied that, although the King might be induced to accept it under the condition of not prejudicing the rights of others, first he wanted to see to whom the investiture belonged by right. On the other hand, wishing to prevent by force the King's entrance into Rome, the Pope asked the Venetian Senate and the Duke of Milan to send help. They immediately dispatched one thousand light horse and two thousand footsoldiers, and promised to send him a thousand men-at-arms. Reinforced by these troops, the Pope hoped to be able to resist.

[*But the Venetians and Duke of Milan consider it too dangerous to send troops so far from their own domains, and remembering the Pope's lack of fidelity in the past when, fearing Charles' approach, he had summoned Ferrando into Rome and then made him leave, they seek to persuade the Pope to withdraw to a place of security rather than risk his person in a vain attempt to defend Rome.*]

The King left Naples on the twentieth day of May, but inasmuch as he had not previously assumed the title and the royal standards, a few days before his departure, the traditional rites were held in the cathedral church with the most solemn pomp and ceremony according to the custom of Neapolitan kings, at which occasion Charles received the royal ensigns and honors and the usual oaths of fidelity given to new kings. In the name of the people of Naples, Giovanni Iovanno Pontano made an oration. That Pontano, a man renowned for his learning and civic action and behavior, should deliver a speech of praise, added no little lustre to the occasion. For Pontano had been secretary to the Aragonese kings for a long time, and very influential among them, and furthermore, had been master in letters and tutor to Alfonso, so that it seemed that, whether he was acting the part of the orator or making himself more acceptable to the French, he extended himself too much in vituperation of those kings by whom he had been so greatly exalted. So difficult is it sometimes for a man to observe in himself that moderation and those precepts which he has taught unto others, though he be overflowing with erudition, and writing of moral virtues, and considered, because of his broad genius in every branch of learning, marvelous in the eyes of the world.

. .

Although the league had advised the Pope to leave Rome, he was still disposed to arrive at some reconciliation with Charles, with whom he was continually negotiating. Ultimately, however, his fears got the better of him, so that two days before the King was to enter Rome, the Pontiff departed, although he had given the King grounds for believing that he would receive him.

Instead, after leaving a sufficient garrison within the Castel Sant' Angelo, the Pope fled to Orvieto, accompanied by the College of Cardinals and two hundred men-at-arms, one thousand light horse and three thousand footsoldiers, leaving as his legate in Rome the Cardinal of Sant' Anastasia to receive and honor the King. Charles entered by Trastevere in order to avoid the Castel Sant' Angelo, and took up quarters in the Borgo, refusing the lodgings offered him by commission of the Pope in the Vatican palace.

When the Pope heard at Orvieto that the King was approaching Viterbo, he fled once more, although he had given the King renewed hope that they would meet at some convenient place between Viterbo and Orvieto. This time Alexander went to Perugia, with the intention that, if Charles should set out on that road, he would then go on to Ancona, from which port he could sail, if need be, to some completely safe place. And yet, although the King was very angry, he gave up the fortresses at Civitavecchia and Terracina, keeping Ostia for himself until his departure from Italy, when he left it in the power of the Cardinal of San Pietro in Vincoli, Bishop of Ostia. The King then passed through the ecclesiastical domain as through a friendly country, except that when his vanguard were refused lodging by the people at Toscanella, they broke into that town by force, put it to the sack and killed many.

After this the King stayed six days at Siena for no good reason, although the Cardinal of San Pietro in Vincoli and Trivulzio had immediately warned him (what he should have realized by himself) how dangerous it was to give his enemies so much time to make provisions and unite their forces.

[*Meanwhile in Lombardy the Venetians and Lodovico Sforza are making great preparations to block Charles' return to France. Sforza arrogantly threatens to expel the French, under the Duke of Orléans, from Asti. Instead, Orléans not only fortifies Asti, but receiving the reinforcements which he had requested from France, leads his troops out of the city, and with the help of conspirators within the town of Novara occupies that town without resistance.*]

The news of the rebellion at Novara caused Charles, who was at Siena, to hasten his march. He wished to avoid any occasion that might cause him to delay his departure; therefore, when he heard that the Florentines—warned by past perils and suspicious because Piero de' Medici was in his ranks and that although they had made preparations to receive him in Florence with the greatest honors—were now, for their own security, filling the city with arms and men, he went on to Pisa through Florentine domain, leaving the city of Florence to his right. In the town of Poggibonsi, Charles was met by Girolamo Savonarola who, in his usual manner, interpolating divine authority into his own words, earnestly exhorted him to restore their towns to the Florentines. To these persuasions he added the gravest threats to the effect that if Charles did not observe those promises which he had sworn with such solemnity, touching the Gospels with his hand and almost before the very eyes of God, he would swiftly and ruthlessly be punished by the Lord.

The King, with his typical inconstancy, gave various replies at that time and the following day in Castel Fiorentino, now promising to restore these towns as soon as he arrived at Pisa, now twisting his pledged word to the contrary, claiming that before he had given his oath in Florence, he had promised the Pisans that he would protect their liberty. Yet all this while, the King was continually giving hope to the Florentine ambassadors of the restitution of their lands as soon as he had arrived at Pisa.

[*At that city, the royal council considers the question again: some for restoring the fortresses to the Florentines, some against. Those opposed stress the advantage of holding Livorno for the defense of the kingdom of Naples.*]

Certainly, although the King's mind was little capable of choosing the healthiest path, these arguments carried some weight: but most influential of all on his decision were the petitions and tears of the Pisans, who gathered in great numbers: men, women, and little children, now prostrating themselves at the King's feet, now supplicating even the least of his courtiers and soldiers with the most moving cries and laments, bewailing their future calamities, the insatiable hatred of the Florentines, and the utter desolation of their country; saying they would not have come to such a pitable condition, had not the King granted them their freedom and promised to maintain it. For, since they believed the word of the most Christian King of France to be inviolable and steadfast, this had given them courage to provoke the enmity of the Florentines to such a degree. These plaints and exclamations so moved everyone, even the private men-at-arms, even the archers of the army and also many of the Swiss, that they flocked in great numbers and tumult to the King, where one of their pensioners, Salzart, speaking in the name of all of them, begged him ardently that for the honor of his own name, and for the glory of the crown of France, and for the consolation of so many of his soldiers who were ready to lay down their lives at any time for him, and who counseled him with more fidelity than those corrupted by Florentine money, that he should not deprive the Pisans of the benefits which he himself had given them. And if it were want of money that was inducing him to consider so great an injustice, he should rather take their chains and their silver and retain the money and pensions which they were receiving from him.

This tumult of the soldiers went so far that a simple archer dared to threaten the Cardinal of San Malò and some others made bold remarks to the Marshal de Gié and the President de Ganay, whom they knew were pressing for the restitution of the Pisans to Florentine rule.

The result of all this was that the King, confused by such a variety of counsels, left matters suspended, indeed so far from any definite resolution, that at the very same time, he renewed his promise to the Pisans never to place them again under Florentine rule; and to the Florentine ambassadors waiting at Lucca, he left it to be understood that that which he was not doing for good reasons at the present moment, he would do as soon as he arrived at Asti; and therefore they should not fail to see to it that their Republic send ambassadors to him at that place.

The King departed from Pisa after having changed the castellan and left the necessary guard at the citadel, doing the same thing in the fortresses of the other towns.

. . .

At that time, the allied army was being diligently assembled in the territory of Parma, numbering about 2,200 men-at-arms, eight thousand footsoldiers and more than two thousand light horse, for the most part Albanians and from the provinces near Greece, who had been brought into Italy by the Venetians, and retaining the same name they had in their country, are called Stradiots. The sinews and nerve of this army were the Venetian troops, for the soldiers of the Duke of Milan, since he had dispatched almost all his forces to Novara, constituted less than a fourth of the army. . .

The vanguard of the French had crossed the mountains much before the rest of the army, hindered by the heavy artillery, very difficult to draw over those sharp Apennine passes: a difficulty that would have been insuperable had it not been for the enormous efforts and promptitude of the Swiss, who were eager to cancel the offense they had made against the King's honor in sacking Pontriemoli.

. . .

The allied princes never believed that the King, with an army so much smaller than theirs, would dare to cross the Apennines by the direct road. Therefore, at first they were convinced that having left most of his men at Pisa, he would return to France by sea with the rest of his army. But afterward, when they understood that he had taken the land route, they believed that, in order not to draw close to their army, he planned to cross the mountains by way of the village of Valditaro and Monte Centocroce, a very steep and difficult pass leading to the Tortonese,* in the hope of joining up with the Duke of Orléans in the neighborhood of Alexandria.

But when it was known for certain that he was marching straight to Fornovo, the Italian army, which previously had been full of spirit and courage as a result of the resolution of so many of their captains and because of the news that the enemy was in such small numbers, lost some good part of its courage when they began to take account of the valor of the French lancers, the skill of the Swiss (to whom, without any comparison, Italian infantry was considered inferior), the skillful handling of the artillery, and (what especially moves men when they have expected otherwise) the unforeseen boldness of the French in approaching them with forces so inferior in numbers. These considera-

* The area around Tortona.

tions had dampened even the spirits of the captains and set them consulting amongst themselves what reply should be given to the trumpeter bearing the challenge sent by the Marshal de Gié [demanding passage for the French army in the name of the King]. On the one hand, it seemed very dangerous to risk the state of all Italy to the discretion of fortune; on the other, it would be the greatest infamy for the Italian militia to show that they lacked courage to oppose the French army which, so fewer in numbers, yet dared to pass right in front of their eyes.

Since in this consultation there was a very great diversity of opinion among the officers, they finally decided, after many disputes, to advise Milan of the King's request and to execute whatever should be determined concurrently by the Duke and the ambassadors of the allies. At their meeting, the Duke and the Venetian ambassador whose states lay nearest the danger came to the same conclusion: that when the enemy wished to depart, they should not close the way, but rather, according to the popular proverb, build a silver bridge for him; otherwise, as might be proved from infinite examples, there was a danger that, fear turned into despair, he might force a passage with the copious bloodshed of those imprudent enough to oppose him. But the Spanish ambassador, wishing to make a try of fortune without any danger to his King, insisted vehemently and almost as if he were protesting, that they should not let the King pass, nor lose an opportunity to smash the French army. For if it safely extricated itself, then Italian affairs remained the same or rather in worse danger than before; since if the King of France held Asti and Novara, then all of Piedmont would be subject to his rule; and having the kingdom of France, so potent and so rich a realm at his shoulders; the Swiss his neighbors, disposed to fight in his pay in whatever numbers he wished; and finding himself increased in reputation and courage if the army of the league, so much superior to his, should thus cowardly yield him passage, he would soon ravage Italy with even more ferocity; and that if the Italians either would not or dared not fight the French, then his sovereigns would be almost obliged to make new decisions. Nevertheless, the most cautious opinion prevailing in the council, it was resolved to write to Venice where the same opinion would prevail.

But already they were consulting in vain. For after the captains of the army had written to Milan, they assumed that it was doubtful that the reply would arrive in time; and considering how dishonorable it would be for the Italian militia if they permitted free passage to the French, they dismissed the trumpeter without any definite reply, and resolved to assail the enemy as he took up the march. The Venetian commissioners concurred in this decision, but Trevisan* more than his colleagues.

---

* Marchionne Trevisan, of a patrician Venetian family. He and Luca Pisano, important members of the Venetian Senate, were part of this commission.

On the other hand, the French marched ahead with great arrogance and audacity; and since up to that time, they had not encountered any resistance whatever in Italy, they were convinced that the enemy army had no intention of opposing them, and even if they did, could be sent flying without any trouble, so little respect did they have for Italian arms. Nevertheless, when they began descending the mountain, they discovered the army encamped in infinite numbers of tents and pavilions, and spread over so wide an area that (according to Italian custom) they could arrange themselves in battle array within the camp ground; and when the French became aware of the great number of the enemy and realized that if they were not determined to fight, they would not have pitched camp so close to them, their overweening arrogance began to cool, so that they would have considered it good news should the Italians be content to let them pass.

And this was especially so, because Charles had written to the Duke of Orleans to continue his march for an eventual meeting with the King on the third of July at Piacenza with as many forces as possible; and although the Duke had replied that he would not fail to be there at the promised time, the King then received fresh notice from the Duke himself that Sforza's army was marching against him, composed of nine hundred men-at-arms, twelve hundred light cavalry and five thousand footsoldiers, and was so powerful that the Duke could not advance without the most manifest peril, especially since he had had to leave part of his forces as garrisons at Novara and Asti. Therefore the King, being forced to arrive at some new decisions, commanded Monsieur Philippe d'Argenton (who a little while before had been Charles' ambassador to the Venetian Senate where, on his departure, he had promised Pisano and Trevisan, just then appointed deputy commissioners, to bend all his efforts to dispose the King's mind to peace) to send a trumpeter to the said commissioners with a letter stating that he desired to speak with them concerning their common welfare. They agreed to meet with him the following morning in a convenient place between both armies. But, either because of a lack of provisions in that place or for some other reason, the King changed his mind and decided that he would not await the decision of this conference.

The Battle of the Taro

The fronts of both camps were less than three miles apart, spread out on the right side of the River Taro (although this should rather be called a brook than a river) which, descending from its source in the Apennines, then runs through a little narrow valley between two hills and spreads out into the wide Lombard plain up to the River Po. On the right of these two hills, descending to the banks of the river, the allied army was encamped, set there rather than on the left bank (which perforce had to be the enemy path) at the advice of the captains, in order to prevent the French from turning toward Parma. For the Duke of Milan distrusted that city, torn by factions, especially since the Florentines had assigned Francesco Secco to accompany the King as far as Asti, and Secco's daughter was married into the house of Torelli, a noble and powerful family in the region of Parma.

The camp of the allies was fortified with ditches and ramparts, and well equipped with artillery, in front of which the French were forced to pass if they wished to retreat into the Asti region (thereby crossing the Taro alongside Fornovo) with nothing but the river between them and the Italians.

All night the French army was greatly harassed, because the Italians attentively saw to it that the Stradiots made incursions right up to the French camp, so that there were frequent calls to arms, everyone leaping up at every noise; in the midst of which, a violent storm suddenly broke, with heavy rains, and the most frightful thunder and lightning, and terrifying cracklings and flashes, which many prognosticated as foretelling the most dire outcome. This storm troubled the French more than the Italian army, not only because they were in the midst of mountains and enemies in a place where, if misfortune struck them, they had no hope whatever of saving themselves, so that they felt themselves in very dire straits indeed (and hence had justifiable reasons for their greater terror); but also because it seemed more likely that threatenings from heaven, which usually manifest themselves only for the most important reasons, were primarily directed against that side where the person of so powerful and majestic a King was to be found.

The following morning, which was the sixth of July, the French army began to cross the river at dawn. Ahead marched most of the artillery, followed by the vanguard wherein the King, believing that it would have to bear the brunt of the main enemy attack, had placed three hundred and fifty French lancers, Gianiacopo da Trivulzio with his hundred lances, and three thousand Swiss who were the sinews and hope of that army; and with the Swiss, on foot, Engilbert, brother of the Duke of Cleves, and the Bailli of Dijon, who had levied them. To these the King had added three hundred archers on foot, and some mounted crossbowmen of his guard, and almost all the other footsoldiers whom he had with him. After the vanguard, marched the main body of the army, in the midst of which was the person of the King, fully armed, and mounted on a fierce courser. Alongside him was Monsieur La Trémouille, a very famous officer in the

French kingdom, who was to command that part of the army with his counsel and authority. After these followed the rear guard led by the Count de Foix, and lastly the supply wagons.

Nevertheless, the King was not without a mind to come to some agreement, and he therefore solicited Argenton to go and treat with the Venetian commissioners at the very moment when the army began to move. But since the Italian army was already in formation and in arms, and the captains determined to fight, the time being so short and the arms so close left neither space nor convenience for a parley. For already the light cavalry were beginning to skirmish on all sides; already the artillery was firing furiously from all quarters; already the Italians had issued out of their tents and extended their squadrons in battle order along the river bank.

Despite these preparations, the French did not cease marching ahead, partly upon the gravel river-bed, and partly along the edge of the hill (because they couldn't deploy their ordnance in so narrow a plain); and already the vanguard was being led directly up to the enemy camp, where the Marquis of Mantua, with a squadron of six hundred men-at-arms, the flower of the army, and a great band of Stradiots and other light horsemen and five thousand footsoldiers, crossed the river behind the French rearguard, leaving on the other bank Antonio da Montefeltro, the natural son of Federigo, late Duke of Urbino, with a large squadron, ready to cross the river when he should be called upon to reinforce the first body of men. Besides that, the Marquis ordered another part of the light horse to strike the enemy on the flank as soon as the battle began, and the rest of the Stradiots to pass the river at Fornovo and attack the French supply wagons, which either for lack of men or at the advice of Trivulzio (as was reputed) had been left without any guard, exposed to whoever wished to capture them.

On the other side, the Count of Gaiazzo crossed the Taro with four hundred men-at-arms (among whom was the company of Don Alfonso d'Este which had come to the camp without Don Alfonso in person, for his father wished it so) and with two thousand footsoldiers in order to attack the French vanguard; similarly, Annibale Bentivoglio with two hundred men-at-arms was left on the other bank as reinforcements when called upon; and two large companies of men-at-arms and a thousand footsoldiers remained to guard the camp, because the Venetian commissioners wanted to keep some reserves intact against all eventualities.

But when the King saw so powerful a force charging his rearguard (contrary to his captains' expectations and convictions), he turned his back on his vanguard and began to move his main forces close to the rearguard, marching so hastily with one of his squadrons that when the assault began, he found himself at the front of his men amongst the first combatants. Some have written that the Marquis' troops crossed the river in disorder because of the height of the banks and the impediments of trees, undergrowth and shoots with which the banks of streams are commonly entangled. Others have added that his footsoldiers reached the main body of the Italian army too late because of these difficulties, and because the stream had swelled as a result of the nocturnal rains; that at any rate, not all the footsoldiers got there, a great part remaining on the other side of the river. But however it was, it is certain that the Marquis' charge was most furious and ferocious, and was met with equal ferocity and valor, the squadrons entering into the thick of the fray from every side, and not according to the custom of Italian wars, which was to pit one squadron against the other, and in place of one that was fatigued or beginning to withdraw, to substitute another, making in the end one big squadron out of several squadrons: so that most of the time battles lasted almost an entire day, always with very little killing, and the fighting was often abruptly broken off by nightfall without any victory for one side or the other.

But now, after the lances had shattered as they clashed and on all sides numerous men-at-arms and horses were toppling to the ground, everyone began with the same fury to make use of their iron maces, their rapiers and other short arms, the horses no less than the men fighting by kicking and biting and charging. Certainly at the beginning the Italians showed outstanding valor, most of all as a result of the courage of the Marquis who, followed by a valiant company of young gentlemen and *lancie spezzate** (these are picked troops outside of any of the regular paid companies), fearlessly placed himself in the forefront of every danger, and did not fail to perform any action which was to be expected of a spirited leader. The French valorously withstood this furious charge, but finding themselves overwhelmed by such greater numbers, they began almost manifestly to give way, not without danger to the King, within a few paces of whom the Bastard of Bourbon was taken prisoner, although he fought fiercely. This capture gave hope to the Marquis that he would have the same success against the person of the King himself (who had been imprudently led to so dangerous a spot without the guard and order proper for so great a prince). The Marquis, therefore, with many of his men made every effort to draw near the King. Against this attack, although Charles had very few of his men around him, he displayed great ardor in nobly defending himself, helped more by the ferocity of his horse than by his soldiers. Nor did he fail, at a time of such great peril, to have recourse to those counsels which fear usually brings to our memories in difficult situations; for finding himself almost abandoned by his men, he turned to heavenly aids, making a vow to Saint Denis and Saint Martin, who are considered the particular protectors of the king-

* Literally, broken lances.

dom of France, that if he passed safely with his army into Piedmont, as soon as he had returned on the other side of the mountains, he would visit, and bestow great gifts on the churches dedicated to their names, one near Paris, and the other at Tours; and that each year, with most solemn celebration and ceremonies, he would make public witness of the grace which he had received through their intervention. Once having made these vows, he felt new courage, and began to fight more bravely, beyond his usual strength and capacity.

But now the King's danger had so enflamed those who were least distant from him that, running to cover with their own persons the person of the King, they even held off the Italians; at the same time, Charles' main battalion, which had remained behind, now intervened, one squadron of which violently struck the enemy on the flank, considerably checking the impetus of their charge.

It has also been stated that Ridolfo da Gonzaga, the uncle of the Marquis of Mantua, a widely experienced condottiere—whilst encouraging his soldiers and reorganizing their ranks wherever there seemed to be the beginning of disorder, and going now here and now there, always playing the role of an outstanding captain—having by chance raised the beaver of his helmet, was wounded by a Frenchman with a dagger thrust in the face and fell from his horse; and since his men were unable to rescue him amidst such confusion and tumult and in the tangle of infuriated horses, other men and other horses fell on him and he lost his life, smothered in the throng rather than as a result of enemy arms. Certainly such a man did not deserve such a death, for that very morning and the day before in council, he had judged it imprudent to risk so much without necessity to the will of fortune, and against his nephew's wish, he had recommended that a battle be avoided.

Thus the battle changing with various acts of chance, and no advantage appearing any more for the Italians than for the French, it was more than ever doubtful who would be the victor. Thus, hope and fear being almost balanced, both sides fought with incredible valor, each believing that victory rested in his right hand and in his strength. The presence and peril of the King aroused the spirits of the French, because, ingrained in the traditions of that nation, the French have always venerated the majesty of their King no differently than they worshiped divinity. Furthermore, they were so situated that only in victory could they hope for safety. The Italians were encouraged by the greed for plunder, the ferocity and example of the Marquis, their initial successes in the battle, the great numbers of troops in their army on whom they relied for reinforcements; a thing the French could not hope for, because all their men were either already mixed up in the fight, or at the very least, expected to be attacked by the enemy at any moment.

But (as everyone knows) the power of fortune is most great in all human affairs, even more in military matters than any others, but inestimable, immense and infinite in actual warfare; where a badly understood command, or a poorly executed order, or an act of rashness, or a false rumor, sometimes coming from even the simplest soldier, will often bring victory to those who already seem to be defeated; and where innumerable accidents unexpectedly occur which cannot be foreseen or controlled by the captain's orders. Thus amidst such indecision, Fortune did not forget her usual role and accomplished what neither the valor of man nor the force of arms had yet been able to accomplish. For the Stradiots, who had been sent to attack the French supply wagons, began plundering without any opposition and concentrated all their efforts on conveying their pillage to the other side of the river: some leading off mules, some horses, some equipment. And when their companions saw them return to camp laden with spoils, not only the other Stradiots who were supposed to strike the French in the flank, but also those who had already been embroiled in combat, now incited by greed for plunder, turned around to rob the supply wagons. And their example was followed by the horsemen and footsoldiers who, for the same reason, broke battle ranks. As a result, the Italians not only lacked their reinforcements which had been ordered, but also the number of combatants was diminished and disintegrated into chaos. Antonio da Montefeltro had not gone into action, no one summoning him, for Ridolfo da Gonzaga, who had been charged with summoning him at the proper time, had been slain. And so the French began to win so much ground that the Italians (who were already obviously giving way) no longer had any support other than the valor of the Marquis. He, for his part, fought most valiantly, still holding off the enemy attack, rallying his men now by his own example and now by ardent speeches, urging them rather to lose their lives than their honor. But it was no longer possible that so few should resist so many; and the enemy already falling upon them from every side in greater numbers, and a great many already slain and many wounded, mostly amongst the Marquis' personal band, they were all forced to flee in order to get back across the river. But because of the storm which had broken the night before, and continued during the battle with thunder and hail and heavy rains, the river had risen so high that those constrained to cross it did so only with great difficulties. The French pursued them headlong down to the river furiously intent upon massacring those who fled, without taking any of them prisoner, and indifferent to spoils or pillage; rather, throughout the field, frequent voices were heard, crying: "Companions, remember Guinegatte!" (Guinegatte is a village in Picardy near Thérouanne, where, during the last years of the reign of Louis XI, the French army, almost victorious in a battle* against Maximilian, King of the Romans,

* August 7, 1479.

broke ranks because they had begun to pillage, and were put to flight.)

But at the same time, while this part of the army was fiercely and valorously fighting, the vanguard of the French against whom the Count of Gaiazzo was leading part of the cavalry, came into the battle with such force that the Italians were terrified, particularly when they saw that their men were not supporting them. Thus, thrown into confusion almost of their own accord, and some of them already slain, amongst whom were Giovanni Piccinino and Galeazzo da Coreggio, they returned to the main squadron in obvious flight.

But the Marshal de Gié, realizing that besides the Count's squadron there was another column of men-at-arms on the other bank preparing for battle, did not permit his men to pursue them. In subsequent discussions, some considered this decision to have been wise and prudent; others (who perhaps paid less attention to the reason than to the event) considered it cowardly rather than circumspect. For there is no doubt that had he pursued them, the Count and his company would have turned their backs, and thus would have struck all the rest of the soldiers remaining on the other side of the stream with such terror that it would have been almost impossible to keep them from fleeing.

For when the Marquis of Mantua, also in flight, recrossed the river with part of his men, keeping ranks closed and in as good order as possible, he found the troops on the other side in such tumult and mutiny that everyone was thinking only of saving his own skin and his possessions; and the high road leading from Piacenza to Parma was already thronged with men, horses and carriages retreating to Parma. This tumult was partly staved off by the presence and authority of the Marquis, who reassembled the men and restabilized their ranks. But even more effective in stanching the agitation was the arrival of the Count of Pitigliano, who had taken advantage of the confusion in both armies, and escaped to the Italian camp, where he reassured and greatly strengthened their spirits, rallying the men and convincing them that the enemy was in an even worse state of disorder and terror. In fact, almost everyone agreed that had it not been for him, almost the entire army would have disintegrated in the greatest terror either then, or at least the following night.

Once the Italians had withdrawn into their own camp, excepting those who, overcome by the confusion and tumult (as happens in such cases) and terrified at the swollen stream, had fled to various places (where many of them fell into the hands of the French scattered throughout the countryside and were cut to pieces), the King with his forces went to join the vanguard which had not budged from its position. There he held council with his captains whether it was advisable to cross the river immediately to attack the enemy camp. Trivulzio and Camillo Vitelli (who, with a few horsemen, had followed the King into the thick of the battle, after having sent the rest of his men to join those who were attacking Genoa) urged Charles to take the assault. Francesco Secco, more than anyone else, was in favor of such an attack, arguing that the road that could be seen from afar was full of men and horses, which indicated that either they were fleeing toward Parma, or having begun to flee, were returning to the camp. But crossing the river offered no little difficulties; and the men, some of whom had fought and some of whom had remained armed in the field, were so weary that the French captains decided to strike camp. So they went to set up their camp at the village of Medesano on a hill not much more than a mile from the battlefield; and there the tents were pitched without any particular order or concern for rank, and with considerable inconvenience, because many of the supply carriages had been stolen by the enemy.

This was the battle between the Italians and the French on the banks of the Taro, memorable because it was the first battle fought in Italy with bloodshed and slaughter for a very long time; before then, very few men had ever died in military action. But in this battle, although the French lost less than two hundred men, the Italians counted more than three hundred men-at-arms dead, and many others slain, bringing the number up to three thousand men; amongst whom were Rinuccio da Farnese, the condottiere of the Venetians, and many gentlemen of note. Bernardino dal Montone, also a condottiere of the Venetians, struck by a mace on his helmet, was left for dead on the battlefield. Bernardino was held in regard more because of his famous grandfather, Braccio dal Montone, one of the first to give luster to the Italian militia, than for his own valor or merit.

And so much slaughter was all the more shocking to the Italians because the battle hadn't lasted more than an hour, and because both sides, having fought with their own forces and short arms, had made little use of artillery. Each side sought to claim the victory and honor of this day for itself. The Italians because their tents and supply carriages had remained untouched, whereas the French, on the contrary, had lost a great many of their supply wagons and tents, among others, part of the King's own pavilions. They also boasted that they would have defeated the enemy if part of their men who had been assigned to enter into battle had not turned aside to plunder: the truth of which the French did not deny. And the Venetians made such efforts to attribute the glory of the day to themselves that, by public proclamation throughout all their domain and especially in Venice, they lighted bonfires and made other signs of celebration. This public celebration was subsequently followed by private examples, for on the tomb of Marchionne Trevisan, in the church of the Friars Minor, were written these words: *He fought successfully upon the River Taro against Charles, King of France.*

Nevertheless, the palm of victory was universally accorded to the French: because of the great difference in the number of dead, and because they had routed the enemy to the other side of the river, and because they had won free passage to advance, which was the very issue for which the battle had been contended.

The King remained all the following day encamped in the same place, and on the next day arranged a parley with the enemy through Argenton, by which a truce until nightfall was agreed upon.

.　.
.

The following morning, the King marched his army before daybreak, without sound of trumpets, in order to conceal his departure as much as possible. The army of the allies did not pursue the French that day, since even had they wished to give chase, they were impeded by the high waters of the river, which had swollen so much during the night because of new rains that it was impassable for the better part of the day.

[*Despite harassments from the rear, the French reach Asti in eight marches without loss of men. Meanwhile those cardinals and captains who had been present at the unsuccessful attempt on Genoa returned to join Charles. By recapturing Rapallo and other places where they had been defeated the year before, the Aragonese gained even greater renown. Apart from La Spezia, the other towns along the Riviera recalled the Genoese to power.*

Meanwhile, in the kingdom of Naples, fighting continues between the French and Ferrando's combined Aragonese-Spanish forces. Secretly summoned by sympathizers within Naples, Ferrando sets out from Messina with eighty ships, reaches the Amalfi coast, then retires to Ischia. An uprising in Naples enables him to enter at last, "received by the multitude with great cries of joy, the women showering him with flowers and perfumes from their windows; indeed many of the most noble ladies ran into the streets to embrace him and wipe the sweat from his brow."

Heavy fighting, however, continues both on land and sea in the kingdom of Naples, the French seeking to recoup their losses.]

About this time at Messina there died Alfonso of Aragon whose glory and fortune, which had rendered his name illustrious everywhere while he was Duke of Calabria, was converted into the greatest infamy and infelicity once he had ascended the throne of Naples. It was reported that a little before his death he had petitioned his son to permit him to return to Naples, where the hatred formerly held against him had now almost become transformed into benevolence; and it was said that Ferrando, whose greed to reign was stronger in him than filial respect (as is typical in mankind), answered no less sharply than shrewdly that it would be best for his father to wait until the kingdom had so settled down by itself that he would not have to flee from it again. And to strengthen his affairs by a closer alliance with the King of Spain, Ferrando took as his wife, with the Pope's dispensation, his aunt Giovanna, daughter of his grandfather Ferdinand and Giovanna, sister of the aforesaid King [of Spain].

[*In the north, meanwhile, the Duke of Milan and the Venetians besiege Novara.*]

While the city of Novara was under attack, the King of France, in order to be closer to that town, had transferred his quarters from Asti to Turin; and although he often went to Chieri, drawn thereto by his love for a lady who lived there, this in no way interfered with his preparations for war, continually pressing for troops to be sent from France with the intention of putting two thousand French lancers into the field. And he was no less diligently soliciting the arrival of ten thousand Swiss whom the Bailli of Dijon had been sent to enlist; planning that as soon as he had these troops in his army, he would make every possible effort to relieve Novara, but without them he would not dare to attempt any serious action. For although the kingdom of France at that time was most powerful in cavalry, and very well furnished with a great number of artillery pieces, and possessed of maximum skill in handling them, its own infantry was very weak. For among the French, the exercise of arms and waging of war was reserved only for the nobility; and therefore there was lacking among the plebians and common people the ancient ferocity of that nation, inasmuch as the multitude of Frenchmen had for a very long time ceased from participating in wars and had devoted themselves to peaceful arts and occupations. Indeed, many of their former kings, who had experienced various conspiracies and rebellions which had occurred in that realm, feared the people's wrath, and had therefore taken the precaution to disarm them and separate them from the use of arms. Consequently, the French no longer had any faith in the valor of their own footsoldiers, and acted very cautiously in war if their army did not contain several bands of Swiss. For the reputation of that nation, at all times ferocious and indomitable, had been greatly increased about twenty years before; when, being assailed by the most mighty army of Charles, Duke of Bourbon (whose might and fierceness struck the greatest terror in the kingdom of France and all its neighbors), the Swiss had defeated him three times within a few months, and at last had taken his life, either in battle or in flight (the circumstances of his death remained unknown). Hence, as a result of their valor, and because the French had no rivalry or differences with them of any kind, nor had they any reason, in terms of their own interests, to suspect them (as they did the Germans), the French never enlisted any other foreign infantrymen but Swiss, and used them in all their important wars; and at this time more willingly than at any other, knowing that the relief of Novara, besieged by such an army and against so many German infantrymen who fought with the same discipline as did the Swiss, was a most difficult and perilous operation.

. .
.

The allies began to have grave doubts about the outcome of the battle of Novara. Therefore, in order to determine more knowledgeably how to proceed in these difficulties, Lodovico Sforza went to the army together with his wife, Beatrice, his constant companion in serious no less than in pleasurable matters. And in her presence, and according to the rumor, primarily as a result of her recommendations, the captains finally after many disputations came to a unanimous agreement [regarding means of carrying on the siege]. . .

These things decided and the entire army mustered, Lodovico returned to Milan in order to make more readily those provisions which might prove necessary from day to day. And in order to favor their temporal forces with spiritual authority and spiritual arms, the Venetians and Lodovico saw to it that the Pope should send one of his macebearers to Charles, commanding him to depart from Italy in ten days with his entire army, and within another brief terminus, to withdraw all his men from the kingdom of Naples. Otherwise, he would have to appear personally before the Pope at Rome under those spiritual penalties with which the Church makes its threats.

Such a remedy had been previously attempted by popes in ancient times. According to written tradition, Adrian, the first of that name, with no arms other than these, constrained Desiderio, King of the Lombards, who was marching with a powerful army to attack Rome, to withdraw to Pavia from Terni, where he had already arrived. But since there was now lacking that reverence and majesty which the sanctity of the popes' lives had aroused in men's hearts, it was ridiculous to expect similar effects from such dissimilar manners and examples. Therefore, scornful of the frivolity of this papal command, Charles replied that inasmuch as when he had returned from Naples the Pontiff had not wanted to wait for him in Rome, where he had gone devoutly to kiss his feet, he marveled that the Pope should make such a demand at this time. However, in obedience, he, Charles, would make every effort to cut his way through to Rome, and lest he take all those pains in vain, he begged the Pope to wait patiently for him.

[*Charles reaches a new agreement with the Florentines. He agrees to return their fortresses and possessions in exchange for certain payments on their part. Meanwhile, the siege of Novara continues under very difficult conditions for the French. Deputies from both camps sound out the possibility of an agreement between the King of France and the Duke of Milan. Charles refers the peace proposals to his council, where the matter is debated pro and con—again with classically modeled speeches written by Guicciardini. The decision is to accept. As soon as the Duke of Milan swears to observe the peace, the King proceeds to Turin; he proposes a meeting with Sforza to stabilize the peace. But Sforza wants "the meeting to take place on some river over which a bridge should be built either of boats or some other material with a strong wooden paling between them: thus the kings of France and England had once met, and other great princes of the West." The King rejects this as "unworthy of himself," and shortly thereafter, together with his court, "takes the road to France with . . . speed and longing. . . ."*]

Thus at the end of October in the year 1495, the King returned to the other side of the mountains, more like one who had been conquered than a conqueror, notwithstanding his victories. As his governor in Asti (which city he pretended to have purchased from the Duke of Orleans) he left Gianiacopo da Trivulzio with five hundred French lancers, almost all of whom followed the King of their own accord within a few days. And for the assistance of the kingdom of Naples, the King made no other provisions than the ships which were arming at Genoa and in Provence, and the assignment of the money and aid promised by the Florentines.

Syphilis Appears in Europe for the First Time

After having narrated so many other things, it seems to me not unworthy of note that those very times when it seemed destined that the woes of Italy should have begun with the passage of the French (or at any rate were attributed to them), was the same period when there first appeared that malady which the French called the Neapolitan disease and the Italians commonly called either boils or the French disease. The reason was that it manifested itself among the French when they were in Naples, and then, as they marched back to France, they spread it all over Italy. This disease, which was either altogether new or at least unknown up to that time in our hemisphere, if not in its most remote and out of the way parts, was for many years especially so horrible that it deserves to be mentioned as one of the gravest calamities. For it showed itself either in the form of the most ugly boils which often became incurable ulcers, or very intense pains at the joints and nerves all over the body. And since the physicians were not experienced in dealing with such a disease, they applied remedies which were not appropriate, indeed often actually harmful, frequently inflaming the infection. Thus, this disease killed many men and women of all ages, and many became terribly deformed and were rendered useless, suffering from almost continuous torments; indeed, most of those who seemed to have been cured, relapsed in a short time into the same miserable state. But after the course of so many years (either because the celestial influence which had produced so virulent a plague, had mitigated, or from long experience, suitable remedies were eventually found to cure it) the disease became much less malignant; also because it transformed itself into other kinds of illness diverse from its original form. This calamity is certainly one which men of our time might justly complain about, if it had been transmitted to them through no fault of their own: but all those who have diligently observed the nature of this illness agree that never, or very rarely, can anyone acquire it except by contagion during coitus. But it would be just to absolve the French from this ignominy because it is obvious that this malady had been carried to Naples from Spain; nor was it really a product of that nation either, for it had been brought there from those islands which (as we shall discuss more pertinently elsewhere) began to be known in our hemisphere almost during those same years as a result of the voyage of Christopher Columbus, the Genoese. In those islands, however, beneficent nature provides a very quick remedy for this disease, for the natives are very easily cured simply by drinking the juice of a wood which grows there, highly valued because of its great medicinal qualities.

BOOK
3

Charles Prepares to Invade Again

[*After Charles' return to France, the affairs of Italy continue to be agitated by the ambitions of the Venetians and the Duke of Milan. French troops remaining in the kingdom of Naples lack aid because Sforza fails to observe the peace conditions he had made with the King. And both the Duke and the Venetians, greedy to control Pisa, lend aid and promises to the Pisans against the Florentines.*

The league also spurs Piero de' Medici to attempt to regain power in Florence. All over the peninsula, factional and other wars break out: in Perugia, in Umbria, around Siena. Piero fails to obtain sufficient backing for his enterprise.

In the kingdom of Naples, Ferrando continues to make progress against the French, as King Charles whiles his time away at Lyons in tournaments and pleasures.

The French castellon consigns the citadel to the Pisans. They demolish the fortress and then beg for help of various powers—the Pope, the King of the Romans, the Venetians, the Duke of Milan, the Sienese, the Luccans—against the Florentines. Finally the Venetians take the city of Pisa under protection but only after considerable debate in the Senate. The Duke of Milan fails to take great account of this, convinced as he is that the Pisans are more devoted to him than to anyone else. He is now so vain that he thinks he has "fortune under his feet, stating publicly that he was fortune's child"; he boasts that the King of France had entered Italy at his invitation and been expelled at his behest; that he, Sforza, had deprived Piero of his authority in Florence; that he had caused his enemies, the Aragonese, first to be driven from Naples, and then to be restored. He presumes now to control the destiny of all Italy.

"Nor did he keep this vain notion hidden . . . but rather took pleasure that it should be believed and heralded by all. Hence Milan resounded day and night with vain voices, and everyone celebrated *in Latin verses and in the vulgar tongue and with public orations and encomiums, the wonderful wisdom of Lodovico Sforza, on whom depended peace and war in Italy; exalting to the skies his name and his nickname 'the Moor' given to him in his youth because of his dark complexion and because of his reputation for cunning. . . ."*

King Ferrando signs an agreement with the Venetians who promise to help him against the French. In the Abruzzi, in Calabria, in Puglia there are various actions.]

THE KING OF FRANCE, ON HIS PART, WAS DEALING WITH THE QUESTION OF SENDING HELP TO HIS PEOPLE. FOR WHEN HE HAD LEARNED OF THE loss of the castles of Naples, and that the Florentines had failed to provide money and help to his men because they had not gotten back their fortresses, Charles roused himself out of that torpor in which he seemed to have sunken since his return to France, and began once again to turn his attention toward Italian affairs. And to be more free of anything that might hold him back, and in order that he might more confidently have recourse again to celestial help (by showing himself grateful for benefits which he had received in his perils), he went posthaste to Tours and then to Paris to satisfy those vows which he had personally made on the day of the battle of Fornovo* to Saint Martin and Saint Denis; and then returning with the same diligence to Lyons, this desire [to return to Italy] became more ardent every day. He was naturally most inclined toward an Italian campaign, considering his acquisition of such a kingdom his greatest glory, being the first of all the French kings to have personally renewed in Italy after so many centuries the memory of French arms and victories; and he was persuaded that the difficulties which he had encountered on his return from Naples proceeded more from the disorders of his own people than from the power or capacity of the Italians, whose reputation in war was no longer held in any estimation by the French. And he was further incited by the Florentine ambassadors, by the Cardinal of San Pietro in Vincoli and Gianiacopo da Trivulzio, who had returned for this very reason to the court; Vitellozzo and Carlo Orsini joined in the same demand; and besides these, the Count of Montorio who had been sent for the same purpose by the barons supporting the French party in the kingdom of Naples; and finally from Gaeta by sea there came the Seneschal of Beaucaire, who pointed out that there were great hopes of victory in case help were sent [to Naples] without any more delay, but that, on the contrary, affairs in that kingdom could not be sustained much longer if they were abandoned. Besides all these, some of the great lords of France

---

* Earlier called the battle on the River Taro.

who had previously been opposed to the Italian campaign were now in favor of it as a result of the ignominy which would result to the French crown by permitting such acquisitions to be lost, and even more so because of the damages which many French noblemen would suffer in the kingdom of Naples. Nor were these proposals checked by the maneuvers which the King of Spain was then manifesting in the region of Perpignan, for his preparations were greater in name than in fact, and the forces of that King were more powerful in defense of their own realm than in attacks on the realms of others; and therefore it was judged sufficient precaution to have sent many men-at-arms as well as a sufficient company of Swiss to Narbonne and other towns on the Spanish frontier.

Then the King convoked all the lords and notable persons of his court in council, where it was decided that Trivulzio should return to Asti as soon as possible, under the title of the King's lieutenant, leading with him eight hundred lancers, two thousand Swiss and two thousand Gascons; and that a short while after him, the Duke of Orleans with other troops should cross the mountains, and finally the person of the King with all the other provisions. Coming with so great an army, there was no doubt but that the states of the Duke of Savoy and of the Marquises of Montferrat and Saluzzo, very fit instruments in waging war against the Duke of Milan, would declare themselves for the King; and it was also believed that, except for the canton of Berne, which had promised the Duke of Milan not to turn against him, all the other Swiss cantons would be more than willing to enlist in the King's service for pay. The King's eagerness spurred a majority approval of these resolutions; for even before he had entered the council, Charles had strongly urged the Duke of Bourbon to set forth with his most efficacious words how necessary it was to undertake a major war, and then in the council he had, with equal ardor, refuted the Admiral who, although followed by very few, had not so much directly contradicted as pointed out many difficulties, and had sought indirectly to mitigate the opinion of the others; and the King publicly affirmed that it was not in his power to come to any other decision, for it was God's will that constrained him to return to Italy in person. The same council also decreed that thirty ships, among which was an enormous carrack called the *Normande*,* and another large carrack belonging to the Knights of Rhodes, should sail from the coast of the Ocean Sea** to the ports of Provence, where there should be armed thirty ships, both light galleys and galleons, and to send that great armada to assist Naples with vast supplies of men, provisions, ammunition and

---

* According to Bembo, a 1200-ton ship.

** A term still used in Guicciardini's day for the Atlantic. In the fifteenth century, before the discovery of America, the Ocean Sea was believed to flow indivisibly around Europe, Asia and Africa.

money. Meanwhile, without waiting until all this should be put into order, some ships laden with soldiers and supplies were to set sail immediately.

Besides all these things, the King's steward, Rigaud, was ordered to go to Milan. For although the Duke had not delivered the two carracks, nor given permission for the King's vessels to be rigged and armed at Genoa, and had only restored the vessels captured at Rapallo but not the twelve galleys held in the port of Genoa, he had tried to excuse himself by throwing the blame on the disobedience of the Genoese and through various devices he continually surrounded the King with his own men. Only recently, he had dispatched Antonio Maria Pallavicini to Charles, declaring that he was disposed to observe the agreement which had been made, but requesting extension of the term for paying the Duke of Orleans the fifty thousand ducats promised in that agreement. But he reaped very little fruit from these tricks, since the King was very familiar with his way of thinking, by example of his previous actions, and because certain of the Duke's letters and instructions which had been intercepted, revealed that he had continually goaded the King of the Romans and the King of Spain to undertake war against France.

Nevertheless, in the hope that perhaps fear would induce Lodovico to do what he willingly would not do, Rigaud was commissioned to indicate to the Duke (without discussing his past inobservances) that it was in his power to cancel the memory of those offenses by beginning to observe his agreements, by yielding the galleys, delivering the carracks and permitting the ships to be armed at Genoa; and that Rigaud should also make known the King's decision to march once more into Italy, which would prove most gravely unfortunate for the Duke if, while the chance was offered him, he failed to reenter into that amity which the King was convinced he had imprudently neglected for foolish suspicions rather than for any other reasons.

Already rumors of these preparations had crossed into Italy and were greatly troubling the allies, especially Lodovico Sforza, since he was the first to be exposed to the fury of the enemy. Thus once again he found himself in a state of the greatest anxiety, especially because after Rigaud's departure from the court, the King had dismissed all the Duke's representatives with most brusque words and actions. The result of this was that, carefully considering the extent of his danger and realizing that his state would bear the brunt and all the travails of the war, he would readily have yielded to the King's demands, were he not held back by a guilty conscience at the offenses he had committed against him, which had generated such distrust on all sides that it would have been more difficult to find a means of assuring each of them than to agree to articles which would accommodate their differences. For taking from the security of the one that which might be agreed upon in order to assure the other, none wished to entrust to the faith of the other that which the other refused to entrust to his own.*

[*French fortunes decline rapidly in the kingdom of Naples; and Ferrando has recaptured practically his entire realm when he suddenly falls ill and dies. Guicciardini praises his courage, ability, nobility of mind and royal virtues. Ferrando's uncle Don Federigo succeeds to the throne of Naples. Charles meanwhile is still dallying at Tours where he had gone ostensibly to worship Saint Martin, but actually, Guicciardini suspects, to worship a lady in the Queen's court.*]

It has already been shown above how fear of French preparations had brought about the beginnings of negotiations to induce Maximilian Caesar** to cross into Italy, more to satisfy Lodovico Sforza than the Venetians. While such fear of the French persisted, an agreement was made with Maximilian to the effect that the Venetians and Lodovico should give him twenty thousand ducats each month for three months in order that he should bring with him a certain number of horsemen and footsoldiers. As soon as the articles had been signed, Lodovico, accompanied by the ambassadors of the confederates, went to Manzo, a place on the other side of the Alps on the German frontier, to discuss the matter with Caesar. After a long conference there, Lodovico returned the same day across the Alps to Bormi, a town in the duchy of Milan, and on the following day, under pretext of going hunting, Maximilian Caesar came to the same place. There they held colloquy for two days, whereby an agreement having been reached with Caesar, stipulating the time and mode of his passage into Italy, he returned to Germany to arrange for the execution of what had been agreed upon.

* Guicciardinian convolutions of this kind lead Goddard to throw up his hands in paraphrase (Goddard, *op. cit.*, Vol. II, p. 75).

** The title used at this point in the text. Later in his famous digression on the historical sources of Church claims to secular power, Guicciardini says that Pope Gregory ". . . transferred to the German nation . . . the right of electing Roman emperors. This tradition and form has been observed up to our own times, forbidding the emperors-elect to use the title of Emperor or Augustus until they have received the imperial crown from the popes. . . . Hence grew the custom of the emperors coming to Rome to be crowned, and before that time not to use any other title than King of the Romans, or Caesar."

Maximilian therefore, although emperor, was entitled to be called only King of the Romans or Caesar at this time. Later, under Pope Julius II, Maximilian obtained leave to assume the title of "Imperator electus," only because the Venetians prevented him from getting to Rome to be crowned. At any event, the whole concept of the Holy Roman Empire was as shadowy as the title.

I have generally followed Guicciardini's usage, with the exception of occasionally adding the name Maximilian for fear that the author's use of Caesar alone might introduce irrelevant classical associations.

But in the meantime, rumors of French preparations having calmed down, Maximilian's march no longer seemed necessary on this account; yet Lodovico determined to employ for his ambition that which he had previously arranged for his own security. Therefore, he continued to solicit Maximilian to march into Italy, and inasmuch as the Venetians were unwilling to share in promising Maximilian the thirty thousand ducats which he was demanding over and above the first sixty thousand promised to him, Sforza obligated himself to that demand. The result was that finally Caesar crossed into Italy shortly before the death of Ferrando.

Apprised of this when he was approaching Milan, Maximilian at once began ruminating how to so manage things that the kingdom of Naples might fall to his son-in-law Juan, the only son of the King of Spain. But being told by Lodovico that this would discontent all Italy, disunite the allies and consequently facilitate the plans of the King of France, not only did [Maximilian] Caesar desist from his first idea, but wrote letters in favor of the succession of Federigo.

Maximilian passed into Italy with a very small number of men, spreading the rumor that very soon there would follow the full forces which he had pledged to bring. He halted at Vigevano; there, in the presence of Lodovico and the Cardinal of Santa Croce, who had been sent to him as papal legate, and other ambassadors of the league, it was proposed that Maximilian should march into Piedmont to take Asti and separate the Duke of Savoy and the Marquis of Monferrato from the King of France.

. . .

The allies had often requested the Florentines to join with them, and at the time when they most feared the passage of the French, they had given the Florentines hope that they would bind themselves to see to it that Pisa would be returned under Florentine dominion. But since the Florentines distrusted the cupidity of the Venetians and of Lodovico, and since they did not wish to lightly alienate themselves from the King of France, they had never readily hearkened to these offers. Furthermore, they were influenced by the hope of securing, through the King's passage, the recovery of Pietrasanta and Serezana, which territories they could not hope to obtain from the allies. They were especially indisposed to join the allies because, judging in terms of their own merits and what they were enduring for the King, rather than on the basis of his nature or his way of doing things, they had come to persuade themselves that as a result of the King's victory, they would obtain not only Pisa, but almost all the rest of Tuscany. These ideas were nourished by the words of

Girolamo Savonarola* who was continually preaching of the great felicity and expansion of power destined for the Florentine Republic after many travails, and of the terrible woes which would afflict the Roman court and all the other Italian powers; and although dissenting voices were not lacking, nevertheless the majority of the people lent utmost faith to his words, and many of the leading citizens were of his party, some out of idealism, some out of ambition, and some out of fear. Thus, since the Florentines were disposed to maintain friendly relations with the King of France, it did not appear unreasonable that the allies should attempt to reduce them by force to that which they were indisposed to follow voluntarily; and this was adjudged to be not so difficult an enterprise because they were hated by all their neighbors, and they could not hope for any help from the King of France (who having abandoned the safety of his own people [at Naples], would most likely be neglectful of the safety of others); furthermore, the very heavy expenses and diminution of income which had weighed upon them already for three years had so exhausted the Florentines that they were not believed capable of undergoing any long-lasting difficulties.

The war against the Pisans had continued all this same year: marked by a variety of troubles, and more memorable because of the military skill displayed by both sides in many operations, and the desperate stubbornness with which the war was being waged, than for the size of the armies or the importance of the places for which they were fighting, since these were ignoble castles of little worth in themselves. Shortly after the citadel had been given to the Pisans and before the arrival of the Venetian reinforcements, Florentine bands captured the castle of Buti and then encamped at Calci; and before they took it, they began to build a bastion on Mount Doloroso to protect their supply line. But the bands of footsoldiers who were on guard there were smashed as a result of their own negligence by Pisan companies. A little later, as Francesco Secco was encamped with a great troop of horsemen on the outskirts of Buti to see to the safe convoy of victuals to Ercole Bentivoglio, encamped with footbands of Florentines around the little castle on Mount Verrucola, he was unexpectedly attacked by infantrymen coming out of Pisa, and his horsemen being unable to maneuver in the difficult terrain, he lost no small part of them.

These successes seemed to bode well for the Pisan side and they had hope of moving on to even greater successes, because Venetian help was already beginning to arrive. Ercole Bentivoglio, who was lodging at the

---

* *"Gigli con gigli dover fiorire"*— "Lilies must flower with lilies." This saying, attributed to Savonarola, has reference to the *fleur de lis* of France and the red lily of the Florentine republic—both heraldic bearings (Bernardo Segni, *Storie Fiorentine,* Augusta, 1723, p. 16).

castle of Bientina, learned that Gianpaolo Manfrone, the Venetian condottiere, had already arrived with the first group of his men at Vico
Pisano, two miles from Bientina; this caused Bentivoglio to simulate fear,
sometimes descending into the field; at other times, as soon as Venetian
forces manifested themselves, he would retire into Bientina. Thus feigning
boldness and rashness, he very astutely one day inviegled the enemy into
an ambush, where he smashed his forces with the loss of most of his
infantrymen and cavalrymen and pursued him up to the walls of Vico
Pisano. And yet the victory was not entirely happy, for when they
wished to withdraw, Francesco Secco, who had joined up with Ercole
that very morning, was killed by an arquebus.

Maximilian Caesar Seeks to Adjudicate the Pisan Affair

After it was resolved that he should march to Pisa, [Maximilian]
Caesar sent two ambassadors to Florence to advise them that because of
the campaign which he had in mind to make in full forces against the
infidels, he had judged it necessary to pass into Italy in order to pacify
and settle conditions there; and for this reason he was requesting the
Florentines to pledge themselves together with all the other confederates
for the defense of Italy, or if they were of contrary mind to this proposal,
they should manifest their intentions. He also wished, for the same reason,
and since it related to imperial authority, to know the differences that
existed between them and the Pisans; and therefore desired that until
he had heard the arguments of both sides, the conflict should be
suspended. He was certain that the Pisans, to whom he had already
given the same orders, would agree to this; and with mild words he
affirmed that he was prepared to administer justice impartially. Having
heard Caesar's proposals, the Florentines commended them with honorable speeches, declaring that they placed great reliance in his good
intentions, and replied that their thinking on the matter would be made
known in detail via ambassadors who would very soon be sent to him.

But in the meanwhile the Venetians, who did not wish to permit
Maximilian or the Duke of Milan a chance to occupy Pisa, sent thither
once more with the consent of the Pisans one hundred fifty men-at-arms
under their condottiere, Annibale Bentivoglio, and soon afterward, some
new Stradiots and a thousand footsoldiers; indicating to the Duke that
they had sent them because their republic, which cherished free cities,
wished to help the Pisans recover their own domain; and indeed by some
means of the help of these forces the Pisans did end by recapturing almost

all the castles on the hills. As a result of this assistance and because of the promptness with which the Venetians had acceded to their frequent pleas—now for men, now for money, now for supplies and ammunitions—the Pisans were entirely at the will of the Venetians, who thus won over for themselves that confidence and love which the Pisans used to have for the Duke of Milan. But although they anxiously desired that the Venetian Senate should continue to defend them, nevertheless the Pisans were soliciting the coming of Maximilian, hoping that by means of the forces in Pisa and those which he was bringing, they would easily be able to capture Livorno.

On the other hand, the Florentines who, besides all their other difficulties, were stricken at that time by the gravest famine, were now in great fear, seeing themselves alone in resisting the power of so many princes; for there was no one in Italy who would help them, and they had received letters from their French ambassadors which certified that they could not hope for any succor whatever from the King, whom they had fervently petitioned to assist them (at least with some sums of money) amidst so many perils. Only Piero de' Medici had ceased to be a threat, because the allies had decided not to make use of his name or support in this action, since experience had taught them that the Florentines would become all the more united in conservation of their own liberties out of fear of the Medici. Nor did Lodovico Sforza, under pretext of being concerned about their safety but really discontent because of the grandeur of the Venetians, cease to urge the Florentines as strongly as possible to place their faith in [Maximilian] Caesar, showing them the great dangers they faced, stressing their fears, and affirming that there was no other way to get the Venetians out of Pisa. This, declared Sforza, would immediately result in their reintegration: a thing very necessary for the peace of Italy, and therefore desired by the King of Spain and all the other allies. Nevertheless, the Florentines, unmoved by the falsity of this subtle flattery, nor frightened by such difficulties and perils, determined not to make any commitment to Caesar nor to refer their rights to his arbitration unless they were first restored to the possession of Pisa. For they placed no confidence either in his will or authority, it being well known that not having forces or money of his own, Maximilian was acting according to the advice of the Duke of Milan, nor were the Florentines able to discern any disposition or necessity on the part of the Venetians to leave Pisa. Therefore, with firm resolution they proceeded to fortify Livorno, making all possible provisions and concentrating all their forces in the area around Pisa. Nevertheless, in order not to show themselves indisposed to a settlement, and making an effort to mitigate Caesar's attitude, they sent ambassadors to him (he having already arrived at Genoa) in order to reply to what his spokesmen had already made known in Florence. The commission of these Florentine ambassadors was to persuade him that there was no necessity to proceed to any declaration, because he could count on the Florentine Republic for anything he might desire, simply out of the devotion they bore to his name. The ambassadors were also instructed to recall to Maximilian that, as for his holy resolution to bring Italy to peace, nothing was more opportune than the immediate restoration of Pisa to the Florentines, because from this root were born all those decisions which were harmful to him and to the allies. For Pisa was the reason that some others were aspiring to rule all of Italy and therefore sought to keep it in a continuous state of war (by which words, although not openly expressed, they meant the Venetians); furthermore, that it was not conformable to his justice that those who had been violently despoiled should, against all the disposition of imperial laws, be constrained to make a compromise, unless firstly their possessions were restored to them. And they concluded that if the Florentine Republic should obtain such a declaration from him, thereby no longer having any reason left for desiring anything but peace with everyone, they would make all such declarations which he might consider pertinent; and that, trusting fully in his justice, they would immediately refer to his hands the recognition of their rights. But this reply did not satisfy Caesar [Maximilian] who desired above all that they should enter into the league, taking his word that Pisa would be restored to them within a fixed period. . . .

[*Maximilian's attempt to seize Livorno ends in ignominious failure; his fleet is shipwrecked; and after characteristic instability, he returns to Germany, "having, with very little dignity to imperial prestige, demonstrated his weakness to all Italy where emperors in arms had not been seen for a very long time."*

The Venetians capture Taranto for Federigo of Naples.]

.   .

While these matters were going on, the Pope, believing that he had a great opportunity to occupy the estates of the Orsini since the heads of that family were retained in Naples, pronounced in consistory Virginio and the others as rebels and confiscated their estates because they had taken pay from the French contrary to his orders. Having done this, he attacked their lands at the beginning of the year 1497, ordering the partisans of the Colonna family to do the same in all those places where their lands were contiguous with the Orsini. This enterprise was strongly supported by Cardinal Ascanio because of his long-standing friendship with the Colonnas and his dissension with the Orsini, and it was approved by the Duke of Milan. But the Venetians were displeased since they desired to win over that family; nevertheless they were not able by any justification whatever to prevent the Pontiff from pursuing his rights; and since they did not consider it useful to alienate him at that time, they agreed that the Duke of Urbino, who was a mercenary both in their service and in that of the Pope, should march to join his men with the forces of the Church whose captain general was the Duke of Gandia, and whose legate was the Cardinal da Luna of Pavia, a cardinal entirely dependent on Ascanio. And King Federigo also sent Fabrizio Colonna to help him.

. .

In this year, nothing much of importance happened between the Florentines and the Pisans (although the war continued without intermission), except that the Pisans sent Gianpaolo Manfrone with four hundred light horse and fifteen hundred infantry to recapture the bastion at the Ponte a Stagno which they had lost when Maximilian departed from Livorno. Having learned of this move, Count Renuccio set out with many horsemen en route to Livorno to support the bastion. The Pisans, who had not expected to be attacked except from Pontedera, being set upon when they had already begun to assault the bastion, were easily put to flight and many captured. But at last, as a result of the truce, even this war ceased, although the truce was accepted by the Florentines with ill will since they judged it inexpedient for their cause to give the Pisans a breathing space, and because—notwithstanding the truce—their suspicion of Piero de' Medici, who was always conspiring something, and their fear of the Venetian troops in Pisa, still compelled them of necessity to continue the same expenses.

Rise in Savonarola's Power. Attempted Medici Plot

THUS, armed actions having come to a halt everywhere, or at least about to cease, the Duke of Milan, although in his latest dangers he had expressed the greatest satisfaction with the Venetians for the prompt aid received from them, and although he publicly exalted with magnificent speeches the capacity and power of the Venetians and greatly commended the foresight of Gian Galeazzo, the first Duke of Milan, who had committed the execution of his last will to the faith of that Senate;

nevertheless not being able to tolerate that the prey of Pisa which he had stalked and flushed with such toilsome maneuvers should fall to them, as it clearly appeared about to happen, he tried to achieve by wile what he could not obtain by force. So, the Duke wrought that the Pope and the ambassadors of the King of Spain, both of whom were threatened by such Venetian power, should propose that, in order to leave the French no possible foundation in Italy and to reduce all of Italy into harmony, it would be necessary to force the Florentines to enter into the common league by returning Pisa to them, since otherwise they could not be so induced. For, he argued, so long as the Florentines were separated from the others they would not cease to goad the King of France to come to Italy, and in case he should come, they would be able, by means of their money and men, especially since they are for the most part situated in the middle of Italy, to bring about consequences of no little importance. But this proposition was rejected by the Venetian ambassador as very harmful to the common welfare, alleging the inclination of the Florentines toward the King of France to be such that, even with this reward, they were not to be trusted if they did not give sufficient security to observe what they might promise, and in matters of such moment no other guarantee would suffice except to place Livorno into the hands of the allies. The Venetian ambassador cunningly proposed this because he knew the Florentines would never consent to place a city of such importance into their hands, and thus he would have all the more reasons to argue against the scheme. The matter then succeeding as he had anticipated, he opposed the proposal so vehemently that the Pope and the Duke of Milan's ambassador did not dare raise objections for fear of alienating the Venetians from their alliance, and so they did not pursue this line of argument further; and the Pope and the Venetians began a new plan to violently divert the Florentines from their friendship with the French: the bad situation within Florence encouraging whoever thought to harm that city, among whose citizens there was no small conflict caused by the form of government.

For at the beginning, when popular authority had been established, there had not also been introduced with it those provisions of moderation which, together with guaranteeing liberty by just means, would also prevent the Republic from being thrown into disorder by the license and ignorance of the multitude. Therefore, since those citizens of greatest quality and condition were held in less esteem than seemed proper, and since their ambition furthermore was suspect to the populace, and since there often intervened in the midst of important deliberations many people of limited capacity, and since every two months the supreme magistracy, to which was referred the bulk of the most difficult problems, was changed, the Republic was governed with much confusion. Added to this was the great authority of Savonarola whose congregations were practically joined in unspoken agreement; and since there were many honorable citizens among them, and since they surpassed in numbers those who were of the contrary opinion, it seemed that the magistracies and public honors would be distributed rather more to his followers than to the others. Thus the city was openly divided: in the public councils one faction fought against the other, and as happens in divided cities, no man took thought of the common good, so intent was he upon smashing his adversary's reputation. These disorders were all the more dangerous since, besides the long travails and serious expenses suffered by that city, there also occurred a very great famine that year as a result of which it might be presumed that the hungry people would desire a new order of things.

Now this evil disposition of civic affairs lent hope to Piero de' Medici (spurred not only by the situation in Florence but also by certain citizens) that he would easily be able to obtain his desires. Therefore, after he had conferred with his old friend Federigo, Cardinal of San Severino, and with Alviano,* and secretly incited by the Venetians, who felt that the situation in Pisa would be stabilized by the troubles of the Florentines, Piero decided to attempt to enter into Florence secretly; especially after he had learned that the Florentines had created as their gonfaloniere of justice, the chief of their supreme magistrates, Bernardo del Nero, a serious man with great authority, who had been for a long time a friend of Piero's father and of himself, and that with him there had been elected to the same magistracy several others who Piero believed would be favorable to his cause out of their old dependence on his family.

The Pope agreed to this plan, since he was eager to separate the Florentines from the King of France by injuring them, since he had been unable to do so by benefices; nor was the Duke of Milan averse, since he felt he could not build any stable foundation or understanding with that city because of the disorders of the present government, although on the other hand he took no pleasure in Piero's return to power, as much for the wrongs he had done him, as well as because he suspected Piero might be too dependent upon Venetian authority.

Therefore, as soon as Piero had gathered together as much money as he could by himself and with the aid of his friends (and it was believed some small sum had been lent to him by the Venetians), he went to Siena, followed by Alviano with the horsemen and infantry, riding always by night and off the main roads so that his coming should be hidden from the Florentines. At Siena, with the help of Gianiacopo

* Bartolommeo d'Alviano, Venetian commander.

and Pandolfo Petrucci, the leading citizens of that government and friends of his father and himself, he secretly gained other forces; so that with six hundred horsemen and four hundred picked footsoldiers, two days after the truce (in which the Sienese were not included), he left for Florence in the hope that arriving there almost unexpectedly at daybreak, he would easily enter the city as a result of the disorders or tumult which he thought would break out in his favor. And this plan perhaps would not have proved vain had not fortune supplemented the negligence of his adversaries. Because, having lodged at nightfall at Tavernelle which consists of several houses on the main road, with the idea of marching most of the night, he was so hindered by a sudden great rainfall that it was impossible for him to arrive at Florence until many hours after sunrise. This delay gave time to those who made it a profession to be his particular enemies (because the plebe and almost all the rest of the citizens were quietly waiting to see how things turned out) to take up arms with their friends and followers, and give orders that suspect citizens should be summoned by the magistrates and held in the public palace, and that they should strengthen their forces at the gate leading to Siena. At the Prior's request, therefore, Paolo Vitelli, who had just by chance returned the previous evening from Mantua, was dispatched to that gate; with the result that no uprising took place in the city, nor was Piero strong enough to force the gate to which he had approached within a bowshot. Thus, after he had remained there four hours, fearing to his great peril the sudden coming of the Florentine men-at-arms whom he thought (and correctly) had been summoned from Pisa, Piero returned to Siena.

Alviano had already departed from Siena and been let by the Guelphs into Todi where he sacked almost all the houses of the Ghibellines and massacred fifty-three of the leaders of that faction; this example was followed by Antonello Savello who entered Terni, and the Gatteschi who were let into Viterbo with the help of the Colonna faction, similar evils being committed in both places and in the surrounding countryside against the Guelphs.* Nor had the Pope taken any provisions against such disorders in the Ecclesiastical State because he hated to spend money on such things, and because his nature was little disturbed by the calamity of others so that he was not at all troubled by those things which offended his honor, provided that his profits and pleasures were in no way impeded.

But yet he could not avoid domestic misfortunes which perturbed his house with tragic examples and lust and horrible cruelty beyond that of all barbarous nations. For, having planned from the beginning of his

---

* The author's failure to take special notice of what seems to be a contradiction is eloquent of his conviction of the impartial distribution of injustice.

pontificate to turn all temporal grandeur over to the Duke of Gandia, his first-born, the Cardinal of Valencia* (whose mind was totally disinclined toward the sacerdotal profession and aspired toward the exercise of arms), not being able to tolerate that this position should be held by his brother, and furthermore envious that Gandia occupied a greater place than himself in the love of Madonna Lucrezia, their common sister, enflamed with lust and ambition (mighty ministers to every great wickedness) one night while his brother was riding alone through Rome, had him killed and secretly cast into the Tiber. It was equally rumored (if however it is possible to believe so great an enormity) that not only the two brothers, but the father himself, competed for the love of Madonna Lucrezia: since, as soon as he was made pontiff, he had separated her from her first husband as having become inferior to her rank, and married her off to Giovanni Sforza, lord of Pesaro. But not being able to tolerate having even her husband as a rival, he dissolved this matrimony which had already been consummated; having proved with false witnesses before judges which he had chosen, and later confirmed by a sentence, that Giovanni was frigid by nature and impotent in coitus.** Above all, the Pope was afflicted by the death of the Duke of Gandia, since he was as ardent as any other father in the love of his children and not accustomed to feel the blows of fortune. For it is obvious that from his youth up to that time, he had known the most happy successes in all things; and he was so grieved by it that in the consistory, after he had with the greatest emotion and tears gravely bewailed his misery and accused many of his own actions and his way of living up to that day, he declared convincingly that he wished to govern his life in the future according to altogether different thoughts and habits: and then he assigned several of the cardinals to join with him in reforming the customs and regulations of the court. But after this work of reform had been under way for a few days, and the author of his son's death now beginning to become plain (at first he had suspected either Cardinal Ascanio or Orsini), the Pope set aside his good intentions and then his tears, and returned more uncontrolledly than ever to those ideas and actions with which he had consumed his years up to that time.

Meanwhile, Florence was afflicted by new travails as a result of the attempt made by Piero de' Medici. For shortly afterward, the sources of information that he had in that city came to light, as a result of which many noble citizens were put in prison and several others fled. After the plan and unfolding of the conspiracy was established by law, there were condemned to death not only Niccolò Ridolfi, Lorenzo Torna-

---

* Cesare Borgia.
** The above passage is omitted in all editions of the *Storia d'Italia* published before the "Friburgo" edition of 1774–76 (see Introduction, footnotes, pp. xxvii, xxviii).

LUCREZIA BORGIA

Painted in the guise of Saint Catherine of Alexandria in Pinturrichio's fresco in the Borgian apartments of the Vatican (COURTESY OF FRATELLI ALINARI)

buoni, Gianozzo Pucci, and Giovanni Cambi, who had urged him to come (for which purpose Lorenzo had lent him money); but also Bernardo del Nero, who was accused of nothing else but having known of this plan and not having revealed it, which error (in itself punishable by capital punishment according to Florentine statutes and according to the interpretation of the common law given by most lawyers) was all the more heinous in his case, since he had been gonfaloniere when Piero came to Florence, and therefore was primarily obliged to carry on this office more as a public person than a private individual. But the relatives of the condemned appealed the sentence to the Grand Council of the people, by virtue of a law set up when the popular government had been established. This appeal induced those who had been the authors of the condemnation (fearing lest compassion for their age and nobility and multitude of kinsmen would moderate in the people's minds the severity of the judgment) to see to it that the question of whether to permit the appeal to follow its course or to prohibit it should be referred to a smaller number of citizens; among whom prevailed the authority and number of those who considered fomenting sedition to be a dangerous and thoughtless thing, and that the laws themselves provided that in order to avoid tumults, the statutes in such a case might be set aside. Thus some of those who were seated in the supreme magistracy were impetuously and almost by force and threats constrained to agree that, notwithstanding the appeal which had been put forward, the executions should be carried out that very night; and more heatedly in favor of this than the others were Savonarola's followers, not without shame for him, that he should have failed to dissuade, especially among his followers, the violation of a law which he himself had proposed a few years earlier as very salutary and almost necessary for the preservation of liberty.

[*The Duke of Milan, the Pope, the Spanish ambassadors and the King of Naples are in favor of returning Pisa to the Florentines to bring them into the league against the French; the Venetians are opposed.*]

Death of King Charles. Trial and Execution of Savonarola

While these things were being debated among the allies with manifest disagreement, a new event occurred which produced effects very different than men had anticipated. For the night before the eighth of April, King Charles died at Amboise of a stroke which the doctors call apoplexy;

the attack (which occurred while he was watching a tennis match) was so strong that within a few hours, at that very place, his life ended— a life which, motivated more by impetuousness than virtue, had upset the world, and was threatening at the time of his death to upset it again. Many believed that because of his ardent desire to return to Italy, he would eventually have resolved all the difficulties that were standing in his way, either following his own inclinations or the counsels of those who vied with the grandeur of the Cardinal of San Malò. The result was that although in Italy, the belief that he would return was sometimes very strong and sometimes very weak, according to the King's vacillating moods, nevertheless there was no one who was not in a state of continuous suspension. Consequently, the Pope, spurred on by his greed to exalt his children, had already begun secretly to deal anew with him; and then it was bruited about (whether true or false) that the Duke of Milan was doing the same thing in order not to remain in a state of continuous fear.

Since Charles died without issue, the kingdom of France fell to Louis, Duke of Orléans, closer in blood than any others in the masculine line. After the King died, the royal guard and all the court immediately hastened to Blois where Louis was at the time; then little by little there arrived all the lords of the kingdom, hailing him and acknowledging him as king, although some were secretly complaining that according to the ancient rules of that realm, Louis was ineligible to the dignity of the crown since he had taken arms against it in the wars of Brittany.

The day following that which ended the life of Charles (a day observed by Christians as Palm Sunday) also marked the end of Savonarola's authority in Florence. For long before this, the Pope had accused Savonarola of slanderously preaching against the comportment of the clergy and the Roman Curia, of stirring up discord in Florence, and of disseminating doctrine that was not entirely Catholic. For these reasons, the Dominican had been several times summoned to Rome by apostolic briefs; but Savonarola had refused to appear, alleging various excuses. Finally, the previous year, the Pope separated him with censure from the fellowship of the Church. As a result of this excommunication, he abstained from preaching for several months, and if he had abstained longer, he would have obtained absolution without any difficulty. For the Pope personally took little account of Savonarola, and was moved to proceed against him more as a result of the suggestions and persuasion of the monk's adversaries than for any other reason.

But it seemed to Savonarola that his reputation was declining as a result of his silence, or that, at any rate, the object of his endeavors was impeded by it, since his purpose was mainly served by his vehemence in preaching. And so, scorning the Pope's commandments, he publicly returned to the same course of action: affirming that the excommunication that had been promulgated against him was unjust and invalid, contrary to the will of God and harmful to the public weal, and castigating the Pope and his entire court with the greatest violence.

His preaching stirred up great dissensions. For on the one hand, his adversaries, whose authority among the people grew greater every day, detested such disobedience and reproved him because his fool-hardiness might result in changing the Pope's mind, especially at a time when negotiations regarding the restitution of Pisa were being discussed with the Pope and the other allies, and when, therefore, it was wise to do everything possible to encourage papal support. On the other hand, his partisans defended him, alleging that divine works should not be interfered with because of concern over human consequences, nor should popes be permitted under such justifications to commence meddling in the affairs of their Republic. This controversy raged for many days, with the result that the Pope became extremely angry and fulminated new briefs and new threats of excommunication against the entire city, so that finally Savonarola was ordered by the magistrates to cease preaching; and although he obeyed this order, many of his friars, nevertheless, continued preaching in the same manner in various churches. But since there was no less dissension among the religious than among the laity, friars of other orders did not cease preaching fervently against him; and finally this quarrel became so heated that one of the Dominican monks who was a disciple of Savonarola and one of the Franciscans agreed upon a trial by fire in the presence of the entire populace, so that the Dominican either being spared or burned would make it clear to everybody whether Savonarola was a prophet or a fraud. For he had earlier preached on many occasions that as a sign of the truth of his predictions, he would obtain, when there was need for it, the grace from God to pass through the fire without harm. And nevertheless, because he was angry that the decision to carry on the experiment now had been made without his knowledge, he cleverly tried to prevent it; but since the matter had already gone so far on its own momentum, urged on, furthermore, by several citizens who wished to have the city freed of all these troubles, it was necessary finally to proceed further. However, on the day chosen, the two friars, accompanied by all the brothers of their Order, having come to the piazza which is in front of the public palace, where not only all the Florentine people but many from neighboring cities had gathered, the Franciscans learned that Savonarola had ordered his friar to bear the Sacrament in hand when he entered into the flames. At this, the Minor friars began to protest, alleging that their opponents were seeking by such means to place the authority of the Christian faith in danger, since if that Host

Medal showing, on one side, Girolamo Savonarola with inscription:
"HIERONXMVS. SAVº-FER. VIR. DOCTISSˢ. ORDINIS. PREDICHA-
TORVM"; on the other, a very free version of a Ptolemaic map of Italy with
Venice, Naples, Rome, etc., indicated by castles, all threatened with judgment
by the hand of God holding a dagger suspended over them. The inscription
reads "GLADIVS. DOMINI. SVP. TERAM. CITO ET VELOCITER"
which might be rendered "Swiftly I summon the sword of God over the land."
(COURTESY OF THE NATIONAL GALLERY, WASHINGTON, D.C., SAMUEL H. KRESS
COLLECTION)

should be burned, the faith of the ignorant would decline considerably;
and since Savonarola (who was present) insisted on his order, so great
a controversy arose that it was impossible for the experiment to proceed.
Savonarola lost so much prestige as a result of this, that on the following
day, a slight tumult happening to break out, his adversaries seized arms
and, the leading magistracy lending their influence to the insurrection,
stormed the monastery of San Marco where Savonarola was living and
led him, together with two of his friars, to the public prison. During these
tumults, the relatives of those who had been decapitated the previous
year slew Francesco Valori, a very important citizen and a leading
supporter of Savonarola, because his authority more than any other's
had been the reason why they had been deprived of the faculty of having
recourse to the judgment of the popular Council.

Savonarola was then examined under torture (although not very
dolorous) and later the deposition of these examinations was published.
According to this trial record (notwithstanding that it cleared the
Dominican of all the calumnies imputed to him, such as covetousness
or corrupt customs or having held secret dealings with princes), the

things which Savonarola had prophesied were declared to have been predicted, not on the basis of divine revelation, but as his own opinion based on deep study of the doctrines of Holy Scripture; nor had he been motivated by any malign intention or cupidity to acquire ecclesiastical eminence by this means, but rather he had greatly desired that his work should result in the convocation of an ecumenical council which would reform the corrupt manners of the clergy and bring back the Church of God (gone so far astray) to a state as similar as possible to what it had been at the time of the Apostles: and that he considered the carrying out of so salutary and complex a task much more glorious than acceding to the papacy. For, his efforts could not succeed unless based on most excellent doctrine and virtue, and by evoking the most unusual reverence of all men, whereas the pontificacy was often obtained either by evil manipulations or the benefits of fortune.

EXECUTION OF SAVONAROLA

Painting by an anonymous Florentine of the period, now in the museum of San Marco, Florence (COURTESY OF FRATELLI ALINARI)

On the basis of this deposition, confirmed by Savonarola in the presence of many religious persons, even of his own Order, but in such concise terms (if what his followers later divulged be true) that his words could be given various interpretations, Savonarola and the two other friars were, by sentence of the General of San Domenico and Bishop Romolino, later Cardinal of Sorrento (commissioners delegated by the Pope), stripped of their holy orders according to the ceremonies instituted by the Roman Church, and left to the jurisdiction of the secular court, by whom they were hanged and burnt. To this spectacle of degradation and torture there thronged no less a multitude of men than those who, on the day appointed for the experiment of entering into the fire, had rushed to the same place in expectation of the miracle which he had promised. Savonarola's death, which he endured with constancy but without expressing any word whatever that might indicate either his guilt or innocence, did not extinguish the diversity of judgments and emotions of the citizens, because many reputed him to be an imposter, and many, on the contrary, believed either that the confession which had been published had been falsely fabricated or else that his very delicate physical state had been much more influenced by the pain of the torture than by the truth: excusing his frailty by citing the example of the Prince of the Apostles who, although he was neither imprisoned nor constrained by torments or any extraordinary force whatever, yet, at the simple words of handmaidens and servants, denied that he was the disciple of that Master whose holy precepts he had heard and whose many miracles he had witnessed.

BOOK

4

THE DEATH OF CHARLES, KING OF FRANCE, FREED
ITALY FROM FEAR OF THE IMMEDIATE THREAT OF
FRENCH POWER, FOR IT WAS NOT BELIEVED THAT
the new King Louis XII would involve himself at the beginning of his
regime in wars beyond the mountains. But the minds of those who
considered future events were not without suspicion that evils deferred
might not become, in the course of time, even greater and more serious,
since so important an empire had now fallen into the hands of a King
mature in years, experienced in many wars, moderate in spending, and
incomparably more self-reliant than his predecessor had been. Furthermore, as King of France, not only did there pertain to Louis the same
rights to the kingdom of Naples, but he also maintained that for personal
reasons the duchy of Milan belonged to him by succession of Madame
Valentina, his grandmother, who had been given in marriage to Louis,
Duke of Orléans, brother of Charles VI, King of France, by her father,
Giovan Galeazzo Visconti before the latter had obtained the title of
duke of Milan instead of imperial vicar. In addition to her dowry (which
consisted of the city and country of Asti and great sums of money), a
specific condition was added to the effect that should at any time the
masculine line be lacking, Valentina would succeed to the duchy of
Milan or, she being deceased, her nearest kith and kin. This clause,
invalid in itself, was (if what the French assert be true) confirmed by
papal authority, the imperial throne then being unoccupied: because the
Roman pontiffs, basing themselves on laws which they themselves had
made, claim that the administration of the Empire, the throne being
unoccupied, belongs to them. And therefore, male descendants of Giovan
Galeazzo lacking after the death of Filippo Maria Visconti, Charles,
Duke of Orléans, son of Valentina, began to lay claim to the succession
of that dukedom. But as the ambition of princes is ready to embrace
any likely reason, at the same time, Frederick [III], the Emperor, was
laying claim to the dukedom as a state which had reverted to the Empire

LOUIS XII

The inscription on this medal, dated 1513, reads "LVDOVICVS D(ei) G(ratia) REX FRANCORVM" (COURTESY OF THE NATIONAL GALLERY, WASHINGTON, D.C., SAMUEL H. KRESS COLLECTION)

since the line named in the investiture made by Wenceslaus, King of the Romans, to Giovan Galeazzo was now extinct; and the duchy was also being claimed by Alfonso, King of Aragon and of Naples, who had been declared heir by Filippo's [Maria Visconti] last will and testament. But the arms, skill and good fortune of Francesco Sforza had proved more powerful. In order that his recourse to arms might be camouflaged by some appearance of right, Sforza alleged that his wife Blanche, an only daughter (if bastard) of Filippo, should succeed to the duchy. Hence, Charles of Orléans (who had been taken prisoner on the day of Agincourt during the wars between the English and the French and been held prisoner twenty-five years in England) could not, as a result of his poverty and ill fortune, attempt to obtain the duchy by himself, nor could he ever obtain any aid from Louis XI, King of France, notwithstanding they were very close kinsmen. For at the beginning of his reign, Louis [XI] had been much molested by the great lords of the kingdom of France (who under pretext of the public weal had conspired against him out of scorn and private interests), so that he always felt that his security and grandeur should be based upon weakening the power of potentates. For this reason, Louis of Orléans, son of Charles, [of Orléans] although he was his [Louis XI's] son-in-law, could not obtain any help from him whatever; and when his father-in-law had died, Louis [of Orléans]—unwilling to tolerate that the King's sister Anne, Duchess of Bourbon, should be preferred before him in the government of Charles VIII, then a minor—had unsuccessfully stirred up new troubles in France and then retired with even less fortune into Brittany. There, joining with those who were unwilling that Charles should acquire Brittany by marrying Anne, heir of that duchy as a result of the death of her father Francis, who had left no male issue (indeed, secretly aspiring to the same matrimony), Louis was captured in

Milan. The Visconti and Sforza.

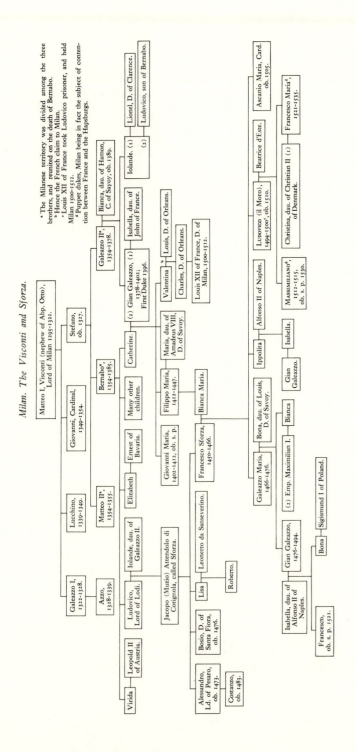

[a] The Milanese territory was divided among the three brothers, and reunited on the death of Bernabo.

[b] Hence the French claim to Milan.

[c] Louis XII of France took Ludovico prisoner, and held Milan 1500-1512.

[d] Puppet dukes, Milan being in fact the subject of contention between France and the Hapsburgs.

a battle between the French and the Bretons which took place near Saint-Aubin [Saint-Aubin-du-Cormier] near Brittany, and taken to France and imprisoned for two years. Hence, lacking all means and, after he had been liberated from prison by royal pardon, finding no help in King Charles, he did not try to play any role in the Milanese campaign, except on the occasion when he had remained at Asti by commission of the King, and marched into Novara with very little success.*

But now having become king of France, his most ardent desire was to acquire as his hereditary right the duchy of Milan; and this desire, which had been nourished in him from his childhood, had now become very much more intensified as a result of the events which had occurred in Novara. Also, the insolent demonstrations manifested against him when he was in Asti had stirred up no little hatred in him against Lodovico Sforza.

Therefore, a few days after the death of King Charles, by deliberations determined by his council, he entitled himself not only king of France, and (in conjunction with the kingdom of Naples) king of Jerusalem and of both Sicilies, but also duke of Milan. And to make known to everyone what his attitude was toward Italian affairs, he immediately wrote congratulatory letters about his own assumption to the Pope, to the Venetians and to the Florentines; and sent entrusted men to stir up hope of new enterprises, making it perfectly clear that he intended to conquer the duchy of Milan.

To this undertaking no small opportunities presented themselves to him, since Charles' death had caused very different attitudes among the Italians than they had held in the past. For the Pope, pricked on by his own interests which he knew could not be satisfied so long as Italy was at peace, desired that affairs should become turbulent again, and the Venetians who, no longer fearful of Charles as a result of the wrongs they had done him, were not disinclined to lend confidence in the new King. This disposition was increasing daily because Lodovico Sforza, although he knew very well that he had to do with a harder and more implacable enemy, still fed himself with the hope with which similarly Federigo of Aragon [King of Naples] had fed himself, namely that the French King would not be able to deal with things beyond the mountains so quickly. Thus Sforza, blinded by present scorn from discerning future perils, was not disposed to refrain from opposing the Venetians in the Pisan affair.

Only the Florentines were beginning to consider estranging themselves from their friendship with the French; because although the new

---

* The Guicciardinian labyrinth here, bestrewed with *suo* and *lui* whose antecedents are shrouded in mist, re- quires, alas, the numerous brackets which I have inserted to unravel the genealogies (see *Storia,* ed. Gherardi, I, 244–45).

France: The House of Valois

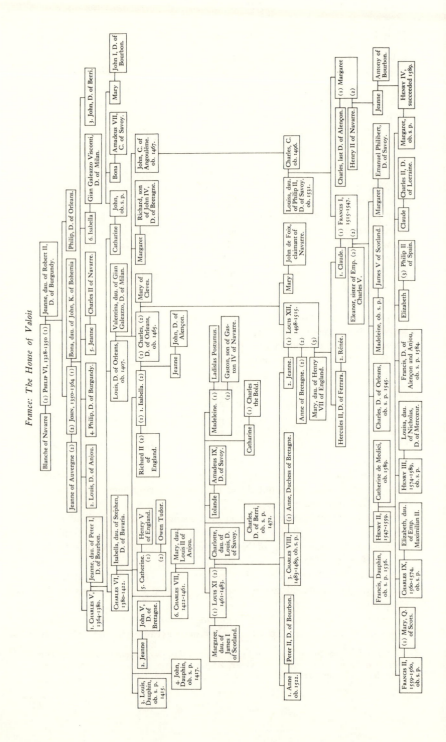

King had earlier been their protector, now, having come to the throne, he had no ties with them whatever, neither for promises given nor benefits received, as had had his predecessor as a result of the treaties made in Florence and in Asti for which the Florentines would have submitted to many perils and hardships rather than abandon their alliance. Furthermore, the continuously increasing discord between the Venetians and the Duke of Milan was the reason that—Florentine fear of the forces of the allies having ceased, and placing more hope in the near and certain favors of Lombardy than in the distant and uncertain assistance of France—they had reason to consider that friendship of less importance.

Just as the disposition of minds was different, no less different were the events set into motion. The Venetian Senate immediately dispatched to the French King a secretary whom they had already sent to the Duke of Savoy; and in order to cast upon such principles the foundations for a well-assured alliance with the French, according as mutual needs might require from day to day, three ambassadors were chosen to go and congratulate him on his succession to the throne, and to offer the excuse that whatever they had done against Charles had not resulted from anything other than a suspicion aroused in them by many indications leading them to believe that the King's thoughts, not content with the kingdom of Naples, were now extending toward the occupation of all Italy. At the same time, the Pope, determined to transfer his son Cesare from the cardinalship to secular grandeur, and his mind now elevated to loftier matters, immediately sent ambassadors to the King, offering to sell him spiritual grace and receive in recompense temporal possessions. For he knew that the King eagerly desired to repudiate his wife Jeanne who was barren and deformed, and who had been almost violently forced on him by her father Louis XI, and he also knew that the King had an equally strong desire to marry Anne, now widow after the death of the past King, not so much for what was left of the old affection that had existed between them before the battle of Saint-Aubin, as the fact that such a marriage would result in his obtaining the duchy of Brittany, a great and very useful dukedom for the crown of France, none of which things could be achieved without papal authorization.

The Florentines similarly did not fail to send ambassadors to the King not only because of their ancient understanding with the crown of France, but also to remind him of their merits and the obligations and promises made by the late King. They were very much urged to this embassy by the Duke of Milan who hoped that Florentine intervention would hinder Venetian negotiations, since both republics were involved in the Pisan affair; and also because if they acquired any promise or authority whatever, they would be able to use it on occasion to bring about an agreement between him (Sforza) and the King of France, a thing which he greatly desired. All these ambassadors were happily received by the King who immediately began to deal with each of them: although his mind was fixed not to set anything in motion in Italy until he had first secured the kingdom of France by means of new leagues with neighboring princes.

. .

But it was inevitable that the blaze of Pisa, kindled and nourished by the Duke of Milan as a result of his immoderate appetite to dominate, should finally burn the author. For his envy, and the danger he foresaw in too much Venetian greatness dominating him and every other potentate in Italy, did not permit him to patiently endure that the fruit of his stratagems and efforts should be gathered by them; and taking advantage of the attitude of the Florentines who were resolved not to give up their offensive against Pisa for any reason, and thinking that as a result of the fall of Savonarola and the death of his opponent Francesco Valori, he could place more confidence in that city than he had done in the past, the Duke of Milan determined to help the Florentines with arms for the recapture of Pisa, since his negotiations and authority, and the negotiations and authority of others, had not been sufficient for this purpose. Sforza vainly persuaded himself either that before any move whatever could be taken by the King of France, Pisa would be reduced to Florentine jurisdiction either by force or agreement, or he truly believed that the Venetian Senate, restrained by that prudence which he, the Duke, had never exercised in himself, would never desire, either out of anger or less important reasons that, to their common peril, French armies should return to Italy, the expulsion of which had cost so much effort.

[*A long passage follows, recounting in detail the efforts of the Florentines to reconquer Pisa. The Duke of Milan, out of envy of the Venetians (who are backing the Pisans), throws his support to the Florentines. All other conflicts in Italy have now ceased. The Venetians try to divert the Florentines from Pisa, by kindling the flames of war at Bologna and Siena. To spare the reader the dilemma of the prisoner who chose the galleys rather than freedom at the price of reading in minutiae Guicciardini's account of the Pisan campaign, I have cut this passage.*]

. .

But while Italy remained in turmoil over the Pisan affair, the new King of France did not cease his preparations for the assault on the state of Milan the following year, in the hope that he would have the Venetians as allies; inasmuch as these latter, inflamed with incredible hatred against the Duke of Milan, were involved in close negotiations with the

King. But even more close were the negotiations between the King and the Pope. For the Pope, excluded from Federigo's alliance and still greedy for the kingdom of Naples, turned all his hopes toward the French, from whose King he sought to obtain for [his son] the Cardinal of Valencia, Federigo's daughter Charlotte* who, not yet married, was still being brought up in the French court.

And since the King, who he believed had the power to marry her off, gave him some hope, the Cardinal of Valencia one morning came to the Consistory and begged his father and the other cardinals that inasmuch as he had never had a mind inclined toward the profession of the priesthood, they should grant him the right to leave the dignity and the habit in order to pursue that occupation to which destiny had drawn him. And thus having assumed secular garb he prepared immediately to go to France; the Pope already having promised the King the right to be divorced from his wife with apostolic authority, and the King for his part having pledged himself to help the Pope (as soon as he had conquered the state of Milan) to reduce those cities possessed by the vicars of Romagna to obedience to the Apostolic See; and to pay him thirty thousand ducats at present, on the grounds that it was necessary to keep greater forces for his custody, since this joining of the Pope with the King would likely stir up many persons in Italy to seek insidiously to harm him. For the execution of these covenants the King began to pay the money and the Pope assigned the problem of the divorce to the Bishop of Setta, his nuncio, and to the Archbishops of Paris and Rouen.** At first, the King's wife through her representatives impugned this judgment; but finally, being no less suspicious of the judges than of the power of her adversary, she agreed to yield up the case, receiving as support for the rest of her life the duchy of Berry with thirty thousand francs revenue. Thus, the divorce having been confirmed by the decision of the judges, nothing else remained for the dispensation and consummation of the new marriage but the coming of Cesare Borgia, who had already been transformed from cardinal and archbishop of Valencia into a soldier and Duke Valentino,*** for the King had given him command of one hundred lancers and twenty thousand francs for provisions, and conceded to him with the title of duke the city of Valence in the Dauphiné with twenty thousand francs revenue.

Cesare Borgia embarked at Ostia on ships sent by the King and at the end of the year arrived at the court, where he entered with incredible pomp and splendor, received most honorably by the King; and he

---

* Charlotte d'Albret, sister of Jean d'Albret, King of Navarre and son of Federigo of Naples.

** Georges d'Amboise (1460–1510), made cardinal in 1498. A minister of Louis XII, he took care of Italian affairs.

*** So Cesare was called henceforth in Italy. His French title was Duc de Valentinois.

brought with him the cardinal's hat for Georges d'Amboise, Archbishop of Rouen, who having previously shared his monarch's perils and fortunes was thereby held in the greatest esteem by him.*

Nevertheless, at first the Duke's manner was not well liked because, carrying out his father's instructions, he denied that he had brought the bull of dispensation with him, in the hope that the desire of obtaining it would make the King more malleable to his designs than would the memory of having received it. But since the Bishop of Setta had secretly revealed the truth to the King, it seemed to him sufficient with respect to God that the bull had been ratified, and so he openly consummated his marriage with his new wife, without making any more requests for the document. This was the reason why Duke Valentino, no longer being able to conceal the bull from him, and learning afterward that the Bishop of Setta had revealed this matter, had the Bishop later secretly put to death by poison.

The King was no less solicitous to renew amity with his neighboring princes. Therefore he made peace with the King of Spain who, no longer concerned with Italian affairs, recalled not only all his ambassadors in that country except the one at the Vatican, but also ordered Consalvo with all his forces to return to Spain, leaving Federigo all the towns in Calabria which he had held up to that day.

[*The second French invasion of the duchy of Milan finally is launched with rapid success. Lodovico tries in vain to arouse the people of Milan to resist, but instead, after the loss of Alessandria, there is an uprising in Milan; and Lodovico flees with his children and brother Ascanio to Germany to implore aid of Maximilian. Milan, and finally the entire duchy, yields to the French. The King comes to that city, where all the potentates of Italy flock to make deals with him, especially the Florentines. Meanwhile the siege of Pisa goes on, as well as Borgia's campaign in the Romagna.*]

Origin of Church Claims to Secular Power**

THE declaration [of the Pope's claims and ambitions in the Romagna] and many other things which subsequently occurred require that men-

---

* Cesare also presented a letter in which the Pope told the King: *"destinamus Maiestati tuae cor nostrum, videlicet dilectum filium ducem Valentinen quo nihil carius habemus."* . . . "my beloved son Duke Valentino than whom we hold no one more dear."

** This section was understandably omitted from all Italian editions of the *Storia d'Italia* prior to the Jacopo Stoer edition, Geneva, 1621 (Gherardi, *op. cit.*, I, p. CLXXV).

tion be made of what rights the Church might have over the cities of Romagna and many other places, which she either has possessed at various times or now possesses; and by what means the Church, originally instituted for the mere purpose of spiritual administration, has attained to worldly states and rule. Likewise, we must set down (as related phenomena) whatever amities and enmities may have existed, for these and other reasons at various times, between popes and emperors.

The Roman pontiffs, of whom the first was the Apostle Peter, whose authority in spiritual matters was laid down by Jesus Christ, and who were great in charity, humility and patience, holy men who worked miracles, were at the beginning not only completely devoid of temporal power but, persecuted by that very power, remained for many years obscure and almost unknown; their names came to the light for no other reason than for the persecutions which they and their followers endured. For although sometimes their proceedings were taken little account of by the innumerable multitude and diversity of nations and religions then in

Popes During Period of Guicciardini's History

PAPAL NAME	SECULAR NAME	PONTIFICATE
Innocent VIII	Giovanni Battista Cibo	1484–1492
Alexander VI	Rodrigo Borgia*	1492–1503
Pius III	Francesco Piccolomini	1503
Julius II	Giuliano della Rovere	1503–1513
Leo X	Giovanni de' Medici	1513–1521
Adrian VI**	Adrian Florensz d'Utrecht	1522–1523
Clement VII	Giulio de' Medici	1523–1534
Paul III	Alessandro Farnese	1534–1549

* Common usage employed this Italian version. In Spanish: Rodrigo Lanzol y Borja.
** The last non-Italian Pope.

Rome, and although several of the emperors did not persecute them except when it seemed that their public actions could not be passed over in silence, nevertheless several other emperors, either because of cruelty or out of love for their own gods, persecuted them atrociously as innovators of new superstitions and destroyers of true religion. In this condition, renowned for their voluntary poverty, for the sanctity of their lives and for their martyrs, they continued up to the time of Pope Sylvester; at which period the Emperor Constantine, having been converted to the Christian faith, moved by the most holy manners and miracles which were continually to be seen among those who followed the name of Christ, the popes were set free of the perils in which they had lived for about three hundred years, and free to publicly exercise the divine cult and Christian rites. So that as a result of reverence for their way of life, the holy precepts which our religion contains in itself, and the readiness with which mankind follows—either out of ambition (most of the time) or fear—the example of their Prince, the name of Christian began to spread marvelously everywhere, and at the same time the poverty of the clerics began to diminish.

For, Constantine, having built in Rome the church of Saint John in the Lateran, Saint Peter in the Vatican, Saint Paul, and many others in various places, endowed them not only with rich vessels and ornaments, but also with possessions and other revenues in order that they would be able to maintain and renovate the buildings and support those who were performing the divine service. Subsequently in later times, many others being persuaded that by alms and legacies to the Church they might easily acquire the kingdom of heaven, either built or endowed other churches or dispensed a great part of their riches to those already built. Thus, either by law or ancient custom, following the example of the Old Testament, each one paid to the Church one-tenth of the earnings from his own property.

And men were stirred to do these things with great zeal because at first the clergy distributed all that remained after the necessary expenses for their moderate maintenance, partly in the construction and decoration of churches, and partly in pious and charitable works. For pride and ambition had not yet entered into their hearts, and Christians universally recognized the Bishop of Rome as the head of all the churches and all spiritual administration, and as the successor of the Apostle Peter; and because that city retained above all others the name and majesty of the Empire in all its ancient dignity and grandeur, and because from Rome the Christian faith had spread to most of Europe, and because Constantine, baptized by Sylvester, had voluntarily recognized that power in him and his successors. And it is furthermore reported that Constantine, having been forced by the troubles in the eastern provinces to transfer the seat of the Empire to the city of Byzantium, called after his name Constantinople, gave the popes the government of Rome and many other cities and regions in Italy.

This report, although diligently nourished by succeeding popes, and because of their authority believed by many people, is rejected by most responsible authors,* and rejected much more by the events themselves. For it is very obvious that at that time and for a long time afterward, Rome and all of Italy were administered as subjects of the Empire and

---

* Notably by Lorenzo Valla (1405–1457), whose treatise *De falso credita et ementita Constantini donatione decla-* *matio* appeared in 1440. Since it was a political pamphlet Guicciardini probably read it.

by magistrates appointed by the emperors. Nor are there lacking those who sharply deny everything that is said about Constantine and Sylvester, affirming that they lived in different epochs; so deeply obscure such ancient things often are.

But nobody denies that the transfer of the imperial seat to Constantinople was the first origin of papal power. Because the authority of the emperors in Italy weakening over the course of time by their continued absence and the difficulties they had in the East, the Roman people, drifting away from the emperors and therefore deferring so much the more to the popes, began to show toward the pontiffs not subjection but rather a kind of spontaneous homage. However, this manifested itself only very slowly because of the inundations of the Goths, Vandals and other barbarous nations who had poured into Italy, and who had taken and sacked Rome more than once. Therefore the name of pontiff was obscure and abject with regard to temporal matters, and the authority of the emperors was very weak in Italy since they had so shamefully left it in prey to the barbarians.

Among these nations, the power of the Goths continued for seventy years, by comparison with whom the force of the others had been almost like a brooklet. Christian by name and faith, the Goths had originally descended from parts of Dacia and Tartaria. When finally the armies of the emperors cast the Goths out of Italy, the country began again to be governed by Greek magistrates; and he who was superior to all the others was called by the Greek word Exarch, and resided at Ravenna, a most ancient city, very rich and populous in those days as a result of the fertility of the countryside. After it had greatly increased in size because of the powerful fleet which Caesar Augustus and other emperors kept almost continuously in the port of Classe which at that time was almost joined to it (and now no longer exists), Ravenna had been inhabited by many captains, and then for a long time Theodoric, King of the Goths, and his successors had resided there. Suspicious of the power of the emperors, the Goths had chosen Ravenna rather than Rome as the seat of their reign because it was more available by sea to Constantinople; and this availability, although for opposite reasons, had also induced the exarchs to continue to make that their seat, sending as their deputies to govern Rome and other Italian cities special magistrates entitled dukes.

Such was the origin of the name of the Exarchate of Ravenna, under which title was included all those who, not having any particular duke, paid direct obedience to the Exarch.

At that time, the Roman popes were deprived of all temporal power; in spiritual matters reverence toward them had waned because of their hypocritical manners which were already beginning to go to excess. Consequently, the popes then were almost like subjects to the emperors, without whose approval, or of their exarchate, they did not dare to exercise or accept the pontificate, although they were elected by the clergy and the people of Rome. Indeed, the bishops of Constantinople and Ravenna often disputed the superiority of the Bishop of Rome, since the seat of religion commonly follows the power of the Empire and of arms.

But the state of things changed shortly afterward, because the Lombards, a most fierce people, entered Italy, occupied Cisalpine Gaul which took the name of Lombardy ·from their rule, Ravenna with the entire exarchate and many other parts of Italy; and extended their armies up to the marches of Ancona, Spoleto, and Benevento, in which two last places they created particular duchies.

At that time the emperors took no heed of these things, partly out of indolence and partly because of the troubles they were facing in Asia. And since Rome was deprived of their help, and the magistracy of the exarchs was no longer in existence, Rome began to govern itself with the advice and authority of the popes. And the popes together with the Romans having become after a long while oppressed by the Lombards, had recourse finally to the help of Pepin, King of France; who, passing into Italy with a powerful army, thrust the Lombards out of part of the empire which they had dominated for more than two hundred years; and gave to the pope and the Roman Church not only Urbino, Fano, Gubbio and many lands near Rome which had become his by fortune of war, but also Ravenna with its exarchate, which they say includes everything contained within the borders of Piacenza contiguous to the territory of Pavia up to Rimini, between the Po River, the Apennine mountains, the Stagni, (or the marsh of the Venetians) and the Adriatic Sea; and in addition to this, from Rimini up to the Foglia River, at that time called the Isauro.

But after Pepin's death the Lombards again threatened the popes and what had been given to them, and therefore Pepin's son, Charles (who was later deservedly surnamed the Great as a result of his great victories), entirely destroyed their empire and confirmed the donation given to the Roman Church by his father; and while he was making war on the Lombards, he approved granting the pope the marquisate of Ancona and the duchy of Spoleto, including the cities of Aquila and part of the Abruzzi.

These things are held for certain, to which some ecclesiastical writers add that Charles had donated to the Church Liguria up to the River Varo, the last frontier of Italy; Mantua, and everything which the Lombards had possessed in Friuli and Istria. Other authors write to the same effect concerning the island of Corsica and all the territory included between the·cities of Luni and Parma.

As a reward, the King of France was celebrated and exalted by the popes and given the title of Most Christian King. Afterward, in the year of our Lord 800, Pope Leo together with the Roman people (with no other authority than as the head of that people) elected the same Charles as Roman emperor: separating, even by name, that part of the Empire from the emperors residing in Constantinople, as if Rome and the western provinces, not being defended by them, had need of being defended by its own prince.

Despite this division, the emperors of Constantinople were not deprived of the island of Sicily, nor of that part of Italy which, reaching from Naples to Manfredonia, ends at the sea; because they had always been under those emperors. Nor because of these things did they abrogate the custom whereby the election of the popes was confirmed by the Roman emperors under whose name the city of Rome was governed. Rather, the popes, in all their bulls, charters and grants, expressed with these formal words the date of the writing: "During the reign of such and such Emperor, our lord."

And they continued in this easy state of subjection or dependence up to the time when things occurred which gave them courage to govern themselves. But the power of the emperors had begun to weaken, first because of dissensions among Charlemagne's descendants while they still held the imperial dignity, and then because the Empire had been transferred to German princes who were not as powerful as had been Charles' successors, borne by the grandeur of the French realm. Hence, the popes and the Roman people (by whose magistrates Rome was beginning, although tumultuously, to be governed) abrogated imperial jurisdiction as much as they could, and made a law that election of popes no longer had to be confirmed by the emperors.

For many years this law was variously interpreted, according as imperial power rose or fell with the fluctuation of events. When the empire devolved upon the house of the Ottos of Saxony, imperial power increased; and Gregory, also of Saxony, who had been elected pope through the favor of Otto III who was then in Rome, and moved by love for his own country and anger over the persecutions he had endured from the Romans, transferred to the German nation, by his decree, the right of electing Roman emperors. This tradition and form has been observed up to our own times, forbidding the emperors-elect to use the title of Emperor or Augustus until they have received the imperial crown from the popes (in order to preserve some prerogative to the popes). Hence grew the custom of the emperors coming to Rome to be crowned, and before that time not to use any other title than King of the Romans, or Caesar.*

But afterward, the Ottos having disappeared and the power of the

* See note p. 114.

emperors diminished because the empire did not continue to be the heritage of great kings, Rome openly withdrew her obedience, and many cities rebelled when Conrad the Swabian ruled; and the popes, intent upon increasing their own authority, almost dominated Rome, although often with great difficulty because of the insolence and unruliness amongst the people. To restrain the people, the popes had already, supported by the Emperor Henry II who was then at Rome, ordained a law that only the cardinals had the authority to create a pope.

A new increase in the pope's grandeur followed. For the Normans, of whom the first was William surnamed Iron-Arm, usurped Apulia and Calabria from the Emperor at Constantinople. Consequently, one of the Normans, Robert Guicciard, restored Benevento as an ecclesiastical territory and recognized the duchies of Apulia and Calabria as feuds of the Roman Church; Guicciard did this either to strengthen himself with some pretext of right or to be better able to defend himself against the emperors, or for some other reason. His example was followed by Roger, one of his successors, who having driven William of the same family out of the duchies of Apulia and Calabria, and then occupying Sicily, recognized, about the year 1130, these provinces as fiefs of the Church under the title of king of both Sicilies, one on this side of the Faro and the other beyond: the Popes not refusing, for their own ambition and advantage, to foment the usurpation and violence of others.

Based on such arguments, and making ever more far-reaching claims (since human greed knows no limits), the Popes began to deprive several kings, disobedient to their commandments, of these realms, and concede them to others.

In this way, Henry, son of Frederick Barbarossa, and Frederick II, son of Henry, became emperors of Rome, all three in succession. But since Frederick became a bitter persecutor of the Church and in his time provoked the Guelph and Ghibelline factions in Italy, one of which was headed by the Pope and the other by the Emperor, after the death of Frederick, the Pope conceded the investiture of these kingdoms to Charles, Count of Anjou and Provence (of which mention has been made above), imposing upon him a yearly tribute of six thousand ounces of gold, with the condition that hereafter none of these kings could accept the title of Roman emperor. This condition has ever since been specified in the investitures [of the kings of Naples]. For the kingdom of the isle of Sicily, occupied by the King of Aragon, after a few years freed itself of that tribute and of acknowledgment of being held in fief to the Church.

It has also been rumored, although not with such certainty as the preceding events, that much earlier the Countess Matilda, a very powerful princess in Italy, gave the Church that part of Tuscany which is limited on one side by the River Pescia and the castle of San Quirico in the county of Siena, and on the other, by the sea below and the Tiber River, and that today this is called the Patrimony of Saint Peter; and others add that the same Countess gave the Church the city of Ferrara.

These latter things are not certain, but even more dubious is what someone has written to the effect that Arithpert, King of the Lombards during their most flourishing reign, gave the Church the Cochian Alps in which they say Genoa is included, and everything between Genoa and the border of Provence; and that Liutprand, King of the same nation, gave the Church Sabina, a country near Rome, Narni and Ancona and certain other territories.

Thus as the state of things varied, similarly varied the relationships between popes and emperors. For at the beginning, having been persecuted a long while by the emperors and then freed of this terror by the conversion of Constantine, they lived tranquilly, attending only to spiritual matters, being for many years little more than subjects living under their shadow. Then for a long time they dwelt in humble condition having absolutely no contact with the emperors because of the greatness of the Lombards in Italy. But afterward, having achieved temporal power with the help of the King of France, they were strictly allied with the emperors, and willingly depended upon their authority so long as the imperial dignity continued in the line of the descendants of Charlemagne. This policy they pursued as much in memory of reciprocal benefits as out of respect for imperial grandeur.

But when the latter power declined, they withdrew their friendship entirely and began to assert that the pontifical dignity should rather give laws to the emperors than receive them. Therefore, having above all else a horror of returning to their ancient state of subjection, and in order that the emperors might not attempt to avow their ancient imperial rights in Rome or elsewhere (as some of the stronger or more ardent ones had tried to do), the popes openly opposed their power with arms; assisted by those tyrants, calling themselves princes, and those cities which, having recovered their liberties, no longer recognized the authority of the Empire.

Hence it came to pass that the popes, arrogating more and more power upon themselves every day, and employing the terror of their spiritual weapons for temporal occasions, and interpreting their role as vicars of Christ on earth as superior to the emperors, and asserting that in many cases the charge of worldly matters belonged to them, sometimes deprived the emperors of their imperial dignity, stirring up the electors to choose others instead; and on the other hand, the emperors either elected or saw to it that there were elected new popes.

The Church was already in a weakened condition, not only because the Roman court had remained in the city of Avignon for seventy years, but also because of the schism that broke out in Italy upon the Pope's return.* And now these controversies between Pope and Emperor gave rise to the fact that in the cities subject to the Church, especially in the Romagna, many powerful citizens seized their own towns and ruled by tyranny. The pontiffs either persecuted these men or, not being powerful enough to suppress them, conceded these cities in fief to these very tyrants or, stirring up other leaders, gave them the investiture. Thus the cities of Romagna began to have particular lords under the title, for the most part, of ecclesiastical vicars. Thus Ferrara, whose government had been given by the Pope to Azzo d'Este, was subsequently granted the title of vicariate, and that family in the course of time was exalted with more illustrious titles. Thus, Giovanni Visconti, Archbishop of Milan, having seized Bologna, was granted the vicarship thereof by the Pope: and for the same reasons in many cities of the marquisate of Ancona, of the Patrimony of Saint Peter and of Umbria, now called the duchy of Spoleto, many particular lords arose, either against the Pope's will, or with his practically forced consent.

These variations happening in the same way among the imperial cities of Lombardy, it sometimes occurred that, according to the shift of things, the vicars of Romagna and other ecclesiastical states, revolting openly against Church rule, would acknowledge that they held those cities as feuds of the Emperor; as sometimes those who held Milan, Mantua and other imperial cities in Lombardy, would acknowledge them as feuds of the Pope.

And in those times, Rome almost governed itself, although it was held ostensibly in the name and dominion of the Church. For although at first, when the Roman pontiffs returned from Avignon to Italy, they were obeyed as lords, nevertheless, soon afterward, the Romans having created a magistracy called the *Banderesi*, they fell into their old contumaciousness, whereupon the popes, retaining very little authority, chose to live there no longer. This lasted until the Romans, impoverished and fallen into the gravest disorders as a result of the absences of the pontifical court, and the year 1400 approaching, in which they hoped (if the Pope were at Rome) there would be a thronging and concourse of people from all parts of Christendom because of the Jubilee, most humbly supplicated

* The so-called "Babylonian captivity" at Avignon lasted sixty-three years (1314–77), according to Pirenne; Gregorovius, without specifying, dates it from the beginning of the pontificate of Clement V, that is, from c. 1305. During this period there were seven French popes in succession.

The "Babylonian captivity" was succeeded by the double election of a pope and antipope, giving rise to the famous crisis known as the Great Schism, which lasted for sixty-one years (Henri Pirenne, *A History of Europe*, New York, 1958, II, 122–35; Ferdinand Gregorovius, *Storia della città di Roma nel medio evo*, Città di Castello, 1943, X, 156; XII, 5–10, 55–59).

Pope Boniface to return, offering to abolish the magistracy of the *Banderesi*, and to submit themselves entirely to his obedience.

Upon these conditions, Boniface returned to Rome, and while the Romans were intent upon their profits of that year, the Pope took absolute command of the city, fortified the Castel Sant' Angelo and placed a garrison there. And although his successors up to Eugenius [IV] had much difficulty, nevertheless their domination was fully fixed thenceforth, and the following popes have, without any further trouble, ruled that city as they wished.

On these foundations and by these means, raised to secular power, little by little forgetting about the salvation of souls and divine precepts, and turning all their thoughts to worldly greatness, and no longer using their spiritual authority except as an instrument and minister of temporal power, they began to appear rather more like secular princes than popes. Their concern and endeavors began to be no longer the sanctity of life or the propagation of religion, no longer zeal and charity toward their neighbors, but armies and wars against Christians, managing their sacrifices with bloody hands and thoughts; they began to accumulate treasures, to make new laws, to invent new tricks, new cunning devices in order to gather money from every side; for this purpose, to use their spiritual arms without respect; for this end, to shamelessly sell sacred and profane things. The great wealth spreading amongst them and throughout their court was followed by pomp, luxury, dishonest customs, lust and abominable pleasures: no concern about their successors, no thought of the perpetual majesty of the pontificate, but instead, an ambitious and pestiferous desire to exalt their children, nephews and kindred, not only to immoderate riches but to principalities, to kingdoms; no longer distributing dignities and emoluments among deserving and virtuous men, but almost always either selling them for the highest price or wasting them on persons opportunistically moved by ambition, avarice, or shameful love of pleasure.

And for all these misdeeds, reverence for the papacy has been utterly lost in the hearts of men, and yet their authority is somewhat sustained by the name and majesty, so powerful and effective, of religion; and mightily by the means they have of gratifying great princes and those powerful personages around them, by conferring dignities and other ecclesiastical concessions. Whence knowing themselves to be held in the greatest respect by men, and that whoever takes arms against them gains grave infamy thereby and often opposition from other princes, and in any event profits very little, and that when victors they employ the victory as they will, and when vanquished they obtain whatever conditions they will, and pricked on by the greed to raise their families from private conditions to principalities, the popes have been for a long time, and very often, the instruments of stirring up wars and new conflagrations in Italy.

But to return to our main purpose, from which my most justified grief over public loss has deflected me more ardently than truly pertains to the laws of history.

The cities of the Romagna, vexed like the other subjects of the Church by these occurrences, had in effect governed themselves for many years now almost as if they were independent of the ecclesiastical domain; for several of the vicars did not pay the tribute due in recognition of superiority; others paid it only with difficulty and sometimes past due, but all of them indifferently, and without permission of the Pope, hired themselves out to other princes, not even stipulating to be exempt from serving them against the Church, and pledging themselves to defend them even against the authority and arms of the popes. These vicars were greedily received by [the princes] that they might take advantage of the forces and resources of their states, as well as to prevent an increase in pontifical power.

Now at that time the Venetians held the cities of Ravenna and Cervia in the Romagna, which they had taken many years before from the family of Polenta, who had first been private citizens in Ravenna and afterward become tyrants of their country and afterward vicars; Faenza, Forlì, Imola and Rimini were ruled by local vicars. Cesena, for a long time ruled by the Malatesta family, was returned to Church domination, Domenico, the last vicar of that city, having died childless not many years before. Therefore the Pope, pretending that those cities had, for various reasons, devolved to the Apostolic See, and wishing to reintegrate them under his ancient jurisdiction (but actually intending to appropriate them for Cesare his son), had agreed with the King of France that when the latter had acquired the duchy of Milan he should help him to obtain only those towns which were held by the vicars; and besides these, the city of Pesaro, whose vicar was Giovanni Sforza, his former son-in-law. For the greatness of the Venetians would not brook the Pope entertaining such ideas in their direction: nor did the Venetians aspire at that time toward those little towns held by the Duke of Ferrara along the Po River. As soon as Valentino had obtained forces from the King and added them to the armies of the Church, he entered Romagna and swiftly took the city of Imola by accord, in the last days of the year 1499.

In this year Italy, shaken by so many perturbations, also felt the shock of Turkish arms. For, Bajazet Ottoman having stormed by sea with a powerful armada, the places which the Venetians held in Greece, sent six thousand horsemen by land to plunder the region of Friuli, and finding that country unguarded and unsuspecting of such an occurrence, the Turks overran it, pillaging and burning up to Liquenza; and having taken an innumerable quantity of prisoners, when on their return they reached the banks of the Tagliamento River, in order to march more easily, they kept those prisoners whom they thought they could lead with them, and cruelly massacred all the rest.

Nor were things in Greece proceeding any more prosperously. Antonio Grimani, captain-general of the armada which the Venetians had mustered against the Turkish fleet, accused of having let slip the opportunity to vanquish the enemy who were leaving the port of Sapienza, and another time at the mouth of the Gulf of Lepanto, was replaced by a successor, summoned to Venice, and the case submitted to the Council of the Pregati where the matter was debated for many months with the utmost care—on one side, his authority and greatness standing in his defense, and on the other, his accusers attacking him with many arguments and witnesses. Finally, when it seemed that his cause was likely to prevail, either because of the man's reputation or the multitude of his relatives; and because in that Council, wherein many prudent men participated, public rumors and insufficiently proved calumnies would not be accorded the same consideration as a desire to arrive maturely at the truth of the matter, the case was thereby transferred by the magistrate of the advocates of the commune to the jurisdiction of the Great Council: where favors ceasing, or where perhaps mass frivolity played more weight than senatorial maturity, he was finally (not, however, before the following year) sent into permanent exile on the island of Ossaro.

.　.
.

Thus amidst great turmoil ended the year 1499. But no less varied and memorable was the year 1500: noteworthy especially for the plenary remission of the Jubilee. This had been originally instituted by the popes to be celebrated according to the example of the Old Testament every hundred years, not for pleasure or pomp, as did the Romans in their secular games, but for the salvation of souls (for according to the pious Christian belief such a Jubilee utterly canceled all the sins of those who, recognizing with true penitence the errors which they had committed, would visit those churches dedicated in Rome to the Princes of the Apostles). Afterward, it was ordained that the Jubilee be celebrated every fifty years, and later still, this was reduced to every twenty-five years; nevertheless, out of memory of its original origin, many more people throng to celebrate it during the hundredth year than in the others.

At the beginning of this year, Valentino took without resistance the city of Forlì, because the Lady of that place [Caterina Sforza], having sent her children and most precious possessions to Florence and abandoned the other things she couldn't hold, determined to defend only the citadel and fortress of Forlì, well provided with men and artillery. But since she alone among so many feminine-spirited defenders possessed manly courage, Valentino soon conquered the citadel as a result of the cowardice of the captains within. And the Duke Valentino, having more regard for the Lady's valor than for her sex, sent her as a prisoner to Rome where she was placed in the Castel Sant' Angelo: although after a little less than a year, as a result of the intercession of Ivo d'Allegri, she obtained her freedom.*

[*The King returns to France while Valentino continues his campaign. Lodovico and his brother recover Milan, whose people have expressed a desire for his return. Sforza raises troops among the Swiss and Burgundians, besieges Novara, and without opposition from French soldiers within the town, captures it.*]

News of the rebellion at Milan aroused the French King's shame and anger. He immediately dispatched La Trémouille into Italy with six hundred lances and sent instructions to levy a great quantity of Swiss. And in order that these necessary provisions be attended to as quickly as possible, he delegated the Cardinal of Rouen as his lieutenant for Italy, and dispatched him immediately to Asti. Since all these things had been expedited with marvelous celerity, by the beginning of April there were already to be found united in Italy fifteen hundred lances, ten thousand Swiss infantry, and six thousand of the King's subjects under La Trémouille, Trivulzio and Ligny. These companies uniting at Mortara, marched toward Novara, placing their reliance no less upon treason than force; because although the Swiss captains who were with Lodovico had shown faith and skill in the attack on Novara, they had now secretly come to an agreement with the French via the Swiss captains serving in that army. Lodovico's suspicions having been aroused,

* The Torrentino edition contains a more detailed and bloodier version of the capture of the citadel; but Gherardi rejects it as an interpolation by another hand, although based on Guicciardini's notes. In this expanded version, *"Madonna"*—nowhere named—entered the citadel, *"e essendo d' animo virile e feroce proccurava, con molto sua gloria, la difesa di quella."* Fenton translates the entire interpolated passage but mistranslates *"considerando in lei più il valore che il sesso"* as "having *lesse* regard to her valour than to her sexe" (emphasis mine—S. A.).

Caterina's valor was famous, winning her the appellation of *"virago"*—a term of praise applied to ladies highly accomplished in bed, in battle, or in belles-lettres.

When her rebellious subjects at Forlì threatened in 1488 to kill her children, held as hostages, Caterina is said to have appeared at the ramparts, lifted her skirts, and shouted: *"A me rimane lo stampo per farne altri!"*—"I've still got the mold to make others!" The *stampo* eventually shaped Giovanni delle Bande Nere, one of the greatest Renaissance military captains (Guicciardini, *La Historia di Italia,* Torrentino edition, Fiorenza, 1561, p. 166; Gherardi, *op. cit.,* I, 313, note 1; Fenton, *The Historie of Guicciardin,* London, 1618, p. 179).

he sought to have four hundred horsemen and eight thousand foot-soldiers levied at Milan and united with his forces. Instigated by their captains, the Swiss now began to mutiny in Novara, their excuse being that the monies due them were not being paid on the day appointed, because of Duke Lodovico's lack of funds. The Duke hastened imme-diately to the place of tumult, and pleading with such timidity that his words aroused no little compassion, he once again gave them all his silver plate and vessels and begged them to be patient and wait until the money came from Milan. But the Swiss captains feared that if the troops being mustered at Milan should join the Duke, this would impede their setting into execution the betrayal which they had determined upon. Therefore they saw to it that the French army, prepared and on the alert, marched up to the walls of Novara. As soon as a great part of the city had been surrounded, the Swiss captains dispatched horsemen between the city and the Tesino River to cut off from the Duke and the others the possibility of fleeing to Milan. The Duke, suspecting that his ill fortune was growing worse every hour, wished to issue out of Novara with his army in order to fight against the enemy, having already sent out his light cavalry and the Burgundians to begin the battle. But he was openly resisted by the Swiss captains, who alleged that without leave of their lords they did not wish to come to blows with their kinsmen and their own brethren and countrymen; and a short while afterward, mingling with the others as if they were all in the same army, they said they wanted to depart immediately in order to return home. And since neither the Duke's prayers nor tears nor promises availed to bend them from their barbarous betrayal, he begged them that at least they might lead him to a safe refuge. But because they had conspired with the French captains to leave and not take him with them, they refused to yield to his demands, although they did agree that he might mingle amongst them in the guise of one of their footsoldiers so that, should he not be recognized, he might perchance save himself. The Duke accepted this condition as a last necessity but this did not prove sufficient for his safety. For, as they were marching in formation through the midst of the French army, he was recognized either by the diligent observation of those assigned to that task or else pointed out by the Swiss themselves, while he was mixed in with the squadron and marching on foot, dressed and armed like a Swiss. And thus the Duke was immediately taken prisoner, a spectacle so abject that it moved even many of his enemies to tears. Besides the Duke, there were captured Galeazzo da San Severino [Count of Gaiazzo], Il Fracassa [Gasparo] and Antonio Maria, his brothers, who were also mingled among the Swiss in the same garb.

LODOVICO IL MORO

*Detail of an altarpiece painted by an unknown Lombard master for the church
of Saint Ambrogio. In the complete work, the Duke and Duchess of Milan
with their two children are seen kneeling at the foot of the Madonna and Child
enthroned, with the four fathers of the church. The hand on the Duke's
shoulder is that of Saint Ambrose, protector and patron saint of Milan. About
1495. Brera Gallery, Milan.* (COURTESY OF FRATELLI ALINARI)

Imprisonment of Lodovico Sforza

L ODOVICO S FORZA was brought to Lyons where the King was, and since he entered that city at noon, a great multitude of people flocked to see a prince who had now fallen into such misery from a state of such greatness and majesty, recently envied by so many for his felicity. And since he could not obtain leave to be brought to the King's presence as he so greatly desired, he was taken after two days to the Tower of Loches where he remained prisoner about ten years, up to the very end of his life. Thus within a narrow prison were enclosed the thoughts and ambitions of one whose ideas earlier could scarcely be contained within the limits of all Italy—a prince certainly most excellent in eloquence, in skill and many other qualities of mind and nature, and worthy of obtaining a name for mildness and clemency if the infamy come upon him as a result of his nephew's death had not blemished that reputation. But on the other hand he was vain, and his mind full of ambitious, restless thoughts, and he violated his promises and his pledges; always presuming so much on the basis of his own knowledge that being highly offended whenever the prudence and counsels of others were praised, he convinced himself that he could turn everyone's ideas in whatever direction he pleased by means of his own industry and manipulations.

Not much later the Cardinal Ascanio followed him. But received with much greater humanity and honor, and graciously visited by the Cardinal of Rouen, Ascanio was sent to a more honorable prison because he was incarcerated in the Tower of Bourges which had been, two years earlier, the prison of the very same King who was now imprisoning him: so varied and miserable is human destiny and so uncertain to everyone are his own conditions in times to come.

BOOK

5

D URING THIS PERIOD CESARE BORGIA'S AFFAIRS
PROCEEDED PROSPEROUSLY. FOR ALTHOUGH THE
KING, VERY DISSATISFIED WITH THE POPE FOR
not having helped him to recover the duchy of Milan, had deferred
lending him assistance to prosecute his enterprise begun against the
ecclesiastical governors of Romagna: yet his desire to keep the Pope
friendly (because of the King's fear of stirrings in Germany) and finding
no means of arriving at an agreement with [Maximilian] Caesar, finally
induced him to change course. The King was especially influenced by
the Cardinal of Rome, who was greedy to obtain the office of legate
of the realm of France. The Pope therefore promised to help the King
with men, and with the person of his son, whenever he wished to undertake an attack against the kingdom of Naples, and to concede to the
Cardinal of Rouen the legation of the kingdom of France for eighteen
months; a concession which was considered a very great thing because it
was new and because it deflected many enterprises and profits out of the
hands of the Roman court (although Brittany was not included in the
concession). For his part, the King sent three hundred lances and two
thousand footsoldiers under Allegri to the Pope, signifying to everyone
that he would consider anyone opposing the pontifical enterprise as
committing an offense against his own person. Supported by public
knowledge of this agreement and by his own forces, which consisted of
seven hundred men-at-arms and six thousand footsoldiers, Valentino
entered the Romagna and without any resistance whatever took the cities
of Pesaro and Rimini, whose lords fled; then he turned toward Faenza
which had no defense other than its own people, because Giovanni
Bentivoglio, grandfather on the maternal side of Astorre [Manfredi], a
little child, was not alone in abstaining from giving them any help in
order not to stir up the armies of the Pope and of his son, and also
because he had been so commanded by the King. The Florentines and
the Duke of Ferrara for the same reasons acted in the same manner, and

even the Venetians, who were bound to his defense, intimated to him (as the King had requested of them) that they had renounced the protection which they bore him, as similarly and for the same reason they had done with Pandolfo Malatesta, lord of Rimini. In fact, in order to demonstrate all the more that they were favorable to the Pope, they created at this very time Duke Valentino as one of their gentlemen, an honor usually granted by that Republic either in recognition of benefits received or in token of close amity.

. .
.

At this time Alexander, Duke Valentino's father, in order that all their efforts might tend toward a common goal, and having that very year created, to his great infamy, twelve cardinals (selected not amongst the most worthy, but amongst those who offered him the highest price); and in order not to neglect any means whatever of getting money, proclaimed throughout Italy and foreign lands the year of Jubilee which was celebrated in Rome with a great influx of people, especially from those nations beyond the mountains. And he granted the possibility of obtaining [absolution]* to anyone who, although he did not go to Rome, would proffer some quantity of money: which, together with the other sums that might be extracted in howsoever a manner from the spiritual treasures as well as the temporal domain of the Church, he sent to Duke Valentino. The Duke remained at Forlì where he was making all necessary preparations for next year's siege; meanwhile, the people of Faenza with no less care were building up the fortifications of their town. These events took place in the year 1500.

[*At the beginning of 1501 the King of France obtains a truce from Maximilian, and focuses all his attention on the Neapolitan enterprise. And to assure the success of this campaign, the French King and the King of Spain agree to attack the kingdom of Naples concurrently and divide that realm.*

Meanwhile Cesare Borgia continues his military activities in central Italy: enters into Bolognese territory, but forbidden to proceed by the King of France, comes to an accord with Bentivoglio; Borgia then threatens the domain of Florence, which results in an agreement; occupies some towns near Piombino, and then returns to Rome to prepare to join the French who are getting ready to attack Naples. King Federigo of Naples prepares to defend himself, "not knowing that the Spanish armies, under pretense of friendship, were

---

* G. is most ambiguous here. He says "of obtaining it," *conseguirlo*—but I have been unable to discover an antecedent to which "it" refers (Gherardi, *op. cit.*, II, 10).

prepared against him. . . ." Federigo appeals to the Spanish general Gonsalvo of Cordova, called "the Great Captain," then with the Spanish fleet in Sicily, to help him.]

In this state of affairs all Italy was certainly full of incredible uncertainties, since everyone judged that this enterprise was bound to be the beginning of the gravest calamities, because the army being prepared by the King of France did not seem to be so powerful that it could easily conquer the united forces of Federigo and Gonsalvo ["the Great Captain"] and it was judged that once the spirits of such mighty kings became agitated, both sides would have to continue the war with greater forces, whence the gravest and most perilous disturbances might break out all over Italy as a result of the various attitudes of the other potentates.

But as soon as the French army came to Rome, all these discourses proved themselves vain. For the French and Spanish ambassadors, entering together into the Consistory, notified the Pope and cardinals of the league and agreement made between their kings in order (as they said) that they might be able to concentrate on a crusade against the enemies of the Christian religion. And they demanded the investiture according to the tenor of the convention which they had drawn up, which was conceded by the Pope without any hesitation.

Therefore, the outcome of this war no longer being in doubt, men's fears were transformed into amazement, everyone finding the King of France greatly wanting in prudence, in that he had preferred rather that half of that realm should fall into the hands of the King of Spain, bringing into Italy, where before he had been the sole arbiter of things, another king as his rival, to whom all his enemies and those discontented with him might have recourse, and furthermore, one who was allied with the King of the Romans by many close interests. And he had done all this rather than endure that Federigo should remain lord of the entire realm, acknowledging to hold it of him and paying him tribute for it, as by sundry means he had sought to obtain.

But the universal judgment was that Ferdinand's integrity and faith were no less wanting, all men marveling that out of his greed to obtain some part of the kingdom he should have conspired against a king of his own blood, and that he might more easily subvert him, he had always fed him with false promises of help, besmirching the splendor of the title of Catholic King (which title he and his Queen, Isabella,* had been granted by the Pope a few years before), and that glory with which their names had been exalted up to the heavens for having driven the

---

* Perhaps Guicciardini has a *lapsus calami* here: he writes *Elizabetta* although   *Isabella* was a not uncommon name in his day.

Moors out of the kingdom of Granada, no less for religious zeal than for their own interests.

To these accusations against both kings, there was no other response in the name of the King of France except that French power was sufficient to provide a remedy at the proper time for all disorders. But as for Ferdinand, it was said that although Federigo had given him just cause for moving against him (knowing that he had secretly negotiated against him with the French King a long time ago), nevertheless, it was not this which had stirred him, but the consideration that the King having determined to undertake at whatever cost a campaign against the kingdom of Naples, he was forced by necessity either to defend it or to abandon it. Taking up its defense would set off a conflagration so great that it would be most pernicious to Christendom, especially now that the Turkish armies were so powerfully arrayed against the Venetians by land and by sea. And abandoning its defense, he knew that his kingdom of Sicily would remain in the gravest peril, and that even without this, it could not but be to his gravest detriment that the King of France should occupy the kingdom of Naples which juridically belonged to him, and that he might also put forth new claims, should Federigo's lineage be lacking.

Therefore in these difficulties he had chosen the way of dividing, in the hope that the bad government of the French would result in their portion also falling to him in a short while. And when that happened, he would either retain it for himself or restore it to Federigo (according as regard for the public welfare counseled him, which he always esteemed more highly than his own interest); rather to Federigo's children, for he didn't deny that he held his name almost in horror, knowing that before the French King took the duchy of Milan, he [Federigo] had been dealing with the Turks.

·   ·
·

The full force of the French was now concentrated around Capua where they encamped, some here, some there near the river, on the upper bank where the river begins to run near the town. Then, having violently battered the city on all sides, they unleashed a most ferocious assault. And although this did not prove successful inasmuch as they were forced to retire from the wall with great loss, nevertheless, the attack having been not without the gravest peril to the defenders, the captains and soldiers began to incline toward a treaty, especially observing as they did that the people of the city and the countrymen who had taken refuge there in great numbers were showing signs of rebellion.

But on the eighth day after the camp had been set up, Fabrizio

FORTRESS UNDER ATTACK

One of the earliest examples of a fortress under attack by two cannon. (From the celebrated treatise Le diverse et artificiose machine *by Agostino Ramelli, an Italian military engineer of the sixteenth century.) An enlargement of the sighting mechanism in the form of a sextant, lower right.*

Colonna having begun to parlay from a bastion on conditions of sur-render with the Count of Gaiazzo, the negligent guard of those within (as often happens at the moment most hopeful for an agreement) gave an opportunity to the enemies to burst in: and these, out of their greed for pillage and anger at the losses they had suffered at the assault, sacked the entire town, slaughtering a great many, and keeping prisoners such as remained after their cruelty. Nor were they any less pitiless and ferocious against the women of every sort or quality, even those dedi-cated to religion, who were the unhappy prey of the lust and avarice of the victors; many of these women were sold afterward at Rome for very low prices: and it has been reported that at Capua, some of them, fearing death less than the loss of their honor, thrust themselves, some into wells, and some into rivers. It has been further revealed that, besides other abominations worthy of eternal infamy, many of the women who had escaped the first assault having taken refuge in a tower, Duke Valentino, who was following the French army with the title of the King's lieutenant, wanted to see all of them; and went there accompanied by no other men than his own gentlemen and guard, and after diligently considering them, kept forty of the most beautiful for himself.

Fabrizio Colonna, Don Ugo di Cardona and all the other captains and important men were taken prisoners, amongst whom Renuccio di Marciano, who had been wounded by a crossbow shot on the day of the assault and kept in the hands of Valentino's soldiers, died within two days, not without suspicion that his death had been helped along. The loss of Capua cut off all Federigo's hopes of being able to defend anything.

. . .
.

At the same time the Pope's affairs were proceeding with their usual prosperity: for he had acquired with the greatest ease all the estates held by the families of the Colonna and Savelli around Rome, part of which he gave to the Orsini. Meanwhile, the Duke Valentino, continuing his campaign against Piombino, sent Vitellozzo and Giovan Pagalo Baglioni there with new forces. Their arrival so frightened Iacopo d'Appiano, lord of that place, that, garrisoning the fortress and the town, he fled by sea to France in order to try to induce the King, who had some time before taken him under his protection, not to permit him to perish, out of regard for the King's own honor. To this the King replied very openly, not concealing his infamy with any artifice whatever, that he had promised the Pope not to oppose him, nor could he oppose him without harming himself.

But in the midst of all this, the town yielded to Valentino through

House of Este

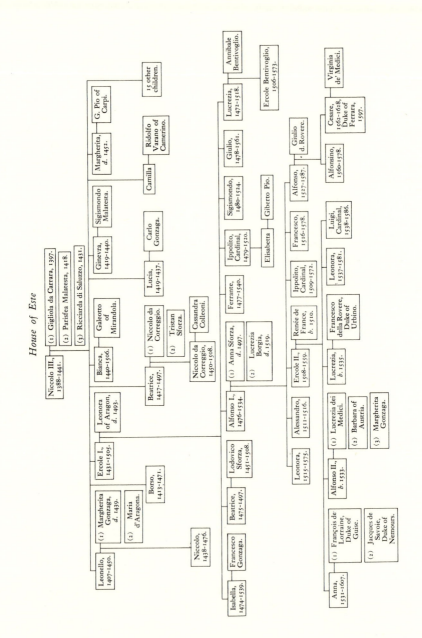

Pandolfo Petrucci's operations, and a few days afterward the castle likewise surrendered. Now the Pope once again married off his daughter Lucrezia: this time to Alfonso, eldest son of Ercole d'Este, with a dowry of 100,000 ducats in cash and many other gifts of the greatest value. This marriage was arranged despite the fact that Lucrezia had already had three other husbands* and was at that time a widow as a result of the death of Gismondo (prince of Bisceglie and bastard son to Alfonso, King of Naples), who had been slain by Duke Valentino. Although this marriage was most unworthy of the house of Este, wont to make the most noble alliances, and all the more unworthy because Lucrezia was illegitimate and stained with great infamy, Ercole and Alfonso consented, because the French King, desiring to satisfy the Pope in all things, made strong importunities for this union. Besides this, they were motivated by a desire for securing themselves by such means from the arms and ambitions of Valentino (if, against such perfidy, any security whatever were sufficient). For Valentino, now powerful with the monies and authority of the Apostolic See and the favor which the French King bore him, was already formidable throughout a great part of Italy, and everyone knew that his cupidity had neither limit nor bridle.

[*Through the rest of this year and the following years 1502 and 1503, "little wars" continue all over the peninsula, all relating to the ambitions of the great powers, France and Spain, as they collide in Italy. The Florentine war against Pisa drags on into its seventh year. French and Spaniard fight in the kingdom of Naples, while in the north the King of France seeks ways to recover the duchy of Milan from the Venetians. Valentino continues to build a Borgian state in central Italy: captures the duchy of Urbino and again threatens Florence. In that city a permanent gonfaloniere, Piero Soderini, is elected; his right-hand man (some say his puppet) is the secretary of the Ten of War, Niccolò Machiavelli.*

Despite a peace treaty signed between the King of France and the Archduke of Austria as procurator of the King of Spain, the war in the kingdom of Naples continues with ever more disastrous French defeats. The Great Captain enters Naples and the Spanish conquer the Abruzzi and practically all of Calabria.

The Pope and his son Cesare, meanwhile, having taken posses-sion of Romagna, now cast their longing eyes on Tuscany, and also plan to seize the estates of the Orsini. The King of France,

---

* Actually two, although there had additionally been two betrothals (at the same time) with formal nuptial contracts, not to mention various fugitive and pos-sibly incestuous affairs.

whose forces have already crossed into Lombardy, has need of the Pope to give passage of the French army through the dominions of the Church on their way to Naples. For this permission Pope Alexander extorts conditions from the King: who consents to Borgian possession of the lands of Giangiordano Orsini and of their conquest of Siena.]

BOOK
6

Death of Pope Alexander VI

BUT NOW AT THE HEIGHT OF HIS GREATEST HOPES (SO VAIN AND FALLACIOUS ARE MEN'S THOUGHTS), THE POPE, WHO HAD GONE TO DINE IN A VINEYARD near the Vatican to escape the heat, was suddenly carried back to the apostolic palace, dying, and soon after him, his son was brought in, also on the brink of death. The following day, which was the eighteenth of August, 1503, the body of the dead Pope was borne according to custom to the Church of Saint Peter: black, swollen, and hideous to behold, most manifest signs of poisoning, but Valentino's life was spared because of the vigor of his youth, and because he had immediately used powerful and suitable antidotes to the poison, although he remained seriously ill for a long time. It was always believed that this episode was the result of poison, and the most widespread rumor was that the affair had taken place in the following way: that Valentino had determined to poison at that selfsame dinner Adriano [Castellesi], the Cardinal of Corneto, in whose vineyard they were supposed to dine (because it is clear that both father and son had frequently and habitually made use of poison, not only to take revenge against their enemies and secure themselves against suspicions, but also because of their wicked greed to despoil the wealthy of their possessions, both amongst the cardinals and other members of the court, heedless of the fact that they had never been harmed in any way by these people, as had been the case with the very rich Cardinal of Sant' Angelo; and equally heedless of the fact that they had been on the very closest terms of friendship with some of them, and that others, like the cardinals of Capua and Modena, had been their most useful and faithful counselors).

Thus it was bruited about that Valentino had prepared in advance certain flacons of wine infected with poison, which he consigned to a steward unaware of the plot, commanding him not to give them to anyone. But by chance it happened that the Pontiff, before the dinner hour, became thirsty as a result of the overwhelming heat and asked that some drink be brought him, and because the supplies for the dinner had not yet arrived from the palace, the steward, who believed that the most precious wine had been set aside for his keeping, gave the Pope that wine to drink which Valentino had sent ahead; and that Valentino, arriving while his father was drinking, began similarly to drink of the same wine.

All Rome thronged with incredible rejoicing to see the dead body of Alexander in Saint Peter's, unable to satiate their eyes enough with seeing spent that serpent who in his boundless ambition and pestiferous perfidy, and with all his examples of horrible cruelty and monstrous sensuality and unheard-of avarice, selling without distinction sacred and profane things, had envenomed the entire world. And nevertheless he had been exalted by the most unusual and almost perpetual good fortune from early youth up to the last days of his life, always desiring the greatest things and always obtaining more than he desired. A powerful example to confound the arrogance of those who, presuming to discern with the weakness of human eyes the depth of divine judgments, affirm that the prosperity or adversity of men proceeds from their own merits or demerits: as if one may not see every day many good men unjustly vexed and many depraved souls unworthily exalted; or as if, interpreting it in another way, one were to derogate from the justice and power of God, whose boundless might cannot be contained within the narrow limits of the present, and who—at another time and in another place— will recognize with a broad sweep, with rewards and eternal punishments, the just from the unjust.

But Valentino, gravely ill in the palace, gathered all his men around him, and although he had always previously thought partly by the terror of his arms and partly by the favor of the new Spanish cardinals, of whom there were eleven, to elect a pontiff of his own choosing after his father's death, now, because of his very dangerous illness, he had much more difficulty than he had earlier imagined in carrying out this or any other of his schemes. For this reason, he complained with the greatest indignation that although he had formerly often anticipated all the difficulties that might result from his father's death and had planned all the remedies against such troubles, it had never occurred to him that he also might happen to be impeded by a dangerous illness at the same time.

Therefore, having to frame his counsels not to plans previously made but to unexpected necessity, and since he deemed it impossible to sustain the enmity of the Colonna and Orsini at the same time, and fearing that they might join together against him, he resolved to place his faith more readily in those whom he had harmed only in their property than in those whom he had harmed both in their property and in their persons; and for this reason, he quickly brought about a reconciliation with the house of Colonna and with the family of the Valle, followers of the same faction, inviting them to return to their own estates and restoring to them their fortresses which had been fortified and enlarged by Alexander at great expense.

But all this sufficed not, neither for his safety, nor to keep peace in the city of Rome, where all was rife with suspicion and agitation. For Prospero Colonna had entered there and all the Colonna party had seized arms; and Fabio Orsini, coming from the houses of his kinsmen in Montegiordano with a great swarm of Orsini partisans, had set afire several warehouses and dwellings of merchants and Spanish courtiers (since almost everyone was stirred up against the very name of that nation out of memory of the insolence which Alexander had employed during his pontificate).

Thirsting for Valentino's blood, Fabio had levied many soldiers from other parts of Italy and was urging Bartolommeo d'Alviano, then in the pay of the Venetians, to come with others of his family and take revenge for the many wrongs done them.

The Borgo and meadows outside the walls were full of Valentino's men; and the cardinals, who did not esteem it safe for them to assemble in the pontifical palace, met at the convent of the Church of the Minerva: at which place, contrary to ancient usage, they began, but much later than usual, to perform the obsequies of Alexander.

The coming of Gonsalvo to Rome was feared, especially because Prospero Colonna had left a certain number of soldiers at Marino, and because as a result of Valentino's reconciliation with the Colonna family it was believed that he had agreed to follow the Spanish party. But much more feared was the arrival of the French army which had been marching slowly till that day, because the public councils of the Swiss (frightened by the ill fortune of the French in the kingdom of Naples) were very wary before they would concede that the King's ministers might enlist their footsoldiers; and almost all the captains and footsoldiers who had been chosen to go there refused for the same reason, and therefore they had been enlisted much later and been slow in setting out.

But as a result of the Pontiff's death, the army, led by the Marquis of Mantua under the title of the King's lieutenant, and by the Bailli of Caen and Monsieur de Sandricourt as co-leaders, in effect, if not in name (because La Trémouille had remained sick at Parma), had marched into the territory of Siena without waiting for the Swiss, with the intention of proceeding to Rome as the King had ordered. He had also commanded the armada at Gaeta to sail to Ostia to block (as was said)

Gonsalvo, should he wish to march with his army to Rome in order to force the cardinals to elect the new pope according to his will.

Nevertheless, they waited several days between Buonconvento and Viterbo because the merchants created difficulties, as a result of the troubles then in Rome, in accepting the bills of exchange sent from France; and therefore the Swiss who had now been brought to Siena refused to march any farther ahead unless they were first paid.

At the same time, there were equally grave uprisings in the territory of Rome and many other places belonging to the Church domain and the domain of Valentino. For the Orsini and all the Roman barons were returning to their estates: the Vitelli had come back to Città di Castello; and Giampaolo* Baglioni had, with hope for a treaty, attacked Perugia, and although he had been put to flight by his enemies, nevertheless he had returned anew with many soldiers and the open help of the Florentines, and more vigorously laid assault again, entering the city not without casualties amongst his enemies and his own forces. The town of Piombino had sprung to arms, and albeit the Sienese attempted to take possession, the old Signoria returned with the favor of the Florentines. The same return to power took place in the states formerly headed by the Duke of Urbino, the lords of Pesaro, Camerino and Sinigaglia. Only Romagna, inclined toward fidelity to Valentino, remained quiet, although it was not without fear of the Venetians, who had mustered many men at Ravenna. The Romagna was inclined to devotion to Valentino because it had learned from experience how much more tolerable it had been for that region to serve all together under a single powerful lord than for each of those cities to remain under a particular prince, who could not defend them because of his weakness or benefit them because of his poverty, but rather was bound to oppress them inasmuch as his small revenues were insufficient for his support.** The Romagnoli*** also remembered that as a result of Valentino's authority and greatness and because of the honest administration of justice, that country had remained at peace and been spared the factional conflicts which had previously vexed them continually and frequently resulted in assassinations. Valentino's measures had served to make the people feel kindly disposed toward him; and similarly he had won many of them over by giving them benefits, by distributing money among picked troops, government officials and magistrates (both of his domain and of the Church), and helping ecclesiastics in matters which

---

* With typical Renaissance indifference to orthographical consistency, G. spells it thus at this point in the text, and as Giovan Pagolo earlier.

** The same idea—almost in the same words—is found in the *Ricordi*. But here in context how much more the maxim resonates!

*** "*Gli uomini*"—"the men," being much too ambiguous in English, I have specified. Romagnoli means the people of Romagna.

would be beneficial to his father: whence neither the example of the other states, where everyone was rebelling, nor the memory of their former lords, estranged them from Valentino.

Thus, although he was oppressed by so many difficulties, both the Spaniards and the French were making great overtures toward him with many promises and offers to join with them. For besides making use of his forces, they hoped to win over the votes of the Spanish cardinals for the future election. But although it was believed that Valentino was an adherent of the Spanish party as a result of the reconciliation he had reached with the Colonna family: nevertheless the Duke had been induced to that agreement only because of fear that they might join with the Orsini. Then, having declared that he did not wish to be held to anything against the King of France, he determined to follow French policy because, both in Rome where he had the French army so near, and in his other states, the King could do more to harm him or to help him than could the Spaniards.

Therefore, on the first day of September he came to an agreement with the Cardinal of San Severino and with Monsieur de Trans (the royal ambassador contracting in the name of the King) promising his troops for the Neapolitan campaign and for any other campaign against anyone except the Church; and for their part, the aforesaid agents obliged the King to protect him together with all the states which he possessed and to help him recover those which he had lost. Besides this, Valentino gave hope to turn the votes of the majority of the Spanish cardinals in favor of the Cardinal of Rouen, who, filled with the greatest hopes of obtaining the pontificate with the authority and money and arms of his King, had left France immediately after the Pope's death to come to Rome, taking the Cardinal Ascanio with him besides the Cardinal of Aragona. Cardinal Ascanio had been released from the Tower of Bourges two years before, and had since been honorably treated at the court and much favored by Rouen, in the hope that at the first vacancy of the papacy, the former reputation and friendships and great many dependents whom Ascanio used to have at the Roman court would be of much use to him: not a very solid basis of reasoning, because Valentino could not entirely dispose of the Spanish cardinals since they were more intent, as men are, on their own purposes than in paying back benefices which they had received from his father or from him, and because many of them, respectful not to offend their own king, would not be so heedless as to elect a French cardinal to the papacy; nor would Ascanio, even if he could, have agreed that Rouen should obtain the pontificate, which would perpetually diminish and extinguish any hope which he might advance for himself and for his house.

Election of New Pope: Pius III

THE ELECTION of the new pope had not yet begun; not only because the funeral of the dead pope had started later than usual (the cardinals not entering into conclave, according to the ancient custom, before the end of the obsequies, which lasted nine days), but also, in order to avoid the possibilities and perils of a schism in the midst of such confusion of affairs and such great dissension amongst princes, the cardinals present had agreed that they should allow time for the absent cardinals to arrive. And although these latter had come, the convocation of the College of Cardinals was still suspended out of suspicion that the election was not likely to be free. They were concerned about Valentino's troops, as well as the French army which had finally assembled all of its forces between Nepi and the Isola. The French, who wanted to march to Rome, refused to cross the Tiber River before the new pope had been created, either out of fear that the adverse party would force the College to elect its candidate, or because the Cardinal of Rouen wanted it thus, for his own greater security, and in the hope that it would favor him for the papacy.

After many disputes these things took shape, the College of Cardinals refusing otherwise to enter into conclave: the Cardinal of Rouen gave his assurance to the entire College that the French army would not pass Nepi and the Isola, and Valentino agreed to go to Nepi and then to Civita Castella, and sent two hundred men-at-arms and three hundred light horse under Lodovico della Mirandola and Alessandro da Trivulzio to the French camp; and the College, having ordered many footsoldiers to guard Rome, gave authority to three prelates appointed as provosts of the conclave to open it if they should hear any disturbances, so that since any of the cardinals might remain free to go whither he pleased, no one could hope to influence him by force.

Finally, the cardinals, thirty-eight in number, entered into conclave, where disagreement, which in other times used to give rise to delays, now so hastened matters that within a few days they created the new pope. Their greed among other things made it impossible for them to agree on the person they had to elect: principally because of the struggle between the cardinals dependent on the King of France, and the Spanish cardinals or those dependent on the King of Spain. But frightened at their own danger, since Roman affairs were in such a state of distrust and tumult, and out of consideration for the dangers which might unexpectedly occur in such difficult times as a result of the absence of an occupant of the Papal See, at last they decided, with the consent even of the Cardinal of Rouen (who lost more hope every day of being elected) to elect as pope Francesco Piccolomini, Cardinal of Siena, who, because he was old and ill at that time, everyone presupposed would end his days in a very short time: a cardinal surely of unblemished repute and, aside from his state of health, not unworthy of so high a post. Piccolomini assumed the name of Pius III, to revive the memory of Pius II, his uncle, who had promoted him to the dignity of the cardinalate.

The Pope having been selected, the French army no longer having any reason to delay, setting out on the march previously planned, immediately crossed the Tiber River; but neither the creation of the Pontiff, nor the setting forth of that army, quieted down the agitation in Rome.

Death of Pius. Election of Julius II

THE AGREEMENT which brought about peace between the house of Orsini and the house of Colonna was stipulated and set down at the same time at the home of the Spanish ambassador who, together with the Venetian ambassador, managed to harmonize all their differences. The union of these two houses frightened Valentino, who determined to leave Rome. Gian Paolo Orsini, who had promised the Cardinal of Rouen to lead him safely to Bracciano,* was already making preparations to go there. But now Gian Paolo and the Orsini determined to attack Valentino, and not being able to break into the Borgo through the bridge of Castel Sant' Angelo, they left Rome and marched in a long circuit to the Torrone gate, which was closed, burnt it, and having broken in, began to skirmish with several of Valentino's horsemen; and although many French soldiers who had not yet left Rome flocked to his help, nevertheless, since the enemies' forces were greater and their attack very powerful, and since Valentino's men (whose numbers had earlier greatly diminished) gave signs of abandoning him, he was forced together with the Prince of Squillace and several of the Spanish cardinals to take refuge in the Vatican palace; whence he immediately withdrew into the Castel Sant' Angelo, receiving, with the Pope's consent, the castellan's pledge (the castellan being the same who had held that post during the days of the previous Pope) to permit him to leave any time he wished; and all his men then dispersed. In this fracas, the Bailli of Caen was

---

* The Orsini were dukes of Bracciano.

wounded, although lightly, and the Cardinal of Rouen that day had great fears for his own safety.

This incident, having removed the cause of the dissensions, similarly dispelled the turmoil in Rome, so that preparations for the election of a new pope were peacefully undertaken. For Pius, not disappointing the hopes which his creation as pope had engendered among the cardinals, now, twenty-six days after his election, passed to a better life. After his death the College of Cardinals deferred entering into conclave for several days because they first wanted the Orsini to leave Rome, who had remained there to make up the number of troops, according to their treaty. The election was determined outside of the conclave; because the Cardinal of San Pietro in Vincoli, powerful in friends, reputation and riches, had drawn to himself the votes of so many cardinals (those of the contrary opinion not daring to oppose him) that entering the conclave with his election as pope already a foregone conclusion, he was raised to the pontificate that very same night (which was the night of the last day of October) without the conclave otherwise going into closed session, an example unheard of before in the memory of mankind. The new Pope assumed the name of Julius, either with reference to his first name, Giuliano, or as was conjectured, to signify the grandeur of his conceptions; or else because he would not yield to Alexander even in the excellence of his name—Julius, the second of that name amongst all past pontiffs.

Certainly everyone marveled greatly that the papacy should have been granted with such widespread agreement to a cardinal who was notoriously very difficult by nature and formidable with everyone; a man always restless, who had consumed his years in continual hardships and had inevitably offended many people and aroused the hatred and stirred up the enmity of many great men. But on the other hand, the reasons were clear why, despite every difficulty, he had been raised to so exalted a state. For he had been a very powerful cardinal for a long while; and the magnificence with which he had always surpassed everyone else, and the unusual loftiness of his spirit had won him not only a great many friends but also outstanding authority in the Roman court, where he had gained reputation of being the chief defender of ecclesiastical dignity and liberty. But his cause was promoted much more by the immoderate and infinite promises which he had made to cardinals and princes and barons, and anyone who might prove useful to him in this affair. Besides, he possessed the means of distributing money and many benefices and ecclesiastical offices, those that were his own as well as those of others, because his reputation for liberality spontaneously drew many people to come to him with offers that he dispose as he liked best of their money, names, offices and benefices. Nor did anybody

JULIUS II

Raphael's portrait in the Uffizi Gallery, Florence, must have been painted
after 1511 since the Pope began to grow his beard only at that time. The
acorn posts of the pontifical throne refer to the oak tree in the escutcheon of
the Della Rovere. Note the six rings. The Pope was very fond of jewels.

consider his promises to be much greater than he could, or should, fulfill subsequently as pope. For so long had he enjoyed the reputation of a generous and veracious man, that Alexander VI, who was such a bitter enemy of his, censuring him on every other account, admitted that Julius was a man of his word. And Julius, knowing that no one can more easily deceive others than one who usually has the reputation of never deceiving anyone, took care as soon as he won the pontificate not to blemish this encomium.

The Cardinal of Rouen was not present at this election because, having despaired of being able to win the pontificate for himself, he hoped that for past services rendered, he would remain in the close friendship of his King, as up to that time he had been reputed to be.

Also absent was the Cardinal Ascanio, although he had previously come to a reconciliation with Julius, setting aside the memory of their former disagreements which they had both had prior to the papacy of Alexander, when they had both frequented the Roman court. The Cardinal Ascanio knew Julius' nature better than did the Cardinal of Rouen, and therefore Ascanio hoped that once Julius became pope, he was likely to be equally or even more restless than he had been in his lesser state of fortune; and that such behavior on Julius' part might open the way for Ascanio's recovery of the duchy of Milan. In like manner, the Spanish cardinals consented to his election, although at first they had been most adverse to it: because observing so many others flocking to Julius' camp and therefore fearing not to be sufficiently strong to block his election, they judged it much safer to mitigate his victory by consenting to it than to exasperate him by fighting against it; and also they placed their trust to some degree in the great promises which he made them. They were further induced by Valentino's persuasions and supplications, since the Duke was now reduced to such a state of calamity that he was obliged to follow any kind of dangerous counsel, and was deceived no less than the others by his expectations; for he had been promised that his daughter would be joined in matrimony with Francesco Maria della Rovere, prefect of Rome and the Pope's nephew; and that Julius would confirm Valentino as captain of the armies of the Church, and (what was more important) would help him recover the states of Romagna, all of which, beginning with the fortresses, had already broken away from fealty to Valentino.

As soon as the Pope had ascertained the intention of the Venetians [in the Romagna], he would have sent Duke Valentino into that region. For when Julius had ascended to the papacy, he had received Duke Valentino with great honor and demonstrations of friendship, and Cesare was now living in the pontifical palace. But the Pope refrained from dispatching the Duke, in the fear that his arrival in Romagna, which previously would have been welcomed by all the people there, would now be most odious in their eyes since almost all of them had already risen in rebellion against him.

Finally, to oppose in some way the advances of the Venetians [in the Romagna], a most dangerous threat to the Ecclesiastical State, and besides, being eager that Valentino leave Rome, the Pope came to an agreement with him (besides the Pope's name, the name of the College of Cardinals participating in this agreement) that Valentino should go to La Spezia by sea, and from thence by land to Ferrara, and then to Imola where there would have arrived one hundred men-at-arms and one hundred fifty light horse who still followed his banner. Valentino having gone to Ostia with this resolution to embark, the Pope regretted that he had not accepted the fortresses; and now disposed to have them for himself in whatever way possible, Julius sent the cardinals of Volterra and Sorrento to Valentino to persuade him that in order to prevent those territories from falling into the hands of the Venetians, the Duke should hand them over to the Pope under the same promise that had been agreed upon in Rome. But since Valentino refused to do this, the Pope became wrathful and had him arrested on the galley which he had already boarded, and then brought, in a decent manner, to Magliana; whence he was taken to the Vatican, the entire court and all Rome rejoicing because of his arrest. However, he was treated honorably and gently (although under a diligent guard) because the Pope feared that the castellans [in Romagna], despairing for his safety, might not sell the fortresses to the Venetians; therefore Julius sought, by humane and peaceful means, to have the fortresses countersigned to him by Valentino.

Thus the power of the Duke Valentino, which had risen, as it were, suddenly by cruelty and fraud as much as by the arms and power of the Church, ended in even more sudden ruin: Cesare now experiencing himself those same tricks and deceits with which his father and himself had tormented so many others. Nor did his soldiers have any better fortune, because having marched to the area of Perugia in the hope of obtaining a safe conduct from the Florentines and others, they discovered the troops of the Baglioni, the Vitelli and the Sienese at their backs, and were forced to withdraw for safety into the domain of the Florentines; where, spread out between Castiglione and Cortona, and reduced to the number of four hundred horse and few footsoldiers, they were plundered by order of the Florentines, and their leader Don Michele,* taken prisoner. The Florentines then gave up Don Michele to the Pope who

---

* Also known as Michelotto. Commenting on his capture, Landucci exclaims: "*Vedi se Valentino rovinava affatto! e se gli era pagato del lume e de'* *dadi delle sue crudeltà*" (Luca Landucci, *Diario Fiorentino*, Florence, 1883, under date of 5 December 1503, p. 263).

had made very strong requests that this be done, since Julius hated all those who had served as agents of the pontificate of Alexander, and since Don Michele had been the most trusted executioner and executor of all of Valentino's villanies: although shortly after, he set him free, as by nature he easily softened with those whom he had the power of dealing with cruelly.

Venetians and Turks

THE SAME YEAR that all these grave events occurred in Italy, Bajazet, the Ottoman, and the Venetians made peace, which was greedily grasped by both sides. For Bajazet, a prince of mild ways, very unlike his ferocious father, and dedicated to literature and to the study of the sacred books of his religion, was by nature very indisposed to warfare. Therefore, although he had begun the war with the greatest preparations by land and by sea, and in the first two years had captured Naupactus, (today called Lepanto), Modon, Corone and Giunco, in the Morea, nevertheless he had not subsequently followed through the war with the same intensity. Perhaps aside from his desire for tranquillity, he was moved in this direction by the suspicion that either their own dangers or their love for their religion might align all the princes of Christendom against him. For Pope Alexander had sent certain light galliots to the aid of the Venetians, and had also stirred up, by means of money, Ladislaus, King of Bohemia and Hungary, to make war on the frontier of the Turks; and the kings of France and Spain had each sent, although not at the same time, their armies to unite with the Venetians.

But this peace was accepted even more eagerly by the Venetians, because the trade and commerce which their agents exercised in many parts of the Levant were being interrupted by the war, to their gravest detriment both public and private. Furthermore, since the city of Venice was accustomed to secure every year great abundance of wheat from lands subject to the Turks, being deprived of such supplies put them in no little difficulty. But far more than this, inasmuch as the Venetians were wont to enlarge their empire in wars with other princes, nothing horrified them so much as the power of the Ottoman Turks by whom they had been beaten every time they had made war with them. Amurathes, grandfather to Bajazet, had occupied the city of Thessalonica, now called Salonica, part of the Venetian domain, and later, Mohammed [II], his father, having been at war with them continuously for sixteen years, seized the island of Negropont from them, and a great part of the Peloponnesus which is now called Morea, Scudri and many other towns in Macedonia and Albania. The result was that, having supported the war against the Turks with the greatest difficulties and boundless expenses and without any hope of gaining any profit therefrom, and besides all this, fearing so much more that they might be attacked at the same time by other Christian princes, the Venetians were always very desirous of reaching an accord of peace with the Turks. According to the conditions of the agreement, Bajazet was given the right to retain everything which he had taken; and the Venetians retaining the island of Cephalonia, anciently called Leucas, were forced to give up to the Turk the island of Nerito, today called Santa Maura.

Importance of the Spice Trade. Discovery of the New World. Explorations of the Portuguese and Spaniards

But the war against the Turks did not create as much harm to the Venetians as did the fact that the King of Portugal had taken away the spice trade from them, to their great detriment and damage. Venetian merchants and ships used to transport spices from Alexandria, a noble city in Egypt, to Venice, and distribute them from there with great profits throughout all the provinces of Christendom. And since this was one of the most memorable things which happened in the world for many centuries, and since the harm it caused the city of Venice has some connection with Italian affairs, it is not entirely irrelevant to discuss it at some length.

Those who have thoughtfully considered and speculated deeply and with a sense of wonderment on the movements and arrangement of heavenly bodies, and have left notice of their observations to posterity, have imagined a line running from west to east through the rotundity of the sky, equally distant at every point from the North and South Poles, which they called the equinoctial line because when the sun is under it, then day and night are equal. The longitude of this line they divided in their imagination into 360 parts which they called degrees; just as the circuit of the heavens via the poles is similarly 360 degrees. After these rules had been set up, the cosmographers measured and divided the earth, drawing an equinoctial line on the earth falling perpendicularly under the celestial line drawn by the astrologers; similarly dividing this and the circumference of the earth with a line falling perpendicularly under the poles with a latitude of 360 degrees. Thus, from our Pole to the South Pole they set a distance of 180 degrees, and from each of the Poles to the equinoctial line, 90 degrees. These were the ideas generally set forth by cosmographers.

But specifically with regard to the habitable earth, given that knowledge which they had of a part of the earth below our hemisphere, they were convinced that that part of the earth below the torrid zone, represented in the astrologers' heaven (in which zone the equinoctial line is contained) as closest to the sun, was therefore uninhabitable because of its heat; and that there was no possibility of passage from our hemisphere to the lands below the torrid zone, nor to those regions lying beyond it toward the South Pole, which Ptolemy, universally considered the prince of cosmographers, called the unknown lands and seas.

Wherefore both he and others presupposed that whoever wished to pass from our hemisphere to the Arabian Sea or to the Persian Gulf, or to those parts of India which the victories of Alexander the Great first made known to our people, would be forced to go there either by land, or else coming as close as he could by the Mediterranean, continue the rest of the trip by land.

But the voyages of the Portuguese in our times have demonstrated the falsity of these opinions and presuppositions. For many years ago, navigators of the Portuguese kings, desirous of earning money by trade, began to sail along the coast of Africa, and little by little reached the Islands of Cape Verde which the ancients, according to the opinion of many, called the Islands of the Hesperides, fourteen degrees distant from the equinox toward the Arctic Pole. Then becoming ever more bold, navigating in a long sweep toward the south, the Portuguese came to the Cape of Good Hope (the promontory in Africa most distant from the equinoctial line, distant thirty-eight degrees from it). Turning from that point toward the east, the Portuguese sailed across the ocean to the Arabian Sea and the Persian Gulf where the merchants of Alexandria used to buy their spices, part of which grew there but most of which were brought thither from the Molucca Islands and other parts of India, and afterward conveyed by land over a long and difficult road and at great expense to Alexandria, where they were sold to Venetian merchants. These merchants would then bring the spices to Venice and supply all Christendom, to their own very great profits: because the Venetians, having the spice trade entirely in their hands, could set the prices as they wished; and the same ships wherein they brought the spices from Alexandria also carried many other kinds of merchandise; and those same vessels with which they conveyed their spices to France, Flanders and England and other places, also returned laden with other merchandise to Venice; and this traffic in like manner greatly increased the revenues of the Republic because of freight charges and tolls.

But now that the Portuguese were going by sea from Lisbon, the capital of Portugal, to those remote regions and making friendships with the kings of Calicut and other nearby regions on the Persian Gulf, and then penetrating by degrees into the interior, and in the course of time building fortresses in advantageous spots, and joining in alliances with some cities of the country, and in other cases reducing them to obedience by force of arms, they had appropriated in their own hands the spice trade which previously the Alexandrian merchants used to have; and bringing these by sea to Portugal, they then sent them, also by sea, to the same places where previously the Venetians had sent them.

Certainly this was marvelous navigation, over a distance of sixteen thousand miles, across seas entirely unknown, under other stars and other skies; and by means of other instruments, because once they had passed the equinoctial line they no longer had the sunset as their guide, and they were entirely deprived of the use of the magnetic compass, nor traveling on such a course could they touch land other than in unknown regions, differing in language, religion and customs, and entirely barbarous, and enemies to strangers. Nevertheless, notwithstanding all these difficulties, in the course of time the Portuguese have made these voyages so familiar, that where before they used to spend ten months on the trip, today they usually complete it in six months and with far less danger.

But even more marvelous were the voyages of the Spaniards beginning in the year 1490 at the initiative of Christopher Columbus, a Genoese. Columbus, having sailed in the Ocean Sea several times, and conjecturing by the observation of certain winds that which afterward actually happened to him, sought and obtained certain ships from the King and Queen of Spain, and sailing toward the west, after thirty-three days discovered certain islands at the extreme end of our hemisphere, about which previously there had been no knowledge: regions fortunate because of the climate, the fertility of the earth, and because (aside from certain savage peoples there who ate human flesh) almost all the inhabitants were most simple in their manners and content with what the beneficence of nature brought forth, nor were they tormented by greed or ambition; but most unfortunate inasmuch as the people, lacking a particular religion, and having no knowledge of learning, nor skill in negotiations, nor arms, nor art of war, nor science, nor experience in anything, are thus not unlike tractable and mild animals, easy prey for whoever attacks them.

Therefore, lured by the ease of taking possession of those islands, and by the richness of the booty (because abundant veins of gold have been found in them), many of the Spaniards began to live there as if in their own country. And Christopher Columbus penetrated even far-

AMERICAN ABORIGINES

The fantastic notion Europeans had of the aborigines of the New World may be seen in this illustration of nude male and female "Indians" combining the characteristics of Christian images of Adam and Eve with classical mythology: the male figure like a Poseidon and the female like an Aphrodite (FROM MONDUS NOVUS, EDITED BY BARCKHUSEN, ROSTOCK, 1505)

ther; and after him, Amerigo Vespucci, Florentine, and successively many others, have discovered other islands, and great countries of terra firma; and in some of them (although the contrary was true for the most part) they found civilized customs and hygiene, both in their public and private edifices, and in their mode of dress and conversation; but almost all these peoples were not warlike, and thus easy prey. These new lands have so much space that they are beyond any comparison far greater in size than the habitable earth previously known to us.

With new voyages and new forces, the Spaniards spread out over these territories, now digging the gold and silver out of the veins lying in many places there and in the sands of the rivers; now purchasing it at ridiculous prices from the inhabitants, and now robbing them of what they had already accumulated. In this way, the Spaniards brought an endless quantity of gold and silver to Spain, many of them sailing [to the new lands] at their own expense as a private undertaking, although with royal license, but each of them giving the King a fifth of everything which they had dug up or otherwise gotten into their hands. In fact, the boldness of the Spaniards went so far that some of their ships, having advanced fifty-three degrees toward the South Pole, always along the coast of the mainland, and then entering into a narrow sea and then sailing towards the east across a very wide ocean, and later returning by means of the navigation that the Portuguese make, have (it is now clear) circled the entire earth.

Surely the Portuguese, the Spaniards and especially Columbus, the first discoverer of this marvelous and dangerous navigation, are worthy

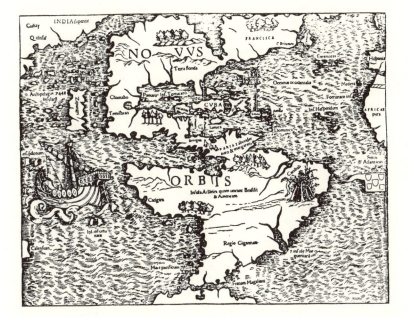

Sebastian Münster woodcut map of the New World from a 1540 edition of Ptolemy's Geographia Universalis

to be celebrated with eternal praise for their skill, their industry, their resoluteness, their vigilance, and their labors, by means of which our century came to know about such great and unforeseen things. But their achievements would have been even more worthy of celebration if they had been induced to undertake such perils and trials, not by an immoderate lust for gold and riches but by a desire, either to gain this knowledge for themselves or for others, or else to propagate the Christian faith: although this happened as a consequence to some degree, inasmuch as in many places the inhabitants have been converted to our religion.

These voyages have made it clear that the ancients were deceived in many ways regarding a knowledge of the earth: that one could pass beyond the equinoctial line; that one could live in the torrid zone; as also, contrary to the opinion of the ancients, we have come to understand through the voyages of others that one can dwell in those zones near the Poles which the ancients affirmed were uninhabitable because of the immoderate cold resulting from the position of the heaven being so remote from the course of the sun. These voyages have also revealed what some of the ancients believed and others denied, namely that there are other inhabitants under our feet whom they called the Antipodes.

These voyages have not only confuted many things which had been affirmed by writers about terrestrial matters, but besides this, they have given some cause for alarm to interpreters of the Holy Scriptures, who are accustomed to interpret those verses of the Psalms in which it is declared that the sound of their songs had gone over all the earth and their words spread to the edges of the world, as meaning that faith in Christ had spread over the entire earth through the mouths of the Apostles: an interpretation contrary to the truth, because since no knowledge of these lands had hitherto been brought to light, nor have any signs or relics of our faith been found there, it is unworthy to be believed, either that faith in Christ had existed there before these times, or that so vast a part of the world had never before been discovered or found by men of our hemisphere.*

The Pope . . . made every effort to have Valentino concede the fortresses of Forlì, Cesena and Bertinoro to him. These were the only fortresses in the Romagna that were still loyal to the Duke because Antonio degli Ordelaffi, a few days before, had taken the fortress of Forlimpopoli by bribing the castellan. Valentino agreed to give the Pope possession of the castle of Cesena, but when Pietro de Oviedo, a Spaniard, went there to take it in the Pontiff's name, the castellan had him hanged,

* This final paragraph is cut out of all editions of the *Storia* before 1774.

declaring that it would be dishonorable for him to obey his lord while the latter was in prison, and that anyone who presumed to make such a request deserved to be punished. For this reason, the Pope, feeling that it was hopeless to be able to obtain these fortresses without first liberating Valentino, came to an agreement with him (which agreement was dispatched to the consistory in the form of a bull for greater security) that Valentino should be placed in the fortress of Ostia under surveillance of the Spaniard Bernardin Carvajial, Cardinal of Santa Croce, who was fully empowered to let him go as soon as he had restored the fortresses of Cesena and Bertinoro to the Pope, and turned over the deed of the fortress of Forlì to the Pontiff, and deposited a security of fifteen thousand ducats in the banks at Rome. The castellan of Forlì promised to render up that castle when he had received the assignation and the aforesaid sum of money to cover expenses which he claimed to have incurred. But the Pope had an altogether different intention. He thought that although he didn't want openly to break the pledge he had given, yet he intended to procrastinate with regard to the Duke's liberation, either out of fear that once freed, the castellan of Forlì would refuse to give up the fortress out of memory of the injuries he had received from his father and himself, or because of the hatred which, with good reason, everybody bore him.

Suspecting this, Valentino secretly sought to have the Great Captain [Gonsalvo] give him safe conduct to go to Naples,* and send two galleys to convey him from Ostia. Gonsalvo having agreed to this request, the Cardinal of Santa Croce, who was equally suspicious, gave the Duke leave to depart without advising the Pope, as soon as the Cardinal learned that besides the fifteen thousand ducats security deposited in Rome, the castellans of Cesena and Bertinoro had turned over the fortresses. Meanwhile, Valentino, without waiting for the galleys which the Great Captain was supposed to have sent him, secretly went by land to Nettuno whence he sailed in a little barque to the fortress of Mondragone and thence overland to Naples, where he was received joyously and with great honor by Gonsalvo. In Naples, after frequent secret consultations with Gonsalvo, the Duke besought him to give him the possibility of proceeding to Pisa with the proposal that if he could stop at that city, the greatest benefits to the cause of the French King would result from it. Gonsalvo seemed to approve of this plan; and offering him galleys to convey him thither, and giving him the power to levy such footsoldiers in the kingdom which he proposed to take with him, he fed the Duke with this hope until such time as Gonsalvo might receive a reply from

---

* After he had practically destroyed the French army on the banks of the Garigliano River (Dec. 1503), in which Piero de' Medici was drowned, Gonsalvo of Cordova took possession of the entire kingdom of Naples on behalf of his sovereign. He governed Naples until 1507.

his King confirming what he had decided to do. Thus every day Gonsalvo was consulting with Valentino with regard to the situation in Pisa and Tuscany, and at the same time Alviano was offering to attack the Florentines because of his desire to bring about the restoration of the Medici in Florence.

But the galleys having already been prepared, and the footsoldiers ready to depart the following day, and although Valentino had spoken at great length that evening with Gonsalvo, who had bidden him farewell with great demonstrations of affection, embracing him as he departed, as soon as the Duke had left the chamber, Gonsalvo (practicing the same deceit that old Ferdinand of Aragon was said to have previously employed against Iacopo Piccinino) had him detained in the castle. At the same time, Gonsalvo dispatched orders to the house where the Duke was lodging to deprive him of the safe conduct that had been made out for him before he left Ostia.

Gonsalvo excused all this with the allegation that since his King had commanded him to take the Duke prisoner, such a royal commandment bore more weight than the safe conduct he had granted, because security given on the sole authority of an official was only valid so far as his lord wished. Furthermore, it was necessary to keep Borgia under arrest because, not satisfied with so many iniquities which he had committed in the past, he was now seeking to alter the possessions of others in the future, to set new plots in motion, to sow seeds of dissension and cause pernicious flames to break out all over Italy. And shortly afterward he sent him in a light galley as a prisoner to Spain (leaving only one page among his followers to serve him), and there he was incarcerated in the fortress of Medina del Campo.

About this time, truce was made by land and by sea, valid for Italy as well as for the nations beyond the mountains, between the King of France and the King of Spain. This truce was greatly desired by the King of France and willingly consented to by the King of Spain, because he judged it better to stabilize in this way, with greater security and tranquillity, those acquisitions which he had already gained, rather than by means of new wars which, being full of danger and expenses, often end differently than one hopes. The conditions were that each of the two parties were to keep what he possessed, [and] that there should be free trade for their subjects throughout all the realms of both parties, except in the kingdom of Naples . . .

And yet although its enemies had all been expelled, the kingdom of Naples did not enjoy the fruits of peace. The Spanish soldiers, who had not been paid for more than a year, were dissatisfied because the Great Captain had, in order that they might be maintained until he could raise their pay, billeted them in various places where they were living at the expense of the people. But since they were indiscreetly left to their own will (which soldiers call lodging at discretion), they had broken the reins of obedience to the displeasure of the Great Captain, and entered into Capua and Castellamare which they refused to leave unless their back wages were paid them. Inasmuch as this involved very great sums of money which could not be raised without laying excessive burdens on the kingdom, which was exhausted and drained by the long wars, the result was that conditions were miserable; the medicine having proved no less harmful than the illness they were seeking to cure, matters all the more grievous insofar as they were new and without any previous examples. Because, although soldiers had always been licentious and troublesome to the people ever since ancient times, when military discipline was severely administered, nevertheless, everything not being as yet entirely chaotic, they lived for the most part on their pay, and their license did not go beyond intolerable limits. But the Spaniards were the first to begin in Italy to live wholly upon the substance of the people, giving as the reason—and perhaps necessity—for their licentiousness the fact that they were poorly paid by their kings who lacked funds. And from this beginning, the depravities grew ever worse, because the imitation of evil is always greater than the example, whereas on the contrary, the imitation of good is always less. Thus the Spaniards themselves and the Italians also began then to act in the same manner whether they were paid or not paid; so that to the great dishonor of the military profession of our day, the possessions of friends are no more secure from the wickedness of soldiers than those of the enemy.

The truce drawn up between the kings of France and Spain, which induced not a few people to believe that peace would follow soon after, and to some degree the capture of Valentino, quieted things down entirely in the Romagna.

But the fact that the wars had ceased in all other parts of Italy did not prevent a resumption of the Florentine war against the Pisans at the beginning of that summer, according to their custom.

The Florence–Pisa War Continues

Still not exhausted by their great expenses, and judging nothing impossible that might give them hope of achieving their desired goal, the Florentines worked out a new way of harming the Pisans, by attempting to deflect the River Arno which runs by Pisa from the tower of Fagiana, five miles from the city via a new bed into the pool which is between Pisa and Livorno. In this way they would cut the supply line from the sea to Pisa via the Arno; and because the surrounding land is low-lying, the rains would not have any exit to the sea and thus Pisa would remain almost as if in the midst of a swamp; furthermore, because of the difficulty of crossing the Arno, the Pisans would not be able in the future to get up into the hills to hinder traffic from Livorno to Florence; and they would have been forced to fortify that part of Pisa through which the river entered and left, lest it be open to enemy attack. But this enterprise, which was begun with the greatest hope and carried on with even greater expenses, proved to be in vain: because as often happens, although such-like projects may be almost palpably demonstrated in the measured plans, yet experience will find them failing (which is the most certain proof of how great a distance there is between planning things and putting them in operation). Besides, there were many other difficulties not previously discussed, caused by the course of the river which, when they thought to narrow it, abated of itself, eating away its channel so that the bottom of the pool where they wanted it to enter proved to be higher than the bed of the Arno, contrary to the predictions of many engineers and hydraulic experts. Furthermore, fortune proved herself malignant and contrary against the Florentines who were so desirous of capturing Pisa. For the galleys which they had manned and sent to Villefranche to capture a ship of the Pisans loaded with grain, on their return were so harassed by winds near Rapallo that they foundered, the captain and crew saving themselves with great difficulty.

But the Florentines having tried arms and terror against the Pisans, now decided (not to leave any method untried) to attempt benignity and gentleness; therefore they passed a new law which granted that whatever Pisan citizen or peasant should, within a certain period, go to live in his house or on his land, would be granted pardon for any fault committed, with full restitution of his goods. Despite this opportunity, very few honestly left Pisa, but a great many, almost all of whom were useless persons, were permitted by the others to take their leave, which would at the same time lighten the burden of the famine ravaging the city, and also make it easier in the future to help with such revenues those who had remained. . . .

In this way, the perils of the Pisans were to some degree diminished, but not so much thereby that they were not still in the gravest straits because of their extreme poverty and famine; but holding any other thing in less horror than the name of the Florentines, although the spirit of the peasants sometimes wavered, they determined to suffer any extremity rather than yield. Therefore they offered to give themselves up to the Genoese, with whom they had fought so many times for reasons of empire or security, and by whom they had been oppressed and over-powered in ancient times.

[*King Federigo of Naples dies in 1504 "entirely bereft of hope to recover by accord the realm of Naples, although he had earlier been convinced (his own desire beguiling him) that the King of Spain would be more inclined to this than the French King, not consider-ing that in our century it was vain to hope for so magnanimous a restitution of so noble a realm, such examples being rare even in ancient times when men were much more disposed than now to acts of virtue and nobility . . ."]**

At the end of this year 1504, Isabella, Queen of Spain, died, a lady of most honorable customs and most lofty ideas, magnanimous and pru-dent during her reign. To her properly belonged the kingdom of Castille, which is the most powerful and greatest part of Spain, which she inherited after the death of her brother Henry, but not without blood and war.

. .

The Queen's death caused new troubles in Spain; but Italian affairs (as will be subsequently told) were disposed toward tranquillity and a new peace. In the year 1505, things continued in the same tranquillity of the previous year; that is, were it not for minor disturbances brought about by the quarrel between the Florentines and the Pisans, this year would have seen a total cessation of arms inasmuch as some of the potentates were eager for peace, and the others who were more inclined to war were impeded for various reasons.

[*The death of Queen Isabella removes certain difficulties touching on the honor of the French King and his fear to make the Archduke his enemy; and peace is established between Spain and France. Among the articles of peace between the French King and Ferdinand, King of Spain, it was agreed that:*]

Neither of the parties would undertake any action against those which either of them might name, and they both named the Pope in Italy, and the King of France named the Florentines; and that to strength-en this treaty, which both kings intended to be a perpetual confedera-tion in defense of their states, the King of France would be bound with one hundred lances and six thousand footsoldiers, and Ferdinand with three hundred lances, two thousand pikemen and six thousand footsoldiers. After peace had been made, wherein the King of England pledged the

---

* A romantic reason which in the name of realism Guicciardini adduces in his criticism of Machiavelli's exemplary use of antiquity.

observance of both parties, almost all of the Angevin barons who were in France, dismissed by the King, went with Queen Germaine* into Spain, having received, at their departure, very few tokens of gratitude from the stubborn King. And Isabella, widow of Federigo, having leave also to depart from the kingdom of France, went to Ferrara because she refused to place her children in the power of the Catholic King.

In Ferrara, Ercole d'Este having died a short time before, and his son Alfonso succeeding to the dukedom, there occurred at the end of this year a tragic occurrence similar to those of the ancient Thebans, but for more trivial reasons if the unbridled fury of love is more trivial than the burning ambition to rule. It so happened that the Cardinal Ippolito d'Este was fervently enamored of a young maid, his kinswoman, who with no less fervor was loved by Don Giulio, bastard brother to Ippolito; when the girl confessed to the Cardinal Ippolito that what attracted her beyond all else and fanned her love to such heat was the beauty of Don Giulio's eyes, the infuriated Cardinal, having waited for a convenient moment when Giulio would be hunting outside of the city, set about him in the field, and forcing him to dismount from his horse, ordered several of his pages to pluck out his brother's eyes as rivals of his love; and he had the heart to remain present during such a horrid act, which later resulted in the most serious troubles among the brothers. Thus ended the year one thousand five hundred and five.

* Germaine de Foix, niece of Louis   Foix. Became second wife of Ferdinand
XII of France and sister of Gaston de   of Spain in 1505.

BOOK

7

[*The years 1506 and 1507 are notable especially for the unexpected sight of a Pope in arms leading his troops to reoccupy the cities of central Italy. Pope Julius II's declaration that he would go in person to "deliver from the hands of tyrants" the cities of Bologna and Perugia seems so ridiculous to the King of France, when he hears about it, that "wishing to criticize him for his notorious drunkenness, he said that the Pope must have been too overheated with wine the night before." Nevertheless, after laying the cornerstone of the new Saint Peter's in April 1506, Julius issues forth from Rome at the head of 500 men-at-arms, marches north, and accepting a capitulation made with Giampaolo Baglioni, tyrant of Perugia, enters "Perugia without any soldiers, so that Giampaolo could have taken him prisoner with his entire court, if he had known how to make resound throughout the world, in a matter of such importance, that perfidy which had already made his name infamous in things of much less moment."* Julius goes on to capture Bologna in the same spectacular fashion. The Vicar of Christ has become Mars.*

Amidst these events Duke Valentino (Cesare Borgia) escapes from prison in Spain and later dies in battle while commanding men-of-war of the King of Navarre. A Genoese rebellion against the French is put down; the King of France makes a triumphal entrance into that city. While this is taking place Maximilian convokes the Diet of Constance, a meeting of the free towns and princes of Germany, where he makes a speech reaffirming German rights to the imperial crown against what he

---

* In *The Discourses*, Chapter XXVII, Machiavelli had earlier made a similar remark: "*Fu notata da gli uomini prudenti, che col Papa erano, la temerità del Papa, e la viltà di Giovampagolo; ne potevano stimare donde si venisse, che quello non havesse con sua perpetua fama oppresso ad un tratto il nimico suo, e se arrichito di preda, sendo col Papa tutti li Cardinali con tutte le loro delitie. . . .* Wise men who were with the Pope remarked on the Pope's temerity and Giampaolo's cowardice; nor could they understand how it happened that he had not, *to his everlasting fame*, overwhelmed his enemy at one blow, and enriched himself with booty, since with the Pope were all the cardinals with all their baubles" (italics mine—s. a.). Both men, one with fire and one with ice, reprove Baglioni for letting a great chance slip by!

considers French encroachments and reaffirms his intention to descend into Italy to receive the crown from the hands of the Pope.

The Venetians debate the question whether to lend their favor to Maximilian or to the King of France; they finally decide to offer Maximilian passage through their territory if he comes without an army, otherwise not. At the beginning of 1508 Maximilian invades their lands and war breaks out in the regions of Trent and Friuli; but the Venetians soon conclude a truce with Maximilian in contradiction to the King of France.]

BOOK

8

The Woes of Italy Caused by the Ambition of Princes

THE DISEASES OF ITALY WERE NOT SUCH, NOR THEIR FORCES SO LITTLE WEAKENED, THAT THEY COULD BE CURED WITH SIMPLE MEDICINES; rather, as often happens in bodies overflowing with corrupt humors, a remedy employed to cure disorder in one part generates even more pernicious and dangerous ills. So it was with the treaty drawn up between the King of the Romans [Maximilian] and the Venetians. Instead of the peace and tranquillity that many hoped must result from it, the truce gave rise to endless calamities among the Italians and even bloodier and more devastating wars than in the past. For although there had already been, for fourteen years in Italy, so many wars and so many changes of state, yet because these things often ended without bloodshed, or else the killings took place, for the most part, amongst the barbarians themselves, the people* had suffered less than the princes. But now the door opening to new discords in the future, there followed throughout Italy, and against the Italians themselves, the cruelest accidents, endless murders, sackings and destruction of many cities and towns, military licentiousness no less pernicious to their friends than to their enemies, religion violated, and holy things trampled under foot with less reverence and respect than for profane things.

The reason for such ills, generally considered, was as almost always, the ambition and greed of princes; but considering the matter more closely, these troubles originated from the rash and overly insolent actions of the Venetian Senate. Hence those difficulties which, up until that time, had kept the King of the Romans and the King of France from joining together against the Venetians, were now removed. One of their enemies,

---

* Guicciardini actually says "*i populi*" —"the peoples"—indicating that he conceived of Italy as plural, a congeries of various populations. Machiavelli was equally aware of this but idealistically sounded the clarion for national unity. Guicciardini was no trumpet player.

DE CAESARE ET VENETIS

The brazen frog dares to make overtures to the eagle who has cast him back into his slimy marsh. Thus every resurgence of the dreaded and envied Venetian power was suspected not only by the other Italian states but also by the Germans. (SATIRICAL ENGRAVING FROM ULRICH VON HUTTEN, AD DIVUM MAXIMILIANUM BELLO IN VENETOS EUNTEM EXHORTATIO, 1517)

exasperated beyond bounds, the Venetians reduced to the greatest desperation; and at the same time, they stirred up the other to a state of the highest indignation, or at least gave him cause to disclose, under an apparent pretext, what he had long desired. For [Maximilian] Caesar, nettled by all the ignominies and harm inflicted on him, and having, instead of acquiring the states of others, lost a part of his own inheritance, was not in the mood to neglect any opportunity whereby he might be indemnified for such insults and losses which he had suffered; and the Venetians imprudently intensified this disposition of his anew after the truce had been drawn up; for, not abstaining to provoke him no less with vain demonstrations than with effects, they received Alviano into Venice with the greatest pomp and almost as a conqueror. The King of France, although at the beginning he had given some hope of ratifying the truce, expressing afterward how greatly he was displeased, complained that the Venetians had presumed to name and include him as adhering to the treaty, and that having seen to their own peace, they had left all of the cares of the war on his shoulders.

· ·
·

In a very short space of time, these states of mind which had been stirred up in both the Caesar and the King began to manifest themselves. For Maximilian, having no confidence in his own strength, nor any more hope that the German princes and people would resent the injuries done him, was inclined to join with the King of France against the Venetians as the only remedy to recover his honor and lost states; and the King was of a similar disposition since this new act of disdain had renewed his memory of the offenses which he convinced himself he had received from them in the Neapolitan wars, and he was incited by his ancient greed for Cremona and other towns which had been possessed for a long time by the dukes of Milan . . .

At the same time, the Pope also stirred up the King against the Venetians, since besides his old reasons, the Pontiff was inflamed against them with new causes of hatred. He was convinced that the Venetians were responsible for the fact that the exiles of Forlì, who had withdrawn to Faenza, had attempted to break into that city, and because the Bentivoglios had found asylum in Venetian domain after they had been expelled by the King out of the duchy of Milan. Furthermore, the Pope was angry because the Venetians were in many ways less respectful than ever regarding the Roman court, and most recently they had greatly agitated the Pope's mind when he had conferred the bishopric of Vicenza (vacated as a result of the death of the Cardinal of San Pietro in Vincoli, his nephew) upon Sisto, likewise his nephew, surrogating him with the dignities of the cardinalate and the benefices thereof.

On this occasion the Venetian Senate, scorning this transfer of legacy, had elected a gentleman of Venice; who, when the Pope refused to confirm him, boldly dared to name himself bishop of Vicenza by election of the most excellent Council of the Pregati. Infuriated by these events, the Pope first sent Maximus, secretary to the Cardinal of Narbonne, to the King, and afterward the Cardinal himself, who newly succeeding the late Cardinal of Aix in his bishopric, was called the Cardinal of Aix; these being well received and heard by the King, brought back to the Pope various schemes to be carried out either without the Emperor or joining with him. But the Pope was more inclined to quarrel than to come to any decisions because, on the one hand, his mind was struggling with an eager desire to set off a war against the Venetians, and on the other, he was held back by the fear of being forced to depend too much on the greatness of others; and much more was he restrained by his long-standing jealousy against the Cardinal of Rouen, wherefore the Pope was greatly troubled that powerful armies of the French King would cross into Italy.

The League of Cambrai

THOSE difficulties which the Pope could not resolve were finally deliberated on by [Maximilian] Caesar and the French King in secret negotiations against the Venetians. And to set these agreements down in a treaty, there assembled in the town of Cambrai, acting for Caesar, Madame Margaret, his daughter—under whose rule Flanders was governed, as well as those other states which had descended to King Philip [I of Spain] through his maternal inheritance—followed by Matthew Lang, very close counselor to the Emperor, to negotiate the treaty; and on the King's side, the Cardinal of Rouen who spread the rumor that the purpose of the negotiations was to draw up a peace treaty between the Archduke and the Duke of Gueldres,* who had agreed on a truce of forty days; taking care that the Venetians should not learn the true reasons for these negotiations. But the Cardinal of Rouen assured the Venetian ambassador with the most solemn oaths that his King wished to maintain his alliance with them.

Following the Cardinal there also came the ambassador of the King of Aragon who tended rather to agree than to set up opposition because, although the King of Aragon had been the prime mover of these conferences between Maximilian and the French King, the negotiations were subsequently carried on without him, since they were both convinced that the good fortune of the King of France would trouble him, just as any increase in Caesar's power would be held in suspicion by the government of Castile; and that therefore, in regard to these things the King of Aragon's thoughts were not in conformity with his words.

At any rate, within a few days a final agreement was reached at

---

* The lands of the Duke of Gueldres were strategically important to the French to permit passage of mercenary German troops.

*DE GIULIO II P. MAX. ORBEM CHRISTIANUM IN
ARMA CONCITANTE*

*Pope Julius, wearing a cuirass and in full armor except for the papal tiara,
instigates the King of France, wearing the crown with the fleur-de-lis, and the
King of Spain and the Emperor, also recognizable by their crowns. At their
feet the Venetian lion.* (SATIRICAL ENGRAVING FROM ULRICH VON HUTTEN, AD
DIVUM MAXIMILIANUM BELLO IN VENETOS EUNTEM EXHORTATIO, 1517)

Cambrai without communicating any part of the agreement to the ambassador of the Catholic King [Ferdinand] until everything had been
settled; and on the following day, which was the tenth of December, the
treaty was confirmed with solemn ceremonies in the cathedral, sworn to
by Madame Margaret, the Cardinal of Rouen and the Spanish ambassador, and nothing else was published except that the Pope and each of these
princes had drawn up a treaty of perpetual peace and confederation. But
in secret articles there were contained very important clauses which were
ambitious and to a great degree and in many ways contrary to the pacts

which Maximilian and the King of France had with the Venetians. Therefore, these secret articles were cloaked with a very pious preamble (as if the diversity of words were sufficient to transmute the substance of facts) in which was set forth a common desire to undertake a war against the enemies of the name of Christ, and the obstacles which the Venetians had set up against this undertaking by ambitiously seizing the lands of the Church. And it was further declared that, wishing to remove this obstacle by henceforth proceeding unitedly toward such a holy and necessary undertaking, and persuaded by the counsels of the Pope, the Cardinal of Rouen acting as his deputy and by his authority, and as deputy and by the authority of the King of France; and by Madame Margaret, delegated and authorized by the King of the Romans, and as ruler of the archduchy and states of Flanders; and with the consent of the ambassador of the King of Aragon, delegated and authorized by his King—they were resolved to wage war against the Venetians in order to recover, each one in his own right, those territories which the Venetians had usurped, set forth as follows: on the part of the Pontiff—Faenza, Rimini, Ravenna and Cervia; for the Emperor—Padua, Vicenza and Verona, belonging to him in the name of the Empire; and Friuli and Trevigi, belonging to the house of Austria; and for the King of France— Cremona, Ghiaradadda, Brescia, Bergamo and Crema; and for the King of Aragon—the towns and seaports given as security by Ferdinand, King of Naples. The secret articles also stipulated that the Most Christian King* was obliged to participate personally in the war and begin it the first day of the next April, at which time also the Pontiff and Catholic King would also enter the war; and that in order that Caesar might have just cause not to observe the truce which he had drawn up [with the Venetians], the Pope should request help of him as protector of the Church; after which request, [Maximilian] Caesar should send him at least one condottiere, and be bound for forty days after the French King had unleashed the war, to personally attack the Venetian state. Furthermore, that whichever of them should have recovered their own territories would be held to help the others until they had entirely recovered theirs, and that all of them were obliged to a defense of whichever of them should be threatened by the Venetians in the lands which they had retaken; that none of them should sign any agreement without common consent; that within three months the Duke of Ferrara, the Marquis of Mantua and anyone who claimed that the Venetians were occupying any lands of theirs might be nominated to join the League; and that once having been nominated, they would enjoy all the benefits of the League as much as

---

* The fact that G. employs the title *Re Cristianissimo* for the first time here, and *Re Cattolico* shortly after, not to mention that *Pontefice* appears in the same context is not without its pinch of irony.

the principals, and would have the right to seize by themselves those things which they had lost; that the Pope should admonish the Venetians under the gravest penalty and censure to restore those Church lands which they had occupied: and that he should be the judge of the contention between Bianca Maria, the Emperor's wife, and the Duke of Ferrara with regard to the inheritance of her sister Anna, former wife of the aforesaid Duke; that the Emperor should invest the King of France, for himself, for Francis of Angoulême, and their male descendants, with the duchy of Milan, for which investiture the King would pay him one hundred thousand ducats; that the Emperor or the Archduke would not make any move during this war and six months thereafter against the Catholic King with regard to the government and titles of the kingdom of Castile; that the Pope should exhort the King of Hungary to enter into the present confederation; that within four months each of the allies should nominate his confederates and adherents, but none of them should be empowered to nominate the Venetians, nor any of the subjects or feudatories of any of the confederates; that each of the contracting parties should be held to ratify the treaty within the next sixty days.

. .
.

The new confederation having been concluded in this form, but those parts of it pertaining to the Venetians being kept as secret as possible, the Cardinal of Rouen departed the following day from Cambrai, the Bishop of Paris and Alberto Pio, Count of Carpi, having first been sent to the Emperor to receive his ratification in the name of the French King, who, without any delay ratified and confirmed the treaty under oath, with the same solemnity with which it had been set forth in the cathedral of Cambrai. And with these seeds of gravest wars ended the year one thousand five hundred and eight.

. .
.

It is certain that this agreement, although declaredly drawn up with the authority of the Pope and the King of Aragon [Ferdinand] was in fact arrived at without either their consent or commission; since Maximilian and the Most Christian King were convinced that they would have to agree, partly for their own benefit, and partly because in the present state of things neither of them would dare reject their authority: especially the King of Aragon to whom, although this agreement was unwelcome (because he feared that it would permit too great an increase in the power of the French King and therefore he, Aragon, considered the security of the entire kingdom of Naples more important than the recovery of the part held by the Venetians), nevertheless, feigning to show a ready disposition contrary to what he really felt, he immediately ratified the treaty with equal solemnity.

Even more doubtful was the Pope, insofar as his mind was typically divided: on the one hand, there was his desire to recover the lands of the Romagna, and his hatred against the Venetians; and on the other, was his fear of the French King. Furthermore, he felt that it would be dangerous for himself and for the Apostolic See if the Emperor's power should begin to spread too far in Italy. Therefore, judging it more useful to obtain part of what he desired by treaty than everything by war, he tried to induce the Venetian Senate to render up Rimini and Faenza to him; admonishing them that the dangers threatening them as a result of the union of so many princes would be even greater if the Pontiff concurred in the League, because he could not refuse to oppress them with arms, spiritual and temporal. But if they restored the lands taken from the Church during his pontificacy, thus restoring his honor together with his lands, he would have just reason not to ratify what had been done in his name but without his consent; and removing papal authority from the alliance would easily reduce it to nothing since it already contained so many difficulties within itself. Julius also assured the Venetians that they could be certain that he would employ all his authority and effort as far as he could, for no other purpose than to see to it that the power of the barbarians should not increase in Italy, a power no less dangerous to the Apostolic See than to the others. Upon this demand, the Venetian Senate assembled several times, some judging it to be of the greatest importance to separate the Pope from his allies; others considering it an unworthy action which would not suffice anyway to deflect war from them. Finally, the wisest and best counsels would have prevailed had not Domenico Trevisan, a senator of the greatest authority and one of the procurators of the very rich church of San Marco (which in the Venetian Republic is an honor next in importance after the doge), rose to his feet and spoke in opposition. With great oratorical skill and careful reasoning, Trevisan sought to convince the senators that it was an action most contrary to the dignity and profits of that renowned and grand Republic to give up those lands demanded by the Pope, since whether the Pontiff was allied or separated from the other confederates would have little effect either to augment or diminish their perils. For although they had used the Pope's name in drawing up the treaty in order that their cause might seem less dishonest, in effect, the treaty of Cambrai had been arrived at without him, and therefore if the Pope should break away, they would not proceed more slowly or with less ardor in carrying out the plans they had already decided upon. On the contrary, the forces of the Pope were not so valorous that they had to be bought at such a price.

Consequently, if the Venetians should be assaulted by the others at the same time, they could defend those cities with very small garrisons. The armies of the Church (the infamy of the military, according to the common proverb) were insufficient in themselves either to conquer or affect in any way whatever the outcome of the war. And amidst the actions and heat of temporal arms, the threats of and reverence for spiritual arms had little effect, since men had no need to fear that the arms of the Church would harm them any more in this war than they had done in many others, especially during the war waged against Ferrara, when the armies of the Church had not been powerful enough to prevent them from obtaining an honorable peace for themselves although infamous for the rest of Italy, which by broad agreement, and at a time when the country flourished with riches and arms and valor, was universally banded against them. And justly so, for it was not likely that the omnipotent God would want the effects of his severity and of his mercy, of his anger and of his peace, to be left in the hands of so ambitious and proud a man, addicted to wine and many other pleasures; and that he should use this power according to his own greed rather than in consideration of justice and the benefit of Christendom. Furthermore, since this pontificate was no more faithful to its sacerdotal pledges than the others had almost always been, he saw no reason why they should feel certain that if they turned over Faenza and Rimini to Julius, he would not join with the others to recover Ravenna and Cervia, since he had no greater respect for promises made than is typical of popes, who, in order to justify their frauds, have decreed, among other laws, that notwithstanding any contract, any promise, any benefit received, the Church could retract and directly impugn any obligations which its own prelates had solemnly made.

And although, argued Trevisan, the League had been drawn up between Maximilian and the King of France with great ardor, the minds of the other allies were not of the same disposition, because the Catholic King had adhered to it unwillingly, and the Pope showed obvious signs of his usual vacillations and suspicions. Therefore the League of Cambrai was no more to be feared than those alliances made at other times at Trent and later at Blois with equal ardor by the selfsame Maximilian and King Louis, since many difficulties stood in the way of the execution of things which had been decided upon, which by their very nature were almost impossible to be carried out. Therefore, the main concern and deliberation of this Senate should be to seek to separate Caesar from this confederacy, which might easily be hoped for in view of Maximilian's nature and his needs, and his long-standing hatred against the French. And once having divided him from the alliance, there was no danger whatever of an outbreak of war; for the King of France, abandoned by him, would not dare attack them any more than he had dared in times past. In all public matters, one must carefully take the beginnings of things into account, because afterward men are unable to deviate from decisions already made and carried on for a long time, without the gravest danger and dishonor. And just as their forefathers, so they also subsequently took advantage of every opportunity to expand their dominion, openly aspiring always to greater glory, and for this reason they had become hated by everyone, partly for fear, partly in grief at what had been taken from them. And although it was known long ago that this hatred might give rise to some great changes of state, yet they had not abstained on that account to seize opportunities as they were offered them, nor was it now a remedy for present dangers to begin to yield up part of what they possessed, since this would not quench but rather kindle the souls of those who hated them, who would take courage from their cowardice. Inasmuch as it was an old maxim all over Italy for many years now that the Venetian Senate never relinquished what had once fallen into their hands, who could fail to understand that acting otherwise at this time, and so cowardly, could only be the result of utmost despair in their capacity to defend themselves against imminent perils? Once having begun to yield anything, no matter how small, would diminish the reputation and ancient splendor of their Republic; and hence greatly increase their peril. And it is incomparably far more difficult for one who has begun to decline, to maintain what he still has, even against the most minimal dangers, than for one who strives to keep his dignity and degree, and thereby acts promptly, making no sign whatever of willingness to yield, against whoever seeks to oppress him. Hence, it was necessary either courageously to reject those first demands, or yielding to them, to keep in mind that they would have to consent to many others. And from this would result in a very short time the total annihilation of their domains, followed by the loss of their own liberty. In the times of their ancestors, and similarly in their own times, the Republic of Venice had withstood the gravest wars with Christian princes; and since they had remained constant and resolute in soul, they had always brought these wars to a most glorious conclusion. So, although their present difficulties might seem even greater, they should hope for the same success; because now their power and prestige were greater, and in wars waged in common by many princes against a single state, the fear is usually more than the effects; once their initial attacks have abated, diverse opinions soon spring up amongst them, and weaken their mutual trust. The Senate should rest its hope in the fact that, aside from all the preparations and remedies that they themselves should set under way, God, the most Just of Judges, would not abandon a republic born and bred in perpetual freedom, the ornament and splendor of all Europe. Nor would He permit that city to be trodden underfoot by the ambition of princes, under the pretense of

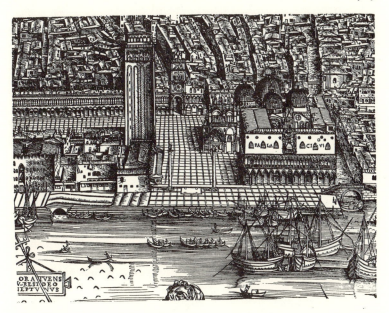

*Detail of a large wood engraving of Venice by Jacopo de' Barberi, 1500, show-
ing the Palace of the Doges facing the Lagoon, the Piazetta with the two
columns bearing the Winged Lion of Saint Mark and Saint Theodore on a
crocodile, the Basilica, the Clock Tower, the Campanile, and the Procuratie
Vecchio on the Piazza of San Marco*

preparing a war against the infidels—that city which had been, with such
piety and religion, for so many years the bulwark of all Christendom.

This speech of Domenico Trevisan so stirred the minds of the
majority that the worst counsels prevailed, despite the arguments of many
senators noted for their prudence and held in great esteem (as had often
been for some years now almost inevitable in that Senate). The result
was that the Pope, who had deferred his ratification till the very last day,
now ratified the League;* but with the express declaration that he would
not commit any unfriendly action against the Venetians until the French
King had begun the war.

> [*The aim of the League of Cambrai, instigated by Pope Julius, is to
> "reduce your Venice to its original condition of a fishing village,"*

* *Però il Pontefice, il quale avevo   one of the most monstrous sentences in
differito insino all'ultimo dì assegnato   the Storia.
alla ratificazione il ratificare, ratificò—

*as the belligerent Pontiff said to the Venetian envoy Pisani. Julius'
quarrel with the republic of the lagoons was over the Venetian's
refusal to restore the cities of Romagna to the Holy See. On April
27, 1509, the Pope fires a bull of excommunication against the now
not so serene republic of Venice. War between the Serenissima and
the forces of the League had already broken out on the fifteenth of
that month.*

*A single battle won by the French (whose army also included
Swiss, Gascons and Italians) at Ghiaradadda—also known as Agna-
dello—on May 14, 1509, suffices to smash the power of the proud
republic. Swiftly Caravaggio, Bergamo, Brescia yield to the King
of France. In desperation the Venetians seek to reconcile themselves
with the Pope, with Maximilian, with the King of Aragon. The Pope
acquires the cities of the Romagna, and other possessions are taken
from the Venetians by the Marquis of Mantua. The Venetians abandon their conquests on the mainland and are reduced indeed to their
canals and lagoons. They beg peace of Maximilian, offer to consign
the ports they hold in the kingdom of Naples to the King of Aragon,
and promise the Pope to restore whatever they still hold in Romagna.]*

The Decline of Venetian Power

THUS, with remarkable and almost unbelievable speed, the good fortunes of the Venetian Republic continued to decline, calamity continually
heaping upon calamity, whatever hopes they clung to proving in vain,
nor was there the slightest indication whereby they might hope to
be able at least to preserve their own liberty after the loss of so great
a domain. Their great ruin affected the Italians in various ways, some
deriving the greatest pleasure from it, remembering that the Venetians
had not sought to conceal their desire to subjugate all of Italy and had
acted in terms of boundless ambition, without respect for justice or
keeping their promises, and seizing everything whenever they had a
chance. These things had made everyone hate the Venetians, a nation
all the more odious because of their widespread reputation for natural
haughtiness. On the other hand, many people, considering the situation
more sensibly, and realizing how wretched and calamitous it would be
for all of Italy to be entirely subjugated under the foreign yoke, heard
the news with incredulity and displeasure that such a city, the fixed seat
of liberty, the glory of the name of Italy throughout the world, should

have fallen to such extremity. For now there no longer remained any check whatever against the fury of those nations from beyond the Alps: the fall of Venice meant the cutting off of their most glorious member, that Italian state which more than any other maintained the fame and reputation of them all.

But so great a fall was particularly disturbing to the Pope, suspicious of the power of the Emperor and the King of France, and desirous of entangling them in other undertakings in order to deflect their minds from oppressing him. Therefore he determined, although secretly, to do all he could so that the misfortunes of that republic should not proceed further, and he accepted the letters written to him in the name of the Doge of Venice, begging him with great submission to deign to receive six ambassadors chosen by the leaders of the Senate, sent to humbly entreat the Pope's pardon and absolution. These letters having been read and their petitions set forth in the Consistory, the Pope agreed to admit the ambassadors, giving as his reason the ancient custom of the Church not to show itself adamant toward those who sought pardon after having repented of the errors they had committed. The ambassadors of Caesar [Maximilian] and of the French King strongly opposed this decision: reminding the Holy Father that according to the League of Cambrai he was expressedly obliged to persecute the Venetians with arms spiritual and temporal until such time as each of the members of the League had recovered what belonged to him. The Pope replied that he had agreed to admit them with the intention of not granting them absolution until Caesar (who alone among the confederates had not recovered all) should first obtain the things that belonged to him.

Florence–Pisa War

At this time the Florentines put their last hand to the war against the Pisans: for after they had cut off grain supplies from the city, they raised new forces, and set themselves diligently and with every effort to block the entrance of any supplies whatever, whether by land or by sea. Nor could they easily carry this out because of the proximity of the Lucchese,* who whenever possible secretly subverted the new agreement they had made with the Florentines. But the lack of provisions grew more serious every day in Pisa; and when the peasants refused to endure. this any longer, those leaders of the city in whose hands resided all public deliberations and whose counsels were followed by most of

* Lucca is fifteen miles from Pisa.

PIAZZA AND BASILICA OF SAINT PETER, ROME

The public ceremony in which Pope Julius II absolved the Venetians of their excommunication took place in front of the Basilica on 24 February 1510. Although this scene of the incoronation of Pope Sixtus V is much later (1585), the view of the Piazza and the church is substantially as it was in Julius' time except for the greater progress in the construction of the new Saint Peter's growing within the shell of the old Constantine church. Here may be seen the Loggia of Benedictions to the right, still part of the old church, and, surmounting all, the drum of the as yet unraised cupola of the new Saint Peter's (from a fresco in the Biblioteca Vaticano). (COURTESY OF FRATELLI ALINARI)

the Pisan youth, introduced, via the Lord of Piombino, a plan for an agreement with the Florentines, in order to lull the peasants with their usual tricks.

Many days were slyly spent in these negotiations; the Florentine secretary, Niccolò Machiavelli,* having gone to Piombino for this purpose, and many Pisan ambassadors chosen by the citizens and peasants. But closing off Pisa was very difficult because the countryside around it is wide, mountainous, full of ditches and swamps, so that it is hardly possible, especially at night, to prevent supplies from getting in. In view of the fact that the Lucchese were expected to send supplies soon, and considering the ferocious determination of the Pisans who would endure

---

* Machiavelli was the secretary of the second chancellery, the board of the Ten (*Dieci*) which managed foreign policy and war. In other words he was Secretary of War, or defense, as we euphemistically like to put it.

SIEGE OF PISA

In this fresco of the siege of Pisa (Palazzo Vecchio, Florence) by Giorgio
Vasari, the painter's manneristic predilection for twisting and twining armies
of seminudes does not entirely deprive his work of documentary interest.
Crossbowmen, trumpeters, cannon, a breach in the wall through which pour
footsoldiers, banners bearing the lily of Florence—all are vividly depicted.
(COURTESY OF FRATELLI ALINARI)

any danger and effort to get them, the Florentine captains decided to
overcome these difficulties by splitting their forces into three parts so
that, distributed over more places, they might more easily block entrance
into Pisa.

. .

The result of this new disposition of forces was that every day the
Pisans suffered more from want of food. Therefore, seeking to obtain
by deceit what they despaired of obtaining by force, the Pisans ordered
Alfonso del Mutolo, a young lower-class Pisan (who had been taken
prisoner earlier by the Florentines and treated very well by his captor)
to offer the Florentines that he would be the means whereby they
might take the gate leading to Lucca by surprise. The Pisans planned
that when the Florentines, encamped at San Iacopo, would march by
night to take the gate, as soon as part of them should enter, not only
would they be attacked, but at the same time, the Pisans would assault

one of the other camps of the Florentines, who, according to the order given, were supposed at that time to be approaching the city.

But because these latter approached the city not rashly or in a disorderly fashion, the Pisans gained nothing by this ruse except the death of a few men who had come to the first gate waiting for the signal to enter the city; among those slain was Canaccio da Pratovecchio, the Florentine who had been Alfonso del Mutolo's captor and to whom the Pisans had confided their scheme. Also killed by a cannon shot was Paolo da Parrana, captain of a Florentine company of light horse.

This hope having failed, and only the smallest quantities of grain entering secretly into Pisa to the greatest danger of those bringing it, and the Florentines not permitting the Pisans to expel useless mouths from their city (tormenting in various ways those who did leave), prices for the necessities of human life rose without limit; and since there weren't enough supplies for all, many were already dying of famine. And yet the stubborn resistance of those citizens leading the government was even greater than these necessities; for they were ready to see the ultimate extinction of their country rather than yield to so horrible a need. Day after day they postponed a parley, seeking every means of giving the multitude now one reason for hope and now another; and especially that the Florentines would be forced to withdraw from their walls, since they expected the Emperor to arrive in Italy at any moment. But part of the peasants, mostly those who had been at Piombino and understood what was in their minds, rebelled and forced them to begin new negotiations with the Florentines. These negotiations were held with Alammano Salviati, commander of that part of the army lodged at San Pietro in Grado, and after a number of disagreements, both sides continually bringing up every possible means of breaking off the discussions, an agreement was reached. The accord was made under very favorable conditions for the Pisans; not only were all their crimes forgiven, but many exemptions were conceded; all debts both public and private remitted; and they were also absolved of restitution of all Florentine property which they had seized during their uprising. So great was the desire of the Florentines to become lords again of that city, so great was their fear of Maximilian who had named the Pisans in the League of Cambrai (although the King of France had not accepted their nomination), so distrustful that some unexpected hindrance might emerge from him or from some other source, that although they were sure the Pisans within a very few days would be forced to yield because of famine, yet the Florentines preferred to be certain of their victory under iniquitous treaty conditions rather than, in order to obtain the city without any treaty whatever, cast any part of their certainty once again into the lap of fortune. And albeit they began to negotiate this agreement in the camp, later it was debated and concluded in Florence by the Pisan ambassadors: the good faith of the Florentines being worthy of memory since, despite being full of hatred and exasperated by the outrages they had supported, nevertheless they were as faithful in observing the promises they made as they had been easy and clement in agreeing to them.

[*Despite their disastrous defeat the Venetians gradually bestir themselves, recapture Padua, and take prisoner the Marquis of Mantua. Maximilian besieges that city, then retires to Verona.*

Pope Julius, meanwhile, in his typical weathervane manner is swinging against the French; his new mood is confirmed by his proposal to absolve the Venetians. Opposition of the other members of the League of Cambrai induces the Pope to postpone this proposal. The Venetians recapture Verona but withdraw when French aid arrives; the war goes on between the Venetians and Maximilian. The Venetians consent to certain conditions and the Pope absolves them of his excommunication.]

BOOK

9

THE POPE HAD DETERMINED, AND FIRMLY AND STUBBORNLY FIXED ALL HIS THOUGHTS, NOT ONLY ON REINTEGRATING INTO CHURCH DO-
main many states which he claimed belonged to it, but beside this, he was resolved to expel the King of France out of all those lands which he possessed in Italy. The Pope was impelled either by his hidden and long-standing enmity toward the French King, or because so many years of distrust were now converted into virulent hatred, or else because of his greed for glory to become (as he said afterward) the liberator of Italy from the barbarians. For these reasons he had absolved the Venetians from censure; for these reasons he had come to an under-standing and close alliance with the Swiss; pretending that he was proceeding along this path more for his own security than out of a desire to harm others; for these reasons, not having been able to separate the Duke of Ferrara from fealty to the French King, the Pope had determined to make every effort to occupy that dukedom; feigning that he had acted only because of a quarrel over the salt taxes and tolls.

And nevertheless, in order that he should not entirely reveal his plans until matters were better prepared, he continued to deal with Alberto Pio* to come to an agreement with the King of France; who, convinced that Julius had no other quarrel with him other than the fact that he had taken the Duke of Ferrara under his protection, and desirous above all to avoid the Pope's enmity, consented to draw up a new agreement with him, referring to the clauses of the treaty of Cambrai wherein it was stated that none of the parties thereof should interfere in matters pertaining to the Church, and inserting such words and clauses within this new agreement as would make it lawful for the Pope to take whatever actions against the Duke that pertained to the specific disputes regarding the salt tax and other duties. The King thought that Julius' plans related only toward these matters: interpreting

---

* Alberto Pio, Count of Carpi, served as Maximilian's ambassador from January 1510 on; he also at various times acted as spokesman for King Louis XII, and was very involved in political negotiations during this period. His mother was the sister of the renowned Pico della Miran-dola.

the obligation that he had taken to protect the Duke of Ferarra in such a manner that it would appear almost as if he could legally deal with the Pope with regard to this. But the closer the King came to the Pope's demands, the further away the Pontiff drew from him. . . .

. .
.

About this time the liberation of the Marquis of Mantua from prison came to pass in a most notable manner. This was achieved by the Pope, who was motivated by the affection which he had earlier

DE FORTUNA VENETORUM

Fortune, her eyes bandaged, turns the wheel: the Papacy triumphs; the Vene-tian lion is at the bottom; the German eagle rises; the Gallic cock, stripped of its feathers, plunges to its ruin. The satirical reference, of course, is to Pope Julius, "Master of the world's game." (SATIRICAL ENGRAVING FROM ULRICH VON HUTTEN, AD DIVUM MAXIMILIANUM BELLO IN VENETOS EUNTEM EXHORTATIO, 1517)

borne him, and also because of his plan to make use of the Marquis' means and the wealth of his state in his war against the King of France. All Italy believed that Julius was the cause of his liberation. Nevertheless I have been informed by an author worthy of belief, and through whose hands at that time the entire government of the state of Mantua passed, that the reason was much different. For suspecting (as was true) that the Venetians were inclined to hold the Marquis forever imprisoned, either because of the hatred or mistrust which they entertained toward the Holy Father; therefore, after many vain efforts had been attempted, the Council of Mantua decided to have recourse to Bajazet, Prince of the Turks; a friend of many years' standing with the Marquis who had often sent him messages and various gifts. When Bajazet heard of his friend's misfortune, he summoned the commissioner of the Venetian merchants then trading at Pera near Constantinople, and sought his promise that the Marquis would be freed. The commissioner refused to promise what was not in his power and offered to write about it to Venice where he had no doubt that a decision would be reached in accordance with Bajazet's request, and since the Turk proudly replied that it was his will that an absolute promise be made, the commissioner was constrained to make it. When this news, sent by the commissioner, arrived in Venice, the Senate considering that this was no time to stir up so mighty a prince, determined to liberate the Marquis; but in order to hide its dishonor, and reap some fruit of the Marquis' liberation, the Senate lent ear to the Pope's request. But in order to assure the Venetians that the Marquis would not move against them, an agreement was reached (although secretly) that the Marquis' eldest son should be held hostage by the Pontiff. The Marquis was then led to Bologna, where having consigned his son to the Pope's agents, the Marquis was thence freed and went to Mantua, making his excuses to the Emperor and the King of France that out of the necessity of setting his own affairs in order, he had not come to serve them. For although he was the feudatory of one and the soldier of the other (having always kept his commission and been supplied by the King of France) actually he wished to remain neutral.

The World's Game*

THUS, up to this day, the Pope succeeded in nothing of all that he had attempted against the King of France: for there had been no

---

* *Il papa vuol essere il signore e maestro del giuoco del mondo*—"The Pope wants to be lord and master of the world's game"—in report of Venetian ambassador Domenico Trevisan, April 1, 1510.

uprising at Genoa as he had most assuredly promised himself; nor did the Venetians, after having attacked Verona in vain, hope any longer to make any progress there; nor had the Swiss moved ahead, since they had been more disposed to display their weapons than employ them; nor did Ferrara consider itself in any danger whatever since they had been promptly helped by the French and survived the winter. The only gain the Pope had made was the surprise capture of Modena, a prize unworthy of such efforts.

Yet it seemed that with the Pope, deceived by so many hopes, there intervened what the writers of fables have left to the memory of posterity about Anteus, namely that no matter how many times he was conquered by the power of Hercules, no sooner did he touch the earth than he was charged with greater strength and vigor. Just so did adversity affect Pope Julius. For when he seemed most cast down and most trampled upon, he rose up with an ever more constant and pertinacious spirit, setting himself more goals in the future than ever. And yet to win these, he had almost no other basis than himself, and his assumption (as he openly declared) that since he was not moved by any particular interests except the simple, single desire to set Italy free, his undertakings must inevitably, with God's help, come to a happy conclusion. He was deprived of valiant and faithful armies; he had no other sure friends than the Venetians who of necessity shared the same fortune; and from whom he could not hope very much since they were drained of money and oppressed with many difficulties; and the Catholic King sent him secret advice rather than open help. . . .

[*On September 15, 1510, the King of France convokes at Tours (G. says "Orliens") a synod of bishops, prelates, doctors and other learned men of his kingdom; this synod declares that the King could with a good conscience "make war upon the Holy Father, in his own defense and in the defense of his allies." There is talk of convoking a general council "to reform the Church, in its head and in its members."*

Julius is now calling for the expulsion of all barbarians from Italy—Fuori i barbari!—and in Rome the saying is that the Pope has cast the keys of Saint Peter into the Tiber to take up the sword of Saint Paul. Bologna becomes the headquarters of the Pope's astonishing campaign, and Michelangelo, who is then painting the Sistine vault, has to come to Bologna on two occasions to extract some money from the tightfisted Ligurian whose thoughts are turned entirely to war. Spiritual arms are now joined with temporal arms: Julius publicly censures Alfonso d'Este and anyone who helps him.

The fortress of Mirandola, key to the duchy of Ferrara, is attacked by papal troops commanded by the Duke of Urbino, Julius' nephew, but valiantly defended.]

Julius at the Siege of Mirandola

THE BEGINNING of the new year [1511] was made memorable by an unexpected occurrence, something unheard of throughout the centuries. For, the attack against Mirandola seeming in Julius' eyes to be proceeding slowly; and attributing this partly to the inexperience and partly to the perfidy of his captains, and especially his nephew, and blaming them for what largely was the result of many difficulties, he decided to speed up the campaign by his own presence. Setting the importunity and violence of his mind above all other considerations, Julius was not restrained by the consideration of how unworthy it was for the majesty of so high a position, that the Roman pontiff should lead armies in person against Christian towns; nor how dangerous this was, scorning the reputation and judgment that the entire world would make of him, and lending apparent reason and almost justification to those who were seeking to convoke the Council and arouse the princes of Christendom against him, on the grounds primarily that his rule was pernicious to the Church and his failings scandalous and incorrigible. Such were the words resounding throughout the papal court; everyone was astonished; everyone criticized him to the utmost, the Venetian ambassadors no less than the others; the cardinals begged him with the greatest insistence not to go. But all these pleas were in vain, and vain everyone's persuasions.*

Julius departed on the second day of January from Bologna, accompanied by three cardinals. When he arrived at the camp he lodged in a farmer's hut lying within range of the enemy artillery, no farther than twice an ordinary crossbow's shot from the walls of Mirandola. And there, wearying and exercising his body no less than his mind and his authority, Julius rode almost continually here and there throughout the camp, ordering the proper placement of the artillery pieces, of which only a small part had been placed until that day; for almost all military operations were impeded by the bitter weather and almost steady snowfall, and because no amount of diligence was sufficient to keep the artillerymen from fleeing, since besides the bitter weather they were under a great deal of cannon fire from the defenders. Therefore, since it was necessary to build new ramparts and call up new artillerymen

* The Pope had only recently recovered from a serious illness.

to the camp in the places where the artillery had to be set, the Pope went, while these things were being carried out, to Concordia in order not to suffer the hardships of the army during this time. At Concordia, Alberto Pio came to him at the commission of Chaumont,* proposing various offers of agreement; but all these were in vain (despite the many goings and comings on both sides) either because of the Pope's usual obdurance, or because Alberto, more suspected all the time, was not carrying out the negotiations with a convincing show of sincerity.

Julius remained at Concordia for a few days; his inveterate impatience bringing him back to the camp: that same ardor whose fires were not in the slightest chilled by the heavy snow which continued to fall from the sky during his march, nor by the bitter cold which his soldiers could scarcely endure. He took lodging in a little church near his artillery and even closer to the wall than had been his former lodging, nor was he satisfied with anything that had been done or was being done, and complained violently about all his captains except Marcantonio Colonna, whom he had summoned again from Modena. And he continued with no less energy moving through the camp, now shouting at this one, now comforting another and acting in all his words and deeds like a military leader, promising his soldiers that if they went about their tasks like men, he would not accept any pact in taking Mirandola, but leave the city for them to sack. And it was certainly a notable thing and very new in men's eyes, that the King of France, a secular prince, still young and very healthy, trained in handling arms, should at that time be reposing in his chambers, and leaving a war waged principally against him, to be led by his captains; and on the other side to see the highest Pontiff, Vicar of Christ on earth, old and infirm and accustomed to comfort and pleasures, personally conducting a war stirred up by him against Christians, and camping in a miserable countryside; where as a leader of soldiers he exposed himself to hardships and perils, retaining of his pontificate nothing but the garb and the name.

By his extreme diligence, by his complaints, promises, and threats, things moved ahead with greater celerity than otherwise; and yet, many difficulties opposing him, they were proceeding slowly withal, what with the small number of sappers and an insufficiency of artillery pieces in the Pope's army (nor were those of the Venetians very large), and also because the gunpowder could accomplish its usual task only with difficulty as a result of the wetness of the season. Those within the walls defended themselves valiantly, led by Alessandro da Trivulzio with four hundred foreign footsoldiers, who supported all dangers with greater resolution because they hoped for help promised by Chaumont.

* Charles d'Amboise, Marshal of Chaumont, and King Louis XII's governor at Milan.

He had been ordered by his King not to permit the Pope to take that town, and had therefore sent for all the Spanish infantrymen who were at Verona, and levied his men from everywhere, continually enlisting footsoldiers. And inducing the Duke of Ferrara to do the same, Chaumont promised to assault the enemy camp before the twentieth of January. But many things made this plan difficult and dangerous: the very limited time he had to gather so many provisions, the opportunity given the enemy to fortify their camp, the difficulty of bringing up artillery, munitions and provisions in so cold a season through terrible roads and the worst snow of many years. And he who should have mitigated these hardships by alertly making up for lost time, augmented them instead. For Chaumont rode suddenly by post to Milan, claiming that he was going there to more swiftly raise money and other necessary provisions; but it was divulged and believed that he had been induced to this sudden departure rather by the love of a Milanese lady; and this sudden departure of his, although he returned quickly, abated the spirits of his soldiers and the hopes of those defending Mirandola. Wherefore many people said openly that Chaumont's hatred against Gianiacopo da Trivulzio was no less harmful perhaps than his negligence or baseness; and that therefore his own passions (as often happens) weighing more with him than his King's welfare, he was pleased that [Trivulzio's] nephews should be deprived of that state [Mirandola].

On the other hand, the Pope spared nothing to gain his victory, roused to greater fury because two of his men had been slain in his kitchen by a cannon shot fired out of the town. This danger caused the Pope to leave that lodging, and then because he could not forebear returning there the next day, he was constrained by new dangers to take the tent of the Cardinal Regino; and those within the walls knowing by chance that the Pope had transferred to that place, directed a big artillery piece against it, not without danger to his life. Finally, the defendants having entirely lost hope of help, the artillery having done great damage, and besides this, the water in the ditches frozen so hard that it could hold up the soldiers, and fearing that they would not be able to resist at the first battle which had been ordered to begin within two days, they sent, on the same day in which Chaumont had promised to join them, ambassadors to the Pope to surrender on condition that everyone's goods and lives be spared.

Although at the beginning, Julius replied that he did not wish to be obliged to spare the lives of the soldiers, yet at last, conquered by the entreaties of all his advisers, he accepted the surrender under the conditions proposed; except that Alessandro da Trivulzio with several of his captains of footsoldiers should remain his prisoners, and that the town should pay him a certain amount of money as recompense for the sack which had been promised the soldiers. Nevertheless, since the soldiers felt that they were due what had been promised them, it was no easy task for the Pope to keep them from sacking it.

This done, the gates being rammed up, the Pope had himself drawn up onto the wall, and from there he descended into the town. The castle yielded at the same time, permission being granted to the Countess to depart with all her goods.

.   .
.

From Mirandola the Pope went to Sermidi in the territory of Mantua, a castle on the banks of the Po. Julius now had the greatest expectations of taking Ferrara without delay. For this reason, on the very day when he won Mirandola, he had answered Alberto Pio resolutely that he had no intention of listening to any discussions about peace unless Ferrara were turned over to him before any other conditions of peace were discussed.

But his thoughts were changed by the new decision of the French. The King, considering how greatly his reputation had fallen with the loss of Mirandola, and despairing that it would be possible to bring the Pope's mind voluntarily to a peaceful settlement, ordered Chaumont that he was not only to see to it that Ferrara be defended but that besides this, he should not abstain whenever an opportune occasion offered itself to attack the Papal State.

In accordance with these instructions, Chaumont mustered his men from all parts and the Pope, at the advice of his captains, retreated to Bologna. There he remained a few days, either because of fear or, as he said, to hasten by his proximity the battering of the bastion of Genivolo, against which he planned to send some soldiers which he had in Romagna. Therefore he went to Lugo and finally to Ravenna, thinking perhaps that so small an operation was not worthy of his presence.

Death of Chaumont

A few days later, Chaumont was struck by a serious illness, and borne to Coreggio where after fifteen days he died. Before his death he had devoutly shown that he greatly repented of the vexations he had done the Church and besought the Pope to grant him absolution by a public declaration which was granted to him, but since death suddenly intervened, he never knew about it while he was still alive. He was a captain who had great authority in Italy during his life, because of the power and prestige of the Cardinal of Rouen, and because of his almost absolute

administration of the duchy of Milan and all the armies of the French
King. But his valor and skill were far inferior to so heavy a burden. Like
men of the lowest degree, he did not understand the arts of war himself,
nor would he lend faith to those who did know them. The result was
that after the death of his uncle, his inadequacies were no longer bolstered
up by favor, and in his last days he was practically scorned by his soldiers,
to whom he permitted the greatest license in order that they should not
speak badly of him to the King. This situation reached such a pass that
Trivulzio, a captain trained in traditional discipline, often affirmed under
oath that he would never more serve with the French armies unless he
himself were in command, or the King were there. Nevertheless, the King
had decided earlier to send as his successor Monseigneur de Longueville,
of the blood royal although illegitimate, the King, in this decision, paying
less heed to Longueville's virtues than to his authority and eminence
resulting from his nobility and riches.

By the death of Chaumont, the leadership of the army fell again to
Gianiacopo da Trivulzio (one of the four marshals of the realm) according to French statutes until the King otherwise disposed. Trivulzio, not
knowing whether he would have to continue the war or not, did not dare
undertake anything of consequence.

. .
.

The fortunes of war fluctuating in this way, it was not yet possible
to discern any signs whereby one might truly judge what would be the
outcome. But the thoughts of the princes, especially [Maximilian] Caesar,
were no less variant and uncertain. Unexpectedly, the Emperor decided
to send the Bishop of Gurk* to Mantua to negotiate a peace. As has been
said above, an agreement had been reached via the aforesaid Bishop,
whereby the King of France and Maximilian would wage war in the
spring with all their forces against the Venetians, and call a Council in
case the Pope should not agree to observe the League of Cambrai. The
Emperor was much inclined toward this Council and, after the return of
the Bishop of Gurk, had summoned all the prelates of his patrimonial
states in order that they might discuss in what manner and in what place
the Council should be held.

But as Maximilian was inconstant and fitful by nature, and an enemy
of the French, he subsequently lent ear to the King of Aragon, who felt
that the union of Caesar Maximilian and the King of France in order to
put down the Venetians with their united forces, and similarly the ruin
of the Pope by means of the Council, would increase the power of the
King of France too much. Therefore, the King of Aragon had endeavored
to persuade Caesar that a universal peace was more to his advantage, since

* Matthew Lang, influential counselor of Maximilian in all imperial politics.

thereby he would obtain either all or most of those places which the Venetians had taken from him. And he advised him that for this purpose he should dispatch an important person with ample authority to Mantua, and see to it that the French King did the same; and that he similarly would send someone there. By this means the Pope could not refrain to do likewise, nor ultimately could he deviate from the will of so many princes; upon whose resolution the decision of the Venetians depending (for being unable to stand alone, they had to follow his authority), it might really he hoped that without any difficulty or recourse to arms or augmenting the fame or power of the King of France, Maximilian, praised by all the world, would reobtain his estate, together with a universal peace. And although there might not happen what reasonably should happen, Caesar would not for this reason be deprived of his capacity to launch the war at the determined time and with the same opportunities: rather, since he was the head of all the Christian princes and the protector of the Church, such a course of action would greatly exalt his glory and justify him all the more. For it would be patent to everyone that his principal desire was to secure peace and unity among all Christians, but that the obstinacy and wicked policies of others had forced him to go to war.

These reasons put forth by the Catholic King were convincing to Maximilian Caesar, who therefore sent letters to the Pope and the French King. To the Pope he wrote that he had determined to send the Bishop of Gurk into Italy because, as was proper for a religious Prince, and by the imperial dignity protector of the Church and head of princes of Christendom, he had resolved to bring about, as much as he could, tranquillity within the Papal See and peace within Christendom. And he urged Julius to proceed in the same manner, as pertained to a true Vicar of Christ, lest failing to fulfill the office of pontiff, he, Caesar Maximilian, should be constrained to think of remedies necessary for the peace of Christendom. He did not approve of depriving the absent cardinals of the dignity of their cardinalships, because they were not absent out of malign reasons nor hatred against him, and therefore did not deserve so great a punishment; nor was the question of depriving cardinals of their office exclusively for the Pope to decide. Furthermore, he reminded Julius that it was a most unworthy and a useless thing to create new cardinals in the midst of such troubles, since this was explicitly forbidden by the agreements made by the cardinals at the time of his election to the pontificate. Maximilian Caesar exhorted the Pope to postpone such a matter to a more tranquil time when he would have no need or cause to promote prelates to so high a dignity unless they were persons broadly agreed upon because of their doctrinal wisdom, discretion and good lives.

To the French King he wrote that knowing he had always been inclined toward an honest and secure peace, he, the Emperor, had decided to send the Bishop of Gurk to Mantua to draw up a universal peace treaty; that he had good grounds to believe the Pope was also inclined toward such a peace; and that the Pope's authority would force the Venetians to do likewise; and that the ambassadors of the King of Aragon promised to do the same. That therefore he desired likewise to send thither his ambassadors with full power; and as soon as all these had assembled, the Bishop of Gurk would entreat the Pope to do the same, and in case he refused, the Council should denounce him in the names of all; ordering that the Bishop should hear everyone's arguments, in order to proceed with more justification and put an end to the universal controversy. But in any case, he should hold this for certain, never to make any agreement with the Venetians unless his differences with the Pope were resolved at the same time.

Maximilian's proposals pleased the Pope, not out of any desire for peace and agreement, but because, convinced that he could induce the Venetian Senate to compose their differences with Caesar, he hoped that Caesar, freed thereby of any need to remain united with the King of France, would break with him; and thus a league of many princes against the French King could more easily be brought about.

But the French King was most displeased with this unexpected proposal, insofar as he had no hope that a general peace would result from it and therefore judged that the least harm that might result would be to protract the carrying out of decisions which he had agreed upon with Caesar Maximilian. The King also feared that the Pope would separate Maximilian from him by promising to help him reconquer the duchy of Milan, and promising the dignity of the cardinalship and other ecclesiastical honors to the Bishop of Gurk. Or at least (reasoned the French King) if, as a result of the Pope's intervention, the accord with the Venetians were no longer favorable to Maximilian, he would be obliged to accept peace under dishonorable conditions.

His suspicions were increased by the fact that Maximilian was newly joined with the Swiss, although only in a defensive alliance. The King of France was convinced that the Catholic King, of whose intentions he was very suspicious for many reasons, had been the author of these new recommendations to Caesar Maximilian. He knew that the [Spanish] ambassador at the Emperor's court had labored, and was laboring openly, for an agreement between Caesar and the Venetians. He believed that he gave secret encouragement to the Pope, in whose army his men had served much longer than he was bound to under the treaties of the investiture of the kingdom of Naples. He knew that to block his actions, he skillfully opposed the convocation of the Council; and under the pretense of honesty, he was openly criticizing the fact that, with weapons in hand, and at a time when Italy was blazing with war, there should be negotiations on a matter which, without agreement of all the princes, could bring forth only the most poisonous fruits. Furthermore, the King of France knew about the Catholic King's new preparations of a very powerful armada, and that although he was letting it be known that he planned to pass personally into Africa, it was not certain whether he wasn't preparing this fleet for other ends. But what made him more suspicious were the smooth words with which the Catholic King beseeched the French King almost in a brotherly fashion that the latter should make peace with the Pope, even setting aside, if it could not be done otherwise, some of his just rights, in order not to show himself as a persecutor of the Church, contrary to the ancient piety of the house of France, and in order not to deflect him [the Catholic King] from that war which he had determined to undertake against the Moors in Africa for the exaltation of the name of Christ. For thus he would be troubling all of Christendom at the same time. And he added that it had been usual for Christian princes, when they were preparing a war against the infidels, to request help from others in such a pious cause, but that it would be sufficient for him, the Catholic King, simply not to be impeded; nor did he request any other help of the French King except that he rest content that Italy remain at peace.

Although these words were conveyed to the King by the Spanish ambassador, and spoken skillfully and with great protestations of friendship by the Catholic King himself to the French ambassador resident with him, nevertheless they appeared to contain a tacit notice that he would take up arms in favor of the Pope; and it seemed unlikely to the King of France that the Spanish King would dare to do this unless he hoped to induce the Emperor to do the same.

The King's mind was no little troubled by these things, and he was filled with suspicion that drawing up a treaty of peace via the Bishop of Gurk would be either useless or pernicious to him. Nevertheless, in order not to give the Emperor any grounds for offense, he resolved to send to Mantua the Bishop of Paris, a prelate of great power and very learned in the laws. At the same time, the King indicated to Gianiacopo da Trivulzio, who had halted at Sermidi because of the better opportunities for shelter and supplies, and had spread his army in other towns in the vicinity, that it was the King's will that Trivulzio continue to command the army, with the proviso that in expectation of the arrival of the Bishop of Gurk, he was not to attack the Ecclesiastical States. Furthermore, the unusually bitter weather also stood in the way of any action, since it was still impossible to camp in the field, even though March had already begun.

.   .
.

But after the Pope understood that the Bishop of Gurk had consented to come to him, Julius was disposed to do him the greatest honors. And since it seemed that there could be no greater honor than for the Roman Pontiff to meet him in person, and to honor him the more by receiving him in a magnificent city, the Pope went from Ravenna to Bologna. The third day after the Pope arrived came the Bishop of Gurk, received with such ceremony that a King could hardly have received more. And the Bishop made no less display of pomp and magnificence; inasmuch as, arriving with the title of Caesar's lieutenant in Italy, he was accompanied by a very large retinue of lords and gentlemen, all with their families, and splendidly garbed and adorned. The Venetian ambassador resident with the Pope met him at the city gate with signs of very great submission; but the Bishop, with incredible ostentation, turned on him with arrogant words and gestures, taking offense that one who represented the enemies of the Emperor should have dared show himself in his presence. With this same pomp, he proceeded to the public consistory where the Pope was waiting with all his cardinals. There the Bishop declared in a brief but very haughty speech that Caesar [Maximilian] had sent him to Italy out of a desire to obtain his rights by peace rather than by war; but this could not take place if the Venetians failed to restore everything that belonged to him in any way whatever.

After the public audience he spoke privately with the Pope to the same effect and with the same arrogance; and on the following day he accompanied these words and gestures with deeds no less haughty. For after the Pope, with his consent, had deputized three cardinals (to wit: San Giorgio, Regino, and de' Medici) to discuss matters with him; and these were waiting for him at the hour set for their meeting, the Bishop sent three of his retinue to deal with them, on the excuse that he was busy with other affairs, as if it were undignified of him to discuss such problems with anyone but the Pope.* Yet the Pope swallowed this indignity together with many others, his incredible hatred against the French conquering his natural disposition.

---

* "*Barbarus est, barbarice egit,*" writes the Pope's master of ceremonies, Paride de Grassis, in his *Diarium* describing the incredible insolence of Maximilian's emissary on this occasion. Matthew Lang behaved with similar haughtiness the following year in Rome, refusing to assume the dignity of the cardinalate, to which Julius had named him, on the grounds that it might cast doubts on the mission with which he was then entrusted. In the same haughty manner he later refused Pope Leo's initial offer of the red hat, and only after his extreme pretensions to first place among the cardinals (Lang only became a priest in 1519!) had been accepted, did the arrogant German become a cardinal, 8 December 1513, accompanied to the Consistory by four hundred knights and numerous ambassadors (Paride de Grassis, *Diarium,* Bologna, 1886, entry of 25 April 1511, p. 271; Ludwig Pastor, *Storia dei Papi,* Rome, 1908, Vol. IV, Part I, pp. 43–46; Julian Klaczko, *Rome and the Renaissance,* New York, 1903, pp. 266 ff.).

But there were many difficulties in arriving at an accord between Maximilian and the Venetians. Although the Bishop of Gurk had first demanded all the towns, he finally agreed that the Venetians might hold Padua and Treviso with all their surrounding countryside and possessions, but in compensation thereof he wanted them to give very great sums of money to Caesar Maximilian. Furthermore, they were to recognize that they held them in fief from Caesar and yield up to him the rights to the other cities.

But the Venetian Senate rejected these proposals, unanimously concluding that since they had so fortified Padua and Treviso, they had no fear of losing them; and it was more useful for the Republic to keep their money because, if this tempest ever passed, some occasion might offer itself when they would easily recuperate the rest of their domain.

On the other hand, the Pope ardently wanted them to come to an agreement with Maximilian, hoping that as a result Maximilian would inevitably break with the King of France. Therefore the Pope goaded them, partly by supplications and partly by threats, to accept the conditions proposed. But his authority had diminished in their eyes not only because they understood what lay behind his importunities, but also because they knew how necessary their company was for him if he were not reconciled with the French King. Thus they held it for certain that the Pope would never abandon them. Still, after they had disputed many days, the Bishop of Gurk somewhat abating his hard conditions and the Venetians yielding more to the Pontiff's urgent requests than they had intended, the ambassador of the King of Aragon also intervening in all the debates, it seemed that they were finally about to come to an agreement: the Venetians (in order that they might retain Padua and Treviso with Maximilian's consent) paying enormous sums of money but over a long term.

There remained the problem of reconciling the Pope and the French King, between whom there seemed to be no controversy other than those touching on the Duke of Ferrara. Unless the problems were solved, Caesar Maximilian was determined not to come to any agreement; therefore the Bishop of Gurk went to speak with the Pope (which had rarely occurred) convinced on the basis of what the Cardinal of Pavia and the Catholic King's ambassadors had told him, that the negotiations would not prove difficult. On the other hand, he knew that the King of France had less regard for dignity than for tranquility and therefore would be disposed to consent to many things of no little prejudice to the Duke. But the Pope, cutting the Bishop off almost as soon as he began to set forth his arguments, insisted on the contrary that having come to an agreement with the Venetians he should leave Ferrarese affairs in the balance; and he complained that Maximilian did not realize that this was the most suitable

DE FOEDERE GALLORUM CUM VENETIS

Federation of the Gallic cock, Venetian lion, and German eagle (SATIRICAL ENGRAVING FROM ULRICH VON HUTTEN, AD DIVUM MAXIMILIANUM BELLO IN VENETOS EUNTEM EXHORTATIO, 1517)

moment to take revenge, by means of other people's power and money, for the many injuries done him by the French. And when the Bishop of Gurk's replies proved unable to budge the Pope from his position, Gurk indicated that he wished to depart without bringing the treaty of peace with the Venetians to a conclusion; and kissing his feet, according to custom, the Bishop left for Modena the next day, which was the fifteenth day after his arrival at Bologna. As soon as he was out of the city, the Pope sent after him, calling him back, but it was all in vain. The Bishop proceeded toward Milan complaining about the Pope in many matters, but especially because, while at his arrival in Italy there had been almost a general cessation of war, the Pope had secretly sent the Bishop of Ventimiglia, son of the late Cardinal Fregosa, to trouble the state of

Genoa. When news of Ventimiglia's mission reached the French, they had him seized at Monferrato, though he was traveling incognito, and taken to Milan where he entirely confessed all the reasons and circumstances of his going.

When the Bishop of Gurk had departed from Bologna, he had requested of the Aragonese ambassadors (who having seemed, at any rate, to have striven greatly for the common peace, now were openly offended by the Pope's inflexibility) that they see to it that the three hundred Spanish lances be returned to the kingdom of Naples, to which they readily consented. And this made men marvel all the more that at a time when the Council was being discussed, and when it was believed that the French and German armies, both accompanied by their kings, would inevitably be all-powerful in Italy; that at such a time the Pope, besides antagonizing the King of France, should alienate Maximilian Caesar and deprive himself of the help of the Catholic King. There were those who wondered whether in this situation as in many others the counsels of the King of Aragon were not different from his deeds, and whether his ambassadors had not operated one way in public and another in secret with the Pope. For, having provoked the French King with new offenses, thereby resuscitating his memory of old grievances, it seemed likely that he would fear that a general peace arrived at by all the others might not give rise to the gravest perils against himself, since the Venetians remained weakened in territory, money, and reputation; and Caesar Maximilian had little power in Italy and was more flighty, unstable, and prodigal than ever. But others, reasoning more subtly, interpreted that it might perchance be that the Pope was confident that, although the Catholic King might declare that he was abandoning him, and withdrawing his forces, yet he would always have to support him in his moments of greatest need, considering how much any decline in papal power would harm him.

The Bishop's departure upset hopes for peace, even though the Pope four days later had sent the Bishop of Murray, the Scottish ambassador, after him to discuss terms of peace with the King of France. Nevertheless, Gurk's leaving eliminated the basic reason that had been holding back Trivulzio from acting, and now he ardently desired to achieve his honorable ambitions, something worthy of his capabilities and former renown, an action which would show the King how dangerous it was to commit the leadership of the war (the most ardent and difficult of all human actions, requiring the most wisdom and experience) to inexperienced youths, whose sole evidence of virtue is favor, rather than to veteran military leaders.

. .
.

At that time the Pope was no longer in Bologna, for after the Bishop's departure, Julius—now displaying audacity and now fear—as soon as he heard that Trivulzio was on the march, determined—even though he no longer had the Spanish lances—to leave Bologna and join up with his troops in order that his presence might induce his captains to give battle against the enemy; which he had never been able to get them to do either by letters or embassies.

[*After Pope Julius had harangued the magistrates of the Forty, the governing body of Bologna, to stand firm with the Papal See against the deposed tyranny of the Bentivoglio, and received assurances of loyal support, from which he drew "more hope than was justified," he left the Cardinal of Pavia as his deputy in Bologna, and went to Ravenna via Forlì.*]

The Bologna Uprising Against Julius

W HEN Trivulzio's forces arrived at Ponte a Lavino, signs of a great uprising manifested themselves in the city of Bologna, the minds of men full of diverse thoughts. Many of the Bolognese, accustomed to live licentiously under the tyranny, supported by other people's money and possessions, and hating the Ecclesiastical State, ardently desired the return of the Bentivoglio. Others, for the harm done them, and which they feared would be done them again; and reduced to desperation at the sight of two such armies marching on their lands close to harvest time, desired anything that would spare them from such evils. Others, fearing the city might be sacked if it were torn by an uprising as a result of the present French advance (remembering vividly as they did, the fury of the French when they first came to Bologna under Chaumont), were willing, so long as they might be spared this peril, to accept any government or dominion whatever. A very few who had earlier shown themselves to be enemies of the Bentivoglio, favored Church rule, but more by desire than deeds.

At any rate, all the people were now beginning to arm themselves, some out of a desire for change, some for security and their own safety, so that everything was full of fear and terror; and the Cardinal of Pavia, papal legate at Bologna, did not possess the spirit or wisdom sufficient to cope with such perils. For in so great and populous a city there were no more than two hundred light horse and a thousand footsoldiers, and persisting more than ever in his disagreement with the Duke of Urbino, encamped with his army at Casalecchio, the Cardinal of Pavia had levied, either by chance or by fate, fifteen captains from amongst the citizenry, to whom, together with their companies and the people, he had committed the guard of the town and the gates. Nor had the Cardinal used wisdom in his choice, most of those he had selected being partisans of the Bentivoglio: among them, Lorenzo degli Ariosti, who had previously been imprisoned and tortured in Rome, suspected of having conspired with the Bentivoglio, and then imprisoned for a long while in the Castel Sant' Angelo.

When these captains had their weapons in hand, they began to hold secret councils and conventicles, sowing new causes for alarm among the people, and only later did the legate begin to become aware of his own imprudence; and in order to avoid the peril into which he had brought himself, he feigned that the Duke of Urbino and the other captains wanted these new captains together with their companies to join their army. But they replied that they would not abandon guarding the city. The Cardinal then tried to bring in Captain Ramazzotto with a thousand footsoldiers, but the people forbade him to enter. These events greatly depressed the Cardinal, aware how much his government was hated by the Bolognese people, and how many enemies he had among the nobility, because not long before he had ordered three honorable citizens decapitated, proceeding of his own regal hand (although it was said that this was done by the Pope's command). Therefore the Cardinal in disguise stole by night out of a secret door of the palace and withdrew into the citadel, and so hastily that he forgot to take his jewels and money with him, sending someone immediately after to get them; and once he had them in his hands, he left by the Soccorso gate toward Imola, accompanied by a hundred horsemen led by Guido Vaina, who had married his sister and was captain of the horsemen appointed as his guard; and a little while after him Ottaviano Fregoso came out of the citadel, with no other company than a guide.

Once the legate's flight was known, a great tumult in the name of the people broke out all over the city; Lorenzo degli Ariosti, not wishing to lose so great an opportunity, together with Francesco Rinucci, also one of the fifteen captains and a Bentivoglio partisan, followed by many of the same faction, ran to the gates called San Felice and Lame, closest to the French camp, broke them open with hatchets, and once having seized them, immediately sent men to summon the Bentivoglio. These having received many French horsemen from Trivulzio, in order to avoid the direct road from the bridge on the Reno (which was guarded by Raffaello de' Pazzi, one of the captains of the Church) crossed the river lower downstream, and arriving at the Lame gate, were immediately led in.

The flight of the army followed the Bologna uprising; for at the third hour of the night, the Duke of Urbino, whose men were spread out from the bridge at Casalecchio to the Siragosa gate, having (it is believed) heard of the legate's flight and the popular uprising, decamped with his entire army so precipitously that he left most of his tents and pavilions pitched; leaving only those troops appointed to guard the camp on the part of the river facing the French, whom he had not advised at all of his departure.

But when the Bentivoglio, already within the town, had learned of his move they immediately advised Trivulzio and sent part of their people out of the town to pursue the Duke's men. These, together with the peasants who were already galloping up from every side, with wild cries and clamors assailed the camp along the wall, and seized their artillery and ammunitions and a great deal of their baggage; although the French by this time had intervened and recaptured most of the booty which the people and the countrymen had taken. By this time also, Teodoro da Trivulzio with his vanguard had arrived at the bridge on the Reno, which Raffaello de' Pazzi was fighting valiantly to defend. For some time he managed to hold out, but finally, not being able to resist the great superiority of his attackers, he was taken prisoner; everyone agreed that Pazzi's defense gave the soldiers of the Church considerable help in saving themselves.

But the Venetian troops and Ramazzotto's men, who only learned very late about the flight of the Duke of Urbino, since they were camped up on the highest mount of Santo Luca, sought safety in the mountain roads, and finally got to the Romagna despite very serious losses. In this victory, won without fighting, fifteen large and many small artillery pieces belonging to the Pope and Venetians were captured, the Duke's own standard together with many other banners, a great part of the baggage trains of the Church and almost all those of the Venetians; some of the men-at-arms fighting for the Church were plundered together with more than one hundred and fifty of the Venetians, and practically all the footsoldiers of both armies were routed. Also Orsino da Mugnano, Giulio Manfrone and several lesser captains were taken prisoner.

Within Bologna there were no killings nor any violence of any sort done either to the nobility or to the people; only the Bishop of Chiusi and many other prelates were taken prisoner, together with their secretaries and other officials who had served the Cardinal and had remained in the resident palace of the legate, since he had concealed his departure from all of them. The same night and the following day, the Bolognese people insulted a bronze statue of the Pope,* dragging it about the piazza with great cries of scorn and derision. Those who committed this deed were

---

* This was Michelangelo's only known work in bronze: a fourteen-foot statue of Pope Julius II, completed and placed in a niche above the central portal of San Petronio only three years before the Bentivoglio uprising. Guicciardini's indifference to art is manifest in his omission of the name of the maker of the statue, a fellow Florentine.

either Bentivoglio partisans, or else people who, weary of the tribulations and destruction of war (and being by nature ungrateful, and eager for change), hated the name and memory of one who had been the cause of their liberation and the felicity of their country.

.   .
.

The Pope, understandably, was greatly disturbed by the loss of Bologna; not only because it was the most important and principal city (with the exception of Rome) of the entire Ecclesiastical State, and because he felt deprived of that glory which the acquisition of Bologna had won for him among mankind and especially in his own mind; besides this, he was also fearful lest the victorious army follow up their victory, for he knew he was not able, at present, to offer resistance . . .

Assassination of Cardinal of Pavia by the Pope's Nephew

At the same time, there occurred another incident which redoubled his woes. Many accusations were laid before the Pope against the Cardinal of Pavia, charging him with unfaithfulness, and cowardice, and lack of foresight.

Meanwhile, the Cardinal himself came to Ravenna to plead his own cause in person. As soon as he arrived, he sent a messenger to the Pope requesting audience; whereupon the Pope, who greatly loved him, replied joyfully that the Cardinal should come and dine with him. But as he was going there, accompanied by Guido Vaina and a guard of his horsemen, he was followed by the Duke of Urbino, who had been his enemy for a long time, and was now enraged because it was being said that the uprising at Bologna had happened through his fault, and also because of the flight of his army. Having intercepted the Cardinal's company, the Duke and a small group of his men forced themselves in amongst his guard of horsemen, who gave way out of respect, whereupon the Duke, with a poignard in his own hands, slew the Cardinal who, perhaps in view of his exalted position, should not have been so violated although he certainly deserved, considering his outrageous and infinite vices, the cruelest punishment whatsoever.*

The Cardinal's death was immediately reported to the Pope, who began lamenting and crying out to heaven and wailing in misery: im-

* ". . . degno, forse, per tanta degnità di non essere violato ma degnissimo, per i suoi vizii enormi e infiniti, di qualunque acerbissimo supplizio." Fenton leaves out the "perhaps." (*Storia*, ed. Gherardi, II, 358; Fenton, *op. cit.*, p. 378.)

measurably moved by the loss of a cardinal who had been so dear to him, and all the more so, that the dignity of the cardinalate should have been outraged in so unheard of a manner, almost before his very eyes and by his own nephew, a matter particularly grievous to him, who made it his profession to conserve and exalt ecclesiastical authority. Unable to bear his grief or contain his fury, the Pope left Ravenna the same day to return to Rome.

And when he had, with great difficulty, reached Rimini, he learned (as if at one and the same time endless and most serious calamities should encompass him) that within Modena, Bologna and many other cities, placards and bulletins announcing the convocation of the Council* and summoning him to appear there in person, had already been hung up in public places.

For after the Bishop of Gurk had left Modena, he had traveled very slowly for several days, awaiting the reply from the Scottish ambassador (who had returned from the Bishop's entourage to Bologna) regarding the proposals which the Pope himself had propounded. But when he returned with very indecisive replies, the Bishop of Gurk immediately dispatched three procurators in the name of Caesar to Milan, where they met with the cardinals and procurators of the King of France, and summoned the Council to be convened at Pisa on the first day of the following September.

The cardinals chose Pisa as a place convenient because of its closeness to the sea for many of those who had to come to the Council, and also safe in view of the confidence the French King placed in the Florentines. For many other places which might have been suitable were either out of the way, or not trusted by them, or might be rejected with just cause by the Pontiff. Nor did it seem honest to convene it in France, or in any place under the King's jurisdiction.

The "Conventicle" of Pisa

THE cardinals claimed that they could legally convoke the Council without papal authorization, because of the obvious necessity of reforming the Church (as they put it) not only in her limbs but also in her head, that is, in the person of the Pontiff, whom they asserted was inveterately given to simony and infamous and dissolute behavior, unfit to govern the papacy, the cause of so many wars, notoriously incorrigible, to the

* The general Council on Church reform, already being discussed at the
synod which Louis XII had convoked
at Tours in September of the previous
year.

universal scandal of Christendom; for the good health whereof no other medicine would suffice than the convocation of the Council. And inasmuch as the Pope was negligent in summoning such a Council, therefore the power of convoking it had legitimately devolved upon them: especially since the authority of the elected Emperor had been joined with theirs, as well as the consent of the Most Christian King, together with the clergy of Germany and France concurring. They added that frequent recourse to this medicine was not only useful but necessary for the very diseased body of the Church, to extirpate old errors, to guard against those that were newly pullulating, to explain and interpret the doubts that every day brought newly forth, and to correct things which although well ordered at the start, had proved in subsequent experience to be harmful. And therefore, the ancient fathers had wholesomely decreed at the Council of Constance that forever afterward a Council should be held every ten years. For what other bridle was there to prevent the Pontiff from swerving off the just path? And in view of the great frailty of mankind amidst so many incitements to evil that happen in our lives, how can we otherwise dwell in safety, if he who has supreme license to do as he wishes, knows that he never will have to render account of his doings?

On the other side, many contested this line of reasoning, and adhering rather to theological rather than canonical doctrine, asserted that the right to convoke councils resides solely in the person of the Pope, even though he be stained by all the vices, provided only that he be not suspected of heresy; and that were it otherwise interpreted, it would be in the power of a few (which should not be permitted in any way) to perturb and change the tranquility of the Church every day either because of ambition or particular hatreds, cloaking their corrupt intentions under false colors. And that all medicines were by their very nature salubrious, but if they were not given in proper dosages or at the proper times, they are poisons rather than medicines; and therefore, condemning those who felt differently, they called this assembly not a Council but a means of dividing the unity of the Apostolic See, the insemination of schism in the Church of God, and a diabolical conventicle.

BOOK
10

Julius-Anteus. Henry VIII of England

WITH MATTERS IN THIS STATE OF SUSPENSION, ALL THE ACTIVITIES UNDER WAY, AND THE MISFORTUNES BEING PREPARED, WERE NEARLY CUT short by the Pope's unexpected death. For, stricken on the fourth day of his illness, he fell into so deep a coma that for several hours those around his bedside were certain he was dead; whereupon, rumor having spread far and wide that he had ended his days, many absent cardinals set out for Rome, and amongst them were those who had convoked the Council.

Nor in Rome was there any less uproar than usually occurs at the death of pontiffs: indeed there appeared seeds of even greater tumults because Pompeo Colonna, Bishop of Rieti, and Antimo Savello, young Roman noblemen who belonged to the party of sedition, summoned the people of Rome to the Campidoglio, and there sought to inflame them with seditious words to recover their liberty.

"The generous Roman spirit has been oppressed long enough. Romans who had formerly ruled the entire world have been slaves long enough. One might perchance justify past times to some degree out of reverence for religion; in whose name, identified with the most sacred customs and miracles, the majority of the people unconstrained by arms or any violence have submitted to the rule of prelates, voluntarily bowing their necks to the sweet yoke of Christian piety. But now, what necessity, what virtue, what dignity can cover in any way the infamy of servitude? Perhaps the integrity of their lives? The holy examples of the priests? Or the miracles which they have performed? But is there in the entire world any generation more corrupt, more iniquitous, more brutal and dissolute? And does it not seem only miraculous that God, the fount of justice, should have so long tolerated such wickedness? Has this tyranny been supported perhaps by skill in arms, or men's industry or assiduous thoughts concerned with maintaining the majesty of the papacy? But what generation has ever been further removed from studies and from military travails? More dedicated to idleness and pleasures? More negligent of the dignity and well-being of their successors? In the entire world there are two similar principalities: the Roman pontiffs and the sultans of Cairo. For neither the dignity of the sultanate nor the highest offices of the Mamelukes are hereditary, but passing from person to person, are granted even to foreigners; and nevertheless the servitude of the Romans is even more ignominious than that of the peoples of Egypt and Syria; insofar as the ignominy of the latter is to some degree understandable because of the bellicose, ferocious nature of the Mamelukes, men inured to toils and lives without any softness or delicacy. But whom are the Romans serving? Persons who are slothful and indolent; foreigners, and often most ignoble not only by blood but also by their mode of behavior. It is high time to awake from so deep a slumber, and to recall that the name of Roman is most glorious when it is accompanied by virtue, but redoubles the shamefulness and infamy of those who have forgotten the honored glory of their forefathers. And now the opportunity easily presents itself, since the Pope's death has occurred when there is discord among the prelates themselves, disunity among the great kings, Italy full of armies and uprisings, and priestly tyranny has become more hateful than ever before to all the princes."*

But Julius came out of his coma; and recovering somewhat (although there was still much greater fear than hope for his life), the day following, in the presence of the cardinals assembled in the form of a consistory, the Pope gave absolution to his nephew of the murder he had committed against the Cardinal of Pavia; not by means of a trial which had been previously discussed (the brevity of time making that impossible), but rather as a penitent, by grace and apostolic indulgence. And in the same consistory the Pope requested that his successor be elected canonically, and wishing to prevent others to rise to so great a height by those means whereby he had so risen, he caused a bull to be published full of dreadful penalties against those who might seek to attain to the papacy either by money or other bribes: declaring any election resulting from such simony to be null and void, thus providing easy grounds for any cardinal to contest it. The Pope had promulgated such a rule even when he was in Bologna, at a time when he was indignant against several cardinals who were almost openly seeking to obtain promises from other cardinals to be elected to the papacy after his death.

On the following day, the Pope's health obviously began to mend, either as a result of his very robust constitution, or else because fate was reserving him as the author and main cause of the longest-lasting and most disastrous calamities of Italy. Certainly one could not attribute his revived health to the skill or remedies of the physicians since he did not

* This speech is omitted in all editions of the *Storia* based on the Torren- tino first edition. Fenton also omits it in all three editions of his translation.

obey them in any way, eating raw apples and other things contrary to their prescriptions, in the midst of his most serious illness.

Spared as he was now from the peril of death, Julius returned to his usual labors and concerns, continuing to negotiate a treaty of peace with the King of France and at the same time a League with the King of Aragon and the Venetian Senate against the French. And although his mind was much more inclined toward war than toward peace, yet various reasons sometimes drew him now in this direction and now in that. He was inclined toward war by his inveterate hatred against the King of France and his failure to obtain all the conditions he wanted in the peace settlement; but besides this, he was all the more incited toward war by the efforts of the King of Aragon to dissuade him from it, since that King was more suspicious than ever that should the King of France come to a peaceful agreement with the Pope, he would attack the kingdom of Naples at the very first opportunity. And in order that his counsels might have a greater effect, he had again sent another fleet out of Spain, besides the first armada which had sailed to Italy from Africa under Pedro Navarro. This new armada was said to consist of five hundred men-at-arms, six hundred horsemen mounted upon jennets, and three thousand footsoldiers; forces which, added to the others, were not to be taken lightly either in terms of numbers or valor.

Nevertheless, the same King proceeding with his usual subtleties, made it seem as if he really wanted a war against the Moors, and that his own personal profit or particular interest did not deflect him from it, but only the devotion which he had always borne toward the Apostolic See. But not being able to maintain his soldiers by himself, he needed the assistance of the Pope and the Venetian Senate. And in order that the Pope and Venetian Senate might more easily concede these things, the forces of the King of Aragon, who had all landed on the island of Capri near Naples, made a show of preparing to sail to Africa.

But the Pope was greatly frightened by his immoderate demands, nor were these sly devices at all to his liking, and he suspected (knowing the man) that the King was not ceasing to give contrary hopes to the King of France. He knew that the Venetians would not withdraw from his side; but he knew at the same time that their financial capacities had been gravely weakened by the devastating war, and that the Senate preferred now rather to look at the defense of their own possessions than to take on a new war which could not be sustained without the heaviest and most intolerable expenses. He hoped that the Swiss, like the great majority of their countrymen, would declare themselves against the King of France, but being uncertain of their disposition in this matter, he did not feel that he should expose himself to such great perils for so uncertain a hope; since it was well known that the Swiss had never broken off dealings with the French King, and that many of their leading men who benefited greatly from French friendship, were laboring all they could in order that the League with the French King might be renewed at the Diet soon to assemble.

As far as the Emperor's intentions were concerned, although he was incessantly goaded by the Catholic King and naturally inimical to France, the Pope rested less hope in him than fear; knowing that the great offers that were being made to him now, were as much against the Venetians as against himself, and that it was possible for the King of France to set more things in action than anyone else; and should the Emperor join with the French King, his authority would render the Council very formidable; and that uniting his armies in good faith with the forces and money of the French King, the joint resources of two such states would deprive the Pope of any hope whatever of victory, which was very difficult to obtain against the French King alone.

But his mind was consoled by the hope that the King of England [Henry VIII] would have to wage war against the French, induced thereto by the counsels and persuasions of his father-in-law, the Catholic King,* and by the prestige of the Apostolic See, very great at that time in the isle of England, and in whose name he, the Pope, had made the most ardent supplications for aid against the King of France, as an oppressor and usurper of the Church.

But that King was much more incited by the innate hatred of the kings and people of England against the French, as well as by his youth and the great sums of money he had inherited from his father; which, according to most reliable sources, was said to be of an almost inestimable amount. All these things so enflamed the mind of this young King, new to the throne, who had never known anything but prosperous fortune in his house, with a great desire to renew the glory of his ancestors, who, entitling themselves kings of France and at various times having vexed that kingdom with great wars from which they emerged victorious, and having for a long time not only possessed Guyenne and Normandy, rich powerful provinces; and in one battle near Poitiers, having captured King John of France with his two sons and many of the greatest lords of that kingdom and also occupied the city of Paris together with most of the realm, accomplishing all this with such success and terror that if their King Henry V had not passed by natural death to another life in the flower of his age and in the midst of his victories, it is believed he would have conquered the entire kingdom of France.

The memory of all these victories stirred the new King's mind with a burning resolution to undertake new enterprises; although when his

---

* Henry had married Catherine of Aragon, his brother's widow, in May 1509. Eighteen years later, his suit for a bill of divorcement resulted in separating England from the Catholic Church and launched Henry on his career of sequential polygamy.

father was dying, he had expressedly advised him above all to maintain peace with the King of France as the only means whereby the kings of England could reign securely and happily. Undoubtedly the war which the English had waged against the King of France (attacked on a wide front at the same time in other parts of his kingdom) was of very great significance; for it struck his kingdom in its very viscera, and remembering these events, the French held the mere name of English in great fear.

Nevertheless the Pope could not safely rest his hopes and build his plans on this basis, because of the incertitude of pledges made by barbarians* and the fact that those countries were so far away.

These, therefore, and under such conditions, were the Pontiff's hopes. On the other side, the King of France abhorred war with the Church, and desired a peace by means of which, besides avoiding the enmity of the Pope, he might also be freed of the importunate demands and necessity of serving Maximilian. Nor did he make any difficulty over annulling the Council of Pisa, which he had set into motion only to force the Pope, by that fear, to peace, provided that he pardon the cardinals and all the others who had participated or consented or adhered to that undertaking.

But on the contrary, the demand for the restitution of Bologna kept him in suspense, since that city was so situated that it could serve as an excellent base of attack against him. The French King feared that the Pope would not sincerely accept an agreement of peace, nor was he by temperament likely to observe it should other opportunities arise, but that he was discussing peace only to free himself of the present danger of the Council and war.

Council of Pisa. Medici Plots Against the Florentine Republic

It was now the first day of September [1511], the day set for the beginning of the Council of Pisa; on which day the cardinals' procurators arrived at Pisa, and in their names celebrated the appropriate inaugural acts. The Pope was furious against the Florentines that they had permitted the Conventicle (by which name he always called it) to be held in their domain. Therefore he declared that the cities of Pisa and Florence were subject to ecclesiastical interdiction, by force of the bull of the Council which he had ordered to be published. In this bull it was declared that whoever favored the Pisan Conventicle would be excommunicated and

---

* In this case, the English; generally used by Italians of that epoch for any people north of the Alps. Guicciardini uses the term descriptively here, as a matter of fact.

placed under interdiction and subject to all the severe penalties ordained by the law against schismatics and heretics. And threatening to invade them with arms, he elected the Cardinal de' Medici as Legate of Perugia, and a few days later the Cardinal Regino, Legate of Bologna, having died, the Pope transferred the Cardinal de' Medici to that legation. His purpose was to throw the Florentines into fear and confusion by assigning near their borders the leader of the opposition to their government. The Pope was hopeful that such a tactic would easily succeed in view of the conditions obtaining in Florence at that time.

For besides the fact that some Florentines desired the return of the Medici family, others among the most eminent citizens were torn by discord and divisions (the ancient malady of that city) caused then by the greatness and prestige of the gonfaloniere.* For some could not endure him because of their ambition and envy, and others were discontented because, taking upon himself in the deliberation of things perhaps more than pertained to his office, he did not leave that role in the government for the others which they deserved in view of their rank. These citizens complained that the government of the city consisted of two extremes: that is, the chief magistrate and the popular council, but there was lacking a well-ordered senate which should exist in a properly instituted republic. For such a senate, besides serving as an institution tempering both extremes, would enable the principal citizens and those better qualified to hold more honorable posts in the Republic. But the gonfaloniere, they charged, who had been elected primarily to set up such an institution, had done just the contrary, either because of his ambition or distrust. Now although this desire was reasonable, it was not, however, of such importance that it should have aroused such dissension (for even lacking such a senate they were obtaining honorable positions, nor were public matters in the long run being handled without them); nevertheless this proved to be the origin and principal cause of the most serious troubles in that city. From this foundation developed all the cleavages among the citizens, and since it seemed to the rivals of the gonfaloniere that he and his brother, the Cardinal of Volterra, were being supported by the King of France and depended on that friendship, they therefore opposed as much as they could those deliberations which were supposed to be made in favor of that King. Instead, this party was favorable to the Pope.

Hence it also came to pass that the name of Medici began to be less odious in that city; because even those important citizens, rivals of the gonfaloniere, who did not desire their return, no longer joined their efforts with others to persecute Medici partisans, nor did they prevent (as at other times they had) other citizens from having dealings with them.

---

* Piero Soderini, gonfaloniere for life, who served from 1502–1512. The gonfaloniere of justice had become the chief prior, or head of the state, long before this but always on a short-term basis.

Rather, in order to put down the gonfaloniere, they showed that they were not lacking in friendship toward them, and even gave some grounds for others to favor the greatness of the house of Medici. Hence it came about that not only were those who were truly friends of the Medici (who had no real strength) hopeful of a change of affairs, but also many noble youths, spurred on either because of the excessive spending, or by particular grievances, or by ambition to surpass others, were hungry for a change of government by means of a return of the Medici. And the Cardinal de' Medici* had nourished and enhanced this disposition with great cunning for several years now. For ever since the death of his brother Piero, whose name was feared and hated, pretending not to wish to interfere in Florentine affairs nor to aspire to the ancient greatness of his family, he had always received all the Florentines who came to Rome with the greatest kindness and willingly busied himself in all their affairs, even of those who had been open enemies of his brother, no less than the others. Thus he managed to transfer all the guilt onto Piero, as if the hatred and offenses had ended with his death; and continuing to act in this way for many years, together with the reputation which he had achieved in the court of Rome of being by nature liberal, affable, and gracious to everyone, he had become acceptable to many people in Florence. And therefore Pope Julius, who was eager for a change in that government, not unwisely proposed him for that legation.

The Florentines appealed from the interdict, not mentioning the Council of Pisa in their appeal, in order to offend the Pope less, but only laying their petition before the Holy Council of the Universal Church. And as if the effect of the interdiction were suspended by the appeal itself, the priests of the four principal churches were compelled by order of the supreme magistrate, to celebrate the divine services publicly in their churches. The result of this was that the divisions among the citizens were all the more brought into the open, because the decision whether to observe or to break the ban now being left to everyone's own discretion, almost everyone was acting with regard to spiritual affairs according to those judgments or passions which moved him in public and temporal affairs.

The Holy League Against the "Barbarians"

HENCE the Pope, setting aside all his thoughts of peace, and because of his long-standing hatreds and covetousness and greed to possess Bologna, and because of his anger at and fear of the Council, and finally, because

* Giovanni de' Medici, the future Pope Leo X.

of his suspicion that if he deferred deliberating any longer, he would be abandoned by everyone (insofar as Spanish soldiers, making a show of having to sail to Africa, were already beginning now to embark at Capri), determined to set up the League which he had discussed with the Catholic King and the Venetian Senate. This treaty was solemnly published on the fifth day of October in the church of Santa Maria del Popolo, the Pope and all the cardinals being present. The articles declared that the parties had formed a confederation primarily to maintain the unity of the Church, and to extirpate the Conventicle at Pisa in order to defend the Church against imminent schism; and to recover the city of Bologna which rightly belonged to the Apostolic See, as well as all other cities and places belonging to the Church directly or indirectly, under which heading Ferrara was included; and that the League would proceed against anyone who might oppose any of these things or attempt to impede their realization (by which words was intended the King of France) and drive them utterly out of Italy with the mightiest armies.

This League made by the Pope for the purpose of liberating Italy from the barbarians aroused various interpretations in the minds of men, according to the diversity of their passions and their judgments. Many, beguiled by the magnificence and splendor of the title of the League, extolled up to the very heaven with the highest praises so lofty an aim, declaring that it was truly a statement of purpose worthy of the pontifical majesty, and that Julius' greatness could not have taken upon itself a more generous enterprise, and that his wisdom was no less than his magnanimity, since by his efforts, he had set the armies of the barbarians against each other. Whence, shedding more foreign than Italian blood against the French, not only would spare our blood, but once one of the enemies had been expelled, it would be much easier for Italian armies to expel the others which would be already weakened and enervated.

But others, perhaps considering the substance of things more deeply, nor allowing their eyes to be dazzled by the League's splendid title, feared that wars begun with the intention of driving the barbarians out of Italy would cause much more harm to the vital spirits of that body than those which had begun with the avowed purpose and resolute intention of subjugating it; and that it was more rash than wise to hope that Italian arms—lacking in skill, discipline, captains of authority and reputation; its princes devoid of common purpose or will—would be sufficient to drive the victor out of Italy. For when all other remedies might fail him, the conqueror could always fall back on the possibility of joining with the conquered to the common ruination of all Italy. Hence, there was much more to fear that these new military agitations might provide other nations with an opportunity to pillage Italy, rather than to hope that the union of the

This unusual sixteenth-century map of Europe appears in a 1575 Cologne edition of Sebastian Münster's Cosmographia Universale. *The upside-down view reflects the German perspective: an amusing example of topographical relativism.*

Pope and the Venetians would be likely to subdue the French and the Spaniards. Italy's desire ought to have been that the discords and unwholesome counsels of our princes had not opened the way for foreign armies to enter; but since, to its misfortune, two of her most noble members had been occupied by the King of France and the King of Spain, she should consider it far less calamitous that both of them remain there, until divine mercy or fortune's favor offered some better-founded occasion. For in pitting one king against the other they were defending the liberty of those who were not yet enslaved. But now they were merely taking up arms against each other, with the result that, as long as the war lasted, those parts of Italy which were still untouched would be torn to pieces by depredations, conflagrations, bloodshed and other terrible disasters. And finally, whichever of them might remain victorious, would afflict all the others with a most bitter and cruel servitude.

But the Pope, who felt otherwise, his spirits roused to greater ardor and inflamed all the more by the new confederation he had formed, as soon as the time limit had passed, which had been set forth in the admonition earlier published against the cardinals promulgating the Council, convoked a public consistory with the greatest solemnity; and sitting in his pontifical habit in the room called the Hall of Kings, declared that the cardinals of Santa Croce, of San Malò, of Cosenza, and of Bayeux were stripped of the dignity of the purple and had incurred all those penalties to which heretics and schismatics were subject. Besides this, he published an admonition of the same form against the Cardinal of San Severino, whom he had not threatened up to that time; and with the same violence he proceeded to plan for his war, continually calling for the coming of the Spaniards, and having more than anything else in mind a desire to launch a war against the Florentines, re-establishing the government in the hands of the Medici, and no less to satisfy his boundless hatred against Piero Soderini, the gonfaloniere, whom he felt was responsible for the fact that the Florentines had never wished to break away from the King of France and that later they had permitted the Council to be held in Pisa.

[*In Florence the Pope's threats result in preparations for war. "Among other things it was proposed, as a most reasonable plan, to resist with the revenues and goods of the Church, the war which the Church was unjustly declaring against them, and therefore the churchmen should be constrained to pay great sums of money."*

The French cardinals wish to bring soldiers to Pisa but the Florentines are opposed. Badly received in Pisa, the Council is transferred to Milan, where it is no better received. Maximilian's attitude with regard to the Council is ambiguous. The French King suspects Maximilian, thinking that if he abandoned him, he would join his enemies; and if he supported him, his alliance would be bought at an excessive price.]

[The French King] hoped that his army would conquer all or parts of the Romagna before the Spaniards approached; and then his forces would either march farther as opportunities offered themselves, or sustain the war in the territories of others until the spring. At that time, he would personally cross into Italy with all the forces of his kingdom, hopeful that his army would prove superior to the enemy in every way. While these matters were being planned, the deliberations proceeding more slowly than perhaps they should have, given the circumstances; and the King, unwilling to lay up great supplies and especially to enlist new footsoldiers because he was instinctively loathe to spend money, there cropped up a suspicion that the Swiss were going to move into action. And since that nation has been mentioned here and there in many of these pages, it would seem to our purpose, and almost necessary, to deal with them in some detail.

History of the Swiss

THE Swiss are those same people whom the ancients called Helvetians, living for generations in the highest mountains of Jura, called St. Claude, and in the Brieg and St. Gotthard range. Ferocious by nature, rustics, the Swiss are shepherds rather than farmers because of the sterility of the country. Formerly they were ruled by the dukes of Austria; but having shaken off their domination a long time ago, they now govern themselves, not recognizing either emperors or any other princes. They are divided into thirteen communities which they call cantons, each self-governing with its own magistrates, laws and ordinances. Every year, or more often, according to the need, they hold a council to discuss all matters, assembling now in one place and now in another, as decided by the deputies of every canton. According to German usage, they call these assemblies Diets; and at these meetings they deliberate on wars, peace, leagues, the requests of those who wish to be granted by public decree the right to levy soldiers, or permission to those who wish to serve as volunteers; and any other things which pertain to the interests of all.

When they agree by public decree to raise troops, the cantons among themselves choose a captain general for the entire army, to whom they give the banners and flags in the public name. The unity and glory of their armies have made this savage uncultured people famous, for as a result of their innate ferocity and their disciplined organization, not only have they always valiantly defended their own country but they have been consummately praised for their military services in foreign wars. Indeed, they would merit incomparably more praise had they served as soldiers for their own domain and not as mercenaries to propagate the rule of others, and if they had more noble aims before their eyes than a constant concern about money; for the love of which they have been corrupted and have lost the opportunity of being feared and respected all over Italy. For since they do not issue forth from their own country except as mercenary soldiers, they have brought back no public fruit of their victories, having become accustomed because of their greed for gain to serve in armies; wherein they are almost intolerable with their voracious ransoms and ever new demands, and besides all this, very troublesome and contumacious in their mode of speech and obedience to those

Another example of sixteenth-century map making: "Looking down" at Italy from the Swiss Alps (SEBASTIAN MÜNSTER'S COSMOGRAPHIA UNIVERSALE, 1575)

who pay them. At home, their chiefs do not abstain from accepting gifts and pensions from princes in order to favor and follow their faction in the Diets. The result has been that since they judge all public things in terms of private profit and make themselves vendible and corruptible, disagreements have also insinuated themselves among their ranks; whereby those things which the majority of the cantons have approved began not to be followed by everyone, and recently, a few years before these times, wars have even come to manifest themselves among them, greatly diminishing their prestige everywhere in the world.

Somewhat lower down the mountains are several towns and villages inhabited by people called the Valaisans* because they live in the valleys; these are much fewer in numbers and in public prestige and valor, since they are not commonly considered bellicose like the Swiss. And even lower than these two, there is another group of people called the Grisons, ruling three cantons, and therefore called Lords of the Three Leagues. The main town of this area is called Coire; they are often leagued with the Swiss, and go to war together with them and are governed almost by the same ordinances and customs; they are preferred to the Valaisans in armies, but are not equals of the Swiss either in numbers or valor.

The Swiss, then, who at this time were not yet so degenerated or corrupt as subsequently they have become, being goaded by the Pope, made preparations to descend into the duchy of Milan . . .

[*The Swiss approach Milan, make demands for money, and then unaccountably withdraw to Como and back to Switzerland. The King of France requests aid of the Florentines against Spanish and papal armies entering the Romagna; pro- and anti-French partisans debate the issue. In Romagna under the inspiring leadership of Gaston de Foix, the youthful French general, Brescia is captured from the Venetians and sacked; then Foix turns toward the region of Bologna against the armies of the Holy League.*

While discussing the Florentine debate, Guicciardini mentions himself for the first time, and with obvious pride. "Amidst these contentions, one faction interrupting the advice of the other, they did not decide to declare themselves or to remain entirely neutral; which gave rise to counsels often uncertain and deliberations repugnant in themselves, without bringing reputation or merit to anyone. Instead, growing out of these uncertainties, they sent as ambassador to the King of Aragon (to the great displeasure of the King of France) Francesco Guicciardini, Doctor of Law, he who wrote this history, who at that time was still so young that in respect of his age, according to the laws of his country, he was unable to exercise any office

* The inhabitants of the canton of Valais in the Rhone Valley.

*whatever; and yet they did not give him commissions such as might
lessen in any way the ill will of the allies." Messer Francesco was
only twenty-eight at the time of his election (October 17, 1511),
and thirty was the legal age for any such post. Since foreign policy
was under the jurisdiction of the Ten (Dieci), Guicciardini therefore
received his instructions from the secretary of that board, who at
that time was Niccolò Machiavelli.]*

The Pope's Ship Visits England

At that time the war planned by the King of England [against France]
was already beginning to make itself manifest, although that King had
earlier specifically denied it and then beclouded his intentions with uncertainties. Nevertheless, the true and very different nature of the facts
could no longer be concealed. For the news came from Rome that King
Henry's ratification of the League had finally arrived by a long maritime
route; and it was known that men and ships were being mobilized, and
that in Spain an armada was being rigged to sail to England [to join
them] and that the minds of all peoples were enflamed to make war
against France. Furthering these preparations there was the timely arrival
of the Pope's galleass laden with Greek wines, cheeses and supplies which,
given in his name to the King and many lords and prelates, were received
by all with great jubilation; and all the people (who are often excited no
less by frivolous than serious things) ran with great delight to see the
galleass, glorying in the fact that never before in that island had there
been seen any ship flying the pontifical banner.

At last the Bishop of Murray, who had negotiated peace between the
Pontiff and the King of France, induced either by his conscience or by
the desire he had to be made cardinal, spoke very favorably and with
ample documentation of the justice of the Pope's cause before a parliament convoked of representatives from all over the island. This parliament decided that prelates should be sent to the Lateran Council in the
name of the kingdom; and at the request of the Pope's ambassadors, the
King ordered the French ambassador to depart, on the grounds that it
was not fitting that one representing a king who was so openly persecut-
ing the Apostolic See, should be seen at the court of a king and in a
realm devoted to the Church.

And now it leaked out that it had been secretly agreed that the King
of England with his maritime forces should attack the coasts of Nor-

mandy and Brittany, and that he should send eight thousand footsoldiers into Spain to join the armies of the King of Aragon and make war against the duchy of Guyenne.

The King of France was greatly afflicted by this suspected action, because knowing how fearful his people were of the English, remembering their ancient wars, he realized that their danger was all the greater now that Spanish armies were joined with those of England; and particularly because he had sent all his men-at-arms, except two hundred lances, into Italy, and if he summoned back either all or part of them, the duchy of Milan, which he prized so much, would be left in manifest danger.

[*Fearful of the English, distrustful of the Swiss, ever more suspicious of Maximilian, his hopes for an agreement with the Pope vanished, Florentine help of little or no importance—all these reasons induce the King of France to order Gaston de Foix to put an end to the war with a single decisive battle, before the Swiss could penetrate into Milanese territory and Ferdinand attack Navarre, and to impede Henry VIII from disembarking in Normandy and Maximilian from openly declaring his enmity.*

By Holy Week, de Foix arrives at Ravenna and on Good Friday the first attack is launched against the walls, forcing the army of the Holy League—basically Spanish—to come to defend the city. On April 10 they are entrenched three miles from Ravenna, facing the French. Both armies are encamped in the great plain where once existed the port of Classe, where the ancient basilica of S. Apollinare in Classe still stands, not far from the great black-green pine grove where in antiquity barbarian kings fought for the control of Italy. On this classic field the French and the Spanish—the armies of the Most Christian King and of the Catholic King with their various Italian and German allies—prepare to dispute the hegemony of Italy (and Europe). Both armies have a cardinal legate in their ranks: with the French, the Cardinal of San Severino in the name of the Schismatic Council of Milan; with the Spanish, Giovanni de' Medici in the name of the Pope. The day is Easter Sunday, April 11, 1512.

With his army drawn up in battle order, the young French commander Gaston de Foix harangues his troops, promising them rich booty not only in Romagna, but afterward in Rome "where the boundless riches of that wicked court, extracted for so many centuries from the bowels of Christians, will be sacked by you: so many stately ornaments, so much silver, so much gold, so many precious stones, so many rich prisoners. . . ." He calls for "divine justice to punish . . . the pride and enormous vices of that false Pope Julius . . . and the perfidious King of Aragon."]

The Battle of Ravenna

A T these stirring words, the air resounded with the sound of trumpets
and drums and the joyful exclamations of the entire army, as the French
began to move toward the enemy camp, less than two miles away from
the place where they had crossed the stream. The armies of the Holy
League were stretched out along the riverbank to their left, in front of
which they had dug as deep a ditch as they could in the brief time available. Winding clockwise, this trench encircled the entire camp, except
for a space of about twenty cubits which they had left open in front of
the ditch so that the cavalry could ride out for skirmishing. As soon as
they heard the French begin to cross the river, the armies of the League
placed themselves in the following battle-order: the vanguard of eight
hundred men-at-arms led by Fabrizio Colonna was disposed along the

BATTLE OF RAVENNA

*Engraving by the Master of the Mousetrap, signed with the monogram "NA
DAT" on a scroll alongside a trap and a mouse, dated 1530* (COURTESY OF
GABINETTO NAZIONALE DELLE STAMPE, ROME)

riverbank, with a squadron of six thousand footsoldiers joined with them on the right. Behind the vanguard, also along the river, was the main body of six hundred lances, flanked by a squadron of four thousand foot-soldiers, led by the Viceroy* together with the Marquis della Palude. The Cardinal de' Medici was also part of this army, although he was naturally very weak-sighted and mild mannered. The Cardinal wore no battle dress and was, both in demeanor and behavior, utterly unlike the Cardinal of San Severino. Also along the riverbank, following the main forces, was the rear guard of four hundred men-at-arms, led by Carvajal, a Spanish captain; alongside them was a squadron of four thousand footsoldiers, and the light cavalry whose captain-general was Fernando Davalos, Marquis of Pescara, still very young but one of whom great things were expected. His forces were posted to the right, back of the footsoldiers, as reinforcements wherever they were needed. The artillery were planted in front of the men-at-arms; and Pedro Navarro, who with five hundred chosen footsoldiers, was not assigned to any particular post, had drawn up along the ditch in front of the infantry, thirty wagons similar to the scythed war chariots of the ancients, loaded with small artillery pieces and with a very long spear on top, in order to more easily bear the brunt of the French assault. In this order they stood firm-ranked within the stronghold of the ditch waiting for the enemy attack: and just as this disposition of forces did not prove successful at the end, similarly, it seemed very harmful at the beginning. For Fabrizio Colonna had advised them to charge the enemy when he began to cross the stream, judging the advantage of engaging in combat with only part of the enemy to be greater than that of having a little ditch in front of them. But Pedro Navarro disagreed, and since his counsels were accepted almost like oracles by the Viceroy, it was very unwisely agreed to permit the enemy to cross.

Therefore, the Frenchmen kept coming on and were already about two hundred cubits from the trench; but when they saw that their enemies were standing firm and didn't want to issue forth out of their position, the French halted in order not to give them that advantage which they sought to have. Thus both armies remained motionless for more than two hours, the artillery shooting from both sides all this time; the French infantry, especially, suffered not a little from this exchange of fire, since Navarro had planted his artillery pieces very effectively. But the Duke of Ferrara, who had been hauling part of the artillery behind the army, quickly brought it up and had it emplaced at the point in the French battle-order where the archers were disposed; and since the army had been arrayed in a crescent, this point was almost at the shoulders of

* Raimondo de Cardona, Spanish Viceroy of Naples.

ALFONSO D'ESTE, DUKE OF FERRARA

The famous gunsmith and military leader (husband of Lucrezia Borgia) here depicted against a background showing Renaissance footsoldiers and horsemen in action. Portrait by Dosso Dossi, Modena, Galleria Estense. (COURTESY OF FRATELLI ALINARI)

the enemy when they now began to batter furiously along the flank. The cavalry of the League especially suffered great losses from this attack, but the Spanish footsoldiers could not be struck, because, at Navarro's orders, they had been withdrawn to a low-lying spot along the riverbank and ordered to stretch out flat upon the ground. Fabrizio cried aloud and sent many messengers, importuning the Viceroy to enter into the battle without waiting until they were all destroyed by artillery fire. But Navarro was opposed, motivated by his perverse ambition, for he pre-supposed that even though all the others should perish, he would emerge victorious because of the valor of his Spanish footsoldiers, believing that the more losses suffered by the army, the greater would be his glory. But the French artillery had already created such havoc among the men-at-arms and light horse that they could hold out no longer. And now there was a most miserable spectacle: horrible cries, and soldiers and horses falling dead to the ground, and heads and arms sundered from the rest of the body, flying up into the air. Then Fabrizio Colonna exclaimed, "Must we all shamefully die here because of the obstinacy and malignity of a Maranno?* Does this entire army have to be destroyed without killing a single one of the enemy? Where are all the victories which we have won against the French? Is the honor of Spain and Italy to be lost because of one man from Navarre?" And with these words, he forced his men-at-arms to move out in front of the trench, without waiting for the Viceroy's leave or orders. Since these men were followed by all the cavalry, Pedro Navarro was obliged to give the signal to his infantrymen who, rising up from the ground, with great ferocity attacked the German footsoldiers who were already coming at them. Thus all the squadrons were now engaged, and a great battle began, undoubtedly the greatest battle that Italy had seen for many years: for the day-long fight at the Taro had been little more than a gallant encounter of lancers, and the deeds of arms in the kingdom of Naples were disorders or rash actions rather than battles, and in Ghiaradadda [Aguadello] only a very small part of the Venetian army had been engaged in combat. But here at Ravenna everyone was intermingled in the battle which was being fought in a flat countryside without any impediments of waters or shelter which might hinder the action, or any place to take cover. Here two armies fought stubbornly for victory or death, enflamed not only by danger, glory and hope but also by the hatred of nation against nation. And it was a memorable spectacle, when in the encounter of the German and Spanish footsoldiers, two very famous captains, Jakob Empser, a German, and Zamudio, a Spaniard, marched out in front of their squadrons and fought

---

* Jews who had ostensibly converted to Christianity to avoid the persecution of the Inquisition in Spain, but continued secretly to practice the religion of their fathers. The word is a term of abuse, literally meaning "pig," most frequently applied by Christians to other Christians.

almost as if it were a duel, the Spaniard emerging victorious, killing his enemy. Ordinarily the cavalry of the League were not equal to the French cavalry, and since their ranks had been so decimated and torn that day by the enemy artillery, they had become even more inferior; therefore, since they had stood off the enemy attack for some time, with stout hearts rather than by strength of arms, and now that Yves d'Allègre was attacking their flank with the rear guard and the thousand footsoldiers called up by La Palisse from Menton, and now that Fabrizio Colonna had already been captured by the soldiers of the Duke of Ferrara while he was valorously fighting, the cavalry of the League could no longer hold out, and they turned their backs and fled. In this they were only following the example of their captains, because the Viceroy and Carvajal, without making a final test of the valor of their men, had already fled, taking almost the entire third squadron with them, as well as Antonio de Leva, a man at that time of very humble position, but who subsequently served in all ranks of the militia for many years and became a famous captain. All the light cavalry had already been routed, and their captain, the Marquis of Pescara, captured, all covered with blood and wounds. Also taken captive was the Marquis della Palude who had led the second squadron into battle with great disorder through a field full of ditches and briars. The terrain was strewn with dead men and horses; nevertheless, the Spanish infantry, abandoned by their cavalry, continued to fight with incredible ferocity; and although at the first encounter with the German footsoldiers, the Spaniards had been somewhat thrown by the firm and close order of the pikes, later coming to swords' point, many of the Spaniards, protected by their shields, had stabbed their way with daggers amidst the legs of the Germans, and managed to penetrate with very great slaughter almost to the center of the squadron. Near them, the Gascon footsoldiers, having occupied the space between the river and the bank, had assailed the Italian infantry who, although artillery fire had raked their ranks, nevertheless would have repulsed them to their great honor had not Yves d'Allègre with a company of horsemen thrust in amongst them with greater valor than fortune. For almost immediately Yves saw his son Nivarais slaughtered before his very eyes, and not wishing to live after so doleful a loss, hurled himself with his horse amidst the thickest swirl of the enemy, where fighting as a great captain should, and after slaying a great many, he was himself slain. The Italian footsoldiers gave way, not being able to hold out against so great a number, but part of the Spanish infantry, racing to their aid, kept them in the battle; and the German footsoldiers, being pressed on the other side by the Spaniards, could scarcely resist any longer. But all of the cavalry having already fled, Monseigneur de Foix now wheeled about to charge against them with a great body of horsemen. The Spaniards, therefore, withdrawing rather than driven out of the battle, and without any disorder, entered the passage between the river and the high bank, marching in step and close ranks, their front unbroken; their discipline and strength beat off the French attack, and the Spaniards began to withdraw. Navarro, however, refused to retreat with the battalion, preferring to die rather than save himself, and was therefore captured at that time. But Monseigneur de Foix could not tolerate the fact that the Spanish infantry was escaping almost as victors, maintaining their order; and knowing that his victory was imperfect unless these were smashed like the others, he furiously went to attack them with a squadron of horsemen, charging upon their rear guard, who suddenly surrounded him and knocked him off his horse or, as some say, his horse falling upon him while he was fighting, he was wounded by a lance thrust in the side and slain. And if, as it is believed, death is desirable when one is at the culmination of one's greatest glory, his was certainly a most happy death, since he died after having already acquired so glorious a victory. He died at a very young age with an unusual reputation all over the world, since in less than three months, having been a commanding officer almost before he had been a soldier, he had won so many victories with incredible speed and ferocity. Lying near him on the earth as if dead was Monseigneur Lautrec with twenty wounds, but later conveyed to Ferrara, his life was saved by the diligent cure of the physicians.

The death of Monseigneur de Foix permitted the Spanish infantry to disengage themselves from the battle without any difficulty: the rest of the army was already scattered and in flight, the baggage taken, the banners and artillery captured, the Papal Legate a prisoner. The Stradiots handed the Papal Legate over to Federico da Bozzole, who in turn presented him to the Legate of the Council. Also captured were Fabrizio Colonna, Pedro Navarro, the Marquis della Palude, the Marquis of Bitonto, the Marquis of Pescara, and many other lords and barons and honorable gentlemen of Spain and of the kingdom of Naples. Nothing is more uncertain than the number of those dying in a battle; nevertheless, among the various opinions, the most common was that both armies counted at least ten thousand men dead, one-third of the French and two-thirds of their enemies; others say the figures are much greater, but undoubtedly almost all of the most valorous and choicest soldiers; among the ecclesiastical forces, Raffaello de' Pazzi, a famous condottiere, was killed; and a great many men wounded.

But with respect to this, the loss of the victors was greater beyond any comparison as a result of the death of Monseigneur de Foix, of Yves d'Allègre, and many French nobles; as well as Captain Jakob and other brave captains of the German infantry, to whose valor, although at a tremendous price of their blood, the victory is in no small part ascribed. And many Gascon and Picard captains also died together with Captain Molard; fighting alongside the French that day, those nations lost the flower of their forces. But the loss beyond all others was the death of Monseigneur de Foix, which deprived that army of all their nerve and sinew.

Most of the vanquished troops who escaped from the battle fled toward Cesena, whence they continued their flight to more distant places. The Viceroy did not halt until he came to Ancona, where he arrived accompanied by a very small troop of horsemen. Many were murdered and plundered in their flight, because mobs of peasants thronged all the roads, and the Duke of Urbino was not only stirring up these peasants against those in flight, but he was also sending soldiers to do the same in the territory of Pesaro. It was believed that the Duke of Urbino had secretly come to an agreement against his uncle, since several days earlier he had sent Baldassare Castiglione to the French King, and had some of his own men with Foix. Only those who fled via Florentine territory passed through unharmed by order of the local magistrates and later of the Republic.

The victorious army having returned to their camp, the people of Ravenna immediately sent representatives to offer up their surrender; but either while they were meeting or had already met, and were waiting to order provisions to be sent to the camp, they neglected to maintain their vigilance in guarding the walls, and German and Gascon footsoldiers entered through the breach in the wall which had been broken down to the ground and cruelly sacked the town; incited to the greatest cruelties because of their fury at the loss which they had received during that day, as well as by their natural hatred against the Italians. Four days later, Marcantonio Colonna surrendered the citadel in which he had taken refuge, saving his person and his possessions; but at the parley he promised that he, together with the other captains would not take up arms either against the King of France or against the Council of Pisa until the next Festival of Mary Magdalen. And a few days afterward, the Bishop Vitello, provost of the fortress, with five hundred footsoldiers, agreed to yield it up under the same conditions. The cities of Imola, Forlì, Cesena and Rimini, and all the fortresses of Romagna except those of Forlì and Imola suffered the same fate: all of them were received by the Legate in the name of the Council of Pisa. But the French army, as if stunned by the death of Foix and the terrible losses they had sustained, remained idle four miles from Ravenna. For the Legate and La Palisse (upon whom the leadership of the army had now devolved because Alfonso d'Este had returned to Ferrara) were uncertain of the King's will and were awaiting his orders, since they had not yet gained sufficient authority over the troops to order the army to move. The soldiers, meanwhile, were involved in distributing and dispatching to safe places the goods which they had plundered; and so weakened and dispirited were they by the victory which they had won with such expenditure of blood, that they seemed

*REVERSE OF MEDAL OF
KING LOUIS XII*

*This medal (on the reverse of the
medal of Louis XII on p. 133)
possibly symbolizes the reversals suffered by the French after their victory
at Ravenna—the mourning figure to
the left being Italy, the* furia francese
*pursuing the victim being herself pur-
sued by Mars* (COURTESY OF GABINETTO
NAZIONALE DELLE STAMPE, ROME)

more like the conquered than the conquerors. And all the soldiers were
calling out the name of Foix with tears and lamentations, for they would
have followed him anywhere, fearing nothing and nothing daunted. And
no one doubted that immediately after the victory, spurred by his
ferocity, as well as by the King's promises (according to the rumor) that
the kingdom of Naples was intended to be acquired for him, he would
have raced with his customary swiftness to Rome, from which the Pope
and his followers, having no other hope of saving themselves, would
have precipitously fled.

[*Enormous is the consternation with which news of the French victory at Ravenna is received by the Vatican. Cardinals fall at the
Pope's feet, imploring him to make peace since the will of God is
obviously against him. The members of the Sacred College also insist
on the gravity of the situation at home, and the growing restlessness
and opposition of the people of Rome. Julius agrees to open negotiations with the Most Christian King, but at the same time assures the
Spanish and Venetian envoys that he is only seeking to gain time, and
that they should remain loyal to the League.*

*Now the wheel of fortune begins to turn in his favor. In May,
twenty thousand Swiss come down from the mountains, and the
French abandon Romagna and retreat to Lombardy. In June, the
French army now commanded by La Palisse has to rush back to
defend French soil, invaded in Navarre by the Spaniards and in
Normandy and Guyenne by the English. Already on the 3rd of May,
sure of himself and with great pomp, Julius had inaugurated the
Lateran Council, which he had convoked against the Council of
Pisa and Milan.*]

BOOK

II

Aftermath of Ravenna

ITALY, THEREFORE, BEING SAFE FOR THIS YEAR [1512] FROM THE ARMIES OF THE FRENCH KING, WHOSE SOLDIERS STILL HELD BRESCIA, CREMA, LEGNAGO, THE castle and lighthouse of Genoa, the castles of Milan, Cremona and several other fortresses of that realm, certain signs of distrust and disunion among the confederates now manifested themselves, so greatly variant were their desires and aims. The Venetians wanted to recover Brescia and Crema, due to them by the articles of capitulation, and because they had so long withstood the dangers and troubles of the war, and the Pope fully shared their desires. On the other hand, Maximilian Caesar (from whose will the King of Aragon could not separate himself in the long run) thought to claim these for himself, and also to despoil the Venetians of everything which had been allotted to them by the League of Cambrai. Caesar and the King of Aragon secretly devised a plan whereby the duchy of Milan should devolve upon one of the nephews they had in common. In opposition to this, the Pope and Swiss strove openly to have Maximilian, son of Lodovico Sforza, who had resided continually in Germany after his father's downfall, restored to his father's position, as had always been the understanding from the very beginning. What primarily moved the Pope was a concern that Italy should not fall entirely under German and Spanish domination; what primarily moved the Swiss was concern for their own profit; hence, they didn't want Italy to be dominated by such powerful princes but rather by those who could not rule without their help. And this depended almost entirely upon them, in whose power Italy lay, because of the fear of their arms, so that the Pope employed every means and effort to keep them friendly, in order to bolster their aims, thus having that bridle ready whereby he could moderate the ambition of Caesar and the Catholic King on any occasion.

For this reason, besides publicly exalting up to the stars the valor of

[253]

the Helvetian nation and magnifying the work which they had done for the safety of the Apostolic See, he honored them with the banners of the Church and granted them the glorious title of champions and defenders of ecclesiastical liberty.*

In addition to these other differences, the Viceroy had re-established order among the Spanish troops who had all withdrawn with him after the rout into the kingdom of Naples, and was now preparing to pass with them into Lombardy. But the Pope and Venetians refused to continue to take upon themselves the payments of forty thousand ducats a month which had been discontinued after the defeat, alleging that since the French army had already crossed beyond the mountains, they were no longer obligated to make those payments which terminated according to the articles of the League every time the French were cast out of Italy. The reply on behalf of the King of Aragon was that one could not say that the French King had been cast out of Italy so long as Brescia, Crema and so many fortresses remained in his power. Furthermore, the King of Aragon and Maximilian Caesar complained that the Pope had appropriated for himself all the prizes of a victory gained in common, and had usurped what clearly belonged to others, occupying, on the grounds of claims either feigned or moldering with age, Parma and Piacenza, cities which had for the longest time been held by whoever ruled Milan as feudatories of the empire. There also appeared a similar difference of opinion with regard to matters concerning the Duke of Ferrara. The Pope was still enflamed with his ancient greed, and on the other hand, the King of Aragon, who desired to protect the Duke, was also angry (as was believed) that an attempt had been made to keep him in Rome contrary to a promise given. Hence the Pope put off attacking Ferrara, hoping that by chance more important matters might be settled first; and Maximilian, wishing to intervene in this situation, sent the Bishop of Gurk into Italy, whom he had planned to send there ever since there had been negotiations for peace between the Pope and the King of France after the battle of Ravenna. Caesar Maximilian dispatched the Bishop to Italy because he feared lest they come to agreements among themselves without taking his interests into consideration; but when afterward the change in the situation occurred, he persisted in his intention to send him.

Similarly, Florentine affairs were taken under consideration. For the Florentines, full of suspicion, were now beginning to taste the fruits of

* Six years earlier, according to Burchard's *Diarium* (22 January 1506), Julius had already taken a personal Swiss Guard into his service at the Vatican. By the end of his pontificate the corps had risen to two hundred. Their uniform consisted at that time of doublet and long hose, with a black velvet cap. The colors were not always the black, red, and yellow of today but varied considerably, judging by Raphael's and other frescoes.

the neutrality which they had unwisely maintained, and to realize that a plenitude of justice in one's cause was insufficient protection when prudence was lacking.

For in the present war they had not acted against the allies nor given any help whatever to the King of France except insofar as they were obliged to the defense of the duchy of Milan according to the treaty drawn up jointly with the Catholic King and the Duke; they had not permitted any harm to be done in their domain to the Spanish soldiers fleeing from the battle of Ravenna (for which the King of Aragon himself had thanked the Florentine ambassador); rather, they had fully satisfied all his demands, so that later, when the Council departed from Pisa, both the King himself and his ministers in Italy had offered the Florentine ambassador a pledge binding them to defend their Republic against anyone, provided that they promised him not to come to the defense of Bologna nor take arms against the Church nor favor the Conventicle of Pisa.

But civic discord prevented the Florentines from choosing the better course, so that they did not join up with the King of France nor anyone else. Instead they chose a course of neutrality which they maintained from day to day with ambiguous and interrupted councils, never deliberating in a unified fashion nor declaring that they wished to observe neutrality. Thus they succeeded in offending to no small degree the mind of the King of France, who from the beginning had expected a great deal of them, nor did they mitigate the hatred the Pontiff felt toward them, and without any compensation whatever on their part, they permitted the King of Aragon to enjoy the fruits of their neutrality, to obtain which he would have gladly come to an agreement with them.

Therefore the Pope, goaded by his hatred against the Gonfaloniere and by the ancient desire of all pontiffs to hold power over that Republic, earnestly requested the restitution of the family of the Medici to their previous glory. And although he used words different than the facts with the Florentine ambassador, the King of Aragon was equally inclined to support this demand, but not with so much vehemence, for fear lest any disturbance whatever in Florence might cause them to lean in favor of the King of France as a result of the authority of the Gonfaloniere; rather it was suspected that even though the Gonfaloniere might be removed, the Republic freely governed would still have the same friendship for the French as a result of both new and ancient dependences.

[Thus, at last] either because of the carelessness or malignity of men, the Florentine cause was entirely abandoned, and it was decided [at an assembly of the Holy League at Mantua where the Bishop of Gurk, Matthew Lang, came as representative of Maximilian] that the Spanish army, together with the Cardinal* and Giuliano de' Medici, should march toward Florence; furthermore, that the Cardinal (whom the Pope declared to be Legate of Tuscany in that campaign) should levy the soldiers of the Church and such others from the neighboring territories as he thought suitable for that purpose.

Spanish Forces (with a Medici Cardinal) March Against Florence

As soon as the affairs of the Diet [the assembly at Mantua] had been expedited, the Viceroy returned to Bologna, where he immediately set his army on the march against the Florentines, who had very little time to make necessary preparations since they did not know previously what had been decided at Mantua. When the Viceroy drew near the frontier, he was joined by the Cardinal, who had had two cannons moved up from Bologna since the Spaniards lacked artillery to batter the walls. Franciotto Orsini and the Vitellis, paid captains of the Church, had also arrived but without their companies, because the Duke of Urbino had forbidden it, both to them and to the other soldiers of the Church. For notwithstanding that Giuliano de' Medici had been brought up for several years in the court of the Duke of Urbino, who had always claimed to desire the greatness of the house of Medici, he had refused (for whatever reason) to furnish them with artillery or any help of any kind, either of soldiers or his subjects, despite the fact that the Pope had commanded the contrary with ample briefs addressed to him and to neighboring towns subject to the Church.

As soon as the Viceroy had entered Florentine territory, an ambassador of the Republic came to him. The ambassador declared that the Florentines had always kept their faith with the King of Aragon, and set forth how the Republic had comported itself in the recent war, and what the King might expect from that city by taking it under his protection, and besought him to indicate, before proceeding any farther, what he wanted of the Florentines, because they would willingly agree to satisfy any

* After his capture at the battle of Ravenna, Cardinal Giovanni de' Medici had been taken prisoner to Milan, where even enemy troops flocked to him to receive the dispensation or absolution which, as papal legate, he was empowered to give. While being led to Lyons by the schismatic cardinals, the Medici cardinal managed to escape from the hands of the French. All this is celebrated symbolically in Raphael's fresco of the meeting of Leo I (the Great) and Attila, wherein Giovanni, then Pope Leo X, is depicted on the white horse he had ridden at Ravenna, and a year later at his grandiose *possesso* of the Lateran. In the fresco, the Huns undoubtedly refer to the French.

reasonable demands that were within their power. The Viceroy replied that his coming had not been decided upon only by the Catholic King but by all the confederates for the common security of Italy; therefore, so long as the Gonfaloniere remained in that administration, there could be no guarantee that on some other occasion, the Florentines would not follow the King of France. Therefore, he was to demand in the name of the whole League that the Gonfaloniere be removed from the magistracy, and that a form of government be set up which would not be suspected by the confederates; and that this could not be done unless the Cardinal and Giuliano de' Medici were restored to their country; and if this were agreed to, they would easily come to an agreement on the other problems. Therefore, the ambassadors should go and report, or otherwise indicate to the Florentines what the Viceroy had in mind, but that he had no intentions of waiting until the reply came.

When the Florentines learned of the coming of the Spaniards, and convinced that they were going to be assailed from some other side by the papal forces, a terrible wave of terror spread throughout the city, for fear of the dissensions among the citizens and the fact that many of them were inclined toward a change of government. They had very few men-at-arms, no infantry except those who had been levied at the last minute or drawn from their garrisons, most of whom were inexperienced in war; they had no excellent captain on whose experience and prestige they could depend; and as for their other captains, never in the memory of man had they had condottieri in their pay from whom they might expect less. Nevertheless, making as careful preparations as they could in the short time available, they assembled their men-at-arms scattered in various places, summoned up footsoldiers wherever they could, and selecting the most useful bands of all their garrisons, they brought all their forces to Florence for the safety of their city and to serve as a base from which supplies might be sent to other places which the enemy might attack.

And although it was late, they did not cease to try to reach an agreement, by means other than the negotiations which the ambassador continued to have with the Viceroy. Hence they wrote to the Cardinal of Volterra, who was at Gradoli near Rome, to go to the Pope and seek to placate him with supplications and offers and every possible means. But the Pope stubbornly replied (with words contrary to his actions) that he was not responsible for this campaign, and that it was being carried out without his forces; but in order not to provoke the entire League against him, he was forced to agree to it, and to permit the Cardinal de' Medici to have artillery brought up from Bologna; and that since he couldn't deflect the campaign before it had begun, much less could he stop it now that it had already begun.

Meanwhile, the Viceroy, who had descended from the mountains at

Barberino, a town fifteen miles from Florence, sent one of his men to indicate that it was not the intention of the League to make any changes either in the government or liberty of the city, provided that the Gonfaloniere be removed from the magistracy for the security of Italy. Furthermore, the League desired that the Medici might be able to enjoy their country, not as heads of the government, but as private citizens living under the law and subject to the magistrates, and in all things like any other citizens.

When this proposal was made known throughout the city, there were as many differences of opinion among the citizens as there are judgments, passions and fears. Some complained that because of one man* only, all the citizens and the entire domain had to be exposed to so much peril; and seeing that removing him from the magistracy, neither the popular Council nor public freedom would be lost, nor would it be difficult to maintain their liberty even should the Medici, deprived of reputation and power, seek to exceed the bounds of their status as private citizens. It was necessary to consider how the city could resist the prestige and power of such a League; certainly their own force was insufficient, with all of Italy their enemies, and there being no hope whatsoever of receiving help from the French, who had abandoned Italy in a cowardly fashion and had all they could do to defend their own kingdom; and aware of their weakness, had replied to the Florentine demands that they [the French] would be satisfied if they came to an agreement with the League.

Others said, on the contrary, that it was absurd to think that so much fuss was being made simply out of hatred for the Gonfaloniere, or in order that the Medici might be permitted to remain in Florence as private citizens; that the allies had other things in mind, namely, to have the entire city at their will and to be able to extract great sums of money from it, and therefore their real aim was nothing less than to reinstate the Medici in their tyranny, but to disguise their intentions with less bitter demands which nevertheless tended toward the same effect. For what else did removing the Gonfaloniere from the palace at this time by threats and fear of arms mean, other than allowing the flock to be lost without a pastor? What else did reinstating the Medici back in Florence amidst such tumults signify, except to raise a standard which those would follow who thought of nothing but expunging the name, the memory, the remains of the Grand Council? and once this was annulled, then liberty was annulled. And how could one prevent the Medici, supported from without by the Spanish army, and from within by ambitious and seditious followers, from oppressing freedom the very day they entered Florence? It was necessary to consider what might be the issue of such things, and what may happen by beginning to yield to unjust and dangerous demands.

* Piero Soderini, the Gonfaloniere for life.

Nor should one be so much in fear of danger that one forgot the security of the city, and how bitter it was for those who had been born and raised in freedom to live in servitude. And that they should remember how valiantly and firmly they had stood in defense of their freedom against Charles VIII, King of France, when he came to Florence with so mighty an army; and that they should consider how much easier it was to resist such small forces, lacking money, supplies, victuals, and with few artillery pieces, and without any means of being able to last out the war (should the Florentines resist their first attack); and who would be disposed toward a treaty under fair terms once they were forced to remain for a while in Tuscany, and saw how vigorously the Florentines were beginning to defend themselves against an enemy who thought (stirred up by hopeful exiles) they would gain victory by a simple assault.

Such were the things being said in the marketplaces and piazzas among the citizens. But the Gonfaloniere, wishing that the people themselves should decide on the reply which the magistrates had to give to the Viceroy's agent, convened the Grand Council, and when the citizens had met, spoke in these terms:

"If I thought that the Viceroy's demands concerned only my interests alone, I myself would have made the decision suitable to my proposal; since I have always been prepared to risk my life for your benefit, and it would be much easier to renounce the magistracy which you have given me, and so free myself of the troubles and dangers of war; especially since in all these years while I have held this position, my body and soul have been riven with toils and troubles. But insofar as something beyond my own interest is involved in this demand, it seemed to my honorable fellow counselors and to me that matters which so concern the interests of all should not be decided without public approval, and that such a serious problem involving everyone should not be deliberated upon by the usual number of citizens with whom other matters are commonly discussed, but rather with you who are the foundation of this city and who alone have the right to deal with such a solemn decision. Nor do I wish to influence you in any way; the recommendation should be yours, the decision yours; I will accept and honor whatever decision you come to. I offer you not only the magistracy which belongs to you, but my person, my very life: and I would consider myself singularly blessed if I thought this might provide for your security. Examine what the Viceroy's demands might mean with regard to your freedom, and God give you grace of understanding that you will come to the best decision. If the Medici were disposed to live in this city as private citizens, patiently accepting the decisions of the magistrates and your laws, their restitution would be praiseworthy, in order that the commonweal might be forged into a single body. But if their intentions are otherwise, be aware of the danger facing you, and do not let any expenses and difficulties seem too heavy to bear when it is a question of maintaining your freedom; how precious freedom is you will realize better, if fruitlessly (I dread to say it) you are deprived of it. Nor should anyone delude himself that government by the Medici would be the same as it was before they were exiled, because the form and basis of things have changed: at that time, raised amongst us almost like private citizens, [possessing] the richest means in view of their position, harmed by no one, they based their rule on the good will of the citizens, discussed public affairs with the outstanding men, and made every effort to cover themselves with the cloak of civic virtue as soon as their ambitions were revealed. But now, having dwelt so many years outside of Florence, brought up in foreign ways, and for this reason out of touch with civic matters, remembering their exile and the harsh manner in which they had been treated, very reduced in means and distrusted by so many families; aware that most, indeed, almost the entire city abhors tyranny, they would not share their counsels with any citizen; and forced by poverty and suspicion, they would arrogate everything to themselves, depending primarily not on good will and love but force and arms, with the result that in a very short time this city would become like Bologna at the time of the Bentivoglio, or like Siena or Perugia. I wanted to say this to those who preach about the time and rule of Lorenzo the Magnificent. For, although conditions were hard then and there was a tyranny (although milder than many others), by comparison with this, Lorenzo's rule would be an age of gold. Now it is your responsibility to deliberate wisely, in terms of the security of your country; and it is my responsibility to give up this magistracy with a resolved and joyous spirit; or should you decide otherwise, honestly to attend to the preservation and defense of your liberty."

There was no question what the Council's decision would be, in view of the fact that almost all the people wanted to maintain popular government. Nevertheless, it was surprisingly agreed that the return of the Medici as private citizens be allowed, but that the Gonfaloniere's removal from the government be denied. And that should the enemy remain pertinacious in this demand [for the Gonfaloniere's dismissal], then the Florentines should make ready to defend their liberty and their country with all their means and their lives.

And so, directing all their thoughts to war and necessary funds, they sent men to Prato, ten miles from Florence, which they believed would be the first place to be attacked by the Viceroy; who, after he had assembled his army at Barberino, as well as the artillery which had been hauled with difficulty because of the harsh Apennine roads, and also because they lacked money to pay for artillerymen and equipment for hauling it, he turned (as it was believed) toward Prato. Arriving there at dawn, he began on the same day to batter the Mercatale gate for several hours with falconets; but because it was well fortified from within, he made no effect whatever. The Florentines had stationed about two thousand footsoldiers within Prato, almost all of their garrison troops, the others levied hastily from all the crafts and humble trades, few of whom had any experience in warfare. There were also a hundred men-at-arms under Luca Savello, an old condottiere who, despite his age and experience, had not achieved any distinction whatever in military science; the men-at-arms were the same who a little while before had been plundered in Lombardy. In addition, there was a very limited number of artillery pieces, scarcity of ammunition and everything necessary for defense, because of the short time available and the inexperience of those responsible for making such provisions. The Viceroy had two hundred men-at-arms, five thousand Spanish footsoldiers, and only two cannon, a very small force in terms of numbers and other provisions, but great in valor. All of the footsoldiers were the very same who had won such praise for their skillful retreat from the battle of Ravenna, when like true soldiers, depending greatly on their valor, they had scornfully taken advantage of their adversary's lack of skill. But having come without any provisions for victuals; and finding that they could not live easily off the country (for although the harvest had just recently been gathered, it was all laid away in safe places), they immediately began to feel the pinch of supplies. Frightened by this, the Viceroy was inclined to come to an agreement, which was continually under discussion: to the effect that the Florentines should consent to the return of the Medici equal with the other citizens, and without speaking any more about deposing the Gonfaloniere, the city should pay the Viceroy a certain sum of money in order that he should depart from Florentine territory; it was believed that this sum would not exceed thirty thousand ducats. Therefore the Viceroy had granted safe conduct to the ambassadors chosen for this purpose, and he would have abstained from attacking Prato until they came, if those within the city had given him some means of provisions.

The Sack of Prato and Return of the Medici to Florence

NOTHING flies away faster than opportunity, nothing more dangerous than to judge other people's intentions, nothing more harmful than immoderate suspicion. All the leading citizens wanted an agreement, accustomed by the example of their forefathers to often defend their liberty against iron with gold. Therefore, they urgently requested that the ambassadors chosen should immediately depart, charged among other things, to see to it that provisions be made available from Prato to the Spanish army, so that the Viceroy might quietly wait if the treaty being negotiated should be drawn up. But the Gonfaloniere, either because he persuaded himself against his natural timidity that the enemy despaired of victory and therefore would have to depart by themselves in any case, or fearing that the Medici might return to Florence by some device, or fate leading him on to be the cause of his own ruin and of the calamity of his country, guilefully delayed dispatching the ambassadors so that they did not depart on the day when they were supposed to go according to the decision.

Hence the Viceroy, pinched by the want of provisions and uncertain if the ambassadors would come any more, shifted camp on the following night from the gate of the Mercatale to the gate called del Serraglio, from which one goes toward the mountains, and there he began to batter the nearest wall with his two cannon; he chose this place because a high turret was joined to the wall from which one could easily climb up to the breach in the wall above that was being bombarded; and this advantage from without became a hindrance from within because the breach that was being made above the turret remained from within very high above the ground. One of the two cannon shattered at the very first salvo, and the other, which they continued to fire alone, had lost so much of its strength because it had been shot off so frequently that the shots reached the walls with weak velocity and to little effect. Nevertheless, after they had, over a period of many hours, made an opening of somewhat more than twelve cubits, some of the Spanish infantry mounted the turret to assail the breach and from there they got up to the top of the wall where they killed two of the footsoldiers who were guarding it. The death of these caused the others to begin to withdraw and the Spaniards were already climbing up the scaling ladders; and although within, near the wall there was a squadron of footsoldiers with pikes and grenades under orders not to permit any of the enemy to stay on the wall and to attack any of those who foolhardily jumped within or got down in any way, yet as soon as they began to see the enemies on the walls, they fled and abandoned the defense. The Spaniards, amazed that military men as well as humble inexpert civilians should show such cowardice and so little skill, broke into the wall without any opposition for the most part, and began to race through the town, where there was no longer any resistance, but only cries, flight, violence, sack, blood and killing, the terrified Florentine footsoldiers casting away their weapons and surrendering to the victors. And nothing would have been spared the avarice, lust and cruelty of the invaders had not the Cardinal de' Medici placed guards at the main church and saved the honor of the women, all of whom had taken refuge there. More than two thousand men died, not fighting (for not one fought) but fleeing or crying for mercy; all the others together with the Florentine representatives were taken prisoner. Once Prato was lost, the Pistoiese* agreed to provide the Viceroy with provisions, and received from him a promise that they would not be harmed. But only in this instance did the Pistoiese depart from Florentine rule.

But as soon as the Florentines heard about the defeat of Prato (so that the ambassadors who were coming to the Viceroy turned back, halfway there), there was great perturbation in the minds of men. The Gonfaloniere, regretting his vain counsels, terrified and having almost completely lost his reputation and prestige, ruled rather than ruling, and irresolute, allowed himself to be led by the will of others, and did not attend to anything, neither protecting himself nor the safety of the citizenry. Others who were looking forward to a change in government waxed bold and publicly laid blame on the present state of affairs: but most of the citizens, unaccustomed to arms and having the miserable example of Prato before their eyes, although they warmly preferred a popular form of government, were exposed because of their fear, as easy prey of anyone who wished to oppress them.

Because of this, Paolo Vettori and Antonio Francesco degli Albizi, young noblemen, seditious and eager for innovations, became more audacious. Many months earlier these two had already secretly conspired with several others in favor of the Medici, and had secretly met and spoken with Giulio de' Medici** in a villa within Florentine territory near Siena, for the purpose of working out a means to restore this family to power. These young men now resolved to get the Gonfaloniere out of the municipal palace by force. Having apprised Bartolomeo Valori of their plans, a young man of the same rank and, like Paolo, deeply in debt because of his excessive expenditures, on the morning of the second day after the loss of Prato, which was the last day of August, they went with a small company to the palace, where they found no guard or resistance whatever, since the Gonfaloniere had surrendered everything to the will of chance and fortune; and entered his chamber and threatened to take his life if he should not leave the palace; in which case they promised to give him their pledge that he would go unharmed. The Gonfaloniere yielded to this, and now there was a tumultuous uprising all over the city, many persons revealing themselves opposed to him and no one in his

* People of Pistoia, a town twenty-two miles from Florence.

** Cardinal Giovanni's cousin, natural son of Giuliano, brother to Lorenzo the Magnificent. Created Cardinal by his cousin when the latter became Pope Leo X, (the illegitimacy of his birth being dispensed with by witnesses who testified that Giulio's mother and father had been secretly married) Giulio himself was elected to the papacy in 1523, assuming the name of Clement VII.

favor. Having at their orders caused the magistrates immediately to convene, who according to the law had the widest authority over the *gonfalonieri*,* the conspirators demanded that Soderini be legally removed from the magistracy, under the threat that otherwise they would take his life. Fearing he would be killed, he was removed from office against his will, and taken for safety to the house of Paolo Vettori whence, on the following night, carefully guarded, he was led to Sienese territory, and from there, pretending to go to Rome with the safe-conduct obtained from the Pope, he secretly took the road to Ancona and went by sea to Ragusa, because his brother the Cardinal had advised him that the Pope would break his promise to him, either out of hatred or greed to plunder his money since he was reputed to be very rich. Once the Gonfaloniere had been removed from the magistracy, the city immediately sent ambassadors to the Viceroy with whom they easily came to an agreement, the Cardinal de' Medici serving as intermediary. The Cardinal was satisfied that with regard to his own interests there should be no mention other than restitution of his family and all their followers within the country as private citizens, with the right to buy back, within a certain time, their properties which had been expropriated by taxation, but restoring the money spent and the [cost of] improvements made by those to whom they had been transferred.

With regard to public affairs, the Florentines joined the League; they obliged themselves, according to what the Medici had promised at Mantua in exchange for their restitution, to pay the Emperor forty thousand ducats as the Bishop of Gurk had demanded; and to pay eighty thousand ducats to the Viceroy for the army, half at the present time and the remaining in two months, and twenty thousand ducats for the Viceroy personally; on condition that having received his first payment, the army would immediately leave Florentine domain, giving up what they had seized. Besides this, they made a league with the King of Aragon with reciprocal obligations of certain numbers of men-at-arms in defense of their states, and that the Florentines should muster two hundred men-at-arms in their pay as subjects of that King; the leadership of this group, although not specified, was intended for the Marquis della Palude, to whom the Cardinal had promised, or at least given hope, to make him a captain-general of the Florentine armies.

The Gonfaloniere having been cast out and the dangers of war having been removed by the agreement, the citizens now began to work to correct the government in certain matters in which the previous

*Gonfaloniers, or standard-bearers. These were the priors among whom Piero Soderini, Gonfaloniere of Justice, the chief prior, had been given an appointment for life ten years before, in emulation of the stability of Venetian government whose doge served in perpetuity.

organization was considered to be useless, but with a universal intention (except for very few, and these either youths or almost all people of low rank), to maintain liberty and the Grand Council. Therefore they decided by new legislation that the Gonfaloniere should no longer be chosen in perpetuity but only for one year, and that in addition to the Council of the Eighty, which was changed every six months and which had the authority to determine the most serious matters, in order that the best-qualified citizens might participate in its councils, there should be added in perpetuity all those who had administered up to that day the chief offices, either at home or abroad: at home those who had been either Gonfaloniere of Justice or of the Ten of the Balìa, of great prestige in that Republic; abroad all those who had been chosen by the Council of Eighty as either ambassadors to princes or general commissioners in war, leaving the organization of the government unchanged in all other respects.

Having established these things, the gonfaloniere elected for the first year was Giovan Battista Ridolfi, a noble citizen reputed to be very wise; the people having respect (as occurs in disturbed times) not so much for those who were more pleasing to them because of their popular touch, but rather those who could hold the trembling Republic firm by their own virtues, and by their great authority in the city, especially among the nobility.

But things had already gone too far, and the commonweal had too many powerful enemies—in the bowels of the domain a distrustful army, within the city the most audacious youth eager to oppress it. And although he demonstrated the contrary with words, the Cardinal de' Medici wanted the same thing. From the very beginning he would not have considered the restitution of his family as private citizens worthy reward for so much toil; furthermore, considering that now especially not even this would prove to be long-lasting, because together with his name, they would be deeply hated by everyone, the other citizens being always goaded by the suspicion that the house of Medici would lay ambush against their freedom, and much more because of the hatred felt against the Medici who had led the Spanish army against their country and been the cause of the most cruel sack of Prato, and because the city out of terror of arms had been forced to accept such base and iniquitous terms. Those who had previously conspired with him had spurred him on, as well as several others who had no honorable position in a well-ordered republic. But the consent of the Viceroy was necessary, who still remained at Prato waiting for the first payment, which the city was having difficulties in meeting because of conditions within Florence. And whatever might be his reason, the Viceroy was not inclined toward any change of government within the city.

Nevertheless, when the Cardinal demonstrated to him (and saw to it that he was seconded by the Marquis della Palude and Andrea Caraffa, Count of Santa Severina, condottiere in the army) that the very name of Spaniard could not help but be most odious to a city where they had caused so much harm; and that on any occasion whatever the Florentines would always support the enemies of the Catholic King (indeed there was danger that once the army withdrew, they would summon back the Gonfaloniere, whom they had been forced to expel), the Viceroy finally consented to the Cardinal's demands. He was also influenced thereto by the fact that the Florentines were having so much difficulty in raising the money which they had promised. Indeed, had they been more prompt in their payments, a firmer foundation for a free government would have been laid down.

As soon as the Cardinal had settled his affairs with the Viceroy, he immediately went to his palace in Florence; and many condottieri and Italian soldiers entered the city, some with the Cardinal and some separately, since the magistrates, for fear of the closeness of the Spaniards, did not dare forbid them to enter.

On the following day, a council of many citizens convened at the public palace to discuss affairs, Giuliano de' Medici* being present at the meeting, when suddenly soldiers assaulted the gate and then climbed the stairs and occupied the palace, pillaging the silver which was kept there for the use of the Signoria. The Signori, together with the Gonfaloniere, were forced to yield to the will of those who could do more with weapons than the magistrates could achieve by respect and unarmed authority; and so as Giuliano de' Medici proposed, the Signori immediately summoned the people to a parliament** in the Piazza Signoria, by ringing the great bell. Those who appeared were surrounded by armed soldiers and young men within the city, who had seized arms for the Medici; and thus they agreed that power over public affairs should be turned over to about fifty citizens chosen according to the Cardinal's will, and that these citizens should have the same authority as had the entire people (which broad form of power the Florentines called Balìa). Now by the decree of these men, the government was reduced to that form which it used to have before the year 1494, and a garrison was set up within the palace, and the Medici seized once again that same position of grandeur, but governed much more imperiously and with much more absolute power than had their forefathers.

Thus the liberty of the Florentines was oppressed by arms, but the Florentines had been led to that situation primarily as a result of the

---

* Cardinal Giovanni's older brother, later Duke of Nemours.

** The Medici always employed the *Parlamento*, or meeting of the Florentine people in the Piazza Signoria, as a means of gaining absolute power (*Balìa*). See footnote * p. 76.

disagreements among the citizens; and it was believed that they would not have fallen to such a state (I pass over the neutrality which they had so unwisely maintained, and the fact that the Gonfaloniere had permitted the enemies of popular government to become too confident) if they had not, also in recent times, so neglected public affairs. For the King of Aragon had not at first so great a desire to subvert liberty as to turn the city away from its loyalty to the King of France and get some money out of it to pay his army. Therefore, as soon as the French had abandoned the duchy of Milan, he commissioned the Viceroy that, when things made it necessary for him to turn to other enterprises, or for whatever other reason he might realize that the restitution of the Medici would prove difficult, he should make his decision according to conditions of the times, and should deal or not deal with the city according as it seemed opportune to him. This had been his order from the beginning; but later, angered against the Pope for what he had attempted to do at Rome against Alfonso d'Este, and suspicious because of the threats which the Pope was publicly making against what he called barbarians, the King openly made it clear to the same Florentine ambassador who had come to him at the beginning of the war, and instructed the Viceroy that there should not be attempted any change in government, either because he judged that it would be safer to maintain the Gonfaloniere, who was an enemy of the Pope, or because he feared that once the Cardinal de' Medici was restored, he would lean far more on the Pope than on him. But this last decision was not known to the Viceroy until the day after the Republic had fallen into the Cardinal's hands. By this it seems clear that if, after the French had been evicted, the Florentines had carefully seen to it, by means of an agreement, that their situation was strengthened; or if they had fortified themselves with arms and trained soldiers, then either the Viceroy would not have marched against them or, finding it difficult to defeat them, would easily have been brought to an agreement with money. But it was destined that they should not act in that fashion, despite the fact that, besides what might have been understood by human reason, they had not also been forewarned of imminent perils by celestial signs: for, a little while earlier, a thunderbolt had struck the Prato gate and knocked the golden lilies, insignia of the King of France, off an ancient marble shield; another lightning bolt had hit the top of the palace and, entering into the Gonfaloniere's chamber, had struck nothing except the great silver box in which votes of the supreme magistracy had been gathered, and then flashing down to the lowest part of the palace, had struck a great stone which held up the whole weight of the building at the foot of the stairs, so that the stone was pushed out of its place unharmed and looked as if it had been drawn out of there by the most skillful architectural experts.

French Affairs

Perhaps it will seem beyond the bounds of my proposal not to deal with affairs occurring outside of Italy, if I make mention of what happened in France that same year [1512]; but because our concerns are affected by what has occurred there, and because the successes of one are often conjoined with the successes and decisions of the other, I cannot pass over French events in silence. At the beginning of May, six thousand English footsoldiers set sail in English and Spanish vessels for Fuenterabia, the last town on the Spanish coast toward France on the Ocean Sea, to attack jointly with Spanish forces, according to an agreement drawn up between father-in-law and son-in-law, the duchy of Guyenne which is part of the province of Aquitaine according to the ancient names and divisions. In reply, the King of France, whose defenses were still insufficient in Picardy, prepared a new levy of eight hundred lances which he had drawn up, and mustered many footsoldiers from the lowest parts of Germany which were not subject to the Emperor; and knowing how important to the defense of the duchy of Guyenne was the kingdom of Navarre (which was the dowry of Catherine de Foix and possessed jointly with her husband Jean, son of Albret [King of Navarre]) he had called Albret to the court and besought with great care to come to an understanding with him. His efforts in this regard were greatly aided by the death of Gaston de Foix, who had not wanted that kingdom to devolve upon the females but upon himself as the next male heir of the house of Foix, and therefore had instigated the French King to oppress Jean.

On the other hand, the Catholic King, who had set his eyes on that realm, demanded that the King of Navarre remain neutral between the French King and himself, and requested also that he permit passage through his realm of Spanish troops that had to enter France; and that as security for the observation of these promises, he should hand over to him certain fortresses which he promised to return as soon as the war was over. The King of Navarre knew where these demands were leading, since the ancient desire of the kings of Spain to occupy Navarre was well known, and therefore the King of Navarre chose to expose himself rather to uncertain dangers than accept a certain loss, hoping that help in cavalry and footsoldiers promised by the King of France would not prove wanting, since restricting the war within Navarre was to the French King's benefit. Meanwhile, either in order to gain time for those forces coming to his aid or to free himself as much as he could from these demands, he continued to negotiate with the King of Aragon who, according to his wont, proceeded in these matters with the greatest cunning.

But the attentiveness and wariness of the King of Aragon did less harm to the King of Navarre than the negligence of the French King who, having taken courage in the fact that the English, having crossed into Fuenterabia, had not made any move for many days now, and trusting that the King of Navarre could defend himself for some time with his own forces, proceeded to send his help very slowly. The result was that the King of Aragon, who had astutely been nourishing Navarre's hopes, swiftly shifted his forces which had been preparing to join with the English, and sent them into Navarre; and the King of Navarre, unprepared and in despair that he would be unable to resist, fled to Béarn beyond the Pyrennes, and the realm of Navarre having been left abandoned, with the exception of certain fortresses which still held loyal to the fled King, fell into the power of the King of Aragon without any expenses or troubles, and more indeed, because of fear that the English were close at hand than because of his own strength.

Inasmuch as the King of Aragon could not legitimately claim this kingdom under any title, he alleged that his occupation was juridically carried out under the authority of the Apostolic See. Because the Pope, not satisfied with the happy successes he was having in Italy, had a little while before published a bull against the King of France in which, no longer addressing him as *Cristianissimo* but *Illustrissimo*, he subjected him and whoever adhered to his cause to all the penalties of heretics and schismatics, permitting anyone the right of occupying legally their possessions, estates and everything belonging to them; and with similar severity, angry because the cardinals and other prelates who had fled from Milan had found asylum in the city of Lyons, he had commanded under pain of most serious censure that the fair which used to be held four times a year with a great gathering of merchants at Lyons should in the future be held in the city of Geneva (from which King Louis XI had formerly removed it for the benefit of his kingdom); and lastly, the Pope had placed the entire kingdom of France under ecclesiastical interdict. But after he had taken possession of the kingdom of Navarre, which although it is a small realm providing very little income, is very important for Spanish security because of its position, the King of Aragon had determined that he would not go any farther since he felt that war with the King of France beyond the mountains was not to his interest. Therefore, at the beginning of his agreement with the English, he had been late in preparing his forces, and after the acquisition of Navarre, when the English urged him to join his army with theirs in order to march together and camp before Bayonne, a city near Fuenterabia, situated almost on the Ocean Sea, he now proposed other campaigns in places far from the seacoast, claiming that Bayonne was so fortified and so manned with soldiers that there was no hope of capturing it. The English rejected these proposals, scornful of any conquest in the duchy of Guyenne other than Bayonne, and when a great deal of time had been consumed in these disputes, the English—angry, irritated and feeling disappointed—without waiting for orders or permission from their prince, set sail and returned to England. Wherefore the King of France now feeling secure in those areas, and no longer fearing English attacks by sea, since at last his navy had become so strong that he ruled the entire seacoast from Spain up to the coast of England, decided to try to recover Navarre; his determination in this regard was strengthened, not only because of the departure of the English, but also because almost his entire army had now returned to France as a result of their ill successes in Italy.

. .

Now followed the year one thousand five hundred and thirteen, characterized by memorable events no less than the previous year. At the beginning whereof, the movement of armies having ceased everywhere, since the Venetians were threatening no one and no one was moving against them, the Viceroy marched with three thousand footsoldiers and set camp at the fortress of Trezzo which yielded to him under the condition that all those within might depart safely with all their goods. But everyone was troubled with premonitions of future events, knowing that the King of France, now being freed of foreign armies in his realm, and taking heart in the fact that he had mustered many German bands of infantry, and increased to no small degree the number of his garrisons of lances, had no greater thought in mind than the recovery of the duchy of Milan. And although the King's desire in this regard was very strong, and although he very much wanted to speed up the war while the castles of Milan and Cremona were still held by his men, nevertheless, considering how many difficulties were created for him by the opposition of so many enemies, and uncertain whether the King of England might not launch a large-scale attack against him the following summer, he decided not to make any move unless he could separate some of the allies from their joint confederation, or else win over the Venetians to his side.

Illness and Death of Pope Julius II Amidst His Ambitions. Character of Julius. Election of Giovanni de' Medici as Leo X

A MIDST such agitated affairs and gravely troubled times, there occurred the Pope's illness. Although the Pontiff had obtained those things which he wanted, nevertheless, with every success, his plans did not diminish but grew ever more ambitious. Thus his illness occurred when he was full of greater schemes and aspirations than perhaps he had had at any time before. For he had decided at the beginning of the spring to undertake his so long-desired campaign against Ferrara, in the belief that the city would not be able to put up much resistance, inasmuch as it had been abandoned of all help, and since the Spanish army was supposed to join with the Pope's men. He had secretly purchased the city of Siena from the Emperor* at a price of thirty thousand ducats for the Duke of Urbino, although he had never wished to grant any part of the Ecclesiastical State to the Duke, with the exception of Pesaro, in order to maintain intact the glory of having thought exclusively of the exaltation of the Church. He agreed to lend forty thousand ducats to the Emperor, receiving Modena as security. He threatened the Lucchese, who had taken advantage of the troubles of the Duke of Ferrara to seize Garfagnana, ordering them to turn it over to him. He was angry with the Cardinal de' Medici because he seemed to lean more toward the Catholic King than to himself; and because he realized that he could not dispose of Florentine affairs as he had thought, he had already concocted new plans and new plots to alter the state of things in Florence. He had become angry with the Cardinal Sedunense, because he had appropriated for himself a yearly revenue of more than thirty thousand ducats derived from property and goods of various people in the state of Milan, and had therefore deprived him of the title of legate and summoned him to Rome. And in order that the position of the Duke of Urbino in Siena might be more stable by knowing what his neighbors were doing, he had again taken Carlo Baglioni into his pay in order to expel Giampaolo from Perugia, since the latter was closely related with the sons of Pandolfo Petrucci, successors to the greatness of their father. He wanted to set up

---

* From this point on in the text I shall use the term Emperor although Guicciardini continues to say Caesar. Maximilian, although not crowned by the Pope, had been given the title of Emperor-Elect by Julius. To sixteenth-century ears Caesar meant Emperor.

as the new Doge of Genoa Ottaviano Fregoso, deposing Janus of that high position; the other members of the Fregoso family consented to this because it seemed that the position belonged more to Ottaviano as a result of the high rank which his ancestors had always held there. The Pope studied assiduously how he could either cast the Spanish army out of Italy or overthrow it with the help of the Swiss, who were the only soldiers whom he praised and welcomed; so that, having seized the kingdom of Naples, Italy would remain free of the barbarians (words which frequently issued from his mouth); and for this purpose he had prevented the Swiss from joining up with the Catholic King.

And nevertheless, as if it were in his power to batter the entire world at one time, he continued to act with his usual fury against the King of France (although he had lent ear to a special legate from the Queen), inciting the King of England to make war against France; for this reason he had by decree of the Lateran Council ordered that the title of Most Christian King be transferred to the King of England; wherefore there was already written a bull removing the King of France of his dignity and title, and granting that realm to whomsoever should seize it. Amidst all these and so many other concerns, and perhaps others more hidden and more far-reaching (because in so ferocious a spirit no concept of any kind, no matter how vast and measureless, was inconceivable), death weighed upon him after an illness lasting many days. And feeling himself forewarned, he convoked the consistory, which his illness prevented him from attending in person, and had them confirm the bull which he had previously published against those who would accede to the pontificate by simony, and declare that the election of his successor was the responsibility of the College of Cardinals and not of the Council, and that the schismatic cardinals could not participate in it; adding that he pardoned the schismatic cardinals for the injuries they had done him and prayed God that he should forgive them the wrongs they had done his Church. He then besought the College of Cardinals that for his sake they should concede the city of Pesaro in vicarship to the Duke of Urbino; recalling that that city, after the death of Giovanni Sforza, had been restored to the Church primarily through the labors of the said Duke. In no other matter did the Pope show any private or personal interest; rather, when his daughter Madonna Felice, many others interceding for her, insistently petitioned that Guido da Montefalco be created a cardinal because they were born of the same mother, the Pope bluntly replied that Guido was not a person worthy of that rank. Thus maintaining in all matters his accustomed constancy and severity, and the same power of judgment and vigorous mind which he had before his illness, he devoutly received the ecclesiastical sacraments, and toward daybreak on the night before the twenty-first day of February, ended the course of these present travails.

A Prince of inestimable spirit and resolution, but impetuous and given to boundless schemes, and if these traits did not hurl him to his ruin, he was sustained more by the feeling of reverence felt toward the Church, the disagreement among princes and the conditions of the times, than by moderation and prudence—worthy undoubtedly of the highest glory had he been a secular prince, or if that same care and purpose which he had used to exalt the Church to temporal greatness by the arts of war had been employed to exalt it in spiritual matters by the arts of peace. Nevertheless his memory is honored and esteemed more than any of his predecessors, especially by those who (having lost the true significance of things, and confusing distinctions and failing to weigh them rightly) consider that the main purpose of pontiffs is to extend, by arms and the blood of Christians, the power of the Apostolic See, rather than to labor by the good example of their lives, and by correcting and curing corrupt manners, for the salvation of those souls for whom they boast that Christ established them as his vicars on earth.

As soon as the Pope was dead, the Viceroy of Naples, who had marched with Spanish troops toward Piacenza, forced that city to return as it used to be under the rule of the dukes of Milan: a similar terror [of the Spanish] induced the city of Parma to follow the example of Piacenza. On the other hand, the Duke of Ferrara, having immediately retaken the towns of the Romagna, drew near Reggio; but since there was no uprising from within, he dared not halt there because the Spanish army had spread out to encamp between Piacenza and Reggio.

There were no other actions in the Church domain, nor did Rome or the College of Cardinals experience any of those difficulties which they had felt at the death of the last two popes. Therefore, when the obsequies had been concluded according to custom, twenty-four cardinals entered peacefully into conclave, having first agreed that the son of the Marquis of Mantua, who had been held by Julius as hostage, should be freed of his pledge and returned to his father.

The first concern in the conclave was to limit with very strict regulations the power of the future pontiff, a power which they said had been too immoderately wielded by the dead Pope: although not much later, the very same cardinals annulled almost all of these restrictions (as amongst men, some do not dare act in opposition to princes, and others ardently desire to enter into their grace). On the seventh day, without any dissenting voices, they chose Giovanni, Cardinal de' Medici, as Pope, who assumed the name of Leo X, then only thirty-seven years old—a startling thing, by comparison with previous custom, and the main reason for which was the industry of the young cardinals who had secretly agreed, a long time before, to create the first pope from amongst their group.

Almost all Christendom was greatly pleased with this election, men

LEO X

Raphael's portrait (1519) in the Uffizi Gallery, Florence, represents the Pope as a humanist. The Pope was myopic; hence the magnifying glass with which he has been examining a manuscript. The dark-haired prelate to the left is his cousin, Cardinal Giulio, the future Clement VII. Another Florentine, Cardinal Luigi de' Rossi, the Pope's secretary, is at the right. (COURTESY OF FRA-TELLI ALINARI)

in general being convinced he would become a most rare pope, because of the untarnished memory of his father's worth, and because of his resounding and widespread reputation for generosity and benignity; he was considered a man of chaste and unblemished morals; and it was hoped that he would follow his father's example as one who loved literary men and all illustrious talents; these expectations grew all the more since the election had been honestly held, without simony or any stain of suspicion.

And it seemed that God was already beginning to approve of this pontificate, because on the fourth day after the election, the cardinals of Santa Croce and San Severino, who had been deprived of the purple, came into his power. For once they had heard of Julius' death, they went by sea to Rome, accompanied by Solier, ambassador of the King of France. When they had arrived at the port of Livorno, and learning that the Cardinal de' Medici had been chosen as the new pope, and trusting in his benignity, especially San Severino because of the close friendship that he had had with him and his brother, they besought a safe-conduct from the captain of Livorno (which did not extend beyond the borders under his jurisdiction), landed, and seeking no other guarantee, came of their own will to Pisa: in which city they were honorably received and then led to Florence where they were courteously kept under guard in such a way that they had no means of leaving: such being the Pope's desire. The Pope then sent the Bishop of Orvieto, who very gently advised them, for their own safety and for the tranquility of the Church, to remain in Florence until it was determined how they should proceed to Rome; and that having been juridically deprived of the purple, and their deprivation confirmed in the Lateran Council, they should not go about in cardinal's habit, so that thus giving indication of humbling themselves, they would facilitate the Pope in his intention (which he already had in mind) of clearing up their situation.

The first action of the new Pope was his coronation, performed according to the custom of his predecessors in the church of Saint John Lateran with so much pomp, not only in his family and court, but also among all the prelates and many lords who had flocked there, and by the Roman people, that everyone admitted that never since the time of the barbarian invasions had Rome seen so magnificent and proud a celebration. In the solemn ceremonies, the standard of the Church was borne by Alfonso d'Este, who having obtained suspension of the censures, had gone to Rome in the great hope, because of the Pope's mild ways, of bringing his affairs to a happy conclusion. The standard of the Knights of Rhodes was borne by Giulio de' Medici, armed and mounted on a great courser, inclined by his nature toward a military career but destined by fate to a sacerdotal life, during which he was to prove a notable example of the vagaries of fortune.* And what made this day all the more memorable and all the more extraordinary was the realization that he who now was accepting, with such unusual pomp and splendor, the banners of so many high dignitaries, had been on the very same day, a year before, miserably taken prisoner [at the battle of Ravenna].

This sumptuous coronation confirmed in the multitude the great expectations which they had of the new Pope, everyone promising himself that Rome was bound to be happy under a Pope bestowed with such liberality and splendor; for it was certain that he had spent for this day 100,000 ducats. But wise men desired greater seriousness and moderation, judging that such pomp was not suitable for popes, nor did present conditions make it advisable to uselessly dissipate the money which had been accumulated by his predecessor.

. .
.

But neither the changing of the pope nor other accidents of fortune sufficed to establish tranquility in Italy; rather, it was already becoming clear that things were heading more toward war than toward peace.

[*Louis XII is impatient to reconquer Milan. To this end he concludes at Blois a league with the Venetians (23 March 1513), who had recently been his enemies. They agree not to depose their arms until the French have recovered Lombardy and the Venetians their territory on the mainland. Against this confederation Pope Leo forms a counter league consisting of Henry VIII of England, the Emperor Maximilian, Spain and the Pope—dedicated to defending Milan and the Church, and to attack King Louis in France itself. With the help of papal gold Girolamo Morone, the chancellor of the Sforza, manages to induce others to join the federation.*

In May 1513 war breaks out again which is to continue practically uninterruptedly for the next decade. The Milanese rise in favor of the French. The French capture Genoa and then lay siege to Novara defended by the Swiss. The French are defeated after a furious battle; Milan returns to the Sforza and Genoa to the Spaniards.]

While the war was proceeding in this way, the Pope made every possible effort to extirpate the split in the Church brought about by the Council of Pisa. And since this depended entirely upon the will of the King of France, he used all his skill to placate him, asserting that the rumor being spread that he had lent money to the Swiss was false, and

---

* The future Pope Clement VII, who was to be imprisoned within the Castel   Sant' Angelo during the Sack of Rome, 1527.

declaring that he desired nothing more than universal peace, and to be the common father to all Christian princes. He was especially grieved that his dissension with the Church should deprive the Pope of the opportunity of showing him how naturally he was inclined toward amity [with the King]; but for the honor of the Apostolic See and for his personal honor, he, the Pope, was obliged to deal differently with him until such time as, having returned to the obedience of the Roman Church, it would be lawful for the Pontiff to receive him as Most Christian King and embrace him as the oldest son of the Church.

The King for his own interest wanted the union of his realm with the Church, a union also insistently urged upon him by the Queen and desired by his court and all his people. Besides this, he knew that he could never hope for an agreement with the Pope in temporal things if first he did not compose their spiritual differences. Therefore, either trusting or feigning to trust his words, he sent as his ambassador to discuss these matters the Bishop of Marseilles; at whose coming, the Pope, by decree of the Council, reinvested the French bishops and other prelates (against whom, as schismatics, his predecessor had rigidly dealt by way of citations to appear under pain of excommunication), with the power to purge themselves of contumacy during all of the coming November.

The same morning in which this was decided, there was read in the council a declaration subscribed under the hand of Bernardino Carvajal and Federico de San Severino in which, not naming themselves cardinals, they approved all the acts of the Lateran Council, promising to cleave to these and obey the Pope; and consequently confessed that they had been lawfully deprived of their status of cardinals; which deprivation, having been carried out by Pope Julius, had been confirmed during his lifetime by the same Council. Previously the question of restoring them to the purple had been debated but deferred as a result of the difference of opinion between the Emperor's ambassadors and the ambassadors of the King of Aragon, together with the cardinals of Sedunense and York, who objected that such restitution was unworthy of the majesty of the Apostolic See, and that it was a very poor example to grant pardon to the authors of such scandals and of so pernicious and abominable a crime; reminding the Council that Julius had constantly opposed them to the end of his life, for no other reason than the public good.

But the present Pope was inclined toward more benign treatment, judging that it was easier to entirely expunge the name of the Council of Pisa by means of clemency than by severity, and in order not to exacerbate the mind of the French King who was insistently interceding for these cardinals. Nor did he feel any particular hatred toward them since the injury had not been done to him; rather, before his pontificacy he and his brothers had been very close friends with Federico. For these reasons, of his own initiative he had caused to be read before the fathers of the Council the written declaration of their humiliation, and then later set aside a day for their restitution, which was carried out in this manner: Bernardino and Federico secretly entered Rome by night, not wearing the habits or insignia of cardinals; the following morning they were to present themselves before the Pope sitting in full Consistory, accompanied by all the cardinals except the Swiss and English, who refused to be present. At first, dressed as simple priests with black berets, they passed through all the public places of the Vatican palace, where they had lodged that night: a great multitude of people thronging to see them, and everyone asserting that so public an ignominy must be a most bitter torment to Bernardino's boundless pride and the no less immeasurable arrogance of Federico. Admitted to the Consistory they fell down on their knees, and with signs of the greatest humility, beseeched pardon of the Pope and of the cardinals, approving everything which Julius had done, namely their removal from the cardinalship and the election of the new Pope as canonically carried out, and damning the Conventicle of Pisa as schismatic and detestable. When this confession had been solemnly registered and subscribed to by their hand, they rose to their feet, made sign of reverence and embraced all the cardinals, who did not stir out of their seats; after this, they were appareled in the habit of cardinals and received in their seats in the same order in which they had been seated before their deprivation. By this act they solemnly recovered the dignity of the cardinalship, but not the churches and other benefices which they used to possess, because these had been transferred to others a long time before, as vacant.

By this act the Pope satisfied the French King, if not fully, at least in part: but he was not satisfying him in other matters . . .

BOOK

12

Henry VIII, King of England, Threatens to Invade France

IN the same year most dangerous wars took place in the regions beyond the mountains, which I will recount for the same reason and with the same brevity with which I touched on them in the narration of the previous year. The origin of these stirrings was the determination of the King of England to invade the kingdom of France that summer with the greatest forces by land and by sea. And to make the victory of that enterprise easier, he had come to an agreement with the Emperor to furnish him with 120,000 ducats, so that he might enter at the same time into Burgundy with an army of three thousand horsemen and eight thousand footsoldiers, part Swiss and part German. He also promised a certain amount of money to the Swiss in order that they might do the same thing, in conjunction with the Emperor, who agreed that they might keep in pawn a part of Burgundy until he had entirely paid them their wages. Besides this, the King of England was convinced that the Catholic King, his father-in-law, adhering to the alliance between the Emperor and himself as he had always asserted he wanted to do, would at the same time launch a war [against France] from his frontiers. Hence the news of the truce drawn up by the King of Spain with the King of France, although this in no way cooled their ardor for war, was received with the greatest indignation not only by the English King but by all his people, which is shown by the fact that had they not been held back by the authorities, the angry multitude would have slain the Spanish ambassador.

Furthermore, the moment was ripe for dealing with the Archduke, not so much that he should not forbid his subjects from taking pay against the French, as in order that he should promise to permit passage of provisions to the English army across his domain.

Against such great preparations and perilous threats, the King of France did not fail to make all sorts of precautions. By sea he organized a powerful navy to oppose the one being prepared in England; by land he mustered armies from every side, making the greatest efforts above all to enroll as many German footsoldiers as he could. Previously he had also requested of the Swiss that although they didn't want to help him in these Italian wars, they should at least agree to furnish him with foot-soldiers for the defense of France. But the Swiss being entirely set upon maintaining the stability of the duchy of Milan, replied that they refused to grant him any soldiers unless he first reunited with the Church, left the castle of Milan which had not yet been rendered up, and yielding his claims to that state, promised no longer to threaten either Milan or Genoa.

Similarly, in order to make the King of England look to his own affairs, the French King had summoned the Duke of Suffolk into France as a claimant to the English crown. For this affront, the King of England cut off the head of his brother, who had been held prisoner till then in England, ever since Philip, King of Castille [d. 1506], sailing into Spain, had delivered him to his father. The King of France was not without hope of achieving peace with the Catholic King: for when that King had learned of the league made between the French and the Venetians, and doubting that he could defend the duchy of Milan, he had sent one of his secretaries to France to propose new agreements: and it was believed that, considering that the Emperor and the Archduke were mighty enough to overthrow his government in Castile, he would not be entirely pleased by a weakening of the French realm.

Besides this [the French King] stirred up James, King of Scotland, his former ally, to make war upon the realm of England. James was more moved by his own interests, inasmuch as French adversities were dangerous to his kingdom, and therefore swiftly made preparations, demanding of the French King nothing other than fifty thousand francs to furnish munitions and food supplies. Nevertheless, the French King was very slow in making these provisions because he had turned his mind toward the Milan campaign, and because of his usual negligence and the vain hopes stirred in him by the truce drawn up with the Catholic King.

[*The King of England is so indignant at the treaty renewed by his father-in-law, the King of Aragon, with the King of France that he complains publicly that Ferdinand had betrayed him three times; therefore Henry is not now inclined to invade France. The Pope also interposes to bring about a peace.*]

Negotiations for an agreement between the King of France and the King of England quickly began to take place, either because of the Pope's authority or at the desire of both parties themselves. The elaborations of this treaty, begun by the Pope with the Bishop of York, were soon transferred to England, whither the General of Normandy was sent for this purpose by the King of France, but under pretext of treating for the liberation of the Marquis of Rothelin. At the General's arrival, and for the entire time he remained on the island, a cease-fire was publicly proclaimed by both Kings, but only on land.

As a result of new losses, the King of England was more inclined toward peace; for the Emperor, who had promised him that he would not ratify the treaty made by the Catholic King without him, sent that King the instrument of ratification. The Catholic King ratified in the Emperor's name by means of a letter sent to the King of France, retaining the instrument to make use of it in his various schemes and devices.

Peace Treaty Between the King of England and the King of France

NEGOTIATIONS having begun between both Kings, the Pope, who wanted to be on good terms with them both, sent the Bishop of Tricarico by post to the King of France, to offer him all his means and prestige; by the King's consent the Bishop crossed over to England for the same purpose. At first, many difficulties manifested themselves in this matter, because the King of England demanded that Boulogne in Picardy be given to him, and a great sum of money. But at last, the difficulties reduced themselves to the question of Tournai, since the King of England insisted on keeping it, and the King of France, on his part, put forth some objections in the matter. Wherefore the English sovereign dispatched the Bishop of Tricarico posthaste to the King of France. Without being notified what the particular difficulty was, the Bishop was commissioned to urge him in his name not to insist so subtly on the matter out of regard for the greater good. But since Tournai was a noble city whose loyalty to the French crown was well known, the French King did not want to discontent his people, and so he referred this matter to the council in which all the leading men of the court participated. There he was unanimously urged to accept the peace, even with this condition, notwithstanding the fact that at that moment the Catholic King was seeking by all possible means to break the negotiations, and therefore proposed many advantages to the French King, especially supporting his claim to the acquisition of the state of Milan. However, since the King's reply had come to England that he was content with the Tournai settlement, at the beginning of August, the peace treaty was concluded between both Kings, valid for their lifetime and one year after their death; with the stipulation that Tournai should be retained by the King of England, to whom the King of France should pay 600,000 scudi, at a rate of 100,000 francs per year; both Kings were obligated to a mutual defense of each other's realms, with ten thousand footsoldiers if the war were by land, and only six thousand if by sea; the King of France was obliged to serve the King of England in all his enterprises with twelve hundred lances, and the latter was bound to serve the former with ten thousand footsoldiers, but in this case, at the expense of whoever had need of them. Both sovereigns nominated the King of Scotland, the Archduke, and the Empire, but neither the Emperor nor the Catholic King was named. The Swiss were also nominated, but on condition that whoever should defend the states of Milan or Genoa or Asti against the King of France should be excluded from nomination.

This peace treaty, drawn up with the greatest speed, was confirmed by a marriage contract: it was agreed that the King of England would give his sister as wife to the King of France once he had acknowledged receipt of the 400,000 scudi for her dowry. The betrothal was immediately celebrated in England, but because of the English sovereign's great hatred for the Catholic King, he did not want the Spanish ambassador present.

No sooner had this peace treaty been concluded when there arrived at the French court the instrument of ratification of truce drawn up by the Emperor, and his mandate and that of the Catholic King for the conclusion of a marriage being solicited between Ferdinand of Austria and the King's second daughter, who was only four years old. But as a result of the peace treaty, these negotiations were completely excluded; furthermore, in order to satisfy the King of England, the French King wished to have the Duke of Suffolk, who was captain-general of the German infantry under his command, depart from the realm; which he did, but most contentedly, honored and praised by the King.

At that time, the Pope had also made new alliances: inasmuch as, full of deceit and dissimulation, on the one hand he did not want the King of France to recover the state of Milan, and on the other, he wanted to restrain him and the other princes as much as he could with sundry devices. Therefore, he had proposed to the King, via the Cardinal San Severino who handled French affairs at the court in Rome, that, since the times were not propitious for drawing up a major and more open alliance between them, at least a beginning and foundation might be laid on which, at some future date, they might hope to come to the closest understanding. And he had sent details of the clauses. But although the King of France showed that he welcomed such negotiations, he had not replied so quickly (waiting fifteen days to make up his mind) either because he was otherwise engaged, or else because he was awaiting some reply from elsewhere to govern himself according to the way things developed. The result was that the Pope drew up a new agreement with the Emperor and the Catholic King for one year; the agreement, however, covered nothing other than defense of their respective states. For the Catholic King had earlier suspected, not without reason, that he [the Pope] had aspirations for the kingdom of Naples for his brother Giuliano, about which matter he had already had some dealings with the Venetians. The new agreement was not quite concluded when the French King's reply arrived, approving of everything the Pontiff had proposed; adding only that, since he was to bind himself to the protection of the Florentines, of Giuliano, the Pope's brother, and Lorenzo de' Medici, his nephew (whom the Pope had appointed for the administration of Florentine affairs), he desired that they in turn should oblige themselves in his defense. Having received this answer, the Pope excused himself on the grounds that he was restrained by the Emperor and the Catholic King, because when he saw the French King dally so long in replying to so befitting a demand, he could not help but begin to doubt. Nevertheless, he had done it* but for a short time, nor did the agreement contain anything prejudicial to him, nor did it impede in any way the negotiations which they had begun. These justifications accepted by the King, they both signed the convention not by instrument, for greater secrecy, but by a covenant subscribed to by each of them in his own hand.

Louis XII Dies and Is Succeeded by Francis I as King of France

AMONG the abovementioned things, it seems worthy of memory that in this same year, Rome saw elephants, an animal perhaps seen no more in Italy after the Roman triumphs and public games. Emanuel, King of Portugal, dispatched a most honorable embassage to declare his obedience to the Pontiff, and among the many gifts presented were these two elephants brought on his ships from India. Enormous throngs celebrated their entry into Rome.

. . .
.

But the already imminent war was delayed by the intervention of death, which customarily cuts short the vain counsels of men, often in the midst of their greatest hopes. For the King of France [Louis XII], greedily making use of the excellent beauty and youth of his new wife, a girl of

* Allied himself with the Emperor and Catholic King for one year.

eighteen, and not considering his own years and weak constitution, was taken with a fever complicated by disorders due to a flux,* and so departed this present life almost regretfully, thus rendering memorable by his death the first day of the year 1515.** A just king, greatly loved by his people, but never, even before his reign or after he became King, did he know constancy and stability either in good or ill fortune. For he had luckily acceded to the throne of France from being a little Duke of Orléans, as a result of the death of Charles, younger than himself, and of his two sons; had acquired the duchy of Milan and then the kingdom of Naples with the greatest of ease, and ruled almost all Italy for many years, almost at his will. He had recovered rebellious Genoa with the greatest good fortune, most gloriously conquered the Venetians, personally participating in both these victories. On the other hand, while he was still young, he had been forced by Louis XI to take his daughter [Joan the Lame], barren and almost monstrous, as his wife, and from this matrimony had acquired neither the good will nor the patronage of his father-in-law. And after his death he was not admitted into the government of the new boy king, because of the grandeur of Madame de Bourbon [Anne of Beaujeu], and was almost obliged to take refuge in Brittany: then captured on the day of Saint-Aubin-du-Cormier, he had been imprisoned for two years. Add to all these things the siege and famine of Novara, the many defeats in the kingdom of Naples, the loss of Milan, of Genoa and all the lands taken from the Venetians, and the rebellion waged against him by most powerful enemies in the kingdom of France; during which time he saw his empire reduced to the gravest perils. Nevertheless, he died at a time when it seemed good fortune was returning to him, having defended his kingdom, made peace and allied himself in a most felicitous union with the King of England, and very hopeful of recuperating the state of Milan.

Louis XII was succeeded by Francis, Lord of Angoulême, close to him in the masculine line of the blood royal, and in the same lineage as the dukes of Orléans. His succession to the throne was preferred over the daughter of the dead king because of the application of the Salique law, a very ancient law in the kingdom of France: according to which females are excluded from the royal dignity while there are males of the same lineage. The new King's virtue, magnanimity, skill and generous spirit had aroused so much hope that it was universally admitted that for many years now no one had come to the throne with greater expectations. For he united the highest grace with the flower of youth (he was twenty-two

---

* G. probably means a dysentery.

** Excessive venery as a cause of death was, not without envy, a commonly held belief. Francesco Vettori, Florentine ambassador to Rome, wrote that King Louis had brought from England a "hackney" so young, so beautiful, and so swift that she had ridden him right out of the world. Raphael's sudden departure at the age of thirty-seven was ascribed to the same mode of transportation.

FRANCIS I, KING OF FRANCE

Portrait by Jean Clouet in the Louvre (COURTESY OF FRATELLI ALINARI)

years old), outstanding physical beauty, the greatest liberality, deep humanity withal, and a thorough knowledge of many things; and above all he was welcomed by the nobility to whom he showed great favor. Together with his title of King of France, he assumed the title of Duke of Milan, belonging to him not only because of the ancient claims of the Duke of Orléans but also as included within the investiture made by the Emperor according to the League of Cambrai; thus he had the same desire to recuperate it as had had his predecessor. He was goaded to this undertaking not only by his own inclination but also by all the youth of the French nobility, the glory of Gaston de Foix, and the memory of so many victories which had been won by recent kings in Italy; although in order not to warn others beforetime to prepare to resist him, he disguised his purpose, as he was advised by his inner council, and employed this interval to draw up treaties of amity with other princes, as is usual in new regimes. Many of these princes immediately sent ambassadors to him, all of whom were affably received, but those sent by the King of England more than all the others. The King of England was still irked by the affronts he had received from the Catholic King, and wanted the friendship which he had begun with King Louis to be continued with Francis. At that same time there arrived a distinguished embassage from the Archduke, among whom the main figure was the Lord of Nassau, who, with signs of great submission, as to his sovereign lord (in that he was possessor of the earldom of Flanders), acknowledged the superiority of the French crown.

Both legations were swiftly and happily expedited: because the alliance made between the King of England and the dead King was reconfirmed with the same clauses, and during the lifetime of each of them, and a period of three years was reserved for the King of Scotland to enter the alliance. And with the Archduke, many difficulties were overcome which many people had felt would impede an agreement.

The French Once Again Invade Italy

But now matters had passed from words and counsels to deeds and executions. For the King had come to Lyons, accompanied by all the nobility of France, and with the dukes of Lorraine and Guelders,* and was marching toward the mountains with a mightier and more flourishing army than had crossed from France into Italy for a long time now. And he was assured that he would have no troubles from beyond the mountains, because the King of Aragon (who previously fearing that such great

---

* Dutch province.

preparations might be turned against him, had armed his frontiers, and united in perpetuity the realm of Navarre to the kingdom of Castile, so that his peoples might be more ready to defend it), as soon as he realized that the war was obviously launched against Italy, dismissed all the companies he had mustered, holding no more reckoning of the promise he had made that year to the confederates to make war upon France than he had done of the pledges he had made those same allies in previous years.

. .
.

At that time a man sent by the King of England came to Francis, who had already departed from Lyons, and strongly urged him in his name not to disturb the peace of Christendom by crossing into Italy. The origin of such a change of mind was that the King of England felt troubled because the King of France had joined with the Archduke, and it seemed to him that French affairs were beginning to proceed too prosperously. On this basis, the King of England had begun to lend ear to the ambassadors of the Catholic King, who did not cease to point out how dangerous the greatness of the King of France was to him; who, by natural hatred, and because he had made his first actions of war against him, could not help but be his greatest enemy. But most of all, the English King was moved by rivalry and envy of Francis' glory, which he felt would greatly increase if he should achieve victory over the state of Milan. He remembered that even though he possessed a tranquil kingdom, very rich as a result of the long peace, and had found so much treasure accumulated by his father, nevertheless he had not dared until after several years to assault the King of France, alone, and surrounded by so many enemies and worn out by so many travails. And now this King, somewhat younger than he was when he was crowned, although he had found his kingdom worn out and exhausted by so many wars, yet had dared in the first months of his reign to enter upon an undertaking opposed by so many princes. He, Henry, with all his mighty preparations and great opportunities, had not brought back to England any other gain than the city of Tournai, and at intolerable and endless expenses. But if (as one might believe) the King of France should gain a victory, the acquisition of so fine a duchy, he would return with great glory into his kingdom; and the road still being open to him, perhaps before he departed from Italy he would seize the opportunity to attack the kingdom of Naples. With such goads and pricks it was easy to resuscitate the ancient hatred in Henry's breast, but there being no time to offer any opposition by arms, and perhaps also seeking more justification, he had sent this embassy to Francis. But this did not delay the King's march, who went from Lyons to the Dauphiné, where on the same day there appeared the landsknechts called the Black Band, led by Robert de la Mark; this band from the lowest part of Germany was held in the greatest estimation in the French army because of its ferocity and its constant demonstrations of loyalty.

At this time Gianiacopo da Trivulzio advised the King that he could lead the artillery across the mountains between the maritime Alps and the Cottian Alps, descending toward the marquisate of Saluzzo where, despite the almost inestimable difficulties, he must finally succeed, because of his great abundance of men and equipment. And since there were no guards in this area, neither at the mountain peaks nor in the mouths of the valleys, it was better to attempt to conquer the rugged mountains and precipitous valleys (which could be done with difficulty but without endangering the men) than to try to force the Swiss to abandon the passes. For the Swiss, so feared, were resolved either to conquer or perish. Most important, the French could not remain there many days if they encountered resistance, because no force or equipment was capable of conveying sufficient supplies for so many men through such bitter and barren places. This recommendation having been accepted, the artillery, which had halted at a spot convenient for turning in any direction, set out immediately on that road. Trivulzio had advised the King that the difficulty of getting the artillery through the passes would be very great, but experience proved it even more difficult. First it was necessary to climb very high and rugged mountains, climbing with the greatest difficulty because there were no paths, and sometimes roads not wide enough for the artillery except when hand to hand the sappers helped. Large numbers of these sappers led the way, now widening the narrow passes, now leveling the impediments on the roads. From the tops of those mountains they descended by very steep cliffs, the mere sight of which struck terror, into the deepest valleys of the Argentiera River. And although there were a great many horses drawing the artillery, they could not sustain the pieces, nor could the shoulders of the sappers accompanying them. Therefore it was often necessary to fasten them to great hempen ropes by which they were lowered down the paths by the hands of the footsoldiers, who amidst such toils applied themselves to every task.

Their labors did not cease even when they had crossed the first mountains and the first valleys, because other mountains and other valleys succeeded, equally difficult to cross. Finally, after five days, the artillery was brought over the mountains to open places of the marquisate of Saluzzo; so toilsome was the passage that it is most certain that had they faced any resistance, or had the mountains been covered with snow, as most of them usually are, their effort would have been in vain. But they were spared human opposition because nobody had ever thought it possible to haul artillery through such bitter mountains. Hence the Swiss lodged at Susa were intent upon guarding the places through which those come who cross Mount Cenis, Mount Genèvre, or the neighboring mountains; and since it was about the tenth of August, the season of the year had already melted the snow, and so that impediment was removed.

[*The defeat of the Swiss at the battle of Marignano (September 13 and 14, 1515) resulted in the capitulation of Milan to the victorious Francis I; and intensified Pope Leo's efforts (already begun before the battle) to secure peace with the French. Flushed with his first triumph beyond the Alps, Francis sends troops to help the Venetians at Brescia and Verona.*]

Meeting of Pope Leo X and King Francis I at Bologna

MEANWHILE, the Pope and King had agreed to meet at Bologna; the King accepted this place rather than Florence in order not to remove himself too far from the duchy of Milan. The Duke of Savoy especially continued to negotiate the agreement between the Swiss and Francis. It was also said that the King opted for Bologna because crossing Tuscany it would be necessary to lead many troops with him; for his honor behooved him not to enter Florence with less pomp than King Charles had entered there.*

In order to arrange this, there intervened several days of delay which were very grave to the King for other reasons as well. For he would have been obliged to keep the entire army mustered so much longer, although it was true that despite very heavy expenses, he had not disbanded (nor had he any intention of doing so up to that day) any of his troops while he was in Italy. The Pope entered Bologna on the eighth day of December; and about two days later the King arrived, received by two apostolic legates, the Cardinal of Fiesco and the Cardinal de' Medici, who had gone to the borders of Reggiano** for that purpose. The King made his entrance without any men-at-arms nor with a very numerous court; and brought, according to the custom, to the public consistory before the Pope, he personally (the Grand Counselor speaking in his name) offered his obedience, which he had not as yet lent. They then remained three days together, lodged in the same palace, manifesting the greatest signs of love and benevolence for each other. At that time, besides reconfirming by words and promises the obligations already undertaken, they discussed many things relating to the kingdom of Naples. Since the King was not ready to attack that kingdom, he took satisfaction in the hope that the

---

* In 1494.
** The country around Reggio.

Pope gave him most clear indications of being favorable to that enterprise, whenever the death of the King of Aragon should occur (which was commonly considered to be imminent), or whenever the alliance that he had with him, that still had sixteen months to go, would be truly ended.

The King interceded once again for the restitution of Modena and Reggio to the Duke of Ferrara, and the Pope promised to restore it to him, the Duke paying him (the Pope) the forty thousand ducats which the Pope had paid the Emperor for Modena, and repaying in addition certain sums of money for expenses incurred in one or the other of these cities. The King also interceded for Francesco Maria,* Duke of Urbino: who having been enlisted by the Church with two hundred men-at-arms, and supposed to join the army with Giuliano de' Medici, when later, because of Giuliano's illness, Lorenzo was proposed in his place, not only had the Duke refused to go, alleging that he did not wish to concede to Lorenzo what he had consented to do even against his dignity, because of his long-lasting friendship with Giuliano (namely to go as a simple condottiere, subordinate to other people's authority in the army of the Church, wherein he had so often been captain general, superior to all); but besides this, having promised to send the men of his company, he ordered them back while they were on the march, because he had already secretly agreed, or was dickering to agree, with the King of France; and ever since the King's victory he had not ceased via his own men to stir him up as much as he could against the Pontiff.

Remembering these affronts, and already having in mind to grant the duchy to his own family, the Pope rejected the King's demand; demonstrating to him with the gentlest words what grievous consequences would result for the Church, stirring up among its subjects boldness to rebel, by such a pernicious example. The King yielded patiently to the Pope's will and arguments: despite the fact that he would have liked, for his own honor, to have saved those who had fallen into peril because they had adhered to his cause. Many of his council and court were advising him to the same course of action, reminding him how unwise was the decision of the past King to have permitted Valentino to oppress the little lords of Italy, as a result of which he had risen to such greatness that if his father Alexander had enjoyed longer life, he (Valentino) would undoubtedly have proved most prejudicial to the King's affairs.

The Pope promised to give the King the power to levy for one year one-tenth of the Church's revenues in the kingdom of France. It was also agreed that the King should have the right of nominating the benefices which previously pertained to colleges and chapters of the Church—a matter very much to the liking of this King, having thereby power of distributing such very rich benefices at his own will. On the other hand,

---

* Della Rovere, nephew of Pope Julius.

it was decided that the annual revenues of the Church in France should be paid in the future to the Pope according to the true value and not according to the ancient taxes, which were very much less; in this, the Pope found himself deceived, because when his deputies and commissioners for the kingdom of France had to take action against those who were concealing the true value, no one wanted to testify, no one wanted to get execution against the parties, with the result that each one continued to pay according to the old taxes.

The King also promised not to take any of the cities of Tuscany under his protection, yet shortly afterward, he requested that the Pope agree to permit him to take on the protection of the Lucchese, who were offering him twenty-five thousand ducats, alleging that he was bound to it by the obligations of his predecessor. But the Pope refused to concede this to him, although he promised the King on his part that he would not molest them in any way.

Besides these matters, they agreed to send Egidio, General of the

A naval battle between the corsairs of Barbarossa (allied with the Turks) and Christian forces in the eastern Mediterranean, in the Gulf of Artha in the Ionian Sea north of Greece where the Battle of Actium had occurred in 31 B.C. From a sixteenth-century print. (COURTESY OF GABINETTO NAZIONALE DELLE STAMPE, ROME)

Friars of Saint Augustine, and a most excellent preacher, to the Emperor in the name of the Pope to induce him to yield up Brescia and Verona to the Venetians, recompensing him with money.

These matters having been expedited, but not in writing (except that which pertained to the naming of benefices and payment of annual taxes according to true value), the Pope, in gratitude to the King, pronounced Adrian de Boissy Cardinal, brother of the Grand Master of France, who in all governmental matters held first place next to the King.

The King departed from this meeting very well content and in great hopes of the Pope's good will, who made a copious outward show of the same sentiments, but felt differently within. For he was no less offended than before that the King possessed the duchy of Milan; he was most offended that he had given up Piacenza and Parma, and similarly he was offended that Ferrara, Modena and Reggio would be restored to the Duke of Ferrara. Not much later, however, this latter agreement turned out to be in vain, for when the Pope came to Florence, where he remained about a month after his departure from Bologna, and when he received from the Duke the promise of the monies which he had to pay as soon as he had entered into possession, and when by common consent the writing of the instruments which had to be drawn up between them had been ordered, the Pontiff refused to carry out the instrumentalities of the agreement, not by denying it but interposing various excuses and delays, continuing to promise all the while.

As soon as the King returned to Milan, he immediately dismissed his army, leaving as guard for that city seven hundred lances and six thousand German infantry and four thousand French, that kind whom they call adventurers. Then with the greatest speed, on the first day of the year 1516 he returned to France, leaving as his lieutenant, Charles [of Montpensier], Duke of Bourbon; believing that he had stabilized his affairs in Italy as a result of the alliance he had contracted with the Pope, and because on that very same day he had come to an agreement with the Swiss. Although the King of England was spurring them to take up arms against the French King, the Swiss renewed their agreement with him, obligating themselves to provide, under their own name and flags, at the King's pay, whatever number of footsoldiers he might demand, whether in Italy or outside, for defense or offense against anyone except the Pope, the Empire and the Emperor. On the other hand, the King confirmed anew to the Swiss their ancient pensions, promised to pay at fixed times the 600,000 ducats agreed upon at Dijon, and 300,000 if they returned to him the towns and valleys belonging to the duchy of Milan. But since the five cantons which possessed these territories refused to do so, and also refused to ratify the agreement, the King began to pay the other eight cantons the installment of the moneys due them; which they accepted but under the express condition of not being obliged to march in his pay and service against footsoldiers of the five cantons.

At the beginning of the same year, the Bishop de' Petrucci, an old and close friend of the Pope, with his help and the help of the Florentines, expelled out of Siena, Borghese, son of Pandolfo Petrucci, his cousin (in whose hands was the government), and arrogated the same authority to himself. What motivated the Pope was a concern that that city, situated between the state of the Church and that of the Florentines, should be ruled by a man in his confidence; and perhaps much more because he hoped that when the time and chance were propitious, he might subject that city, with the willing consent of the Bishop himself, to the rule of either his brother or his nephew.

[*On 15 January 1516, dies Ferdinand the Catholic, who had exercised so potent an influence on European politics for more than twenty years. The Great Captain had died about a month earlier. The Pope wishes to despoil the Duke of Urbino from his state, giving as reasons that Francesco Maria della Rovere had killed others besides the Cardinal of Pavia, and that he had secretly compounded with the enemies of the Church while he was in the pay of the Church as captain of its army. Leo had been deterred in carrying out this plan so long as his brother Giuliano lived, since Giuliano had been an honored guest at the court of Urbino for many years while in exile (he figures as one of the leading participants in Baldassare Castiglione's* Il Cortigiano, *which relates the witty conversations that took place at that brilliant refined court). But now Giuliano has died after a long illness. Leo excommunicates the Duke. A papal army assails the duchy, and Francesco Maria is forced to capitulate. The Pope names his nephew Lorenzo as Duke of Urbino (18 August 1516).*

But although it seems as though Italy might at last have rest and tranquility, since arms have been laid down between the Emperor and the Venetians, and the French king has no opportunity to make war against Maximilian or the Catholic king, central Italy now breaks out into war as the ousted Duke of Urbino emerges from exile and recovers his entire domain. The Pope seeks everywhere for help, and fighting takes place in various localities of Umbria and Romagna. Because of Urbino the Vatican is overladen with debts.]

BOOK

13

The Cardinal of Siena Plots to Assassinate the Pope

AT THIS TIME, THE POPE'S CONCERNS PROCEEDED NO
MORE FELICITOUSLY IN OTHER ACTIONS THAN IN
THE TRAVAILS OF WAR. FOR A PLOT WAS LAID
against his life by Alfonso, Cardinal of Siena, who was offended because
the Pontiff had quite forgotten the toils and dangers which the Cardinal's
father, Pandolfo Petrucci, had endured in order that his brothers and
himself might return to power in Florence, as well as the efforts which
he, Alfonso, together with the other young cardinals in the conclave,
had made in order that Leo might be raised to the pontificate. And as
recompense for so many favors, the Pope had had his brother Borghese
and himself expelled from Siena, so that now, deprived of his paternal
goods, he could not maintain the dignity of the cardinalate in splendor as
he was wont to do. Therefore, burning with hatred, and almost reduced
to desperation, he had even had the adolescent idea of himself violently
attacking the Pope with arms. But being restrained more by the danger
and difficulty of the enterprise than by the example and scandal that
would be universally felt throughout all Christendom should a cardinal
by his own hand assassinate a pope, he turned all his thoughts to taking
his life by poison by means of Batista da Vercelli, a famous surgeon and
very intimate with him. The idea (if such frightful mad rage deserves
the name) was to be put into effect as follows: to celebrate the surgeon's
skill with the highest praise (since he had no other opportunity), and
thus bring it about that the Pontiff, who was constantly calling upon
physicians because of an old fistula which he had under his buttocks,
would hear of his high reputation and summon him to his cure.

But Alfonso's impatience created difficulties in their hopes of executing this plot. For while the plan was being worked out at length, Alfonso,
unable to contain himself from openly complaining of the Pope's ingratitude, and every day becoming more irksome and odious, and falling

under suspicion that he might be plotting something against the Papal State, was finally almost forced to leave Rome for his own security. But he left his secretary Antonio Nino there; between the secretary and the Cardinal there was a steady stream of letters and by several of these that were intercepted, the Pope understood that there was a conspiracy against his life. Therefore, under cover of wanting to make some provision for Alfonso's affairs, he called him to Rome under a safe conduct, and promised by his own words given to the ambassador of the King of Spain not to harm him. Under this security, although he was aware of how much wickedness was afoot, the Cardinal imprudently went before the Pontiff where he, together with Bandinello, Cardinal de' Sauli, a Genoese, also a factor in Leo's assumption to the pontificate but so involved with Alfonso that it was felt that he must be aware of everything that was going on, were apprehended in the Pope's chamber, whence they were led to prison in the Castel Sant' Angelo; and an order was immediately given that Batista da Vercelli, who was then practicing medicine in Florence, should be arrested and brought to Rome at once. The ambassador of the King of Spain made the strongest efforts to have Alfonso liberated, protesting and complaining most strongly that a pledge given to him as ambassador of that King was the same as a pledge given to the King himself. But the Pope replied that a safe-conduct, no matter how broad and provided with the strongest and most specific clauses, was never intended to provide assurance in crimes against the life of the Pope, unless specifically so mentioned: and that the same prerogative (of requiring a particular and separate clause) held true in case of poison, so abhorred by divine and human laws and all the sentiments of mankind.

The Pontiff proposed Mario Perusco, a Roman, and fiscal procurator, to conduct their examination. The result of the rigorous examination was that they confessed to the plot planned by Alfonso with Bandinello's knowledge; this confession was confirmed by Batista the surgeon and by Pocointesta da Bagnacavallo who, under Pandolfo, the Cardinal's father, and Borghese his brother, had been captain of the guard at the piazza of Siena for a long time. These two were publicly drawn and quartered. But after this confession, at the next Consistory, Raffaello Riario, the Cardinal of San Giorgio, treasurer of the Apostolic See, was arrested and brought to the Castello. Riario was undoubtedly the leading cardinal of the College as a result of his wealth, the magnificence of his court, and because of the long time he had held that dignity; he confessed that he had never been advised of the plot, but the Cardinal of Siena, complaining and threatening the Pope, had several times spoken to him in a way in which he could understand what he had in mind: namely, that if he had a chance, he would do harm to the Pope in person.

Subsequently, the Pope complained at another Consistory (in which the cardinals, unaccustomed to such violation of their dignity, were all perturbed and frightened) that his life should have been threatened so cruelly and wickedly by those who, above all others, were obliged to defend it, since they were raised to so high a dignity and were the principal members of the Apostolic See. Bitterly lamenting his misfortune, the Pope complained that it had stood him in no stead that he had always been beneficent and kind with everyone, even to the point that many criticized him for it. He added that there were still other cardinals involved in this crime and if, before the Consistory was dissolved, they would frankly confess their guilt, he would be prepared to use clemency and pardon them; but once the Consistory was over, severity and justice would be applied against anyone involved in such a crime. At these words, Adrian, Cardinal of Corneto, and Francesco Soderini, Cardinal of Volterra, kneeling before the papal throne, said that the Cardinal of Siena had spoken the same words to them that he had used with the Cardinal of San Giorgio.

When the examinations were completed and made known in the Consistory, Alfonso and Bandinello were deprived of the dignity of cardinals, degraded and turned over to the secular court, by sentence declared in public Consistory. The following night Alfonso was secretly strangled in prison; Bandinello's sentence was commuted by papal grace to perpetual imprisonment. Not much later the Pope not only liberated him from prison, but having been paid a certain amount of money, restored him to the dignity of the cardinalate; although in his case the Pope had just cause for indignation in that he had always been benefited by Leo who looked upon him most benignly, and had turned against him for no other reason than the great friendship which he bore to Alfonso, and because of his anger that the Cardinal de' Medici had been preferred before him in the petition for certain benefices. Nevertheless, there were those who interpreted the matter, perhaps malignly, to the effect that before he had been released from prison he had been given, by order of the Pope, that kind of poison which does not kill immediately, but in time consumes the life of him who has taken it.

As for the Cardinal of San Giorgio, whose crime was minor, the Pope proceeded more mildly, although the laws which have been passed and interpreted by princes for the security of their state would have it that in the crime of lese-majesty, capital punishment should be applied not only to those actively involved in the plot, but also against those who know of what is being brewed against the state; and much more when it is a question of plotting against the life of the prince. But the Pope had respect for the age and prestige of the Cardinal of San Giorgio, and for the great friendship and connections that had existed between them for a long time before Leo became pope. Therefore, although he was by the same sentence deprived of the cardinalate (in order to maintain authority by severity), he was almost immediately restored by grace (except that he could not vote, either actively or passively) to his office, being obliged to pay a very great sum of money; and before a year had passed, he took his full place again in the College of Cardinals.

Adrian and Volterra did not suffer any penalties, except that secretly they paid a certain amount of money; but since neither of them had confidence of being able to remain safely in Rome nor with the dignity of office that pertained to them, Volterra went to Fondi with the Pope's permission, where, under the shadow of Prospero Colonna, he remained until the Pope died; and Adrian secretly departed, but whatever became of him, he was never more found or seen anywhere as far as is known.

The bitterness of this episode forced the Pope to think about creating new cardinals, since he knew that practically the entire College was antagonistic to him because of the punishments of the conspirators and other reasons. He proceeded in this design so immoderately that in a single morning in Consistory he named thirty-one cardinals, the College agreeing out of fear and not of their own will; in the abundance of this number, the Pope had the opportunity to satisfy many of his aims and to elect from among men of all qualities. For he promoted two of his sister's sons, and some of those who had been in his service either during his pontificate or before, and were grateful to him and to the Cardinal de' Medici for various reasons, but in no other respect were worthy of such high office. He made many cardinals to satisfy great princes, creating them at their request; many were created by payments of money, since he found himself without funds and in dire necessity; some were distinguished for their knowledge of doctrine; and there were three generals (this is the highest rank among them) of the Orders of Saint Augustine, Saint Dominic and Saint Francis; and (what was most rare in a single promotion) two of the family of the Trivulzio, whose selection was motivated in one case by the fact that he was Leo's chamberlain, and the Pope wanted to satisfy Gianiacopo; and in the other, a reputation for ecclesiastical learning, aided by a certain sum of money.

But what created the greatest surprise was the elevation of Franciotto Orsini and Pompeo Colonna to the cardinalate, and five other Romans of the principal families who followed either the former or the latter faction: in this, the Pope followed counsels contrary to the decisions of his predecessor, but this was considered unwise and turned out quite unhappily for him and his kindred. For since the greatness of the Roman barons had always been a cause of concern and preoccupation for the pontiffs, Julius had never wanted to appoint any of them to the cardinalate, once the old cardinals of those families were gone, who had been bitterly persecuted by Alexander VI to despoil them of their estates. But

Leo, most unwisely, did just the contrary; nor could it be said that he was drawn to do so because of the merits of those persons; Franciotto was promoted to the dignity of cardinal from the profession of arms, and Pompeo should have been undone by recalling that although he had been a bishop, he had on the occasion of Julius' illness sought to stir up the Roman people against the rule of priests, and furthermore had openly rebelled in arms against the same Pope who had deprived him of his episcopal dignity for this reason.

The Ottoman Turks under Selim

Now followed the year 1518, during which time Italy knew no movements of war, even the slightest, something which had not happened for many years. On the contrary, all the Christian princes seemed to be of the same disposition; and among these, the Pope being the promulgator thereof, plans were being made (with more seeming argumentation than substantial recommendations) for a unified expedition of all Christendom against Selim, Prince of the Turks. Selim's power had so grown the previous year that, considering his might and his greed for domination, his skill and ferocity, it might well be suspected that if the Christian powers did not take steps to attack him, he would turn his victorious arms against them before much time passed.

For when Selim had previously learned that his father, Bajazet, already very old, was thinking of fixing the succession of the empire upon Ahmed, his first-born, he had constrained him by arms and by bribing the praetorian guard to turn the government over to him. And it was also universally believed that in order to be completely safe, Selim had had him wickedly put to death by poison. Later he was victorious over his brother in a contest of arms, and openly took his life; he did the same thing to the youngest of his brothers, Corcud; nor content with having killed, according to Ottoman custom, his nephews and any other descendants of that stock, it was believed (so bitter and implacable was his temperament) that he sometimes thought of taking the life of his only son Suleiman.

Proceeding from war to war according to these principles, he conquered the Adulians, a ferocious mountain people; then crossed over into Persia against the Sophi to whom he gave battle and defeated, and occupied the city of Tabriz, seat of that empire, together with most of Persia. And if he was forced to abandon Persia, it was not because of his enemies (who, fearing they would be unable to bear the shock of his armies, had withdrawn to mountainous wild places), but because he lacked victuals, that year having been most barren and unfertile.

After this expedition, he returned to Constantinople and punished many soldiers guilty of sedition; then when he had rested his armies for several months, he feigned that he wished to return to the war against Persia, but turned his forces instead against the Sultan of Syria and Egypt, a prince not only held in ancient reverence and esteem by those adhering to that religion, but also very powerful because of the extent of his domain, his great revenues, and the military prowess of the Mamelukes by whose arms that empire had been held with the greatest reputation for three hundred years. For their dominion was governed by sultans who attained the supreme rule not by succession but by election, and where only men of manifest worth, proved and proficient in all military undertakings, were appointed to govern the provinces or lead the armies; the nerves and sinews of their armies being made up not of mercenary soldiers and foreigners, but picked men who had been kidnapped as boys from the neighboring provinces, raised for many years on short rations, accustomed to hardships, and continuously trained in arms, horsemanship, and all those exercises pertaining to military discipline. They were then enrolled in the order of the Mamelukes (in which order, little by little, there succeeded not the sons of those Mamelukes who had died, but others who had been captured as boys to serve as slaves, and then attained to that position by the same discipline and training as had their predecessors). These men, numbering no more than sixteen or eighteen thousand, held in subjugation under their most stringent rule all the peoples of Egypt and Syria, despoiled of all their arms and forbidden to ride horses. And since they were men of such ability and ferocity, who made war for themselves (for amongst their ranks and by them were the sultans elected, and theirs were the honors, the emoluments, and the administration of all that most opulent and rich empire), not only had they subjected many neighboring nations, beaten the Arabs, but waged many wars with the Turks, defeating them often and rarely or never being vanquished.

Against these, therefore, Selim moved with his forces, and shattered them in several battles fought in the country, during which the Sultan was slain. Afterward, the other Sultan, his successor, was captured in a battle, and publicly put to death with ignominious torture. Thus slaughtered in great numbers by the Turks, the name of Mameluke was practically wiped out; Cairo, a most populous city in which the sultans resided, was overthrown, and all Syria and Egypt occupied in a short time. Hence, having so swiftly increased his empire, practically doubled his revenues, and eliminated the obstacle of such powerful and famous rivals, Selim was not without reason feared as a formidable foe of Christendom. And this fear was understandably increased by the fact that, together with his overwhelming power and valor, Selim was driven by a burning desire to rule, and by his victories to hand down a most glorious name to his descendants.

For this reason, having often read, as rumor had it, of the deeds done by Alexander the Great and Julius Caesar, his soul was greatly tormented because those deeds performed by him were in no way comparable to their numerous victories and triumphs. And continually reorganizing his armies and militia, building anew a great number of ships and making new provisions necessary for war, it was feared that he was thinking of attacking, whenever he was ready, either Rhodes, as some thought, bulwark of Christendom in the east, or (as others thought) the kingdom of Hungary, heretofore feared by the Turks because of the ferocity of its inhabitants, but at that time weakened because it was in the hands of a child-king governed by prelates and barons of the realm, who were in disaccord among themselves.

Others affirmed that Selim's thoughts were entirely turned toward Italy, and that his idea of attacking it was emboldened by the disagreement amongst the princes and his knowledge of how much Italy had been lacerated by many years of war. Furthermore, he was incited by the memory of his grandfather Mohammed, who with much weaker forces and a little navy sent to the kingdom of Naples, had by an improvised attack conquered the city of Otranto, and opened a door and fixed a position from which he might continuously vex the Italians (if death had not intervened).

Now therefore, the Pope, together with the entire Roman court, was terrified by such successes, and in order to provide against so grave a peril, he demonstrated that first he wished to have recourse to divine aid; and so he caused most devout processions to be celebrated in Rome, wherein he went barefooted; after which he turned his mind to the consideration and organization of human aid, and wrote briefs to all the Christian princes, admonishing them against the great peril and exhorting them to put aside their disagreements and contentions and promptly attend to the defense of religion and the common safety, which would be continuously subjected to the most terrible dangers if, with unity of purpose and forces, the war were not shifted to the Turkish empire, and the enemy assailed in his own house.

After having consulted the opinions of military men and experts who knew the towns, the disposition of the provinces, and the forces and arms of the Turkish empire, it was decided necessary that a very large provision of money be voluntarily contributed by the princes, and a universal tax imposed on all Christian peoples; after which, the Emperor, accompanied by Hungarian and Polish cavalry (bellicose nations trained in continuous wars against the Turks), and with an army of cavalry and German infantry suitable for such an undertaking, should sail down the

Danube into Bossina (called Misia in ancient times) and from there go to Thrace and approach Constantinople, seat of the Ottoman empire; and that the King of France with all the forces of his realm, with the Venetians and other Italians, accompanied by Swiss footsoldiers, should sail from the port of Brindisi to Albania (an easy and very short passage) to invade Greece, which was full of Christian inhabitants, and for this reason, as well as the bitterness of being under Turkish domination, most disposed to rebel; and that the Kings of Spain, of Portugal and of England, joining their armadas at Cartagena and neighboring ports, should sail with two hundred ships full of Spanish infantry and other soldiers to the Strait of Gallipoli to attack Constantinople, once the Dardanelles (that is, the castle situated above the mouth of the strait) had been captured: and that the Pope should sail along that same route, departing from Ancona with one hundred high-prowed galleys.

Earth and land covered with these preparations, and the empire of the Turks (who base their defense primarily on land actions) attacked from so many sides, it seemed legitimate to hope, especially with the addition of divine help, that so fearful a war would have a most felicitous conclusion.

In order to deal with these matters, or at least not to be impugned as failing in his pontifical office, Leo, after first sounding out the minds of the princes, published in consistory a universal truce for five years amongst all the Christian potentates, under pain of most serious censure against those who might violate it. And in order that there might be agreements and resolutions on matters pertaining to so great an enterprise (regarding which the Pope was also in continual consultation with the ambassadors of the princes), he dispatched as legates the Cardinal of Santo Sisto to the Emperor, the Cardinal of Santa Maria in Portico to the King of France, the Cardinal Egidio to the King of Spain, and Lorenzo Cardinal Campeggio, to the King of England, all highly reputed cardinals, either because of their experience in such affairs, or because of their reputation as theologians, or because they were very close to the Pope.

Now, although all these preliminaries were set in motion with great hopes, and although everyone accepted the truce, and everyone declared himself, with ostentatious and magnificent speeches, to be against the Turk and to be ready (if the others concurred) to lend all their strength to so just a cause, nevertheless, since each of them considered the danger uncertain and very far off, and relating more to one state than to another, and since it was very difficult, and required a long time to introduce such a sense of zeal and so universal a union, private interests and advantages prevailed.

The result was that all these negotiations not only did not lead to any hopeful conclusion, but also were dealt with only frivolously and, as it were, ceremoniously. Furthermore, it is natural among mankind that those things which at first seem most terrifying, diminish and cancel themselves out from day to day, so that unless new occurrences supervene to rekindle the terror, in the space of a very short time men convince themselves that they are practically out of danger.

This negligence of public affairs and excessive concern for one's own interests was confirmed all the more by Selim's death, which took place shortly after. The Turk's long illness had forced him to suspend all his preparations for war, and finally consumed by sickness, he passed to the other life, leaving his great empire to Suleiman, his son, a young man but reputed to be more mild-spirited (although the results demonstrated otherwise) and not disposed to make war.

. .
.

At that time the Pope and the King of France revealed that they were very closely allied. For the King gave his niece Madeleine [de La Tour d'Auvergne], born of royal blood of the house of Boulogne, as wife to Lorenzo [de' Medici], with a dowry of ten thousand scudi, part given to him by the King and part belonging to her patrimony; and a male child having been born to the King, he requested of the Pope that he should have him baptized in his name. For this reason, Lorenzo, who was making preparations to go marry his new wife, hastening his departure, went by post to the French court, where he was warmly received and honored by the King. By showing that he was entirely devoted to him, and promising to follow his fortune in every situation, Lorenzo greatly won over the King's favor. He brought Francis a papal brief granting him the right to spend at his pleasure the moneys raised by tithe or for the crusade until they had to be used against the Turk, with the proviso, however, that he promise to make these sums available whenever the purpose for which they had been raised required it.

Nevertheless, fifty thousand scudi were set aside for Lorenzo's use; and the King, who up to that day had feigned not to notice that the Pope was not carrying out the promise which he had made to him by brief of the restitution of Modena and Reggio, although the terminal date of seven months had already passed; and knowing that he could not create more difficulties for the Pope than by raising the question of this restitution, and taking more account, as often happens, of the stronger than of the weaker, returned the writ of promise into Lorenzo's hands.

Almost at the same time, the Venetians also prolonged, by intervention of the French King, the truce they had with the Emperor for five years, on condition that they should pay twenty thousand scudi for each of the five years; and in which it was expressedly stated that each year they should pay the Venetian exiles who had followed the Emperor, one quarter of the revenues which they had had before; paying for this purpose five thousand ducats, to be raised out of taxes. And the Emperor would have been induced perchance to make peace, if they had given him a greater sum of money. But the truce was more welcome to the King because the Venetians, not entirely assured, would have more reason to hold his friendship dear; and because the Emperor, having received money from them, would not be able to stir up any changes of government.

And since affairs everywhere were tending toward peace, the differences between the kings of France and England were also composed and confirmed by new dynastic marriages in order that the agreements might be made more permanent. For the King of England promised to give his only daughter [Mary Tudor] to the Dauphin, first-born of the King of France, together with 400,000 ducats dowry. Since the English King had no other children, it was expected that the succession to the throne would have to go to her. Both these children were so young that an infinite number of things might occur before they were old enough to celebrate the marriage.

A defensive league was set up between the two kings, naming the Emperor and the King of Spain as the major powers to be included, in case they should ratify it within a certain time. The King of England bound himself to return Tournai, the guarding of which cost him very heavily, receiving as immediate payment from the French King 260,000 ducats for his expenditures. The King of France would declare that he had received 300,000 ducats in dowry from his daughter-in-law to be, and that he would pay 300,000 ducats more within twelve years. He also promised to give Tournai back if the peace and marriage should fail to take place. In order to carry out this league and marriage agreement, both parties sent ambassadors to receive the ratifications and oaths, and these documents were expedited in both courts with the greatest solemnity and ceremony; and it was resolved that both kings should meet together personally between Calais and Boulogne,* not long after the restitution of Tournai.

At the same time, since the French King's daughter, who had been destined to marry the King of Spain, had died, the peace and mutual agreement were reconfirmed between them, with the promise of the matrimony of the second daughter. Both princes celebrated this union with grand demonstrations manifesting their amity. The King of Spain, who had already paid the 100,000 ducats to him at Lyons, publicly wore the Order of Saint Michael on the feast day of that saint, and the French King publicly wore the Order of the Golden Fleece on Saint Andrew's day.

Thus conditions were at peace in Italy and beyond the mountains;

---

* A small seaport on the English Channel.

and only Gianiacopo da Trivulzio was afflicted and discontent: taking no satisfaction either of his years, now that he was reduced almost to extreme old age, or of his capacities and virtues, so often tried in the service of the house of France. For caused perhaps to some degree by his ambition and restlessness, opposed by the subtle humors of his rivals, and persecuted in many things by Lautrec, a suspicion had been aroused in the King's mind that he and his house were too acceptable to the Venetians because of the interests of the Guelph faction and ancient understandings. Furthermore, Teodoro da Trivulzio was the governor of Venetian troops, and Renato of the same family had recently entered their service.

Therefore the King granted the Order of Saint Michael to Galeazzo Visconti who had remained the head of the Ghibelline faction after the death of Francesco Bernardino Visconti, in order that he might oppose Trivulzio with greater authority, and had set up a pension for him; and the King and Lautrec praised him on every occasion. These developments did not take place without depressing Trivulzio, who was poorly disposed to conceal his feelings, and who frequently complained, thus becoming every day more suspect and hated. But what gave Lautrec and the others all the more reasons to calumniate him in the King's presence, was the fact that he had himself created a burgess of the Swiss,* as if he wished by their help to have defense against the King, and perhaps he was aspiring to even loftier heights. The result of these slanders was that, old as he was, he went to France to justify himself. As soon as he left, not only did Lautrec, by order of the King, take into custody at Vigevano, his wife and grandchild born to the Count of Musocco, his only son (now deceased), but he was not even received by the King with his usual honors and welcome. Rather, reproving him for having become a Swiss, the King told him that the only thing that kept him from punishing him as he deserved was his widespread reputation (more indeed than was true) for services rendered to the crown of France. He was required to retract what he had done; and a few days later, following the court, he fell sick at Chartres and passed to that other world.

A man universally considered of singular worth in military discipline (proved by many trials); and subjected all his life to the inconstancies of fortune, now embracing him with prosperous successes, and now chafing and troubling him with adversity; one who fittingly deserved what was inscribed on his tomb at his orders:

IN THIS TOMB RESTS GIANIACOPO DA TRIVULZIO

WHO PREVIOUSLY HAD NEVER RESTED

* A Swiss citizen.

Death of the Emperor Maximilian

IN this same year the Emperor, wishing to establish the succession of the Holy Roman Empire after his death on one of his nephews, negotiated with the Electors to choose one of them as King of the Romans. Whoever achieved this title immediately succeeded to the Empire without any other election or confirmation, once the Emperor was dead. And since no such election can be held until he who has been chosen for the Empire has obtained the imperial crown, he petitioned the Pope that, by a new example, he should be crowned in Germany at the hand of several cardinals deputized as apostolic legates for this act.*

And although the Emperor had first desired that this dignity should be conferred upon his grandchild Ferdinand, for it seemed proper that since so many states and so much power had been lavished on the older brother, the other should be bolstered by this position; and his judgment was that in order to maintain his house in greater honor, and against all the misfortunes that might befall the older grandson, it would be better to have two persons of high rank rather than one; nevertheless, urged to the contrary by many of his courtiers and by the Cardinal Sedunense, and by all those who feared and hated the power of the French, his first recommendation was rejected, and he turned his mind to see to it that this dignity should be assumed by the King of Spain. Those who counseled the Emperor proved that it would be much more useful for the exaltation of the house of Austria to concentrate all that power in a single person, than to divide it in several parts, which would make them less capable of carrying out their designs. And they argued that Charles' greatness resting upon such mighty foundations, one might hope that, having achieved the imperial crown, he would perforce reduce all of Italy and a great part of Christendom into a single monarchy: a state of affairs which not only would redound to the greatness of his descendants, but also to the peace of his subjects, and with respect to the infidels, to the benefit of all Christendom.**

* This paragraph is so bestrewed with *Elettori, elezione, eletto, Imperio, Imperadore, imperiale* that the ambiguity is as much a result of repetitious diction as legalistic mentality. I have stuck closely to the original text (*Storia*, Gherardi ed., III, 203).

** Charles, born 1500 (hence eighteen years old at this time) had inherited from his paternal grandmother the extensive domains of Burgundy—equivalent approximately to present-day Belgium and Holland; and from his mother the realms of Castille and Aragon, that is, Spain, of which he entered into effective possession at the death of his maternal grandfather Ferdinand (January 1516). This accumulation of territory from the north to the south of Europe was the result of the wise Hapsburg marriages for which was created the motto: "*Arma gerant alii, tu, felix Austria, nube*" (cf. Luigi Salvatorelli, *Sommario della storia d'Italia*, Turin, 1955, p. 356).

IMPERATOR CAESAR
DIVVS MAXI MILIANVS
PIVS FELIX AVGVSTVS.

MAXIMILIAN I

Wood engraving by Albrecht Dürer, dated 1518, one year before the Emperor's death (COURTESY OF GABINETTO NAZIONALE DELLE STAMPE, ROME)

Furthermore, it was the Emperor's office and duty to think about the expansion and exaltation of the imperial dignity which had resided for so many years in his person and the house of Austria. Up to that time the house of Austria had been greater in title and name than in substance and effect, because of his weakness and that of his predecessors, nor could it hope to be resurrected or returned to its pristine splendor except by transferring itself to the person of Charles and joining itself with his power: nor was it his office to impede but rather to augment this opportunity which had been brought to him by the order of nature and fortune. One might note by the examples of the ancient emperors, Julius Caesar, Augustus and many of their successors,* that, lacking sons or persons of the same line, and concerned that the dignity residing in their person should not be extinguished or diminished, they had sought by means of adoptions for successors distantly related, or not even related at all.

Still fresh was the example of the Catholic King who, although he loved Ferdinand like a son, always kept him near him, and having but rarely seen Charles—indeed finding him quite disobedient to his commands in his last years—nevertheless, he had not had any compassion for the poverty of one whom he loved as a son; had not given him any part of his state, not even those lands which, having been acquired by him personally, it was in his power to dispose of; rather, had left everything to one whom he scarcely knew, except as a stranger.

The Emperor should remember how the same King had always advised him to acquire new states for Ferdinand but to leave the imperial dignity to Charles; and take note that to aggrandize the glory of his successor and moved by no other reason, he had despoiled his own so noble and illustrious house of the kingdom of Aragon, perhaps doing so at the harmful advice of many courtiers, and perchance unjustly; and had thus consented, against the common desire of most men, that the name of his house should be extinguished and annihilated.

The King of France opposed the Emperor's request with all his might and skill, considering himself greatly threatened that the King of Spain should add the imperial dignity to so many kingdoms and states, so that gaining more vigor from so much power he would become formidable to everyone. Therefore, seeking to block this project secretly among the electors, he beseeched the Pontiff not to agree to send the crown to the Emperor Maximilian, setting thereby a new example; and he dispatched ambassadors to the Venetians in order that they might join with him in opposition, admonishing both the Pontiff and them of the danger such greatness would bring.

Nevertheless, for the most part, the Electors were already drawn to

---

* Another reading might be Caesar Augustus.

The Hapsburgs: from Maximilian I

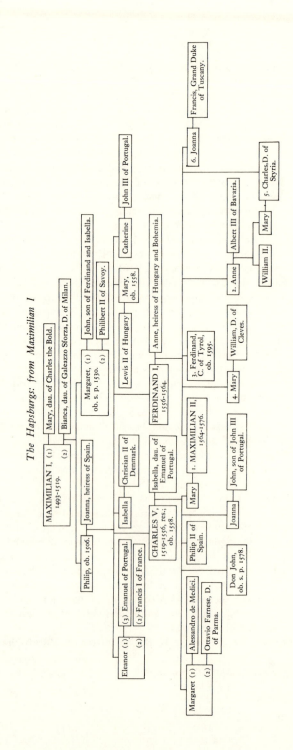

the Emperor's opinion, and were already almost guaranteed the money that the King of Spain had promised them for this election, 200,000 ducats for this purpose having been sent to Germany. Nor could they honestly, or perhaps without danger of scandal (with respect to past examples) deny this petition; nor was it believed that the Pope (although he was disturbed by it) would refuse to concede that the Emperor should receive the imperial crown in Germany in his name by the hand of the Apostolic Legate; seeing that his going to be crowned in Rome, although it brought greater prestige to the Apostolic See, would be in every other respect ceremonial rather than substantial fact.

With these thoughts and actions ended the year 1518, the deliberation among the Electors not yet having taken place. Furthermore, as a result of a new event, this meeting became ever more dubious and difficult. For the Emperor died during the first days of the year 1519. He died at Linz, a city situated at the frontiers of Austria, intent as always in hunting wild beasts; and with the same fortune with which he had almost always lived. For, that very fortune which had been most kind in offering him the greatest opportunities, I do not know if she was not equally averse in not letting them succeed; or if that which fortune had brought him, even to his own house, he had been deprived of by his inconstancy and immoderate ideas, often different from other men's judgments, together with boundless prodigality and waste of money—all these things undid all his successes and opportunities. Otherwise, he was a prince most expert in war, diligent, secretive, most laborious, clement, benign, and full of many outstanding gifts and graces.

Rivalry Between King Charles of Spain and King Francis of France for the Imperial Crown

At Maximilian's death, the King of France and the King of Spain began openly to aspire to the imperial crown. Although this controversy was a matter of such importance, and between such mighty princes, nevertheless it was waged between them in a modest manner, neither of them engaging in contumacious words or threat of arms, but rather, each with the force at his disposal, making every effort to attract the minds of the Electors toward his side. Indeed, the King of France, most laudably, speaking about this election with the ambassadors of the King of Spain, said that it was commendable that each of them should seek honestly to increase his honor by the splendor of such dignity, which had resided at sundry times in the families of their predecessors. But this was no reason for either of them to

TRIUMPHAL CHARIOT OF MAXIMILIAN I

*Detail of the Triumphal Chariot of Maximilian I, woodcut by Albrecht Dürer,
c. 1518. The inscription at the head: "As the sun is in heaven so is the Emperor
on earth." The numerous virtues ascribed to the belaureled and crowned
Maximilian in the guise of allegorical maidens entitled Justice, Temperance,
Liberality, Fidelity, Goodness, Intelligence, etc.; the feathers of conquests*

*worn by Victory: France, Switzerland, Hungary, Bohemia, Germany, Venice;
the chariot driven by Reason holding the reins of Nobility and Power; the
wheels of Magnificence, Honor, Dignity, and Glory—all this overplush rhetoric, reflected in the overcrowded imagery of Dürer's print, is in marked
contrast to Guicciardini's icy, terse profile of Maximilian's character and
career.*

insult the other, nor should the amity and alliance between them be diminished. Rather they should follow the example that one sometimes sees between two lovers who, although they love the same lady, and are making every effort to win her with all their skill and means, do not fall into contention with each other for this reason.

The King of Spain felt that the Empire rightfully belonged to him because it had continued for many years within the house of Austria, nor was it the custom of the Electors to deprive the descendants of the deceased Emperor of it without evident reason of their incapacity. There did not seem to be anyone in Germany of such prestige and power that he might have to compete with him in this election; nor did it seem just or very likely to him that the Electors should have to transfer so great a dignity, which had continued for many centuries within the German nation, to a foreign prince. And should any among them, corrupted by money or for some other reason, prove to be of a different mind, he hoped either to frighten him with arms prepared at an opportune time, or that the other Electors would oppose him, and at least that all the other princes and free towns of Germany would not tolerate that such infamy and ignominy should befall all of them, especially when it became a question of transferring the Empire to the person of a French king, which would be to increase the power of a king inimical to their nation, and from whom they could be certain that that dignity would never again return to Germany. He thought, therefore, that it would be easy to bring about what had already been arranged by his grandfather, who had agreed upon certain rewards and gifts for each of the Electors.

On the other hand, the King of France was no less eager and hopeful, based primarily on the belief that he could acquire the Electors' votes with enormous sums of money. Several of the Electors, joined to him by ancient bonds of friendship and favors, pointed out how easily he might gain his end and spurred him on to make an effort; and (inasmuch as men are apt to persuade themselves of that which they desire) he nourished this hope with reasons more apparent than true. For he knew that ordinarily the German princes took it ill that the Emperor should be too powerful, for fear that he would not want to take cognizance, either in sum or in part, of the imperial jurisdictions and powers which many of them were exercising; and therefore he was convinced that they would not consent to the election of a king of Spain under any circumstances, thus subjecting themselves by their own actions to an Emperor who would be more powerful than any Emperor had ever been from the time of the ancients to the present. But such [objections] did not seem altogether pertinent in his case, since having had no states nor any ancient connections in Germany, they could not have so much suspicion of his grandeur. For this reason, likewise, he believed that regard for national glory would prove not only a counterweight but actually a source of concern to the free towns, as usually the goads of self-interest are incomparably more powerful among men than respect for the common welfare. He was aware that many illustrious German families were greatly offended that the imperial crown should have continued for so many years in the same house, while they considered themselves worthy of that dignity, and he knew that they took it amiss that an election which should have gone today to one and tomorrow to another should instead have begun almost by succession to perpetuate itself in the same stock; and one could call a succession that election which did not dare to deviate from the closest relative of the lineage of the Emperors: thus the empire had passed from Albert of Austria to Frederick his brother, from Frederick to his son Maximilian, and now they were considering transferring it from Maximilian to the person of his grandson Charles.

These humors and sense of indignation among the German princes gave the French King hope that their disagreements and rivalries might aid his cause, since it often happens in contentions that whoever considers himself, or the party he favors, ruled out, will hasten (regardless of everything else) to support any third party whatever, rather than yield to the one who has been opposed to his intention.

Besides this, the King of France hoped for pontifical favor, both because of the agreement and good will that he believed he had contracted with the Pope, as well as because he didn't believe that the Pontiff could take pleasure that Charles, so powerful a prince, contiguous to the states of the Church in the kingdom of Naples, and who had, by the support of the Ghibelline barons, thus opened the road to the very gates of Rome, should also gain the imperial throne.

But he did not consider that this line of reasoning, although very true with regard to Charles, also militated against his claims: because should he gain the imperial throne, the result would be no less formidable to the Pontiff and to everyone else, than had the crown gone to Charles; notwithstanding that if one of them perhaps possessed more realms and more states, the other was not to be estimated any the less because his power was not dispersed and separated in various places, but his realm was all together and united, with a remarkable obedience of his people, and provided with the greatest riches. Nevertheless, not recognizing in himself what he easily realized in others, he had recourse to the Pope, entreating him to favor his cause, for he could count on the King personally and on his realm, as on his own son.

The matter of this election weighed very heavily upon the Pope, since he considered the security of the Apostolic See and the rest of Italy endangered, whichever of the two kings should accede to the imperial throne. And since his power and prestige among the Electors was not such that he could hope to prevail much with them, he judged it necessary to make use of all his prudence and skills in a matter of such moment. He was convinced that the King of France, fooled by several of the Electors, did not have any chance in this election, nor, despite the fact that he was among venal men, did he have any possibility of dishonestly transferring the empire from the German nation to France by means of bribery.

It seemed to him, however, that the King of Spain, because he was of the same nation, and because of the negotiations begun by Maximilian and for many other reasons, was much more likely to gain his end, unless he stirred a very powerful opposition against him; and the Pope judged that such opposition could not be raised in any way except that the King of France should prepare to deflect to one of the Electors those same favors and money which he was using to elect himself. It seemed impossible to him to induce the King to this course of action so long as he was still fervid with vain hopes. Therefore, he hoped that the more ardently and confidently the King of France plunged into these maneuvers, the more easily (once he began to realize that all his hopes were in vain, and finding himself already in the open, and vexed, and out of the race) would he be forced to suddenly favor the election of a third party with no less ardor than he had supported his own claim; and when the Pope had already gained the King's faith of being favorable to him and desiring only what he himself desired, then it would be possible at such time to make his councils and authority heard. And it might likewise happen that by strongly favoring the claims of the King of France at the beginning, the other King, seeing his desire difficult of attainment, and doubting that the King, his adversary, might not have some possibility, should, in like sort, hasten to support a third claimant.

Therefore, the Pope not only signified to the French King that it was his highest desire that he should attain the imperial crown, but encouraged him with many lines of reasoning to proceed resolutely in this enterprise, promising that he would favor him with all the authority of the papacy. And since he thought that he could make no greater impression that such was his intention than by using in this action an instrument whom the French King would judge depended more on himself than on others, the Pope immediately assigned as his Nuncio in Germany, Roberto Orsini, Archbishop of Reggio, a person in the King's confidence; with a commission that, both on his own part, and together with the King's agents there, he should foster as much favor as possible among the Electors for the Pope's wishes in this election; cautioning him however to proceed with more or less moderation, according as he found the Electors disposed in Germany, and the general situation.

These actions, being discreetly discoursed upon by the Pope, and concealed under the subtlest camouflage, would have required greater prudence on the part of the French King and his ministers in Germany, and more gravity and fidelity on the part of the Pope's ministers.

But while these matters were proceeding with negotiations and with arms, the King of France gave orders for Pedro Navarro to take to the high seas with an armada of twenty galleys and other vessels, and with four thousand paid infantry, under pretense of suppressing the corsairs of the Moors (who having already for many years overrun our seas without any opposition, were infesting them this year more than ever) and to attack, if the Pope thought it advisable, the Moors in Africa; but principally in order that the Pope, having shown himself entirely for him in the competition for the Empire, should have no cause for fearing the forces of the Catholic King: who more because of the fear he had of being attacked than out of a desire of attacking others, was carefully preparing a fleet to be sent to guard the kingdom of Naples.

And nevertheless, amidst these distrusts and suspicions, both kings continued to feign friendship, and at Montpelier, in their name, the Grand Master of France [Gouffier of Boissy] and Monseigneur de Ceures, each of whom was in the closest counsels and confidence of his respective King, agreed to negotiate on fixing the marriage of the second daughter of the King of France with the King of Spain. And what was more important, they were to resolve affairs in the kingdom of Navarre, the restitution of which, promised to the ancient king in the accord made at Noyon, although greatly desired by the King of France, had been deferred up to that time by the King of Spain with various excuses: but the death of the Grand Master, which occurred before they could speak together, interrupted the hopeful outcome of this meeting.

At this time there also died Lorenzo de' Medici, weakened by almost continuous illness since he had returned from France where he had consummated his marriage with unhappy auspices, because a very few days before his death, his wife having given birth, prepared the way for him by dying. Because of Lorenzo's death, the Pope—desirous of keeping the power of the Florentines conjoined with that of the Church so long as he lived, and lending no ear to the counsels of some who advised him that since there no longer remained any legitimate descendants (except himself) of the masculine line of Cosimo de' Medici, founder of their glory, he should restore liberty to his country—proposed the Cardinal de' Medici* for the administration of that state: either out of a desire to perpetuate the name of his house or out of hatred, caused by exile, against the name of the Republic. And thinking that it would be difficult, because of the love the people bore toward their former Duke, to hold the duchy of Urbino in the name of Lorenzo's remaining daughter [Catherine de'

---

* Giulio de' Medici, the Pope's cousin.

Medici], included in the paternal investiture, he restored it together with Pesaro and Sinigallia to the Apostolic See; and judging that this was not sufficient to curb the people's ardor, he had the walls of the city of Urbino and other principal places of the duchy, with the exception of Gubbio, razed to the ground. Gubbio was not so sympathetically inclined toward Francesco Maria [della Rovere], because of its rivalry with Urbino; and therefore the Pope bestowed upon it his favor and prestige, setting it up as the head of the duchy. And in order to weaken the duchy so much the more, he gave the Florentines (whom he had already established as creditors in the apostolic chamber) in payment for monies expended for him in the war with Urbino, the fortress of Santo Leo with all Montefeltro and the parishes of Sestina, which used to be in the territory of Cesena. The Florentines took little satisfaction and contentment out of this settlement, but were in no position to oppose his will.

Election of Charles of Austria, King of Spain, as Emperor

THERE still remained the controversy over the imperial succession, all Christianity looking on with bated breath while both kings put forth their claims more ardently than ever. In this contest, the King of France deceived himself more every day, beguiled by the grand promises of the Marquis [Joachim] of Brandenburg, one of the Electors who, having received a very great offer of money from him and perhaps a certain amount in down payment, had not only pledged by secret agreements to give him his vote, but promised that his brother, the Archbishop of Mainz, one of the three Prelate Electors, would do the same. The King also anticipated a great deal from another group of Electors, and in case the votes should be even, rested his hope on the ballot of the King of Bohemia. For should the six Electors (of whom three are prelates, three princes) fail to agree, the vote of the King of Bohemia settles the controversy. Therefore he sent the Admiral,* who had gone to Germany earlier for this election, a very great sum of money to give the Electors. And understanding that many of the free towns, together with the Duke of Wirtenberg, threatening whoever might wish to transfer the Empire upon foreigners, were mustering many troops, the King made provision of other moneys to oppose by force of arms anyone who tried to prevent the Electors from choosing him.

But the desire of the German people that the imperial dignity should

---

* Guillaume Gouffier, Lord of Bonnivet, younger brother of the Grand Master (Boissy). Made Admiral of France in 1515. Died in 1525 at battle of Pavia.

not be removed from that nation was very great; indeed, together with the Swiss, motivated by love for their common Germanic fatherland, they had begged the Pope not to lend his favor in this election to anyone who was not of German tongue. But the Pope nevertheless continued to favor the King of France, hoping thereby that since he showed himself so ardent in his support, the French King would have to hearken with greater trust to his counsels. By such reasoning the Pope managed to persuade himself that once the King's hope of being elected was set aside, he would endeavor with similar urgency to see to it that some other German prince would be elected.

But this counsel proved fruitless, because the Admiral and Roberto Orsini, deceived by the promises of those who made the most positive promises in order to get money from the hands of the French, and both of them passionately involved—one because he was an ingenious Frenchman and the King's minister, the other frivolous by nature and eager to get in his good graces—every day more, with vain opinions, confirmed the King's hope that he could carry the election.

With these practices, those who have the right of electing the Emperor of Rome (not by any ancient custom or well-founded reason, but by concession of Gregory V, a German who was Roman Pontiff) came according to tradition to Frankfurt, a town of lower Germany. And while various disputes were continuing in anticipation of arriving at a decision in due time, according to their orders, an army was put into the field by command of the King of Spain (who was more ready to spend money for mustering troops than giving it to the Electors) and approached Frankfurt under pretext of preventing anyone from seeking to violate the election. This so increased the courage of those Electors favoring his cause, attracted others who were doubtful into their camp, and so frightened the Marquis of Brandenburg, who was inclined toward the King of France, that despairing that the other Electors would concur with his choice, and wishing to avoid the hatred and infamy of the entire nation, he had not dared to disclose his intention: with the result that finally coming to the act of election on the twenty-eighth day of June, Charles of Austria, King of Spain, was elected as Emperor by the united votes of four Electors, viz: the Archbishop of Mainz, the Archbishop of Cologne, the Count Palatine and the Duke of Saxony. But the Archbishop of Trier voted for the Marquis of Brandenburg, who also voted for himself. Nor was it doubted that if the votes had been equal, and the election then depended on the seventh Elector, the outcome would have been the same, for Louis, King of Bohemia, who was also King of Hungary, had promised his vote to Charles.

This election greatly depressed the King of France and his dependants in Italy, and on the contrary, greatly lifted the spirits of those of contrary hopes or thoughts, in seeing so much power united in a single prince, a young man about whom many predictions were heard, promising him a great empire and stupendous opportunities. And although he was not as well provided with money as the King of France, nevertheless his power of furnishing his armies with German and Spanish infantry was considered of the greatest importance, since these were footsoldiers of the highest valor and reputation. But the contrary was true with regard to the King of France, because not having in his realm infantrymen to oppose the others, he could not involve himself in powerful wars except by gathering up footsoldiers from foreign countries at the greatest expense and sometimes with the greatest difficulty. Therefore he was obliged to deal cautiously with the Swiss at great cost, and tolerate much of their insolence, and yet he was never entirely sure either of their constancy or of their fidelity.

Nor did anyone doubt that between two princes, both young and with many reasons for rivalry and contention, a most serious war must inevitably result. For the King of France still maintained his desire to recuperate the kingdom of Naples, claiming to have just title to it: and he also took greatly to heart the restitution of King John to the realm of Navarre, concerning which he now realized he had been fed vain hopes.

The Emperor was troubled by the payment of 100,000 ducats which he had promised at the treaty of Noyon; and it seemed to him that the King, having violated the agreement previously drawn up at Paris, and immoderately taking advantage of having to march into Spain, had almost forced him to draw up a new accord. The cause of the Duke of Guelders was ever fresh between them, a contention which alone might prove sufficient to stir up a war, since the King of France held this duchy under his protection and the state of Flanders considered him a deadly enemy. But above all, the new Emperor was ardently aroused by the duchy of Burgundy, which had been occupied by Louis XI on the occasion of the death of Charles, Duke of Burgundy, grandfather on the maternal side of the Emperor's father, a matter which had always troubled the minds of his successors.

Nor were there lacking goads and reasons for dissension with regard to the duchy of Milan: the present King had not obtained this or demanded its investiture after the death of Louis XII, and claiming that there were many exceptions to those rights coming down to him out of the investiture made to his predecessor, and the invalidity and loss of those rights—all this was sufficient to stir up war between them.

Nevertheless, neither time nor opportunity were propitious then for setting armies in motion. For, aside from the fact that it was necessary for the Emperor to return first to Germany in order to take the imperial crown at Aachen, according to the custom of other emperors-elect, there was the additional fact that since each of them was so powerful, he was restrained from attack by the mutual danger, until he had first thoroughly sounded out the minds and dispositions of the other princes, and especially (should it be a question of waging war in Italy) that of the Pope. But the intentions of the Pope were so hidden under camouflage and manipulations that they were not known to anyone, and perhaps sometimes not even resolved in his own mind; although he had given dispensation to Charles to accept his election to the Empire, contrary to the tenor of the investiture of the kingdom of Naples, wherein (according to the form of the ancient investitures) that was expressedly forbidden him. However, the Pope had done this less out of free will, than in order not to be put in a position of denying it, without gravely offending Charles.

Martin Luther Attacks the Authority of the Roman Church with Regard to the Sale of Indulgences. Spread of His Doctrine

Now followed the year 1520; during which time and for the same reasons, the peace in Italy continued which had been maintained during the previous year. But in 1520 new doctrines began to spread widely, first against the authority of the Roman Church and then against the authority of the Christian religion. This pestiferous poison originated in Germany in the province of Saxony as a result of the preaching of Martin Luther, a friar professor of the Augustinian Order, whose doctrines, for the most part, revived the ancient errors of the Bohemians. For these latter had been reproved by the universal Council of the Church held at Constance, by whose authority John Huss and Jerome of Prague had been burned, two of the principal heads of that heresy which had been for a long time restricted within the confines of Bohemia.

But the authority of the Apostolic See, used so licentiously by Leo, had been the cause of stirring up this heresy anew in Germany. For Leo, following the advice of Lorenzo Pucci, Cardinal of Santi Quattro, with regard to the granting of graces which the court of Rome concedes in things both spiritual and beneficial, had spread throughout the world, with no distinction of times or places, the broadest indulgences, not only for the benefit of those still living, but also with the power of liberating the souls of the dead from the pains of Purgatory. Since there was no precedent or truth of any sort in this procedure, for it was notorious that these indulgences were being granted only to extort money from men

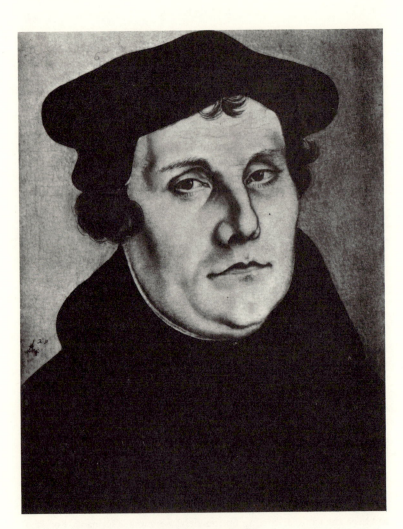

MARTIN LUTHER

*Portrait by Lucas Cranach, dated 1529 (Uffizi Gallery, Florence). The artist was an ardent disciple of the Reformer and his friend as well. Luther stood witness at Cranach's marriage and was godfather to his children. The artist served for nearly fifty years as court painter of Frederick the Wise, Elector of Saxony (first at Wittenberg and later at Weimar), producing numerous severe portraits of Luther and other leaders of the Reformation and, at the same time, many mythological pictures populated by archly libidinous female nudes—a dualism not uncommon among the reformers. (*COURTESY OF FRATELLI ALINARI*)*

who yielded more out of simplicity than out of wisdom, and since the practice was being impudently carried on by commissioners deputized for these exactions, most of whom purchased the right of selling indulgences at the court, they had stirred up a great deal of scandal and indignation in many places; and especially in Germany where many of the Pope's ministers were seen selling at a cheap price, or gambling away in the taverns, the power of delivering the souls of the dead out of Purgatory.

And the indignation grew because the Pope (easygoing by nature, and hence exercising his pontifical office in many things with little majesty) gave his sister Maddalena the emoluments and exactions of the indulgences of many parts of Germany. She had deputized as her commissioner the Bishop Aremboddo, a minister worthy of this commission, which he carried on with great avarice and extortions. And inasmuch as it was known all over Germany that the money being raised was not going to the Pope or to the apostolic chamber (where it might even have been possible that some of the money might have been spent for good uses), but was destined to satisfy a woman's greed, not only had the exactions and the ministers thereof become detestable, but also the name and prestige of him who had so ill-advisedly granted them.

Luther seized upon this opportunity, and by condemning these indulgences and laying charges against the Pope's authority because of them, his cause gained ever more favor in the ears of the populace, the great number of his auditors multiplied, and he began more openly every day to deny the Pope's authority.

From these beginnings, perhaps honest, or at least in some part excusable, considering the just cause which had given rise to them, carried away by ambition and popular acclaim, and the favor of the Duke of Saxony, not only did Luther become too immoderate in his opposition to the power of the popes and the authority of the Roman Church, but falling once again into the errors of the Bohemians, he began in time to remove the images out of the churches, to despoil ecclesiastical places of their goods, to permit monks and nuns to enter into matrimony, confirming these opinions not only by precedent and arguments but even by personal example; he denied that the Pope's power extended beyond the bishopric of Rome, and affirmed that every other bishop had the same authority in his diocese that the Pope had in Rome. He scorned and rejected all those things which had been determined by the councils, all those things written by those who are called the Doctors of the Church, all the canonical laws and decrees of the popes, returning solely to the Old Testament, the books of the Gospels, the Acts of the Apostles, and all that included under the name of the New Testament and the Epistles of Saint Paul; but giving all these writings new and unsuspected meanings and unheard of interpretations.

Nor did the madness of Luther and his followers remain within these bounds, but being supported one might say by almost all of Germany, they were led into more pernicious and detestable errors every day; went so far as to wound the sacraments of the church; to despise fasts, penances, and confessions; and at last, several people of his sect went on (but they already differed in some ways from Luther's opinions) to invent poisonous and diabolic lies about the Eucharist.

All these things, based upon rejection of the authority of the Councils and the holy Doctors, have opened the way to every sort of new and perverse interpretation or invention; and in many places, even out of Germany, these interpretations are extended so that they contain doctrines that release men of many precepts established for the salvation of all by the ecumenical councils of the Church, the decrees of the popes, the authority of the canons, and the salubrious interpretations of the holy Doctors; with the result that people are reduced to an almost free and willful mode of life.

The Pope strove at first to extinguish this poisonous doctrine, but he did not employ those remedies and medicines suitable for curing such a malady. For he summoned Martin Luther to Rome, suspended him from his office of preaching, and then because of his disobedience subjected him to ecclesiastical censure. But he did not abstain from continuing to set a bad example in many things, which were offensive to all men, and which Luther had damned with good reason. Whence, proceeding against him with ecclesiastical arms did not diminish Martin's reputation among the people, but rather augmented it, as if the persecutions arose more out of the innocence of his life and the soundness of his doctrine than for any other reason. The Pope sent many priests and monks to preach against Luther in Germany; he addressed many briefs to princes and prelates; but neither these nor any other methods used to suppress Luther were of any avail (because of the people's support, and the great favor shown him by the Duke of Saxony in his own lands).

Thus this situation began to seem more grave every day at the court of Rome, and nurtured suspicions that there might be born therefrom the most serious threat against the grandeur of the popes, the usefulness of the Roman court, and the unity of the Christian religion.

For this reason, many consistories were held that year at Rome, and frequent consultations of cardinals and theological disputes in the Pope's chamber, in order to find remedies for this malady which was continually growing. And although there were not lacking those who recalled that since the persecution made against him up to that time had not been accompanied by correcting blamable behavior in their own ranks, they had only increased his reputation and the people's support, and that it would have been a lesser evil to have feigned unawareness of this folly (which perhaps might have disappeared of itself) rather than by blowing on the fire, to kindle it, and make it blaze all the more. Nevertheless, as it is within the nature of man to proceed voluntarily to fiery remedies, not only were the persecutions against Luther and the other members of his sect, vulgarly called Lutherans, intensified, but furthermore, a most solemn admonition was launched against the Duke of Saxony who, exasperated by this, became the most vehement promoter of Luther's cause.

Thus in a space of a few years, things went on multiplying so that there was great danger that almost all of Christendom might become infected by this contagion. Nor has Luther's course been curbed so much by anything as by it becoming known that the sect supporting this doctrine is no less hostile against temporal princes than against the authority of the Roman pontiffs; with the result that many princes for their own interest have vigilantly and severely prohibited the introduction of this contagion into their realms; and on the contrary, nothing has so sustained the stubbornness of these errors (which were sometimes close to confusion and collapse, because the heads of these heresies went too far, and because of the various and even contradictory opinions among themselves) as the licentious liberty which the people have begun to manifest in their mode of living, and the greed of potentates not to be deprived of the goods and property which they have seized from the churches.

. .

Nothing worthy of memory happened in Italy this year except that Giampaolo expelled Gentile (both of the same family of the Baglioni) from Perugia, either because some contention had arisen between them or because Giampaolo, not satisfied to play a greater role and possess more authority in the government, wished to arrogate everything for himself. This antagonized the Pope, who summoned Giampaolo to appear personally in Rome. But Giampaolo, fearing to go there, sent his son Malatesta to justify his actions, and to offer ready obedience to all the Pope's commandments. But since the Pope still insisted on his coming, after many days of perplexity, he resolved to go, placing his confidence partly in the long-standing devotion which at all times he had displayed toward the Pope's house, and partly persuaded by his son-in-law Camillo Orsini and others of his friends, who, employing their influence and making use of powerful means close to the Pope, had either obtained from him an explicit pledge (although not in writing), or at any rate the Pope had used such words with the greatest astuteness, and given such indications that those who confided in him could deduce his state of mind, with the result that Camillo and his friends encouraged Giampaolo to appear, giving him to understand that he could do so safely.

But when he arrived in Rome he found that the Pope, under the pretense of recreation, as at other times he was wont to do, had entered the Castel Sant' Angelo a few days before. Going there the following morning to present himself, Giampaolo was arrested by the castellan before ever arriving at the Pope's presence, and then having been rigorously examined by appointed judges, he confessed to the gravest crimes, not only with regard to matters pertaining to the preservation of the tyranny, but also for nefarious pleasures, and others of his particular interests.

For these reasons, after he had been imprisoned for more than two months, he was beheaded according to the sentence of the law. It was believed that the Pope was motivated in this situation because during the war over Urbino, he had understood by many signs that Giampaolo was opposed to him, and that he had come to a secret understanding with Francesco Maria [della Rovere], and that he could not rely on him in any situation that might occur, and that consequently he could not be certain of Perugian affairs so long as Giampaolo remained in that state. In order to reorganize matters there as he desired, and since the sons of Giampaolo had fled as soon as they had news of their father's arrest, the Pope gave this legation to Silvio, Cardinal of Cortona, an old servitor whom he had trained. He placed Gentile back in Perugia, to whom he gave the goods which Giampaolo had possessed, and leaning on a very weak subject, he deflected reputation and greatness upon him.

. .
.

In this same year [while the Pope continued to make new attempts against the Duke of Ferrara] the Emperor sailed from Spain to Flanders. In his passage he touched at England, not out of necessity as his father had done, but voluntarily in order to speak with the English King with whom he was in good agreement. From Flanders he went to Germany in the month of October, where at Aachen (a noble city renowned as the ancient residence and sepulchre of Charlemagne) he received the first crown, the very same, according to tradition, with which Charlemagne was crowned; and according to the ancient tradition it was given to him by the authority of the princes of Germany.

But this felicity of his was disturbed by new incidents in Spain. For the people of that realm were troubled by his accession to the imperial throne, because they knew that he would be forced, for various reasons, to spend no little part of his time outside of Spain, to the greatest detriment and inconvenience of them all. But they were particularly aroused by the great hatred which they had conceived against the avarice of those who governed for him, especially against Monseigneur de Ceures, who showing himself insatiable, had accumulated by every possible means an enormous sum of money, as the other Flemings had likewise done, selling for ready money to foreigners those offices which usually went to Spaniards, and putting up for sale all the favors, privileges, and expeditions that were being sought for at the court. Consequently, all the people were stirred up against the Flemings, and at the Emperor's departure, the population of Valladolid had rebelled. And he was hardly out of Spain, when everyone broke into insurrection, not against the King (they said) but against his bad governors; and taking counsel together, they would no longer obey the King's officers, and had summoned a meeting of the majority of the population, who formed a government and ruled in the name of the Holy Junta (as the popular universal council was called). The royal captains and ministers opposed the popular government with arms, and so matters were reduced to open warfare, and disorders multiplied so much that the Emperor retained very little authority in Spain; whilst in Italy and elsewhere, hopes grew among those who wished to diminish his grandeur. Nevertheless, his fleet had conquered the island of Jerbe from the Moors, and in Germany, the reputation of the French King had somewhat declined.

[*Although Italy has been more or less at peace for three years, now new wars break out, more dangerous than before. The fundamental cause is the "ambition of two most mighty kings, puffed up with mutual jealousies and hatred, which incited them to exercise all their power and all their disdain in Italy." Up to now various interests have maintained a balance between the King of France and the Emperor: the Venetians are leagued to help Francis I in defense of the duchy of Milan; the Swiss are disposed only to serve as soldiers to whoever gives them pay. Therefore, the French King does not fear the Emperor, and on the other hand the Emperor does not fear French attacks in Naples unless Pope Leo joins in the action.*

But Leo's policy is to come to agreements—written or secret— with both camps simultaneously in the hope that his own ambitions (the recovery of Parma and Piacenza, and the seizure of Ferrara) might be fulfilled by maneuvering amidst greater antagonists. Leo's double-dealing and ambition become the immediate cause of new wars. Guicciardini condemns this Pope who had "no reason or necessity to . . . stir up war. . . . The Pope possessed tranquilly, and with great obedience, the very large estate of the Church; and Rome and all the court were flourishing and in a state of felicity. He had full authority over the state of Florence, which at that time was powerful and very rich; and he was naturally inclined to ease and pleasures, and now, because of too much licentiousness and greatness, he was especially indisposed to attend to affairs; immersed all day long in music, jests and buffoonery; also being inclined, much more than was honest, to pleasures which are enjoyed [only] with great infamy, he seemed altogether estranged from war." Leo's immoderate spending and burden of debts would also seem to restrain him. "But it is right truly spoken there is no greater enemy to a man than too much prosperity. . . ." Leo's duplicity unleashes the war between Emperor and King of France.

Meanwhile on 3 January 1521, the Pope pronounces anathema against Martin Luther, and in February Charles V attends the Diet of Worms. On the 16th of April, Luther, armed with an imperial safe-conduct, arrives at Worms, and for two days—the 17th and 18th of April—fiercely defends his doctrine in the presence of the Emperor, who, on May 26, signs the decree banning Luther, calling him "Lucifer incarnate." In Rome Luther is burned in effigy. The break with the Church is now definite; the Reformation is in full swing. Thanks to this edict of Worms, Pope Leo breaks his alliance with France and openly joins the ranks of the Emperor Charles. The armies of the league enter Milan, and Parma and Piacenza are recaptured for the Church.]

Death of Pope Leo X. His Character Weighed

THE WAR HAD BEEN REDUCED TO THESE TERMS, WITH THE PONTIFF AND THE EMPEROR IN GREAT HOPES OF STABILIZING THEIR VICTORY; FOR THE King of France would require a long time to send new forces into Italy, and the power of those who had won Milan from him, together with most of that duchy, seemed sufficient not only to hold it but to win whatever still remained in the hands of the enemy. Indeed, the Venetian Senate, frightened at such success and fearing lest the war which had been launched against others should be transferred into their own house, had already given the Pope hope of making the French troops leave their domain.

But an unforeseen occurrence had suddenly given rise to unforeseen thoughts. For on the first of December, Pope Leo unexpectedly died. Whilst at his villa at Magliana, where he often went for relaxation, the Pope had received news of the conquest of Milan, and taking from it such extraordinary joy, he was that very night overcome by a slight fever and the following day had himself brought to Rome. Although the physicians considered this onset of his illness of slight importance, he died within a few days; not without very great suspicion of poison, given to him (as was suspected) by Bernabo Malaspina, his chamberlain, whose office was to give him drink. Although Malaspina was imprisoned on this suspicion, the matter was not examined any further because the Cardinal de' Medici arrived at Rome and had him freed, in order not to give occasion for arousing greater enmity with the King of France, at whose instigation, it was whispered (by uncertain sources and conjectures), Bernabo had given him the poison.

The Pope died, if you pay any attention to the opinion of men, in the greatest glory and felicity, not only because the victory over Milan had freed him of perils and inestimable expenses (his lack of money having constrained him to raise it by any means whatever), but also because a few days before his death, he had learned of the taking of Piacenza and, on the very day that he died, of the capture of Parma. All this was so greatly desired by him that it is certain that when he decided to set off the war against the French, he had told the Cardinal de' Medici, who was dissuading him against it, that he was principally moved by a desire to recuperate these two cities for the Church, and should such a blessing be conceded him, not even death would be unwelcome.

A Prince in whom were many things worthy of praise and great blame; one who greatly failed to fulfill the expectations that had been aroused at his assumption to the pontificate, since he governed with more prudence but much less goodness than everyone had foreseen.

A Surprising Election in the Conclave

At this time the election of a new pope had not been decided because of the great dissension among the cardinals, caused principally by the Cardinal de' Medici, who aspired to the pontificate and had employed his power, based on his reputation for greatness, his revenues and the glory gained in the conquest of Milan, to unite for himself the votes of fifteen other cardinals, moved either by self-interest, or the friendship they bore him, or the memory of benefices which they had received from Leo; and some in the hope that when he despaired of winning the pontificate for himself, he would support those who had been ready to favor him.

But many things militated against the Cardinal's ambitions; many felt that it was pernicious for the new pope to be of the same family as his predecessor, since this would serve as a precedent of beginning to pass on the papacy by succession. All the old cardinals were opposed, for they sought that dignity for themselves, nor could they tolerate that one less than fifty years old should be chosen. All those partisans of the French cause were against him; as well as several of those who supported the imperial faction, because the Cardinal Colonna, although at first he had made a show of wanting to be favorable to him, had then very openly come out in opposition. And those cardinals who had been dissatisfied with Leo were bitter enemies. Nevertheless, in these difficulties, he was sustained by a most efficacious hope, for since more than one-third of the College of Cardinals supported him, it was not possible to elect anyone without their consent so long as they remained united; whence he hoped that over a period of time his adversaries would inevitably either grow weary or become divided, there being many among them who were unable because of their age to tolerate a long period of discomfort; and because although they were agreed among themselves not to create him pope, they were in disagreement about the creation of anyone else, each one thinking to elect either himself or his friends; or many of them were most stubborn in not yielding one to the other.

But the change of government in Perugia somewhat mollified the Cardinal de' Medici's obstinacy, at the intervention of the Cardinal de' Petrucci, one of the cardinals who supported him. Petrucci, head of the state of Siena, fearing that as a result of his absence there might be a revolution in that city, against which the Duke of Urbino, it was understood, wished to turn his army, strongly urged that the new pope be decided upon. Petrucci's intervention, and also the danger which a change of government in Siena would incur for Florentine interests, influenced the Cardinal de' Medici, who began to come to the same conclusion; but he was not entirely resolved whom he wished chosen.

But as one morning the scrutiny was being made in conclave, according to the custom, Adrian, Cardinal of Tortosa,* was proposed: a cardinal of the Flemish nation, but since he had been schoolmaster to the Emperor during his adolescence, and had been promoted to the cardinalate by Leo through the Emperor's influence, he represented Charles in Spain. His name was proposed without anyone having any inclination to elect him, but just to waste that morning. But as several votes in his favor began to disclose themselves, the Cardinal of San Sisto began to dwell upon Adrian's virtues and knowledge, almost in a perpetual oration; whereupon several cardinals beginning to yield to his cause, little by little the others followed, more by impulse than by deliberation; with the result that he was created Pope that morning by unanimous vote; those who had chosen him not even being able to give any reason why, amidst so many travails and perils for the Church, they should have elected as Pope a foreigner,** so far distant from the country, who had not won any favor either because of his merits in the past, or conversations that he might have had with several other cardinals (who scarcely knew his name) and who had never been in Italy, and had no thought or desire to see that land. Since this extravagance could not be explained by any sort of reason, they attributed its cause to the Holy Ghost, which usually (as they put it)

---

* Adrian was from Utrecht in Flanders; his cardinalate was of a town on the Ebro River, in Terragona province, Spain.

** Guicciardini's (and the Italians' in general) dismay at the election of a foreigner seems to overlook the election of another foreigner in 1492—Roderigo Borgia of Spain, who became Alexander VI. Could it have been that Borgian vices were more assimilable to *Italianità* than Flemish virtues?

POPE ADRIAN VI

Contemporary engraving by Daniel Hopfer. The inscription reads: "Pope Adrian of the Cimbrian [German] nation, born at Utrecht."

inspired the hearts of the cardinals in the election of popes: as if the Holy Ghost, which above all loves the purest hearts and spirits, would not disdain to enter into souls full of ambition and incredible greed, and almost all dedicated to the most refined, not to say most dishonest, pleasures.*

The new Pope learned the news of his election at Victoria, a city in Biscay; upon receipt of which he had himself designated Adrian VI, not changing the name that he previously held.

* The final clause of this paragraph —"as if the Holy Ghost . . . pleasures"— was expurgated from the Torrentino *editio princeps*, 1561, and consequently from all subsequent editions based on it. It is also missing in Fenton (*La Historia di Italia*, Fiorenza, 1561, p. 571; Fenton, *op. cit.*, p. 582).

BOOK

15

THUS WHILE ITALY WAS OPPRESSED BY CONTINUAL ADVERSITIES, AND TERRIFIED WITH THE FEAR OF EVEN GREATER FUTURE EVILS, THE POPE'S ARrival was eagerly awaited, pontifical authority being considered an opportune instrument for composing all these disagreements and providing against so many disorders.

During those same days, the Emperor had sailed to Spain, conferring with the King of England en route. Now he begged the Pope to wait for him at Barcelona, where Charles wished to go personally to pay his obeisance and acknowledge him as Pontiff.

But Adrian refused to wait for him, either because he feared that because of the great distance which the Emperor had to cross (he was still on the other side of Spain) he, Adrian, would lose so much time that later he would have to sail in a bad season; or else out of the suspicion that the Emperor might be seeking to have him defer his trip to Italy; or (as many said) in order not to lend too much credit to that judgment which people had held of him from the beginning (namely, that he owed so much to the Emperor), which would hinder his efforts to establish a universal Christian peace as he had determined to do.

Therefore he crossed by sea to Rome where he made his entry on the twenty-ninth day of August, with an enormous concourse of people and the entire court. Although his arrival was very greatly desired (for Rome without the presence of the Pope is much more like a desert than a city), yet this spectacle troubled the minds of everyone, considering that they had a Pope of a foreign nation,* altogether inexperienced with regard to the affairs of Italy and the Curia, and not even a member of one of those nations which were familiar with Italy because of long years of relationships. All these forebodings grew when, at his arrival, the plague

* "... *uno Pontefice di nazione barbaro* ..." Reminiscent of the ancient Romans (and Greeks), all foreigners are called barbarians. Guicciardini used the same term in the previous section dealing with Adrian's election.

SIEGE OF RHODES *1522*
From a contemporary print

began in Rome (which was interpreted as a very bad portent of his pontificacy, and caused the gravest losses throughout the autumn).

. .

But the most unhappy event at the end of the year 1522 was the capture of the island of Rhodes, to the greatest infamy of Christian princes, by Suleiman Ottoman. This island had been organized under the rule of the Knights of Rhodes, formerly called the Knights of Saint John of Jerusalem. Residing in that place ever since they had been driven out of Jerusalem, although they were set in the midst of the Turk and the Sultan, both very powerful princes, they had maintained themselves for a long time to the greatest glory of their Order and had been, as it were, a bulwark of the Christian religion in those seas, although they were somewhat notorious for the fact that, spending all their days in piracy against the ships of the infidels, they also at times pillaged Christian vessels.

The island was surrounded for many months by an enormous army, and the Turk* in person, never losing the least opportunity to torment them, now by launching violent attacks, now by digging mines and trenches, sometimes by constructing great earthen or wooden platforms overtopping the walls of the town. As a result of these efforts and operations, which the Turks pushed ahead despite very great losses, the number of those within the walls was also notably diminished; so that, exhausted by the continuous struggles and lacking powder for their artillery, and being able no longer to resist against such hardships, and a great part of the wall having been knocked down by the artillery, and the mines had been infiltrated into many places of the city (within which the defenders found themselves continually restricted because their outworks had been destroyed), finally reduced to the last necessity, they capitulated to the Turk with the agreement that the Grand Master of Rhodes would leave the city to him, but that he together with all the Knights and people of Rhodes could depart safely with the right to bear with them as many of their possessions as they could; and that they might have some security, the Turk would order his fleet to sail out of those waters, and withdraw his land army five miles from Rhodes.

As a result of this capitulation, Rhodes fell to the Turks, who observed the pledges made, so that the Christians crossed to Sicily and then into Italy. In Sicily they found a fleet of certain ships being fitted up (but late because of the Pope's fault) to set sail for Rhodes as soon as they had a prosperous wind, supplies of victuals and munitions.

* Suleiman Ottoman.

And once they had departed from Rhodes, Suleiman, for the greater contempt of the Christian religion, made his entrance into that city on the birthday of the Son of God; on which day, celebrated with endless songs and music in Christian churches, he had all the churches of Rhodes, dedicated to the cult of Christ, converted into mosques dedicated to the Mohammedan religion, and according to their custom all Christian rites exterminated. Thus ended the year 1522, ignominiously for Christendom; such fruit reaped the discord of our princes, which would have been tolerable if at least the example of the harms suffered had served them as a lesson for the future. But the disagreement among our princes continued, and therefore the troubles of the year 1523 proved no less than before.

[*Despite all efforts of the King of France to block agreement, the Venetians finally—after delays and impassioned debate in the Senate—shift their alliance from France to the Emperor. The King of France then prepares to return to Italy for the reconquest of Milan, and his adversaries form a new confederation against him, accepting the Pope as head. This confederation against France includes the Pope, the Emperor, the King of England, the Archduke of Austria, the Duke of Milan, the Florentines and the Genoese. Once again the French army crosses the mountains, and soon Novara and all the towns near the Ticino River fall to the French, who, losing a chance to take Milan, think of besieging rather than assaulting it.*]

In this state of affairs, Pope Adrian passed to that other life on the fourteenth day of September, not without inconveniencing the allies, who besides the Pope's prestige, also felt the loss of his pecuniary contributions, to which he was bound according to the agreement of the confederation. He died, leaving a very small reputation of himself, either because of the brief time he had reigned or because he was inexpert in handling affairs; but with the boundless joy of the entire court who were very eager to see an Italian, or at least someone brought up in Italy, on the papal throne.*

. .
.

At the Pope's death, the Church lands began to stir into resurrection. Before his illness, tiny sparks of the future blaze started to appear, which was likely to have spread while he was alive, if partly by chance and partly because of the watchfulness of others it had not been checked.

---

* When he died, the Romans attached this inscription on his physician's door: *Liberator patriae Senatus Popu-* *lusque Romanus.*—Liberator of his country SPQR. Adrian was indeed the last non-Italian Pope.

For before the Pope went to Italy, the College of Cardinals had turned over the custody of Reggio and Rubiera to Alberto Pio, so that he still held the fortresses of those places. Under various pretenses and excuses, taking advantage of Adrian's limited experience, for many months he had scoffed at the Pope's request that these places be restored to him. Therefore it had been agreed that as soon as the war broke out, Renzo da Ceri, followed by several horsemen and a good number of footsoldiers, should halt at Rubiera, to control from that strategic place the Roman road between Modena and Reggio, for the purpose of blocking the money and dispatches going to Milan from Rome, Naples and Florence, and to proceed to greater enterprises as the occasion afforded. But since the governor of those cities, Francesco Guicciardini,* had a premonition of this plan in good time, and had shown the Pontiff where Alberto's mild words and requests were tending, and the danger which the entire Ecclesiastical State would incur from that direction, he had prevailed so much that the Pope was offended and, both by threats and showing that he was ready to use force, constrained Alberto to restore these fortresses to him. Albert had not dared to oppose the Pope since the French campaign was not very far advanced.

[*War continues between Ecclesiastical forces and the Duke of Ferrara, and in the duchy of Milan against the French. Guicciardini, governor of Modena and Reggio, defends those cities for the Church against the Duke of Ferrara. Guicciardini writes of his own actions here with icy praise, as if he were talking about someone else. Nevertheless the Duke captures Reggio by default. Meanwhile the Admiral of France, Bonnivet, not expecting to take Milan by force, but that his enemies "would dissolve for want of money . . . or victuals," withdraws his forces.*]

Election of Giulio de' Medici as Clement VII

But a very few days after the Admiral had departed from his quarters near Milan, there succeeded the creation of the new Pope, the conclave having already been in session for fifty days. At the beginning there had entered into conclave thirty-six cardinals, and later three more arrived, consuming all their time in various quarrels; their minds were divided not only between the diverse wills and desires of the Emperor and the King of France, but also by the greatness of the Cardinal de' Medici.

* The author of this *History*.

For although the Cardinal was opposed by all those who supported the King's authority, and by some of those who still depended on the Emperor, he had at his command and devotion the united votes of sixteen cardinals, absolutely determined to elect him and not to elect anyone else without his consent; and he had the secret promises of five others to give their votes to him personally in the election that would be held. Besides this, he was favored by the Emperor's ambassador and all the others who followed his authority.

Although he had had almost all these basic sources of support at the death of Pope Leo, nevertheless, he now entered into the conclave with a much more constant resolution not to abandon his hopes, either because of the length of time that might be consumed, or for any other reason, basing his expectations principally on the fact that two-thirds of the votes of the cardinals present is necessary for the election of the pope. Nor did either the common danger of Italy or the specific danger to the states of the Church cause the cardinals to withdraw from their quarrels; rather, according as the fortunes of the war varied, both sides went on postponing the election, hoping to be favored by the victory of those propitious to their cause; and the election would have been deferred even much longer if, among the cardinals opposed to the Cardinal de' Medici, almost all of whom were the oldest in the College, there had been the same agreement to choose anyone whatever of their group, as there was not to choose him; and if setting aside their personal greed, they had contented themselves with this aim, namely, that the Cardinal de' Medici should not ascend to the papacy. But it is very difficult to attain a commonly desired end by means of an agreement in which disagreement and ambition are mixed. Cardinal Colonna, the bitterest enemy of the Cardinal de' Medici, an impetuous and very proud man by nature, was angry at the cardinals joined in his camp because they had refused to elect as Pope the Cardinal Iacobaccio, a Roman, and a man of the same faction and very dependent on Colonna. Therefore, Colonna went spontaneously to offer his help to the Cardinal de' Medici that he might win the election; the Cardinal de' Medici, by a document written in his own hand, with the greatest secrecy, promised Colonna the office of the vice chancellery which he held, as well as the extremely sumptuous palace formerly built by the Cardinal di San Giorgio, and given to him by Pope Leo. This increased the ardor of the Cardinal Colonna all the more, so that he induced the Cardinal Cornaro and two others to agree with him and vote for the Cardinal de' Medici. And as soon as their leanings in this direction were known, many others (as often happens in conclaves), influenced by cowardice or ambition, began to compete not to be the last to favor him; with the result that the same night he was unanimously honored as Pope; and the following morning, which was the nineteenth day of November, the election was consummated according to tradition by a solemn balloting: the very same day precisely whereon two years before he had made his victorious entrance into Milan.

It was believed that among the other reasons which had helped him were his very great income from benefices and ecclesiastical offices, for when the cardinals entered into conclave, they had made a written agreement that the revenues of whoever should be elected pope should be evenly distributed among the others.

He wanted to keep his name of Giulio; but admonished by several cardinals that he should be aware of the fact that those who had not changed their names on their election to the papacy had all finished their lives within a year,* he therefore assumed the name of Clement VII, either because it was close to the name day of that saint, or else because he wanted to allude to the fact that as soon as he was elected, he had pardoned and received into grace the Cardinal of Volterra and all his faction. For although the previous Pope, Adrian, in the last days of his life had declared the Cardinal of Volterra unable to participate in the conclave, yet he had entered there at the permission of the College, and had been stubborn to the end in opposition to Giulio's election.

There was certainly throughout the world the highest estimation for this new Pope; hence, the tardiness of the election, much more drawn-out than had occurred for the longest time, seemed to be compensated for by having placed a person of the highest value and prestige in the Papal See: for at his will and pleasure were conjoined the power of the state of Florence with the mighty power of the Church; and because for so many years during the period of Leo he had governed practically the entire pontificate, and because he was reputed to be a serious person, constant in his judgments; and since many things which had occurred during Leo's reign were attributed to him, everyone affirmed him to be a man full of ambition, lofty minded, restless, and most eager for innovations; to these qualities were added the fact that he abstained from pleasures and was assiduous in his duties, so that there was no one who did not expect from him the greatest and most extraordinary achievements. His election immediately restabilized and secured the state of the Church.

* Not exactly true: Adrian wore the triple tiara from 9 January 1522 to 14 September 1523.

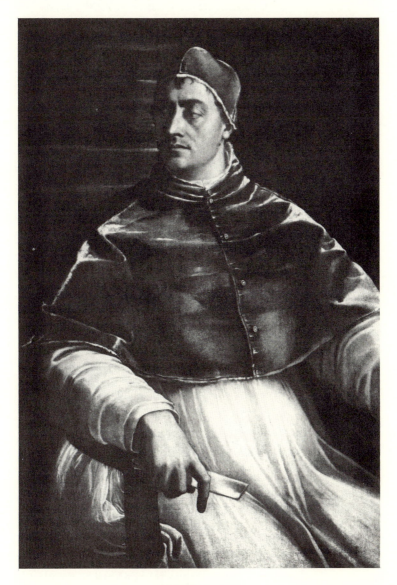

CLEMENT VII

Portrait by Sebastiano del Piombo in the National Gallery of Capodimonte,
Naples (COURTESY OF FRATELLI ALINARI)

Character of Prospero Colonna.*
Changes in the Nature of Warfare

AT that time, Prospero Colonna was drawing toward death after an illness of eight months, not without suspicion of poison or of some amorous potion. Hence, whereas before he could not abide the coming of the Viceroy, later, no longer being able to manage the war, he had continuously requested it. The Viceroy therefore came; but when he approached Milan, he waited several days before entering, to pay his respects to the virtue and fame of such a captain. And yet when he understood that Prospero was at the last gasp and already losing his mind, the Viceroy entered with the desire of seeing him, but just in time for Colonna to survive a few hours more: although others said that he delayed his entrance until after the Captain's death, which occurred on the penultimate day of that year.

Prospero Colonna was certainly a famous captain throughout his life, but during his last years his reputation and authority had soared to new heights; skillful and possessing great experience in the art of war, but not ready to seize quickly enough those opportunities which the enemy's weakness and lack of unity might offer, just as his cautious procedure did not offer them any easy opportunity to overpower him; very slow by nature in all his actions, one to whom you would deservedly give the title of malingerer**; but he deserved praise for having managed the wars more with counsels than with the sword, and he had taught men to defend their states without exposing themselves, except of necessity, to the fortunes of war. For in our age methods of warfare have undergone the greatest changes: in that before King Charles of France marched into Italy, the brunt of battle was borne much more by horsemen heavily armed at all points, than by footsoldiers; and since the weapons that were used against the towns were very difficult to move and manage, therefore, although armies frequently engaged in battles, there was very little killing, and most rare was the blood that was shed, and the cities under attack defended themselves so easily (not because of skillful defense but because of the lack of skill of the attack) that there was no town so small or so weak that it could not hold out for many days against the greatest armies of their enemies; with the result that only with the greatest

---

* Famous *condottiere*, most lately at Milan, where he commanded the imperial forces. His ambition to be leader was at the back of his opposition to the arrival of the Viceroy of Naples.

** "... *il titolo di cuntatore* ..." i.e., one who counts every move.

difficulties could one make armed seizure of states belonging to others.

But after King Charles had come to Italy, the terror of unknown nations, the ferocity of infantry organized in waging war in another way, but above all, the fury of the artillery, filled all of Italy with so much dread that no hope of defending oneself remained for those not powerful enough to resist in the countryside; for, men who were unskilled in defending their towns, surrendered as soon as the enemy approached, and even if some put up resistance, they were taken within a very few days. Thus the kingdom of Naples and the duchy of Milan were attacked and conquered almost in a single day; thus the Venetians, beaten in one battle only, suddenly abandoned the entire empire that they had on the mainland; thus the French, having scarcely seen their enemies, left the duchy of Milan.

Then terrified by the ferocity of the attacks, men began to whet their wits and contrive more subtle means of defense, fortifying their towns with banks, ditches, moats, flanks, ramparts, bastions; whence (the great number of infantry pieces also helping to this purpose very much, more effective in defense than in attack) the towns now being defended have been made very safe and cannot be taken by storm.

Scythed war chariots and armored tanks invented by Leonardo da Vinci
(COURTESY OF FRATELLI ALINARI)

Perhaps these inventions began at the time of our fathers when the town of Otranto was recovered from the Turks. Afterward, Alfonso, Duke of Calabria, entered there, and found many types of fortifications built by the Turks and unknown to the Italians; but they remained more in men's memories than served as examples. Prospero alone, or before anyone else, by these means twice provided notable defense for the duchy of Milan. For either by attacking or defending, by cutting the enemy's line of supply, by prolonging the war so that they were ground down by tedium, the length of the war, poverty and disorders; he conquered and maintained his defenses without venturing into battle, without drawing forth anything but the sword, nor breaking a single lance; whence the road having been opened by him and his followers, many wars which

Detail showing the siege of a fortress in the sixteenth century, from an engraving by Albrecht Dürer

continued for many months were won more by industry, and stratagems, and knowing how to take advantage, than by arms.

These were the events that occurred in Italy during the year 1523. That same year many things beyond the mountains were being prepared with the greatest hopes, which did not give rise to results worthy of such princes. For the Emperor and the King of England had agreed and promised [Charles] Duke of Bourbon to unleash war with powerful armies, one in Picardy and the other in Guyenne; but the actions of the King of England in Picardy were almost of no importance, and the Duke of Bourbon's attempted invasion of Burgundy immediately proved to be useless, because lacking money to pay his German infantry, some of the captains, who had come to an agreement with the King of France, withdrew part of the landsknechts, with the result that the Duke despaired of achieving his aims in France and went to Milan. The Emperor did not like the idea of the Duke's crossing into Spain, perhaps because he didn't want his [sister's] marriage to go ahead, as the Duke desired. Therefore he dispatched [Count] Büren to bring him the title of his lieutenant general in Italy, and to persuade him to stay there.

Nor did matters proceed happily for the Emperor with regard to Spain. For although in his fervent desire for war, he had come to Pamplona to enter personally into France, and had already sent his army beyond the Pyrenees and they had occupied Salvatierra, not far from Saint-Jean-Pied-de-Port, nevertheless, his readiness being greater than his power (since, for lack of money, he could not maintain such forces as would be necessary for such an undertaking, nor for the same reason could he assemble his army until almost the end of the year, so that in the cold places the season multiplied his difficulties, impeded by shortage of provisions which were difficult to convey over so long a supply line), therefore he was forced to disband his army, which had been drawn up against the counsel of almost everyone: so much so that Federico of Toledo, Duke of Alva, an old and prestigious prince, said in the heat of the war that the Emperor Charles, who in many ways resembled his maternal grandfather, King Ferdinand, in this present instance was more like his paternal grandfather, Maximilian.

[*Following a series of encounters in Lombardy, the French finally retreat from their Milanese enterprise, cross the mountains again, and all that they have won in the duchy falls once more under imperial dominion. The war against the French being now finished in Italy, the Emperor Charles thinks of transferring it to France itself. The King of England is also ready to participate in such a war, not so much because of his pretensions to that realm as his desire to arbitrate the peace between the French King and the Emperor.*

In July 1524 the imperial armies of the Duke of Bourbon with

SIEGE OF MILAN AND EXPULSION OF THE FRENCH
Fresco by Giorgio Vasari and aides in the Palazzo Vecchio, Florence

*certain allies invade France; Aix falls; Marseilles is laid under siege.
But when the King of France raises a powerful army at Avignon,
which seems to threaten simultaneously the imperials at the bastions
of Marseilles and northern Italy, the forces of the Emperor decide
to lift their siege and return to Italy. At the same time, Francis I sets
out to invade Italy once more, deeming he can get there first and
recapture the duchy of Milan. Thus two powerful armies converge
in the Lombard plain.*

*At the battle of Pavia (24 February 1525), the Emperor's birth-
day, his army, which includes Spaniards, Italians, and the feared
German landsknechts, attacks the French army which has been encamped there for three weeks, well protected on the right by the
Ticino River, and on the left by a broad park surrounded by a high
wall in which is the celebrated Certosa of Pavia. Within a few hours
the bloody battle results in a disastrous defeat for the French: more
than eight thousand men killed or drowned as against seven hundred
imperials. Twenty of the "most noble Lords" of France are captured.
Most spectacularly, the King himself "is taken by five soldiers who
did not know who he was; but the Viceroy happening to come, he
made himself known to him, who kissing his hand with great reverence, took him prisoner in the name of the Emperor . . . the same
day the battle was fought, all the duchy of Milan was freed from
the French . . . The following day the King was led to the fortress
of Pizzichitone; since, for his own safety, the Duke of Milan was
unwilling that he should be brought to the Castle of Milan; and
there [at Pizzichitone] except for his liberty (for he was very carefully guarded), he was in all other things treated and honored as a
King."*

*Guicciardini, whose counsels helped induce Clement to espouse
the French cause (in fact, an alliance between the Pope and Francis
I had been openly published on the 5th of January 1525, to the uncon-
cealed displeasure of the Emperor), blames the defeat of Pavia on the
"avarice or pusillanimity of the Pontiff," whose "irresolution" resulted in failure to arm in time and hence an inability to intervene
with sufficient authority in the quarrel between the two great adversaries.]*

BOOK

16

Aftermath of the Battle of Pavia. Italian Fears of the Emperor

SINCE AT THE BATTLE FOUGHT IN THE PARK OF PAVIA, NOT ONLY HAD THE FRENCH ARMY BEEN SHATTERED BY THE IMPERIAL FORCES, BUT ALSO the Most Christian King taken prisoner, and most of the captains and nobility of France around him either captured or killed, and the Swiss, who in times past had waged war in Italy to their great fame, behaved most cowardly; the rest of the army, despoiled of their tents, did not stop until they reached the foot of the mountains. And (what marvelously increased the reputation of the victors) after the imperial captains had won so memorable a victory with so little loss of blood, it is impossible to express how astonished were all the potentates of Italy; who finding themselves almost completely disarmed, fell into the greatest terror, since the imperial armies remained very powerful in the field and now faced no enemies.

They were less reassured by what many divulged regarding the good intentions of the Emperor, and of his inclination toward peace, and not to usurp the states of others, than terrorized by considering the great danger that he, moved either by ambition which ordinarily is natural among all princes, or by the insolence which commonly accompanies victories, and spurred likewise by the hotheadedness of those who governed his affairs in Italy, and finally by the persuasions of his council and all his court, would on such an occasion (which was sufficient to kindle the coldest spirit) turn his thoughts toward making himself lord of all Italy; knowing especially how easy it is for every great prince, and most of all for a Roman emperor, to justify his enterprises with appearances that seem honest and reasonable.

Nor were only those of lesser prestige and force troubled by this fear, but the Pontiff and the Venetians almost more than the others. The

Venetians not only had a bad conscience for having failed him without just cause and not adhering to the stipulations of their alliance, but much more because they recalled the ancient hatreds and frequent quarrels between them and the house of Austria, and the grave wars which they had waged a few years earlier with Maximilian, his grandfather, in the course of which the name and memory of the rights of the empire, almost forgotten, had been remarkably resurrected in the state which they possessed on terra firma. Besides, they knew that whoever intended to become great in Italy had to think about battering down their power.

The Pope found himself on every other count laid wide open to all sorts of dangers. For aside from the majesty of the pontificate (often ill secure from the grandeurs of the emperors even in those days when the world displayed an ancient reverence toward the Apostolic See), now he was disarmed, without money, and the Church state very weak, with very few strong towns, the people not united or firm in their devotion to their prince, but almost the entire ecclesiastical domain divided into Guelph and Ghibelline parties, and the Ghibellines by an inveterate and almost natural state of mind partial to the emperors, and the city of Rome, above all the rest, weak and infected by these seeds.

Furthermore, the Pope was concerned with Florentine affairs which, depending on him and being the specific and traditional glory of his house, were no less close to his heart than those of the Church. Nor was it less easy to alter that situation, for that city which had expelled the Medici at the passage of King Charles, having tasted eighteen years of popular government under the name of liberty, had been discontent at their return, so that there were few who truly were pleased at their restoration to power.

The Pope greatly feared lest there be added to these already dangerous possibilities no small desire to cause him harm. He also had just cause to fear not only because he who is less powerful is never entirely safe from the ambitions of the more powerful, but also because he dreaded whether his name might not have now become odious to the Emperor for various reasons. He reflected that although during the life of Pope Leo, while he himself was a cardinal, he had labored greatly for the Emperor's glory—indeed Leo and he had with very great expenses and dangers opened the road to his great power in Italy—and that when he became Pope he had given money to his captains and made the Florentines contribute while the Admiral was in Italy, without removing from his army the forces of the Church and of that Republic; nevertheless, either considering that it pertained to his office to be rather father and common pastor among all Christian princes and the author of peace rather than the fomenter of wars; or else having begun very late to fear such greatness, he had soon withdrawn from running the same fortunes with the Em-

peror, so that he had not wanted to renew the confederation made for
the defense of Italy by his predecessor, nor help him with money when
the Duke of Bourbon had entered with his army into Provence the
previous year.

. .
.

The capitulation having been drawn up, the Pope sent, with the
permission of the Viceroy, the Bishop of Pistoia to visit and console the
King of France in his name, in order not to be lacking in respect due such
a prince. After having spoken together in general terms in the presence
of Captain Alarcon, and after the King had besought the Pontiff (via the
Bishop of Pistoia) to intercede in his behalf with the Emperor, the King
of France humbly asked what had happened to the Duke of Albania;*
and he was greatly disturbed by the reply to the effect that one part of
the army having melted away, he had crossed into France with the other.

The Emperor Charles' Prudent Acceptance of Victory over the French. Debate Among His Counselors with Regard to the Disposition of the Captured King of France

As far as one could understand from external signs, the Emperor's actions
appeared clearly to indicate a very moderate state of mind, a man not
easily swept away by his good luck, an attitude that seemed incredible in
so powerful and young a prince, who had never known anything but
felicity. For when he had been advised of his great victory [at Pavia],
the news of which reached him on the tenth of March, together with
humble and imploring letters written by the King of France in his own
hand more in the tone of a prisoner than that of a king, he went immediately to church to render thanks to God with much solemnity for such
success, and the following morning with signs of the greatest devotion
he received the sacrament of the Eucharist and went in procession to the
church of Notre Dame outside of Madrid, where he was at that time
with his court. Nor did he permit, as was the tradition of others, that
they should make great show of jubilee with bells and fireworks and

* John Stuart, Duke of Albania, of the blood royal of the kings of Scotland, had been dispatched by Francis I to attack Naples at the same time as Francis marched into the duchy of Milan. Francis hoped this would draw off imperial forces from Milan.

other ways, saying that it was fitting to celebrate victories over the
infidels, but not those won against Christians. And he did not show either
by gesture or word any sign whatever of too much joy, or being puffed
up with pride, replying to the congratulations of the ambassadors and
important personages around him that he was pleased because the fact
that God had aided him so openly seemed to be a sign of being, although
undeservedly, in his grace; and because he hoped that now would be the
opportunity to establish a general peace in Christendom, and to prepare
for a war against the infidels; and because he would have greater means
to do good for his friends and to pardon his enemies.

He added that although this victory might seem to be entirely his,
since none of his friends had helped him gain it, yet he wanted it to be
shared by all. Indeed, having heard the Venetian ambassador justifying
the actions of his Republic, he told the people present that these excuses
were not true, but that he wished to accept them and adjudge them as
true. By such words and actions, so revealing of the highest wisdom and
goodness, since he continued in this way for several days, the Emperor,
proceeding soberly as was his wont, called his council together one day
and requested that they advise him what he should do with the King of
France, and to what end he should direct this victory; ordering that
everyone should freely give his advice in his presence. After which
command, the Bishop of Osma, who was his confessor, spoke as follows:

"Although, most glorious Prince, all things which happen in this
lower world proceed from the providence of Almighty God, and are
thereby daily governed and have their source, yet this sometimes may
be more clearly discerned in some particular; but if ever it has been seen
and manifested in anything, it is seen in the present victory. For, because
of its greatness and the facility with which it was won, and since this
victory was gained over most powerful enemies, much more provided
than we are in the necessary supplies of war, no one can deny that it was
the express will of God and almost a miracle. Therefore, the more manifest and greater is his goodness, so much the more is your Majesty
obliged to acknowledge it and show your gratitude which you owe;
which consists principally in directing the victory so that it might be
more at the service of God, and to that end for which (it may be
thought) he conceded it to you.

"And certainly, when I consider to what state Christianity has been
reduced, I see nothing more holy and more necessary and more welcome
to God than a universal peace among Christian princes; for it is clear
that lacking this, religion, faith, a worthy life for mankind, are all sink-
ing into obvious ruin.

"On the one side we have the Turks, who have made such progress
against Christians because of our discords, and who are now threatening

Hungary, the kingdom of your sister's husband; and if they capture Hungary (as they will undoubtedly do unless the princes of Christendom unite) the road to Germany and Italy will be open.

"On the other hand, there is this Lutheran heresy, so great an enemy of God, so vituperous against those who would put it down, so dangerous for all princes, which has already taken such root that unless provisions are made against it, the world will be filled with heretics, nor can it be guarded against except by your authority and power; which, while you are engaged in other wars, cannot be adopted to extirpate this most pernicious poison.

"Furthermore, although at present there is no fear of either Turks or heretics, how much more wicked, more poisonous, more foul is it that so much Christian blood, which could be gloriously shed to strengthen faith in Christ or at least reserved for more necessary times, is being shed uselessly for our passions, accompanied by so much rapaciousness and violations, so many acts of sacrilege and nefarious deeds; evils for which those who have willfully caused them cannot hope for any pardon from God, and those who cause them out of necessity do not deserve to be excused, unless at least they have determined to remedy them as soon as they can.

"Universal peace in Christendom must therefore be your aim and goal, as things which are honorable, holy and necessary above all else. Now we see in what way this can be achieved. There are three decisions which your Majesty can take with regard to the King of France: firstly, to keep him perpetually imprisoned; secondly, to free him in a loving and fraternal spirit, without any other conditions than those relating to the signing between you of a pact of perpetual peace and amity, and healing the ills of Christendom; thirdly, to free him, but seeking to derive therefrom as much profit as possible.

"Of these three possible courses of action, if I do not deceive myself, the other two would prolong and intensify the war, whereas a loving and brotherly liberation is the only solution which could extirpate wars forever. For who can doubt that the King of France, if he is treated with such generosity, with such singular liberality, would not as a result of such goodness remain more bound to you in his soul, and more in your power, than he is now in his body?

"And if between you and him there should be a true union and concord, all the rest of Christendom would embark upon that road which you two have shown. But if you resolve to keep him always imprisoned, besides the fact that it would be too infamous, too cruel, and the sign of a spirit that does not know the power of fortune, would it not breed wars upon wars? For it presupposes a desire to acquire either all or part of France, which cannot be done without new and very great conflicts.

If one takes the middle road, that is, liberate him, but with the most advantageous conditions possible, I believe that it would be the most intricate and dangerous game of all. For establishing whatever relationship, whatever clauses, whatever obligations one might wish, he will always remain an enemy, nor will he ever be lacking in the company of all those who fear your greatness; with the result that here again we have new wars, and more bloody and more dangerous than those in the past.

"I know how far this opinion differs from men's taste, and how new and unparalleled it may be; but extraordinary and singular decisions are very suitable for an Emperor. Nor is it to be marveled at that the Caesarian soul be capable of that which other men's minds cannot arrive at, for to the degree that he exceeds them in dignity, so much should he exceed them in magnanimity. And therefore, one should know above all others how much true glory resides in such generosity, how much more it is the office of the Emperor to pardon and to benefit others rather than to get for oneself; and that God has not given him in vain, and almost miraculously, this power to set the world at peace; and after so many victories, and after so much grace which God has shed upon him, and after seeing everyone kneel at his feet, it should be the part of the Emperor to proceed no longer as an enemy to any man, but to act as the common father for the safety of all. The magnanimity of pardoning their enemies, of restoring the kingdoms to the conquered, rendered more glorious the names of Alexander the Great and of Julius Caesar than all their victories and all their triumphs: whose example should be all the more followed by one who, not having glory as his only end (although it is a very great reward), desires principally to do that which is the true and proper office of every Christian prince.

"But let us consider further, to convince those who measure human affairs solely by human ends, what decision would be more suitable to these ends. Certainly I believe that the most wonderful and worthy aspect of your Majesty's greatness is the glory of having been invincible up to now, and of having guided all your enterprises to most happy conclusions, with such reputation and prosperity. This is undoubtedly the most precious jewel, the most singular treasure among all your treasures. Then how much firmer would it be established, how much better secured, with how much more certainty would it be preserved, than by calming and crowning the wars with so generous and magnanimous an end, by removing your glory from the hazards of chance, and bringing this vessel laden with merchandise of inestimable value from the high seas securely into port?

"But let us say more: is not that grandeur which is voluntarily maintained more desirable than that which is maintained by force? No one doubts it, because it is more stable, easier, more pleasant, more honorable.

If the Emperor place the King of France under his obligation by such liberality, by such kindness, would he not always be his master and lord, both of him and of his kingdom? If he gives the Pope and other princes a clear sense of certainty that he is satisfied with the realm he now possesses and has no other thought than the security of all, will they not remain without any suspicion? And having no more cause to fear him nor contend with him, they will not only love, but also will adore such goodness. Thus, by the good will of all, he will give laws to all and beyond comparison he will prevail more amongst Christians by benevolence and prestige than he could do by force and domination. He will have the opportunity, aided and followed by everyone, to turn his arms against the Lutherans and against the infidel, with more glory and more opportunity of greater conquests. I don't know why this should not also be desired in Africa or in Greece, or in the Levant, even though enlarging his dominion among Christians might be as easy as many, in my judgment, vainly imagine. For your Majesty's power is so augmented that it is too formidable for everyone; and when it is observed that even greater designs are planned, everyone of necessity will unite against you. The Pope fears your power, the Venetians fear it, all Italy fears it; and by signs often discerned, it is to be believed that the King of England also feels threatened by it. The French may be held back for several months by hopes and vain dealings, but in the end it will be necessary to free the King or else they will be reduced to a state of desperation; and in that state they will unite with all the others. If the King is freed under conditions of little profit to your Majesty, what gain will have been made in losing the chance of employing so great a magnanimity? And if it be not shown now at the beginning, although it might be shown later, it will no longer bring with it equal praise or glory or grace. If the King be liberated under conditions which are useful to you, he will not observe them, because no guarantee that might be given you could be of such importance to him as the fact that his enemy should not become so great that later on he might oppress him.

"Thus we have either a useless peace or a perilous war, whose ends are uncertain; and he who has been lucky for a long time in the vicissitudes of fortune is more to be feared, and is more displeased when things go badly, than he who has had the power to establish everything on a firm basis.

"I think, O Emperor, that I have satisfied your command, if not with wisdom, at least with affection and fidelity; nor does there remain anything but to pray to God that he should give you the mind and ability to make that decision which will be most according to his will, most according to your glory, and most, finally, according to the welfare of

Christendom: of which you, by your supreme dignity, and because it is clear that such is God's will, must serve as father and protector."

. .

The Emperor listened to this counsel with great attention, without making any sign of being pleased or displeased. But after he had been somewhat silent for a while, he indicated that others might proceed to speak, and Federico, Duke of Alva, a man of great authority spoke as follows:

"I will be excused, invincible Emperor, if I confess that my judgment is no different than common judgment, nor am I capable of arriving with my intellect at that degree of understanding which the intellects of other men have not arrived at; rather I will be perhaps more praised if I should recommend that one should proceed along those same roads that your fathers and ancestors have always followed, for new and unheard of counsels can at first glance seem perhaps more glorious and more magnanimous, but later undoubtedly they prove to be more dangerous and more fallacious than those which have at all times, and among all men, been confirmed by reason and experience. The will of God principally, and then the valor of your captains and army, have given you the greatest victory that any Christian prince has won for a very long time. But all the fruits of victory consist in using it well, and not to do this is an even greater infamy than not to conquer, just as it is much more blameworthy to be fooled by those things which are in one's power than by those which depend on fortune. Therefore, so much the more heed should be taken not to make decisions that at the end will shame you in the eyes of others and cause you regret in your own eyes; and the more serious is the importance of what is being so much discussed, so much the more circumspectly should one proceed; and arrive maturely at those decisions wherein errors once made can no longer be corrected.

"And it should be remembered that if the King is freed he can no longer be restrained, but so long as he is in prison, it is always in your power to free him: nor should he be astonished at the delay, for (if I am not deceived) he is himself conscious of what he would do if the Emperor were his prisoner.

"It has certainly been a very important thing to capture the King of France, but whoever will consider the matter well will find it infinitely better to leave him in prison; it will never be considered wise to make a decision of such importance without lengthy deliberations and without weighing the matter an infinite number of times in one's mind. Nor perhaps would I hold to this opinion were I persuaded that the King, freed now, would recognize such an act of grace with due gratitude; and that the Pope and others in Italy would set aside their greed and ambition together with their suspicion. But who does not know how dangerous it is to base so important a resolution on so fallacious and uncertain a presumption? Rather, whoever carefully considers the condition and customs of men would more readily judge the contrary, because nothing by its nature is more brief, nothing has shorter life, than the memory of benefits received; and the greater these are, so much the more, as the proverb says, are they repaid with ingratitude; for whoever cannot or will not cancel them with remuneration, often seeks to cancel them either by forgetting them, or by convincing himself that they were not so great; and those who are ashamed of having been reduced to the condition that they had need of the good will of others, are also angry and offended for having received them; so that there can be more hatred in them because of the memory of the necessity into which they have fallen, than obligation in consideration of the kindness with which they have been treated.*

"Furthermore, who is naturally more insolent and more truly frivolous than the French? Where there is insolence, there is blindness; where there is frivolity, there is no awareness of virtue, no judgment in evaluating the actions of others, no gravity in measuring that which concerns oneself. What, therefore, can one hope of a king of France, inflated with as much pomp and ostentation as might be expected in a king of the French, other than that he would be burning with scorn and rage for having been made captive of the Emperor at a time when he thought of conquering him? He would always have this infamy before his eyes, nor, once liberated, would he ever believe that the way of extinguishing this disgrace is by gratitude; rather, he would always seek to gain the upper hand; he will convince himself that you have let him go because of the difficulty of keeping him, not out of kindness or magnanimity. This is almost always the nature of all men, this is always the nature of the French; and anyone who expects seriousness or magnanimity from the French expects a new order and law in human affairs.

"Instead of peace, therefore, and reducing the world to order, greater wars would arise more dangerous than those in the past, because your reputation will be lessened and your army which expects the deserved fruits of its great victories, deceived in its hopes, will no longer have the same virtue and vigor, nor will your affairs have the same good fortune,

---

* The same idea is found in the *Ricordi,* second series, No. 24 (*op. cit.,* p. 74), and in somewhat different form in Machiavelli's *The Prince.* It might be very revealing to investigate how many of Machiavelli's and Guicciardini's celebrated (or infamous) acerbities are, as Guicciardini declares above, merely echoings of Tuscan folk-sayings. The Floren-tines are famous all over Italy for speaking "without hair on their tongues"—that is, saying what they believe to be the truth without concern for accepted pieties. Guicciardini's and Machiavelli's notion of how the political animal, man, will behave is frequently closer to the peasant who cropped their olive trees than to the savants of antiquity.

which even those who cling to her find difficult to retain, let alone those who cast her away.

"Nor will the Pope and Venetians be any better; rather, regretful for having permitted you to gain victory in the past, they will seek to block you in the future, and the fear they have now of you will force them to do everything possible not to have to fall again into new fear; and whereas it is in your power to hold all men bound and astounded, you yourself by means of a profligate act of kindness will be the one who will unbind them and give them courage. I do not know what God's will is, nor do I believe any others know; for it is usually said that His judgments are secret and deep. But, if one can conjecture from that which is clearly shown, I believe that He is favorable to your grandeur; I do not believe that His graces have been granted so abundantly that you should dissipate them yourself, but rather to make you superior to the others, as well in effect as by title and reason. Therefore, to lose so rare an occasion that God has sent you is nothing else but to tempt Him, to render yourself unworthy of His grace.

"Experience has always shown and reason demonstrated that things which depend on many never succeed well; therefore, whoever believes that the union of many princes will suppress the heretics and conquer the infidel does not, I would hazard, measure the nature of the world very well. There are enterprises which have need of a prince so mighty that he should lay down rules to others; they will be debated and dealt with in the future with the same success with which they have been debated and dealt with in the past. For this reason, I believe God sent you so many victories; for this, I believe God opened the road to the monarchy for you, by means of which alone such holy results may be achieved; and it is better not to hurry in laying down the principles of these things, in order to establish better and more certain foundations.

"Let not the fear of so many menacing alliances deflect you from this decision, because the opportunity which you have in hand is too great; and if things are well negotiated, the King's mother* will never— because of her pity as a mother and the necessity of recovering her son— cast off all hopes of getting him back from you by an agreement. Nor will the Italian princes ever unite with the government of France, knowing that by setting the King free, it will always be in your power to separate him, rather turn him against them. Thus forced to remain startled, so to speak, and in suspension, at the end they will compete as to receiving laws from you: then it will be indeed glorious for you to show clemency and magnanimity when things are so stabilized that they cannot fail but recognize you as superior.

"Thus did Alexander and Caesar, who were liberal in pardoning

* His mother, Louise of Savoy, became Regent, for Queen Claude, his wife, had died in 1524.

affronts, but not so thoughtless as to put themselves back into those very difficulties and dangers which they had already superseded. Who acts in that fashion is praiseworthy because he does something which has few examples, but whoever does what has no example acts unwisely and by chance alone.

"Therefore, O Emperor, my opinion is that one should reap as much fruit as possible of this victory; and that for this purpose the King should be conducted, if it is not possible to Spain, at least to Naples, treating him always with those honors suitable to a king. In reply to his letter, one should send a man to him with the most gracious words, proposing the conditions of his liberation—conditions which, worked out in detail, would be worthy rewards for so great a victory. Thus having established these foundations and proceeding toward these aims, daily developments and incidents as they reveal themselves will determine the King's liberation sooner or later; or whether we remain at war or at peace with the Italians. At present, we may rest good hopes in the Italians; we should increase the reputation and favor of our armies as much as possible by art and industry in order not to tempt fortune anew every day; and we are ready to come to an agreement with anyone or with all of them together or with no one, according to the situation.

"These are the roads which wise princes have always followed, and particularly those who have founded the bases of your grandeur; for they have never thrown away their instruments of growth nor slackened their hold on fortune's favor when she was propitious to them. And thus should you also act, since what might appear ambition in some of them justly pertains to your actions. Remember, O Emperor, that you are a prince, and that it is your office to act in a princely way; and that no line of reasoning, whether divine or human, should urge you to let slip the opportunity of reaffirming the usurped and exploited authority of the empire, but you are only obliged to show courage and the intention to use this power correctly. And above all, remember how easy it is to lose great opportunities and how difficult to acquire them; and therefore, whilst you have them, it is necessary to work at all times to retain them and not depend on the goodness or wisdom of the conquered, since the world is full of wickedness and folly; and judging that, and considering that the Christian religion can be defended either by your greatness or by nothing, therefore you must not fail to increase your power as much as you can, not so much in the interests of your own authority and glory, but for the service of God and zeal for the common good."

It would be impossible to express how favorably this speech of the Duke of Alva was heard by the entire council, since each one had already set forth in his mind the idea of an empire of almost all Christendom. Hence, none of the others—even without replying—did anything but confirm the same recommendation. The Emperor also approved, although more to show that he didn't want to part from the counsels of his advisers than to disclose his own intentions in the matter. He therefore dispatched Büren, his chamberlain, very close to the King and in his favor, to notify the captains of his decision and to visit the King of France in his name, and to propose conditions whereby he might obtain his freedom. Büren traveled by land because the King's mother no longer impeded the transit of men and couriers that came and went from the Emperor, in order that the negotiations for her son might more commodiously be effected. He went together with Bourbon and the Viceroy to Pizzichitone, where the King still remained, and offered him his liberation, but on conditions so harsh that the King heard them with the greatest dismay. For besides giving up those regions which he claimed to hold in Italy, the Emperor demanded restitution of the duchy of Burgundy as properly belonging to him, and that he should give Provence to the Duke of Bourbon, and there were other conditions of the most serious kind with regard to the King of France and to himself.

The King firmly replied to these demands that he had decided rather to die in prison than deprive his sons of any part of the kingdom of France; but that even though he might decide otherwise, it was not in his power to carry it out, since the ancient French constitutions did not permit that anything belonging to the crown might be disposed of without the consent of the parliaments and others in whom resided the authority of the entire realm; and that these usually in similar cases placed the security of all ahead of the particular interests of the King's person.

. . .

When the news of the defeat of the army and the King's capture reached France, so great was everyone's dismay and desperation that it would be almost impossible to imagine. For in addition to the boundless grief which the King's unhappy situation brought that nation, naturally most affectionate and devoted to the crown, were added infinite private and public griefs—private, insofar as there were very few in the court and among the nobility who had not, on that day of battle, lost sons, brothers and other relatives or friends among their own ranks; public, for the decline of the power and splendor of so glorious a realm (a thing all the more grievous unto them since by nature they were so arrogant and presumptuous), and because they feared that so dreadful a calamity might not be the beginning of greater ruin, the King imprisoned, and captured with him or slain in the battle the heads of the government and almost all the main captains of the war, the kingdom's financial affairs in disorder and surrounded by most powerful enemies.

For the King of England, although he had undertaken numerous negotiations and showed a change of spirit in many things, nevertheless, a few days before the battle of Pavia, cut off all negotiations which he had had with the King, and announced that he intended to cross over into France if Italian affairs took a good turn. Therefore, there was very great fear that in such circumstance he and the Emperor might unleash the war in France, where, since there was no leadership other than a woman and the King's little sons, the eldest of whom had not yet ended his eighth year, and since they had the Duke of Bourbon with them, a lord of such power and prestige in the kingdom of France, any action which they might embark upon would be most dangerous for the French. Nor amidst all the tribulations she suffered for love of her son, and the dangers to the kingdom, did the mother lack her own personal passions: for, ambitious and most tenacious in ruling, she feared that if the King's liberation involved a long period of time and new difficulties should break out in France, she might be forced to yield the administration to those deputized by the realm. Nevertheless, amidst all these perturbations, she and her closest advisers having taken heart, fortified the French frontiers as soon as they could, setting aside notable provisions of money; in addition to which, Madame the Regent, in whose name and at whose commands all matters were expedited, wrote to the Emperor supplicating letters full of compassion, bringing up, and then successively urging as much as she could that negotiations for an agreement be initiated.

. .

These reasons, besides the desire which they had always had, all the more intensified the conviction of the Viceroy and the other captains to transfer the King of France to a safe place: judging that because of the enmity of all the others, he could not be safely kept in the duchy of Milan. Therefore they decided to take him to Genoa, and from Genoa by sea to Naples, to keep him under guard in the Castelnuovo, where they were already preparing quarters for him. This was most disturbing to the King, who from the very beginning had strongly wanted to be brought to Spain; for he was convinced (I don't know whether because he measured other people by his own nature, or because men easily delude themselves when their desires are involved) that once he was brought into the Emperor's presence, he would easily gain his liberation, either because of the Emperor's kindness or because of the conditions which he (the King) had in mind to propose.

The Viceroy warmly desired the same thing to increase his own glory; but inasmuch as he was held back by fear of the French fleet, Montmorency went by common consent to Madame the Regent and secured six light galleys from her, of those that were in the port at Marseilles (with the promise that they would be returned as soon as he had arrived in Spain), and with them he returned to Portofino, where the King had already been brought. These ships were added to the sixteen galleys of the Emperor, on which they had previously decided to bring him to Naples, and arming all of them with Spanish infantry, they set sail for Spain on the seventh day of June, at a time when not only the Italian princes but all the other imperial captains and the Duke of Bourbon held it for certain that the King was being brought to Naples. With fair winds they arrived in eight days at Rosa, a port in Catalonia, to the Emperor's great joy, since he had up to that day known nothing of these deliberations.

As soon as the Emperor learned of the King's arrival, he ordered that although he should be received with the greatest honors wherever he might pass, nevertheless he should be kept in custody, until such time as other decisions were reached, in the fortress of Sciativa near Valencia, a fortress which in ancient times had been used by the kings of Aragon to keep great men in custody, and in which more recently the Duke of Calabria had been kept imprisoned for many years. But since this decision seemed cruel to the Viceroy and very different from the promises which he had made him in Italy, he obtained permission by letter from the Emperor that until further decision, the King should be kept in a villa near Valencia, where there were opportunities for hunting and other entertainment. Later, when the King had been set up there with a suitable guard, under Captain Alarcon, who had always had him under his custody, the Viceroy, together with Montmorency, went to the Emperor to report to him on the situation in Italy and matters which had been discussed with the King up to that time, recommending with strong arguments that the Emperor turn his mind toward coming to an agreement with the King of France, because he could not look forward to faithful friendship and alliance with the Italians.

Wherefore, after the Emperor had heard the Viceroy and Montmorency, he decided that the King of France should be brought to Castile to the fortress of Madrid, a place very far from the sea and from the French border, where, honored with the ceremonies and reverence due so great a prince, he should nevertheless be kept under diligent and strict guard, although he would have the right of issuing forth from the fortress at certain times of the day, riding on a mule. Nor would the Emperor admit the King to his presence unless first an agreement were reached, or it was certain that it would be reached.

·　·

But at the same time, because of new occurrences in Spain, almost everything changed. For the King of France, very unhappy since he had tried in vain to be received by the Emperor, fell so ill while in the fortress of Madrid, and was reduced to such extremity of life that the doctors assigned to cure him informed the Emperor that they had lost all hope for the King of France's health, unless Charles came in person to comfort him and give him some hope of being liberated. Whereupon the Emperor preparing to go, his Grand Chancellor dissuaded him from it, saying that his honor obliged him not to go unless he went with the intention of immediately freeing him without any treaty; otherwise it was an act of humanity not regal but mercenary, and a desire to see that he was cured, not out of charity for his health but moved only by self-interest, in order not to lose by his death the opportunity of gains hoped for from the victory.

This was certainly a memorable bit of advice, and worthy of being accepted by so great a prince. Nevertheless, advised differently by others, he went by post to visit him. The visit was brief, since the Most Christian King was already almost at death's door, but the Emperor was full of gracious words, and gave the King most certain hope of being freed as soon as he regained his health; and indeed after this visit (whatever might be the reason, either the comfort he took from it or the fact that his youth was in itself stronger than his illness), his health began to mend to such a degree that in a few days he was out of danger, although not until later did he regain his former good spirits.

. .

In these negotiations, what caused the greatest difficulties above all, and the greatest fears, was the suspicion that every time the Emperor, finding himself in dire straits, might offer to free their King, the French would not only abandon the League but would also help the Emperor against the allies. And although the King of England gave his promise for all of them, that they would not come to an agreement; and they were negotiating that in Rome, Florence or Venice they should give a security in payment for three months, yet they found no way of being sure that their suspicions were ill-founded. For since the French had no other purpose than the King's liberation, and since it was well known that they had no inclination to wage war until they had lost all hope of an agreement, it seemed most likely that whenever the Emperor should consent, they would propose an alliance with him over any other interest and consideration. Indeed, it was known that no matter how superior might be the preparations and forces of the League, so much the more would the Emperor be inclined to come to an agreement with the King of France. And therefore it seemed most dangerous to unite in a war in which the powerful preparations of the allies might cause as much harm as good. Ambassadors and agents of princes assailed the Pope on every side with these arguments, and his own ministers as well, since his family and his counsel were divided. Each one favored his own inclination with that much less regard, the more authority they had arrogated to themselves with the Pope,* who was accustomed up to that time to allow himself to be carried along in great part by those who should have obeyed his every nod, and been no other than ministers and executors of their master's will and orders.

To understand this and many other things that happened, it is necessary to set forth this matter more fully.

Analysis of the Papacy of Leo X. The Relative Roles of the Pope and Giulio de' Medici

Leo, who brought the sovereign ecclesiastical honor to the house of the Medici, and so bolstered by his prestige as cardinal both his own fortunes and those of his family (which had fallen from so high a place into great decline) that they might hope for a return of good fortune, was a man of very great liberality, if such be the proper name for excessive and boundless spending.

Having won the pontificate, the spirit of Leo's papacy appeared so magnificent and splendid and truly regal, that it would have been marvelous even in one who had by long succession descended from kings or emperors: not only was he profligate with money, but with all those graces which are in the power of a pope: which he conceded with so little restraint that he caused the spiritual authority to become defiled, upset the style of the court, and by spending too much, put himself in a position where he always had to look for money by extraordinary means. To this excessive easy-goingness of his was added the deepest dissimulation, whereby he turned the heads of everyone at the beginning of his pontificate and made himself seem to be an excellent prince (I don't speak of apostolic goodness, for according to our own corrupt customs the goodness of a pope is praised when it does not exceed the malignancy of other men). But Leo was reputed to be clement,** eager to benefit everyone and most indisposed from all those things which might harm anyone. The same Leo was most devoted to music, to jests, and to buffoons; in suchlike

---

* ". . . *ciascuno favoriva la propria inclinazione con tanto minore rispetto quanto era maggiore l'autorità che s'avevano arrogata con lui . . .*" (*Storia,* ed. Gherardi, III, 432). Guicciardini's roundabout style here is perfectly congruous with the twinings and self-justification of Clement's advisers.

** *Ma era riputato clemente . . .* Is Guicciardini indulging in a sly pun here?

amusements he immersed his soul and spent most of his time that otherwise would have been devoted to great enterprises and ends, for which he
had a most capable intellect. In the early years of his papacy, a great many
believed that he was most chaste; but later it was discovered that he was
excessively given, and every day more shamelessly, to those pleasures
which cannot honestly be mentioned.

Among his other sources of good luck, which were numerous, Leo
had no little fortune in always having his cousin, Giulio de' Medici, at his
side; whom he had raised to the cardinalate from being a Knight of
Rhodes, although he was not of legitimate birth. For being by nature
grave, diligent, and assiduous in his undertakings, disinterested in pleasure,
orderly and dedicated in everything, and having, by the will of Pope Leo,
all the important business of the pontificate in his hand, Giulio put to
rights and moderated many disorders that proceeded from the Pope's
largesse and easy ways; and what is more, not following the custom of
other nephews and brothers of popes, putting Leo's honor and grandeur
ahead of whatever support he might make use of after his death, he was
so faithful and obedient that he seemed indeed to be the Pope's second
self; for which reason he was always most honored and advanced by the
Pontiff, who entrusted him more every day with his affairs; which being
in the hands of two different natures, sometimes showed how well the
mixture of two contraries go together. The assiduousness, the diligence,
the order, the gravity of habits of the one; the easy-goingness, the
prodigality, the pleasures and sense of honor of the other, made many
people think that Leo was ruled by Giulio, and that in himself he was not
the man to hold so heavy a responsibility, nor to do harm to anyone, but
simply most desirous to enjoy the comforts of the pontificate; and on the
contrary, that Giulio was ambitious, thirsting for innovations, with the
result that all the severity, all the agitation, all the enterprises that took
place during the time of Leo, were believed to have proceeded at Giulio's
instigation, who was reputed to be a malevolent man, but of great mind
and capacity.*

This opinion of his value was confirmed and grew after Leo's death;
for amidst so many contradictions and difficulties that befell him, he supported and managed his affairs with such dignity that he almost seemed
to be pope, and he maintained his authority among many of the cardinals
to such a degree that he entered into two conclaves absolute master of
sixteen votes, and finally, notwithstanding endless contradictions of the
majority, especially the older members of the College, he attained to the
papacy when Adrian died, less than two years after the death of Leo. He

---

* Machiavelli suggests that a wise
ruler leaves onerous tasks to his ministers
but performs generous acts himself. By
this definition Leo was very wise. (Niccolò Machiavelli, *Il Principe*, "Testino"
edition, Florence, 1550, p. 44 *et passim*.)

entered his new office with the greatest expectations. It was universally believed that he would be a greater pope and accomplish greater deeds than any of those who till that day had been seated in that chair. But soon it was known how vain were the judgments made about Leo and him. For Giulio had many characteristics different from those which had previously been believed: he did not possess either that desire for change, or grandeur, or tendency of mind for generous and magnanimous ends that had previously been supposed, and had been rather Leo's executor and minister of his plans far more than the director and initiator of his counsels and of his will. And although he had a most capable intelligence and marvelous knowledge of world affairs, yet he lacked the corresponding resolution and execution. For he was impeded not only by his timidity of spirit, which was by no means small, and by a strong reluctance to spend, but also by a certain innate irresolution and perplexity, so that he remained almost always in suspension and ambiguous when he was faced with deciding those things which from afar he had many times foreseen, considered, and almost resolved. Whence, both in his deliberations and in executing what he had already decided upon, any small aspect newly revealing itself, any slight impediment that might cross his path, seemed sufficient to make him fall back into that confusion wherein he was before he had come to a decision, since it always seemed to him, once he had decided, that the counsel which he had rejected was better. For afterward, summoning up in his mind only those reasons which he had neglected, he did not recall those reasons which had motivated his choice: the conflict and comparison of which would have weakened the weight of the opposing reasons. And although he remembered having often been the prey to foolish fears, he had not learned the lesson not to permit himself to be overcome by fear. Thus as a result of his complicated nature and confused way of proceeding, he often permitted himself to be led by his ministers, and seemed directed rather than counseled by them.

. .

[*The Emperor, feeling that it is dangerous to have to cope with too many enemies at once (the Pope and the Venetians pressing him for the restitution of Francesco Sforza to the duchy of Milan), decides to come to an agreement with the French King, who, despairing to obtain his liberty by any other means, and after fruitlessly arguing for Burgundy, offers to render it up to the Emperor, and to renounce all his rights to the kingdom of Naples and the duchy of Milan, and to deliver two of his sons as hostages for his pledged word.*

A vigorous debate follows in the presence of the Emperor be-

*tween his Grand Chancellor (contra) and Viceroy (pro) on the
proposal to come to an accord with the King of France. Finally on the
14th of February 1526, terms of peace are signed between the Emperor
and the King of France, some of the principal articles of which are:
that the French King would be set at liberty on March 6, and within
six weeks would consign to the Emperor the duchy of Burgundy
among other possessions; that when the King was delivered there
should be put into the Emperor's hands the Dauphin of France and
with him either the Duke of Orléans, the King's second son, or
twelve of the chief lords of France, to be held as hostages until the
articles were signed and ratified within four months, at which time
the King's third son, the Duke of Angoulême, would be turned over
to be brought up with the Emperor "to assure the peace"; that the
French King would renounce his rights to Naples and Milan; that he
would renounce his sovereignty of Flanders and all places which the
Emperor possessed; that a mutual defense league would be drawn up
between both potentates; that the Emperor would promise to give his
sister Madame Eleanor in marriage to the Most Christian King; that a
marriage would be drawn up between the Dauphin and the daughter
of the King of Portugal, born of Madame Eleanor, as soon as their
age would permit; that the King of France would furnish and rig
ships for the Emperor when he decided to cross into Italy.*

*The Pope was named as the conservator—we would say guar-
antor—of this agreement, more for ceremony's sake than true meaning. And in case the King for any reason should not carry out his
promises, he would return voluntarily to prison.]*

The Treaty of Madrid Sets Free the King of France

This accord created the greatest surprise throughout Christendom. For,
when it was understood that its implementation involved, first of all, the
liberation of the Most Christian King, everyone felt that as soon as he had
regained his liberty, he should not have to give up Burgundy, as being too
important a region of the French kingdom; and except for those few who
had urged the Emperor to it, his entire court were of the same opinion.
And the Grand Chancellor,* more than any of the others, opposed and
rejected this clause with such vehemence that, although he was ordered

---

* Guicciardini had characterized him earlier at the time of the debate: "Mercurio da Gattinara, the Grand Chancellor, a man who, although of base parentage from Piedmont, was highly reputed and experienced, so that he had managed for many years now all the important affairs of that court."

to sign the articles of capitulation (which is the office of a grand chancellor), he refused to do so, alleging that the authority entrusted in him should not be used in matters as dangerous and pernicious as this; nor could all the Emperor's indignation move him from his refusal: so that when the Emperor saw that he was remaining fixed to this stubborn determination, he himself signed it; and a few days later went to Madrid to confirm the family alliance, and by conversing familiarly and, as it were, domestically, with the King, lay the foundation for their amity and good will. Great were the ceremonies and shows of love between them: they appeared together oftentimes in public, and they held very long discussions oftentimes alone in secret; in the same carriage they went to a castle a half day's journey away, where there was Queen Eleanor with whom they drew up, I believe, the marriage contract. But with all these signs of peace and friendship, the guard about the King was never slackened, nor was he given more liberty, so that he was at one and the same time cherished as a brother-in-law, and kept under guard as a prisoner. Hence it was easy to understand that this was an accord full of discord, a family alliance without love, and that their ancient rivalries and passions might at any time weigh more with them, than regard for things accomplished more by violence than any other reason.

Now, having spent several days in these proceedings, and the ratification of Madame the Regent already having arrived, together with the declaration that with the Dauphin of France they would sooner give [in hostage] their secondborn son than the twelve barons, the King departed from Madrid to go to the frontier, where his person was to be exchanged for his little sons; and accompanying him was the Viceroy, the author of his liberation, to whom the Emperor had given the city of Asti and other states in Flanders and in the kingdom of Naples.

．．
．

At this time the Emperor wrote a ceremonial letter to the Pope, indicating to him that out of a desire for peace and the common good of Christendom, having forgiven and forgotten so many affronts and acts of enmity, he had set free the King of France and given him his sister as wife, and had chosen as the conservator of the peace the Pope, to whom he always wished to be a most obedient son. . .

[*The Emperor also replies to the Pope regarding the restitution of the Duke of Milan and other details of the accord pending between them. But the Pope does not accept his proposals; he fears that "the Emperor's greatness would inevitably mean his servitude." He dispatches the Florentine Paolo Vettori to France, to arrive there when the*

King does, to sound out Francis' mind in the hope of getting him to join with the Venetians and the pontifical forces against the Emperor. Clement also sends a deputy to Henry VIII in England for the same purpose.]

By this time the French King had arrived at Fonterabia, a town belonging to the Emperor located on the Ocean Sea on the frontier between Biscay and the duchy of Guyenne; and on the other side his mother with the two children had come to Bayonne, a few leagues from Fonterabia. There she had remained a few days beyond the day appointed to make the exchange, because she had suffered from gout along the way.

Then, on the eighteenth day of March, the King, accompanied by the Viceroy and Captain Alarcon and with about fifty horses, was brought to the shore of the river that divides the realm of France from the kingdom of Spain; at the same time, Lautrec with a similar number of horses and the two little sons appeared on the other bank. In the midst of the river there was a great barque held fast with anchors, in which there was no one. The King approached this barque in a little boat, wherein there were also the Viceroy, Alarcon and eight others, all armed with short weapons; and approaching the barque on the other side in another small boat came Lautrec with the hostages and eight other companions armed in the same manner.

Then the Viceroy went into the barque with all his company, and the King with them, and immediately thereafter Lautrec with his eight companions; so that within the barque there was a like number from both sides, Alarcon and his eight being with the Viceroy, and Lautrec and his eight with the King. As soon as they had all leaped into the barque Lautrec drew the Dauphin out of the little boat into the barque, who was then given to the Viceroy and by him consigned to Alarcon who immediately put him in their boat: and at the same time the little Duke of Orléans was fetched into the barque. No sooner was this done when the Most Christian King leaped out of the barque into his boat with such swiftness that this exchange seemed to have occurred at the same moment; and then brought to shore, the King suddenly mounted—as if he feared an ambush—upon a marvelously swift Turkish horse prepared for this purpose, and raced without stopping to Saint-Jean-de-Luz, a town belonging to him, four leagues away. Whence, after a short rest, he galloped with the same speed to Bayonne where he was received with incredible joy by his entire court.

From there he immediately dispatched by diligence a man to the King of England, explaining to him, with letters in his own hand, how he was liberated. The messenger was also commissioned to acknowledge that the King's freedom was entirely of his own doing; and to express his desire to be inseparable from him and to be guided in all occurrences by his counsel; and soon after he sent him other ambassadors to solemnly ratify the peace which his mother had made with him, because he placed the greatest reliance on the amity of that King.*

* Here ends the first printed editions of the *Storia d'Italia*. The editions of 1561, 1562 and 1563 contain only Books I–XVI; the last four books were first published separately in 1564 in Venice. Only in 1567, again in Venice, did the complete *Storia* appear, the last four books appended with a separate frontispiece and numeration. But this edition is otherwise mutilated by various deletions of ecclesiastical censors—especially the famous section of Book IV dealing with Church claims to temporal power.

In his dedication to the Torrentino edition of 1561, Agnolo Guicciardini had declared that since his uncle's untimely death had prevented him from bringing to perfection the last four books—*"più presto abbozzati che finiti"*—these were not being published at that time. However, writes the same Agnolo in his new dedication (1564) to the separate publication of the last four books, so much interest had been aroused by the publication of the first sixteen books of the *Storia*, and so much desire to read the last four books "as sons of the same father, and containing things closer to our times, and because their quality and grandeur are perhaps greater than the former," he had conscientiously transcribed the rough copy and published it "without adding or removing anything, preferring to leave some vacant places rather than insert the ideas or words of others into this history" (*Historia di Italia*, Fiorenza, Torrentino, 1561, Dedication; Gherardi, *op. cit.*, I, p. CLXX).

Fair copy by amanuensis of the opening section of the Storia d'Italia *with marginal and interlinear corrections in Guicciardini's own hand* (FROM THE CODEX IN THE ARCHIVE, THROUGH THE COURTESY OF THE BIBLIOTECA MEDICEA LAURENZIANA, FLORENCE)

[*No one in Italy really believes that Francis I will abide by the crushing and humiliating terms of the Treaty of Madrid. The Pope himself is of the opinion that since the oath was exacted by force, the King is not bound by it. And in fact, once back on his home soil, Francis begins overtures with the Pope and other Italian states to renew the war against Spain. Efforts are even made to draw Henry VIII of England into this grand alliance against the Emperor; he fails to join only because the potential allies will not accede to his persistent request that the league be drawn up in England.*

All Italy is now stirred up to embark on a kind of crusade for national freedom. Machiavelli calls for the extirpation of these "ferocious beasts who resemble man only in aspect and speech." One of the chief architects of the anti-imperial alliance is Francesco Guicciardini, President of the Romagna, convinced like everyone else that the struggle against Spanish domination is a necessary and holy war of independence.

Finally a new coalition is formed in the so-called holy league of Cognac (22 May 1526) adhered to by Clement VII, Francis I, Venice and the Sforza of Milan. Clement of course controls Florence as well as the papacy, and so that state is inevitably committed to the league; Venice also joins.

But French military fire soon proves far less tangible than their agitated diplomatic smoke; no French army turns up in Italy, and the Pope, revealing his indecisiveness more every day, tries to arouse Francis from his dallying, both amorous and military; asks money from the King of England and seeks to come to an agreement with the Duke of Ferrara. Military actions break out in Lombardy and Tuscany.]

*The Pope Pleads for Unity of Christendom Against the
Turkish Threat in Hungary. Colonna Uprising
Against the Pope in Rome*

NOW THAT PUBLIC CALAMITIES MIGHT BE ADDED
TO THE POPE'S PRIVATE AFFLICTIONS, CAME THE
NEWS THAT SULEIMAN OTTOMAN, PRINCE OF
the Turks, had defeated Louis King of Hungary in ranked battle, his victory resulting no less through the enemy's temerity than by his own forces.
For although small in numbers by comparison with so great a foe, the
Hungarians placed more confidence in the victories which they had often
achieved against the Turks in the past, than in the present situation, and
they convinced the King, who was young in years but in counsel even
younger than his age, that he should not dim the fame and ancient military
glory of his people; and without waiting for the help which was coming
from Transylvania, he should confront the enemy, not refusing even to
fight in the open countryside, wherein the Turks are practically invincible
because of their great number of horsemen. The outcome therefore cor-
responded to his rashness and imprudence; the army, gathered of all the
nobility and brave men in Hungary, was shattered, a great many killed,
and the King himself was slain, together with many of the leading prelates
and barons of the realm.

As a result of this victory the Pope was greatly disturbed, it being
considered certain that the Turk would take permanent possession of the
entire Hungarian kingdom to the greatest detriment of all Christendom,
for whom that realm had been a shield and rampart for many years. The
Holy Father was especially troubled, for new setbacks make a greater
impression on minds which are already perturbed and afflicted than they
do on minds devoid of other passions. Therefore, meditating new ideas
and plans, and expressing boundless grief in his gestures, his words, his
countenance; and having called the cardinals into consistory, he bitterly
lamented of the great ignominy and harm that had come to all of
Christendom; which he himself had not failed to foresee, whether by
strongly urging and recommending peace among Christian princes, or by
assisting that realm with no small amounts of money when he himself had
so many grave needs of his own. Indeed, he had foretold that the present
war would be very inopportune and importunate for the defense of that
kingdom, and dangerous for the rest of Christendom, and he had said it
and known it from the beginning. But necessity had induced him (since

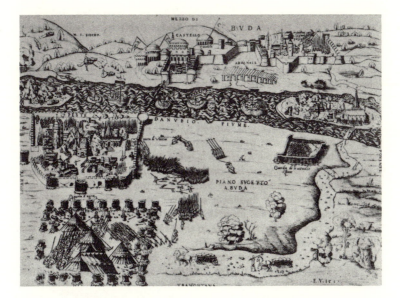

The city of Buda, from a print dated 1542, showing various aspects of Renaissance warfare (COURTESY OF GABINETTO NAZIONALE DELLE STAMPE, ROME)

he saw that all honest conditions for peace and security of the Apostolic See and of Italy were being shattered) to seize arms, against what had always been his intention. For both the neutrality which he had maintained before this necessity, and the conditions of the league which he had organized, all concerned with the common welfare, served sufficiently to show that he had not been moved by any considerations of personal interest, and particularly those of his family. But since, perhaps for some good end, it had pleased God that the body of Christendom should be wounded, and at a time when all the other members of this body were distracted by other thoughts than those relating to the security of all, he was forced to believe that it was the will of God that the curing of so great a malady be sought by other means.

And therefore, since this cure was more the obligation of his pastoral office than anyone else's responsibility, he was prepared to set aside all considerations of discomfort, peril and his dignity, and having brought about a suspension of the wars in Italy as soon as he could under certain conditions, to embark upon his galleys, and in person go to meet the princes of Christendom to obtain from them by persuasion, prayers and tears, a universal peace among Christians. He exhorted the cardinals to gird themselves for this expedition, and to aid their common father in so pious a duty; and to pray God that he be favorable to so holy a work; and if this could not be carried out successfully because of the sins they all shared, that it please Him at least to grant the Pope grace that he might die during such negotiations, before all hope was ruled out. For, no unhappiness, no misery, could be greater to him than to lose hope and the possibility of being able to lend his hand to quench so pernicious and pestiferous a fire.*

The Pope's proposal was listened to with great attention and no less compassion, and greatly praised. But it would have been praised even more had his words aroused as much belief as the dignity they possessed in themselves. For most of the cardinals interpreted them to mean that, having taken up arms against the Emperor at the time when the danger to Hungary was already imminent and clear because of the Turk's open preparations, the Pope was more disturbed by the difficulties into which the war had fallen than the dangers to the Hungarian kingdom. But it was impossible to make a real test of that.

For the Colonna, beginning to carry out their nefarious design, had sent their follower Cesare Filettino with two thousand foot-soldiers to Anagnia, where there were two hundred paid infantrymen of the Pope; claiming, to hide their intentions, that they wished to capture that town. But since they had in fact another idea, they occupied all the passes, and taking great care that no news of their progress reach Rome, they assembled all their forces around Anagnia, and with these soldiers and others (in all, about eight hundred horsemen and three thousand foot-soldiers, but almost all seasoned troops) they marched swiftly toward Rome, no one there having any presentiment of their coming, arrived on the night before the twentieth of September, and took by surprise three gates of Rome. Their entry into the city was by the gate of Saint John Lateran, and with them in person were not only Ascanio and Don Ugo di Moncada** (for the Duke of Sessa had died many days before at Marino) but also Vespasiano, who had solicited the accord and been the inter-mediary and given his pledge for himself and all the others. Also present was the Cardinal Pompeo Colonna, so carried away by ambition and fury that he had conspired to bring about the Pope's violent death, and (as was commonly and firmly believed) to seize with bloody hands and most wicked deeds the vacant pontifical seat, forcing the cardinals to elect him by force of arms.

* Much of the above two paragraphs is imperfect in the text: verbs are missing or in the form of infinitives (Gherardi, *op. cit.*, IV, 67–68).

** Deputized by Charles V to go to Italy to break up the new holy league formed against the Emperor at Cognac. Moncada was infamous for his cruelty and considered an *Exaltado*: one of those who wished to subjugate all of Italy under Spanish military despotism.

VIEW OF ROME AT THE BEGINNING OF THE
SIXTEENTH CENTURY

A. Hadrian's Tomb (Castel Sant' Angelo) B. Vatican C. Saint Peter's
D. Column of the Antinines (Marcus Aurelius) and the nearby Pantheon
E. Trajan's Column F. Arch of Septimus G. Temple of Peace H. Baths
of Diocletian I. Tiber River Bridge K. Capitol (with Gothic Tower of
Senator's Palace) L. Isola Tiberina M. Saint John Lateran with statue of
Marcus Aurelius N. Aqueduct, branch of Aqua Martia, and fed baths of
Diocletian O. Arch of Titus P. Santa Susanna Q. Santa Maria del Popolo
R. San Lorenzo S. San Sebastian T. San Vitale V. Cecilia Metella

Judging by the relative distances among these various monuments, Münster's
map is more the product of conjecture and aesthetics than measurement

When at daybreak the Pope learned of their coming (the Colonna forces were already gathered around Saints Cosimo and Damiano), he was terrified and thrown into confusion, and vainly tried to quell this tumult. For the Pope had neither his own forces to defend himself; nor did the Roman people, partly happy at his misfortune and partly judging that public disturbances would not affect them, make any sign of moving in his support.

Encouraged by this, his enemies advanced, finally halting with all their bands at Sant' Apostolo, whence about five hundred infantry with some cavalrymen pushed ahead across the Ponte Sisto into Trastevere. These forces were repulsed from the gate of Santo Spirito, after some resistance by Stefano Colonna, who had been enlisted into the Pope's service, and stationed there with two hundred infantry. The rebels headed for the old Borgo toward Saint Peter's and the pontifical palace, the Pope still being in the palace. Vainly calling for God's help and the help of men, ready to die on his throne, the Pope was preparing to take his place on the pontifical throne, vested in his pontifical garb and ornaments, following the example of Boniface VIII when he suffered the attack of Sciarra Colonna.

But the cardinals around him with great difficulty dissuaded him from this proposition, warning him not to move, if not for himself at least for the safety of the Papal See, and in order that the honor of God might not be wickedly violated in the person of his Vicar. Therefore the Pope, together with several of the cardinals closest to him, withdrew into the Castello at the seventeenth hour,* and just in time, too, for not only had the footsoldiers and horsemen already arrived, but also all the rest of the troops were sacking the ecclesiastical palace and the sacred ornaments of the church of Saint Peter: having no greater respect for the majesty of religion and no more horror at sacrilege than had the Turks in the churches of the kingdom of Hungary.

Then they entered into the new Borgo of which they sacked about a third; proceeding no farther ahead for fear of the artillery in the castle. Later, when the tumult had quieted down, which had lasted a little more than three hours (for within Rome they did no damage nor harmed anyone), Don Ugo, under the Pope's pledge, and receiving as hostages for his security the cardinals Cibo and Ridolfi, the Pope's distant cousins, went into the Castello to speak with him. Using words suitable for a conqueror, Don Ugo proposed conditions for a truce. On the basis of the reply, deferred till the following day, an agreement—that is, a truce—for four months was concluded between the Pope in his name and the name of the allies, and the Emperor, with another two months notice, and giving the allies the right to enter into the agreement within two months. The truce covered not only the Ecclesiastical State and the kingdom of Naples, but also the duchy of Milan, the Florentines, the Genoese, the Sienese, the Duke of Ferrara and all the subjects of the Church, indirect and direct. The Pope was obliged to immediately withdraw his forces around Milan to this side of the Po River, and recall Andrea Doria**

---

* About 1 P.M. The hours were computed, on a 24-hour basis, from nightfall to nightfall. At this season, nightfall in Rome would be about 8 P.M.

** Andrea Doria, the celebrated admiral of the Genoese galleys, was in the service of the French. His navy was of fundamental importance in the western Mediterranean.

and his galleys from the fleet. The imperial and Colonna troops were obliged to leave Rome and the entire Ecclesiastical State and withdraw into the kingdom of Naples. The Colonna and anyone else who had participated in this uprising were to be pardoned; Filippo Strozzi and one of the sons of Iacopo Salviati were to be given as hostages of observance, the Pope pledging to send them to Naples within two months under pain of thirty thousand ducats.

Both sides eagerly agreed on drawing up this truce: the Pope because there were no victuals in the Castello to maintain him, Don Ugo (although the Colonna protested) because he felt that he had done enough for the Emperor's benefit, and because almost all the troops with whom he had entered into Rome, now laden with booty, had dispersed and disappeared.

[*By the fall of 1526, the Emperor, who has also been impeded for want of funds, gathers together an army of German landsknechts under their leader, George Frundsberg, and Spanish troops under the Duke of Bourbon, the Constable of France, who has deserted his king to serve the Emperor. At the end of November Frundsberg's hordes, sacking and marauding as they go, make the difficult crossing of the Po and invade the territory of Parma and Piacenza. Guicciardini is now in command of all ecclesiastical armies as the Pope's Lieutenant General. In February 1527 both imperial armies have joined forces near Piacenza; their march southward is made easy by the active help of the Duke of Ferrara and the Duke of Urbino's tactics of procrastination, ancient grudges against Medici popes now being fatefully paid off.*]

BOOK

18

Agitation in Florence at the Approach of the Imperial Troops under the Duke of Bourbon

THE YEAR 1527 WILL BE FULL OF ATROCITIES AND EVENTS UNHEARD OF FOR MANY CENTURIES: OVERTHROW OF GOVERNMENTS, WICKEDNESS of princes, most frightful sacks of cities, great famines, a most terrible plague almost everywhere in Italy; everything full of death, flight and rapine.

. . .

Now all the armies were in Tuscany, and when the allies learned that the Duke of Bourbon had marched in one day (the twenty-third of April) from Pieve to Santo Stefano to encamp at Chiasso near Arezzo, a march of eighteen miles, their captains met at Barberino to decide what was to be done. Many of them, together with agents of the Pope and of the Florentines, urged that the united armies should march and set up quarters beyond Florence, in order not to afford the Duke of Bourbon an excuse to approach that city. It was resolved that the troops be allowed to remain where they were, but that on the following day the captains should go to Ancisa, thirteen miles from Florence, and later transfer the troops there if they found safe quarters for them, as Federico da Bozzole, who had put forward this recommendation, affirmed they might.

But as they were marching the next day, and already near Florence, an unexpected incident which might have given rise to the most serious results had it not been settled, greatly impeded carrying out this plan and others which they had in mind.

For there was great agitation and passions kindled, and almost all the people were most discontent with the present government, and the young people were insisting that the magistrates (even before they passed a law to that effect) should give them the public arms to defend themselves (as they said) from the troops. The result was that before a resolution was made, a sort of tumult flared up almost by chance, on April 26, in the Piazza Signoria; most of the people and almost all of the armed youth began to run toward the public palace. And to this uprising, no little encouragement was given by the imprudence or timidity of Silvio, Cardinal of Cortona who, having arranged to go forth from the city to meet the Duke of Urbino and do him honor, did not change his decision, even though before he left he learned that this uprising had begun; whence the rumor spreading throughout the city that he had fled, many people were more ready than ever to attack the Palazzo [Signoria]. The palace was already occupied by the youth, and the piazza filled with an armed multitude, who forced the Chief Magistrate to declare by solemn decree Ippolito and Alessandro [de' Medici], the Pope's nephews, as rebels; thus manifesting their intention to reintroduce popular government.

But meanwhile, the Duke and the Marquis with many captains entered into Florence, and with them the Cardinal of Cortona and Ippolito de' Medici, and having armed fifteen hundred footsoldiers who had been stationed several days in the city for fear [of Bourbon], all these forces closed ranks and marched toward the piazza which fell into their power because the crowds immediately abandoned it.

Nevertheless, since those who were in the palace were throwing stones and firing arquebuses, no one dared remain in the piazza, but they occupied the surrounding streets. But since the Duke of Urbino judged there were not sufficient forces in Florence to seize the palace, and considering it dangerous unless the palace were captured before nightfall, lest the people regain their courage and rise up again in arms, he decided with the consent of the three cardinals present—Cibo, Cortona and Ridolfi—and the Marquis of Saluzzo and the Venetian commissioners, all congregated in the Street of Garbo contiguous to the palace, to call up part of the Venetian infantry who were quartered in the Florentine plain near the city.

Thus preparations were being made for the dangerous contest, for the palace could not be captured without the death of almost all the nobility within it, and also there was the peril that once having set their hand to arms and killing, the victorious soldiers would sack the rest of the city. Thus the Florentines prepared for many bitter and unhappy days. However the Lieutenant General [Guicciardini]* swiftly cut this most difficult knot, for having seen Federico da Bozzole come toward them,

---

* Francesco Guicciardini had arrived in Florence on April 23, after the defense against the imperials in the north had collapsed. Giovanni de' Medici (Giovanni of the Black Bands), the celebrated young captain, lost his life in that campaign.

and realizing who he was, he immediately left the others and met him, to be the first to speak to him. Although this seemed of no importance, it proved to be the main reason for freeing the city of Florence that day from so evident a danger. At the beginning of the uprising, Federico had gone to the palace, hoping to quiet down this tumult by his authority and the good reputation he held among many of the youth; but having no success in this—rather, having met with insults from some of them—he had been kept for several hours, and only with no little difficulty did he obtain the right to leave. Therefore he left the palace full of anger, and knowing how easy it was to take it because of their small forces and disorder, he was coming to incite the others to attack it immediately. But the Lieutenant General, showing him with very few words how harmful to the Pope would be all the disorders which might result, and how detrimental to the common cause of the allies, and how much better it was to wait for the people's spirits to calm down, rather than to incite them again, and therefore how dangerous it was to show the Duke of Urbino and the others how easy it was to capture the palace, he managed without difficulty to convince him. So much so, indeed, that Federico spoke to the others precisely as the Lieutenant General wished, and expounded the matter in such a way, and aroused so much hope of settling the affair without arms, that having chosen this as the better path, they entreated both of them to go together into the palace to endeavor to appease the tumult, giving assurances to everyone against whatever they might be charged with having conspired that day against the state.

Thus, not without difficulty, they went into the palace with the safe-conducts of those who were within and induced them to abandon the palace, which they were unable to defend. Thus the tumult was put down and things returned as before.* And nevertheless (as ingratitude and calumny are more present than remuneration and praise for good works), although everyone greatly commended the Lieutenant General at that time, nevertheless the Cardinal of Cortona complained a little later that he was more concerned about the safety of the citizens than the grandeur of the Medici and had acted cunningly, and that this had been the reason why Medici rule had not been established permanently on that day by arms and the blood of citizens. And the multitude also blamed him afterward, because when he went to the palace, presenting the dangers to be greater than they were, he had induced them unnecessarily to give up for the benefit of the Medici.

The Florentine uprising, although it was settled the same day and without bloodshed, was nevertheless the origin of the gravest disorders;

* Although Guicciardini writes objectively about his role in this affair, a certain amount of self-complacency is visible through the ice. His brother Luigi was gonfaloniere at the time.

and perhaps one could say that had it not been for this incident, the ruin that quickly followed would not have occurred.

[*Before marching into Tuscany, the Duke had promised to meet with the Viceroy (who had made a truce with the Pope after inconclusive fighting in the kingdom of Naples) and with Guicciardini. The Viceroy wanted to induce Bourbon to accept the accord; Bourbon however failed to show up for the appointment, and tried to cross the Alps the same day.*]

In this state of affairs the Pope, having learned how the Duke of Bourbon had deceived the Viceroy, and of his passage into Tuscany, of necessity turned his thoughts to war. On the twenty-fifth of April he concluded a new alliance with the King of France and the Venetians, obliging them to give him subventions of great amounts of money; and not wishing to oblige the Florentines or himself to anything other than that which they might be able to carry out, he alleged that they were both drained because of their excessive expenses. Although these were onerous conditions, they were approved by the ambassadors of the allies in order to entirely separate the Pope from the agreements made with the Viceroy.

But they were not approved by the principals: the Venetians blamed Domenico Venereo, their ambassador, for having concluded without approval of the Senate an alliance which cost so much and bore so little fruit, considering the Pope's vacillation, who they thought would return on every occasion to his original lack of faith and desire for an agreement [with the Viceroy]. And the King of France, out of money, and more intent on wearing the Emperor down by a protracted war rather than by a victory, considered it sufficient at this time that the war involve very small expense. In fact, if at first he took it greatly amiss when he heard of the truce made by the Pope, later, considering the state of affairs more carefully, he wanted the Pope to convince the Venetians (without whom he would not enter into any agreement whatever) to accept the truce.

.   .

But at this time the Pope, greatly troubled that the war had been transferred to Tuscany, but nevertheless less troubled than if it had been transferred to Rome, raised infantry and made provisions for money, but slowly. His plan was to send Renzo da Ceri with troops against the Sienese, and also attack them by sea,* so that the Duke of Bourbon would

---

* Guicciardini probably means from the seacoast although the text states "*per mare.*" Siena is inland. The domain of the republic of Siena, however, extended along the coast; most likely Guicciardini refers to actual landings.

become involved in Tuscany, and thereby be blocked from taking the road to Rome.

In fact, every day the Pope grew less fearful of this, hoping that, because of the difficulties which the Duke of Bourbon had in marching his troops to Rome without supplies and without money, and because of the opportunities that he had in the state of Siena, where at least his soldiers could be fed, he would call a halt, with this enterprise against the Florentines.

But either because Bourbon's first decision had been different, secretly decided upon (as many have said) before Finale, with the authority of the Duke of Ferrara and Girolamo Morone; or else doubting that he could gain anything in that undertaking, since the forces of the entire league had been brought to the defense of Florence; and being unable to maintain his army any longer without money, an army which up to that day he had led through so many difficulties by vain promises and vain hopes; and obliged either to perish or try his fortune, the Duke of Bourbon decided unexpectedly to march ahead at the greatest speed to attack the city of Rome; where the rewards of victory, both for the Emperor and for the soldiers, would be inestimable, and the hope of achieving it was not small, since the Pontiff, poorly advised, had discharged first the Swiss and then the footsoldiers of the Black Bands, and begun to prepare again so slowly (when the accord was in desperate straits), that it was thought he would not assemble sufficient defenses and garrisons in time.

Therefore the Duke of Bourbon departed with his entire army from the country around Arezzo on the twenty-sixth day of April, swiftly, without artillery, without baggage trains; and marching with incredible speed, not held back either by the rain which was very heavy during that season, or by the want of victuals, he approached Rome so rapidly that the Pope was hardly aware of his arrival. Neither at Viterbo, where the Pope had not dispatched troops in time, nor any other place did he face any opposition whatever.

Hence the Pope had recourse to those remedies which, had he taken them in time, would have been of the greatest importance for his safety. His wisest advisers had warned him that this was bound to happen; but now he acted out of direst necessity, and when he could no longer profit by those remedies which he should earlier have applied. Thus he created three cardinals for money, but the money could not be paid to him because of the difficult situation, and even if it had been paid, it could no longer have borne any fruit because the peril was so nigh. He also called together the people of Rome, urging them immediately to take up arms in defense of their country against so terrible a danger, and demanding that the richest among them lend money to raise troops; but all of this had no results whatever. Rather, it is remembered that Domenico di Massimo, the richest of all the Romans, offered to lend a hundred ducats:

for which avariciousness he paid a price, for his daughters fell into the clutches of the soldiers, and he and his sons were taken prisoner and had to pay the highest ransoms.

But in Florence the news of Bourbon's departure arrived from Vitello in Arezzo, from which it took one day more than it should have. At receipt of this news, the captains decided that Count Guido Rangoni, with his horsemen and those of the Count of Caiazzo, and with five thousand footsoldiers of the Florentines and of the Church, should immediately march toward Rome, closely following the other army, in the hope that if the Duke of Bourbon was marching with artillery, these reinforcements would arrive in Rome before him; if he was marching lightly, they would be so closely on his heels that, since he had no artillery and there was some slight defense in Rome, where the Pope had written that he had six thousand footsoldiers, the city could hold out until the first help arrived; and once arrived, there was no danger whatever that Rome would perish.

But the celerity of the Duke of Bourbon and the inadequate provisions made at Rome upset all these plans. For Renzo da Ceri, to whom the Pope had entrusted the main responsibility for the defense of Rome, had, because of the short time at his disposal, levied very few useful footsoldiers, mustering instead an unskilled and unmilitary mob gathered up out of the stables of the cardinals and prelates, and in artisans' workshops and taverns. And having fortified the Borgo—weakly, in everyone's opinion, but sufficient in his—Renzo da Ceri was so confident in his defensive measures that he didn't permit the bridges of the Tiber to be cut to save Rome, in case they could not defend the Borgo and Trastevere. Indeed, considering help to be superfluous and having a foreboding about Count Guido's arrival, he had the Bishop of Verona, in the name of the Pope, write him on the fourth of May that, since Rome was sufficiently fortified and provided for, he should only send six hundred or eight hundred arquebusiers there, and that he with the rest of the troops should go and join the army of the league, which would do more good than to be enclosed within Rome.

Although this did not cause any harm because the Count was not so far on the march that he could arrive in time, nevertheless it indicates what poor calculations Renzo da Ceri was making of the present danger. But it was no less to be wondered at (if it be cause for wonder that men know not how to, or cannot, resist destiny) that the Pope, who used to denigrate Renzo da Ceri more than any of the other captains, should now put himself entirely into his hands and his judgment; and much more, that he, usually fearful in lesser dangers, had many times been tempted to abandon Rome when the Viceroy set up his camp at Frusolone, now in so great a danger, contrary to his nature, should stand firmly in Rome with such hope of defending it that he had become almost an agent of the enemy, not only prohibiting the men from leaving, but giving orders that no goods should be taken out, which many merchants and others were seeking to unburden themselves of by way of the river.

The Sack of Rome

ON the fifth of May, Bourbon and his army took up quarters in Prati near Rome. From there, with military insolence, he sent a trumpeter to demand passage of the Pope through the city of Rome, to march with his army into the kingdom of Naples. The following morning at daybreak, he determined either to conquer or die (for certainly he had little other hope left in his undertakings), and approaching the Borgo on the side toward the hills and Santo Spirito, a bitter battle began. And fortune favored him because a thick fog which had risen before daybreak made it possible for him to approach the city more safely, covering his movements until the army reached the position where the battle began. At the beginning of this battle, Bourbon, goaded by ultimate desperation, was at the forefront of his troops, not only because if he failed to obtain a victory, no refuge remained to him, but also because he saw how the German foot-soldiers were marching coldly into battle. At the onset of the assault, he was wounded by a shot from an arquebus and fell dead to the ground.* But his death did not chill his soldiers' ardor, but rather caused them to fight with the greatest fury so that after two hours they finally broke into the Borgo, aided not only by the great weakness of the fortifications but also by the poor resistance put up against them. This battle demonstrated—as has been demonstrated many other times to those who have not yet learned to evaluate present situations from examples of antiquity— how much the virtues of men trained in warfare differ from new armies picked up here and there at random, and from a popular multitude.** For among the defenders were part of the youth of Rome under their

---

* In his *Autobiography*, Benvenuto Cellini claims to have fired this fatal shot that killed the Duke of Bourbon. The Florentine sculptor-goldsmith claims he aimed his arquebus at someone *sollevato degli altri*, and it is generally agreed that Bourbon was shot as he was climbing a scaling ladder. Perhaps this is one of the rare times when Cellini's psychopathic boasting bears some resemblance to the truth (Benvenuto Cellini, *La Vita*, Florence, 1937, p. 64).

** This remark is undoubtedly ad-dressed to the shade of Niccolò Machiavelli, who had argued for the institution of a popular draft militia. I think Guicciardini is being ironical of his friend Niccolò, who made too much exemplary use of Greek and Roman history. Another reading might be: ". . . those who, *because of* past examples, have not yet learned to evaluate present situations . . ." (my italics, S. A.). Machiavelli died 22 June 1527 (cf. *Ricordi, op. cit.,* second series 117, p. 97).

CASTEL SANT' ANGELO: ROME

Engraving by Antonio Salamanca, about 1530. At the left, a small section of the wall that runs from the Vatican palace to the castle; atop the wall is a secret corridor used by the pontiffs in times of peril.

local leaders and carrying the flag of the people; although many Ghibellines and those of the Colonna faction might have desired, or at least did not fear, an imperial victory, hoping not to be harmed out of respect for their faction. This was also a reason why defense actions were carried out rather coldly. Nevertheless, because it is difficult to capture a town without artillery, about a thousand footsoldiers of the attacking forces were killed. As soon as the assailants had broken in, the defenders took to their heels, many running to the Castello, and the outskirts were totally abandoned as prey to the victors; and the Pope, who was waiting at the Vatican palace to learn what had happened, as soon as he heard that the enemy had broken into the city, fled immediately with many cardinals into the Castello. There he deliberated whether he should remain in the castle, or else, accompanied through the streets of Rome by the light cavalry of his guard, try to make for a safe place. Thus he was destined to serve as an example of the calamities that can happen to popes, and also how difficult it is to extinguish their majesty and power. For while debating this matter, the Pope received news of Bourbon's death from Berardo of Padua (who had fled from the imperial army), and also was told that the entire army, thrown into confusion by their captain's death, desired to make peace with him. Therefore he sent out men to parley with their chiefs, and foolishly ignored those who had counseled that he depart: he and his captains proving no less irresolute in taking measures for their defense than they had been in launching attacks.

Therefore, the same day, the Spaniards meeting with no resistance whatever and encountering neither order nor planned defense, entered Trastevere; and from there without any difficulty, on the same afternoon at twenty-three hours* broke into the city of Rome by the Ponte Sisto. Almost the entire papal court and the citizens, as is usual in such terrifying situations, were in flight or in confusion, except for those who placed their confidence in the reputation of their faction, or some cardinals who were reputed to be followers of the Emperor and therefore believed themselves safer than the others.

As soon as they had entered the city, the imperials began to run about tumultuously in search of booty, respecting neither friends nor the authority and dignity of prelates, nor even churches, monasteries, and relics, honored by pilgrims from all over the world, nor sacred things. Therefore it would be impossible not only to narrate but even to imagine the calamity of that city, destined by heaven's orders to consummate greatness, but also to drastic shifts of fortune, having been sacked by the Goths 980 years before. And impossible also to describe the enormous booty, since such riches were accumulated there, and so many rare and precious things belonging to merchants and courtiers.

But an even greater source of booty were the large number of important captives who had to buy back their liberty with enormous ransoms. And to bring their misery and infamy to overflowing, many prelates were captured by soldiers, especially by the German landsknechts, who because of their hatred for the Roman Church, were cruel and insolent, contemptuously leading priests throughout the city of Rome mounted on asses and mules, wearing the robes and insignia of their ecclesiastical dignity. Many were most cruelly tormented and either died in the torture or were treated in such way that their lives ended within a few days after they had paid their ransom. About four thousand men perished in the battle and in the furor of the sack. The palaces of all the cardinals (even that of the Cardinal Colonna who was not with the army) were sacked, except those wherein enormous sums of money were raised to save the merchants who had taken refuge there with their goods, together with the persons and goods of many others.

And some of those who came to an agreement with the Spaniards were later either plundered by the Germans or had to make a settlement with them. The Marquise of Mantua settled for her palace at a price of

---

* An hour before sunset.

GERMAN LANDSKNECHTS

Engraving by Hans Sebald Beham,
1544 (COURTESY OF GABINETTO NAZION-
ALE DELLE STAMPE, ROME)

fifty thousand ducats, which were paid by merchants and others who had
taken refuge there: the rumor ran that her son Don Ferrando participated
in it to the sum of ten thousand. The Cardinal of Siena who, by ancient
tradition of his forefathers, was devoted to the empire, was taken prisoner
by the Germans after he had paid the Spaniards for his own safety, and
for his palace; he had to pay a ransom of five thousand ducats to the
Germans after they had sacked his palace and led him about the Borgo
bareheaded, buffeting him. The cardinals della Minerva and Ponsetta
suffered almost similar indignities, taken prisoner by the Germans, paying
ransoms, and then first one and then the other led in procession all through
the city of Rome. The Spanish and German prelates and cardinals who
felt safe from receiving indignities of their own nations, were captured
and treated no less cruelly than the others. Hearing the cries and miserable
shrieks of Roman women, and nuns led in droves by the soldiers to satisfy
their lust, one could not but say that God's judgments were beclouded
and concealed from mortal men, inasmuch as He allowed the renowned
chastity of the Roman women to be so miserably and brutally violated.
On every side were heard the endless lamentations of those being cruelly
tormented, partly to force them to pay ransoms, and partly to reveal
where they had hidden their possessions. All sacred objects, the sacraments and the relics of the saints with which all the churches were full,
were bespoiled of their ornaments and thrown on the ground; to which
German barbarism added infinite insults. And whatever remained after
the soldiers' plunder (which were the basest things), were carried off

by those peasants of the lands of the Colonnas, who came afterward. Even the Cardinal Colonna, who arrived (I believe) on the following day, saved many women who had fled into his house. And it was said that, counting money, gold, silver and jewels, the sack amounted to more than one million ducats, but that an even greater sum had been extracted by ransoms.

The same day that the imperial troops took Rome, Count Guido [Rangoni] arrived with the light cavalry and eight hundred arquebusiers at the Ponte Salario to enter Rome the same evening; but when he heard of what had happened, he withdrew to Otricoli where the rest of his troops joined him. For notwithstanding the letters received from Rome scorning his help, he had nevertheless continued his march, not wishing to besmirch his reputation to be the man who had saved Rome. Nor were those people lacking (as it is within the nature of men to judge their own actions benignly and mildly, but severely censure the actions of others) who reprehended Count Guido for not having known how to take advantage of a noble opportunity. For the imperials, all of them so intent on rich booty, and emptying houses in their search for hidden treasure, and in taking prisoners, and carrying off to safe places what they had already plundered, were dispersed all over the city, without orderly fixed quarters, without recognizing their ensigns, without obeying the commandments of their captains; so that many believed that if Count Guido and his troops had quickly marched into Rome, not only would they have brought about the Pope's liberation simply by presenting themselves at the Castello, which was neither besieged nor guarded outside by anyone, but also some glorious feat of arms would have befallen them, the enemy being so busy pillaging that it would have been difficult for them to put together any sizeable force for whatever reason: it was more than certain that for some days longer, at any rate, no soldier was going to report to his post and flag, should he be so ordered by his captains or should he be called to arms because of some incident. But men often persuade themselves that if such and such a thing were done, or not done, certain effects would follow, but if one could see the actual results thereof, such judgments would often be found fallacious.

The Pope Remains in Captivity While the Duke of Urbino Dallies

MEANWHILE the Duke of Urbino, having heard of what had happened at Rome, although he affirmed that he wished to help the Pope with all his forces, nevertheless, considering this to be an opportunity to seize Perugia from the hands of Gentile Baglioni, who was maintained in power there by the Pope's authority, and to restore it to the rule of Giampaolo's sons, approached Perugia with the Venetian regiments, and by threats, forced Gentile to leave. A guard under commanders dependent on Malatesta and Orazio, one of whom was in the Castel Sant' Angelo and the other in Lombardy with Venetian troops, was left in Perugia by the Duke; and after three days had been spent in this affair, he marched on the 15th or 16th of May to Orvieto. The road which he took from his quarters at Cortona to go beyond the Tiber toward Rome had resulted in great delay.

At Orvieto all the leaders of the army met together to decide on future actions. At these discussions, the Duke of Urbino showed great ardor at the beginning of his speech, but then set forth many difficulties, calling upon all of them to remember to think about a safe path of retreat if they should not succeed in bringing help to the Castello; therefore he wanted hostages from Orvieto for assurance that on his return they would not fail to provide food supplies for his army. And a great deal of time being consumed in these discussions, he finally resolved to be at Nepi on the 19th, and that on the same day the Marquis with his forces, and Count Guido with his Italian infantry, should be at Bracciano, so that all of them would go on the following day to Isola, nine miles from Rome . . . The Pope knew about the coming of these armies through letters written by his Lieutenant General, Guicciardini, from Viterbo. This was why, the accord being almost concluded between him and the imperials, he refused to subscribe to the articles . . .

The French were ready to come to the help of the Castello, and the Venetians intensified their disposition with warm letters, the Prince having spoken to them ardently in the Council of the Pregati. Therefore, no other excuse remaining to the Duke, he wanted a muster of all the armies to be made on the following day, hoping perchance to find the number so diminished he would have good cause to refuse to give battle. But this stratagem proved in vain, because although many were gone, there still remained more than fifteen thousand footsoldiers in the army, goodspirited, and all resolved to fight. The muster having been taken, they held a council on what should be done. Many proposed that they go and encamp at the Cross of Montemario (as those from the Castello strongly urged), alleging that being in strong quarters and three miles from Rome, there was nothing to fear that the imperials would issue forth to set up quarters outside of Rome. They could therefore remain there and retire without danger, and from that place they might know better what to do, and better execute their plans of succoring the Castello when the opportunity occurred.

But this resolution did not please the Duke, who accepted a proposal put forward earlier by Guido Rangoni, offering to march that same night to the Castello with all the horsemen and footsoldiers of the Church to attempt to liberate the Pope; provided that the Duke of Urbino with the rest of the army would march up to Tre Capanne to lend him support. But this plan was not carried out that night because the Duke, goaded by the others, rode ahead to reconnoiter the quarters at Montemario; nevertheless, night approaching, he did not pass Tre Capanne. But since many hours had been vainly lost in these proceedings, it was necessary to defer for a future night the carrying out of their decision.

But the same day, the Duke, referring to certain spies (whether true or suborned) who had informed him that the trenches dug by the imperials in Prati were better than they actually were, and that the wall of the corridor going from the Vatican palace to the Castel Sant' Angelo had been broken in several places (which was also false) in order to immediately rush help from all sides, should troops be discovered, pointed out many difficulties, all of which were seconded by Guido and approved by almost all the other captains. Hence it was concluded that it was impossible to come to the aid of the Castello at that time, and some of the other captains who disputed this decision and strove to defend the opposite opinion were bitterly rebutted by the Duke.

Thus the Pope remained in captivity, not even a single lance being broken to free from imprisonment one who had levied so many soldiers, spent infinite sums of money, and stirred almost the entire world into war.

Nevertheless, they did discuss whether that which was not being done at present might not be done in the future with much greater forces; regarding this plan, proposed by the Duke, he himself pointed out that undoubtedly the Castello would be saved whenever there should be a true number of sixteen thousand Swiss in the army levied by decree of the cantons, not reckoning among these those that were already in the army, as they had already been rendered useless because of their long stay in Italy; and besides the Swiss, ten thousand Italian arquebusiers, three thousand sappers and forty artillery pieces. He requested the Pontiff's deputy Guicciardini to recommend to the Pope (who, it was understood, had enough food supplies for several weeks) that he defer coming to an agreement until they could put together these forces. The Lieutenant General [Guicciardini] replied that he agreed with his proposal, in case the state of affairs should not change in the meantime, but it was very likely that those in Rome at this time would make the rescue more difficult by constructing new trenches and fortifications, and also that the troops that had been brought to Naples in the Viceroy's fleet would come to Rome. The Lieutenant General wanted to know what hope he could give the Holy Father should these things occur, as was likely. He replied that in such a case he would do as much as possible, adding that by joining the forces at Naples with those in Rome, there would be in all more than twelve thousand German landsknechts, and eight to ten thousand Spanish footsoldiers; and so if the Castello were lost, one could not count on winning the war unless they actually had at least twenty-two or twenty-four thousand Swiss.

Everyone having rejected these demands as impossible, the army withdrew on June 1st to Monteruosi, notwithstanding the fact that the Pope, in order to gain advantage in the negotiations for an agreement, had strongly requested that it postpone its departure; and the same night, Piermaria Rosso and Alessandro Vitello with two hundred light cavalry went to face the enemy at Rome.

Ever less hopeful of receiving help, and fearing for his life at the hands of the Germans and the Colonna footsoldiers, the Pope had sent a message to Siena calling the Viceroy to Rome, hoping also to receive better conditions from him. The Viceroy came eagerly, believing that he was to be made captain-general of the army. But when he arrived at Rome, where he entered under a safe-conduct from the captains of the army, and found that the German and Spanish infantry (who had elected the Prince of Orange as their captain-general after the death of Bourbon) were ill disposed toward him, he had not dared remain there. But as he was marching toward Naples, he met the Marquis del Guasto, Don Ugo [di Moncada] and Alarcon en route, and returned to Rome at their advice. Nevertheless, not being welcome to the army, he no longer possessed any authority either in the affairs of the war, or with regard to the treaty of peace with the Pontiff.

Thus, having finally lost all hope, the Pope came to an agreement with the imperials on the 6th of June, almost under the same conditions with which he might have come to an agreement earlier; namely, that the Pontiff was to pay 400,000 ducats to the army, that is 100,000 now (which would be paid out of the silver and gold money hidden in the Castello), 50,000 within twenty days and 250,000 within two months, assigning for these payments a pecuniary tax to be levied on the entire Ecclesiastical Domain; that he should place the Castel Sant' Angelo, the fortresses of Ostia, Civitavecchia and Civita Castellana, and the cities of Piacenza, Parma and Modena in the hands of the Emperor to hold as long as he saw fit; that he should remain prisoner in the Castello with all the cardinals who were with him—that is, thirteen—until such time as the first 150,000 ducats had been paid; then the Pope and the cardinals in the castle should go to Naples or Gaeta and wait there until the Emperor determined what further action should be taken with regard to them; that he should hand over the archbishops Sipontino and Pisano, the bishops of Pistoia and Verona, Iacopo Salviati, Simone da Circasoli and Lorenzo, the brother of the Cardinal de' Ridolfi, as hostages to the army by way of guarantees of the payments (of which one-third belonged to the Spaniards). That Renzo da Ceri, Alberto Pio, Orazio Baglioni,

Cavalier Casale, ambassador of the King of England, and all the others who had taken refuge in the Castello, except the Pope and the cardinals, should have freedom to depart safely. That the Pope should absolve the Colonnas of the censures which they had incurred, and that when he would be led outside of Rome, a legate should remain there in his name, and the Provost of the Sacred Roman Rota* to administer justice.

When this agreement had been reached, Captain Alarcon entered into the Castello with three companies of Spanish footsoldiers and three companies of German footsoldiers. Assigned to guard the Castello and the person of the Pontiff, Alarcon performed his duty with the greatest diligence, keeping the Pope under very strict guard, restricting him to very narrow quarters, and allowing him very little liberty.

But the other fortresses and towns which had been promised were not so easily consigned; for the castle of Civita Castellana was held in the name of the allies; and Andrea Doria refused to turn over the castle of Civitavecchia, although the Pope had commanded him to do so, unless he were first paid 14,000 ducats, which he claimed were owing to him in salary. The architect, Giuliano Leno, a Roman, went to Parma and Piacenza in the name of the Pope; and Ludwig, Count of Lodron, in the name of the captains; commanding those cities to obey the will of the Emperor, although the Pope had secretly advised them to the contrary. But these cities, abhorring Spanish domination, refused to permit them to enter. But the Modenese were no longer in command of their own city, for the Duke of Ferrara, not neglecting the opportunity which the Pope's misfortunes threw his way, was threatening to destroy the already mature grain harvest, and on the 6th of June forced them to render up the city to him. And although the Duke had but small forces with him, Count Lodovico** Rangoni, to his shame, departed without making any show of resistance. The Duke's action showed how much he scorned the authority of the Venetians, who had counseled him not to undertake any innovations against the Church at such a time. Nevertheless they did not forbear doing what they were dissuading others not to do. For they came to an agreement with the Guelfs of Ravenna, sent footsoldiers there under the pretext of guarding it against the Cotignuolo Guelfs, and thus appropriated that city for themselves; and having secretly slain the castellan, they also occupied the fortress, making it known that they wished to hold it in the name of the entire League. A few days later they seized Cervia and the Pope's salt flats that were there. And since the Pope's domain was neither guarded nor defended by anyone, except insofar as the people did so in their own interest, Sigismondo Malatesta seized the city and fortress of Rimini with similar ease.

* The Supreme Court of the Church.
** Thus in the text. G. probably means Guido.

Medici Rule Overthrown Again and the Third Florentine Republic Established

Nor did the Pope have any better fortune in the city of Florence. For as soon as news of the fall of Rome arrived, the Cardinal of Cortona, terrified at finding himself abandoned by those citizens who professed to be friends of the Medici, and having no way of providing the money, except by violent and extraordinary means, and unwilling out of avarice to dip into his own purse, at least until something were known about the progress of the armies marching to help the Pope, and without being forced by necessity (for there were many soldiers in the city, and the people, terrified at the incidents following upon the seizure of the palace, would not have dared make a move), decided to yield to fortune; and when he had convoked the citizenry, he left the administration of the Republic freely up to them, having obtained certain privileges and exemptions, and the right for the Pope's nephews to remain in Florence as private citizens, each of them to be pardoned for all the things which he had committed against the state in the past.

These matters settled, the Cardinal and the Pope's nephews went to Lucca on the 16th of May; where quickly repenting for having departed so pusillanimously, the Cardinal tried to retain the fortresses of Pisa and Livorno which were in the hands of castellans friendly to the Pope; nevertheless within a very few days these castellans, having lost all hope of help because of the Pope's captivity, and also having received some money, delivered these fortresses to the Florentines.

Meanwhile, the Florentines having brought the city back to popular government, created Niccolò Capponi, a citizen of great authority and a lover of liberty, as Gonfaloniere of Justice for one year, with the right to be confirmed within three years. Above all, Capponi desired harmony among the citizens and wanted the government to be organized as a republic in the most perfect form possible; and when on the following day he had convoked the Grand Council, in which resided the absolute power of establishing laws and creating all the magistrates, he spoke as follows:*

[* This speech is lacking in the oldest Codex, the author writing "leave space of three pages." Subsequent printed editions of the *Storia d'Italia* either indicate the missing speech with asterisks, or substitute the speech found in Benedetto Varchi: *Storia Fiorentina*.]

* * *

The Gonfaloniere's words were most grave and his advice certainly most wise, and had the citizens lent faith to them, their new-found liberty perhaps would have endured longer. But since there is more disdain in those who regain their liberty than in those who defend it, and since the hatred against the name of the Medici was great for many reasons, most of all for having had to support, in large part with their own monies, ventures begun by the Medici (for it is manifest that the Florentines had spent in the seizure, and later defense of the duchy of Urbino, more than 500,000 ducats, and the same amount in the war made by Leo against the King of France; and that they had spent 300,000 ducats in those things resulting from the same war after his death, which were paid to the imperial captains and the Viceroy before the creation of Clement and after; and now, more than 600,000 ducats in the war against the Emperor); for these reasons, they began to persecute excessively those citizens who had been friends of the Medici, and to vilify the name of the Pope. They violently defaced and destroyed the insignia of the Medici family all over the city, even those placed on edifices built by them; smashed the images of Leo and Clement which were in the church of the Annunziata, famous all over the world; they confiscated pontifical properties in exaction and collection of old debts, omitting nothing, most of them, likely to arouse the Pope to anger and stir up dissension and discord in the city; and disorders would have multiplied if the authority and wisdom of the Gonfaloniere had not interposed, which however was not sufficient to remedy such widespread turmoil.

Treaty Between France and England

In France preparation for a new war had been made long before; and on the 23rd of April, the treaty which had been under consideration for many months was drawn up between the King of France and the King of England, as follows: that [Mary] the daughter of the King of England should marry either the King of France or the Duke of Orléans, his second son, and that when the two kings met, which was planned to take place during Pentecost, between Calais and Boulogne, they would decide which of the two should marry her. The King of England would relinquish his claim to the kingdom of France, receiving in compensation thereof a yearly pension of 50,000 ducats. That the King of England would enter the League drawn up at Rome, obliging himself to engage in war against the Emperor beyond the mountains all through next

July with nine thousand footsoldiers, and the King of France with eighteen thousand and a suitable number of lances and artillery. That in the meanwhile both should send ambassadors to the Emperor advising him of the confederation which they had entered into, demanding that he set free the King's children and sign a peace treaty with honorable conditions; and if, within a month, he refused to accept these proposals, they would declare war against him.

As soon as this agreement was reached, the King of England immediately entered the League, and he and the King of France sent two men by post to advise the Emperor of their intentions. These actions were carried out by the French and English ambassadors more promptly than they had been done at the Pope's commission. For his nuncio, Baldassare da Castiglione,* declaring that it was better not to exacerbate the Emperor's mind too much, had refused to go along with the declaration of war.

But then when news of the loss of Rome reached France, the great pleasure the King took in learning about Bourbon's death tempered his lesser displeasure in learning of the Pope's imprisonment. The King thought it inadvisable to permit Italian affairs to run their course, and so he came to an agreement on the 15th of May with the Venetians to raise ten thousand Swiss in common, he paying the first payment and the Venetians the second and thus successively; and to send ten thousand French footsoldiers under Pedro Navarro,** and the Venetians should raise ten thousand Italian footsoldiers between them and the Duke of Milan; and to send again five hundred lances and eighteen pieces of artillery.

But the King of England, despite the agreement reached, did not concur in waging war outside of Italy, a war which was also not satisfactory to the King of France, since each of them wanted to keep the conflict as far as possible from his own realm. Therefore, they dispensed with that obligation and agreed that the King of England should pay for the maintenance of ten thousand footsoldiers to be employed in the Italian wars over a period of six months. It was also primarily at the English King's insistence that Lautrec was declared captain-general of the entire army, although almost against his will.

While Lautrec was making preparations to cross the mountains with

---

*Author of *The Courtier*, one of the most celebrated "model" books of the Renaissance.

** Navarro, captured by the French at the battle of Ravenna in 1515, was imprisoned in the Castle of Loches. King Ferdinand would not pay his ransom; and after three years Navarro entered the army of Francis I. He spent the rest of his life as a French officer. Such fluid loyalties were not uncommon at the time; the Duke of Bourbon being the conspicuous example in the other direction.

the necessary supplies of money and other provisions, nothing of great moment took place in Italy. For the imperial army did not leave Rome, despite the fact that every day more of them were dying because of the bitter plague, which at that time was raging also in Florence and many parts of Italy.

. .
.

The plague also invaded the Castel Sant' Angelo to the great peril of the Pontiff's life, several of whose personal retainers died. Afflicted by so many woes, and having no hope in anything except the clemency of the Emperor, the Pope (with the consent of the captains) appointed as his legate Alexander, Cardinal Farnese; although when the latter had by this opportunity gotten out of the Castello and left Rome, he refused to go on the legation. The captains wanted to bring the Pope to Gaeta with the thirteen cardinals who were with him, but he managed to convince them otherwise with much adroitness, petitions and diligence.

Meanwhile, the Emperor had learned of the Pope's captivity, by letters which the Grand Chancellor, who was coming to Italy at the Emperor's orders, had written to him from Munich (the Emperor recalling him at once). And although Charles showed in words how greatly he was disturbed by this news, nevertheless it could be gathered that in secret he was most pleased. Indeed, he did not entirely abstain from giving outward sign of this, since the receipt of this news did not interrupt the festivities which were already under way for the birth of his son. But since the Pontiff's liberation was so greatly desired by the King of England and the Cardinal of York, and since the concern of such authoritative persons also influenced the King of France (who otherwise, if he had recovered his sons, would have been little moved by the Pope's woes and those of all of Italy), they both sent conjointly ambassadors to the Emperor demanding his liberation as a thing which was the common concern of all Christian princes and the particular responsibility of the Emperor, under whose pledge and by whose captains and army the Pope had been reduced to such misery. And at the same time, they requested that the cardinals who were in Italy, together with those outside, should meet at Avignon to consult at so difficult a time what was to be done for the good of the Church. But the cardinals refused to go there in order not to place themselves entirely in the hands of such powerful princes, although they offered various excuses. On the other hand the Cardinal de' Salviati, Legate at the French court, whom the Pope asked to go to the Emperor to help his situation, at the arrival of Don Ugo [di Moncada] (whose coming there had been agreed upon in the capitulation), refused to do so, as if it were a pernicious thing that so many cardinals should be in the Emperor's power; but he sent by one of his chamberlains the instructions which he had received from Rome, to the auditor of the chamber* who reported back with words most gracious, but of ambiguous import, that could be variously interpreted. The Emperor would have desired that the Pontiff in person be led to Spain; nevertheless—both because it was an infamous thing and in order not to irritate the King of England too much, and because all the grandees of Spain, especially the prelates and lords, were greatly displeased that he who represented Christ on earth should be held in prison by the Roman Emperor, protector and advocate of the Church— therefore, having replied in kindly fashion to those ambassadors, and to the request for peace they were making of him, that he was content that this should be negotiated by the King of England (which was accepted by them), on the 3rd of August he sent the General** to Italy, and four days later, Veri di Miglau, each of them (according to rumor) with instructions to the Viceroy for the liberation of the Pontiff and restitution of all towns and fortresses which had been taken from him. In support of these instructions, he also agreed that his Nuncio should send him certain sums of money, exacted from the collections of those realms wherein the courts had refused to contribute money to the Emperor.

. .
.

Meanwhile there were very few actions of war in Italy, since there was great anxiety over Lautrec's arrival. For the imperial army—all in disorder and having rejected obedience to their captains, a heavy trial to their friends and to the towns surrendered—moved not, nor frightened their enemies in the slightest. The Spanish and Italian footsoldiers, fleeing the contagion of the plague, remained scattered about Rome; the Prince of Orange with a hundred and fifty horsemen had gone to Siena to flee the plague and to keep that city loyal to the Emperor. Earlier they had sent some infantry there because the Sienese, stirred up by seditious leaders, had tumultuously sacked the houses of the citizens of the Monte de' Nove and slain Pietro Borghesi, a notable citizen, together with one of his sons, and sixteen or eighteen others.

In Rome there only remained the Germans contaminated with the plague; the Pope had had the greatest difficulty in satisfying them with the first 150,000 ducats, partly with money, partly with agreements made with Genoese merchants for the tithes of the realm of Naples and for the sale of Benevento. For the rest of the money due them, the Germans demanded other guarantees and allotment of sums other than the impost taxes on the Ecclesiastical State, things which were impossible for the imprisoned Pope.

Therefore, after direfully threatening the hostages, keeping them

* Resident with the Emperor.
** Of the Franciscans.

enchained with great cruelty, they led them ignominiously to the Campo de' Fiore, where they erected a gallows, as if they were about to immediately inflict that punishment upon them. Then they departed from Rome without any captains of authority, wandering about and renewing their supplies rather than stirring up any real trouble: and when they had sacked the cities of Terni and Narni, the city of Spoleto agreed to give them passage and provisions. Therefore, the army of the allies went to establish its quarters at Pontenuovo beyond Perugia, for the protection of Perugia. First the army encamped near the Lake of Perugia, but very diminished in numbers with respect to its obligation to the allies. For with the Marquis of Saluzzo there were three hundred lances and three hundred French archers, three thousand Swiss and a thousand Italian infantry; with the Duke of Urbino fifty thousand men-at-arms, three hundred light horse, one thousand German infantry and two thousand Italians. The Venetians impudently and dishonestly offered the excuse that they were fulfilling their obligations with the troops that they kept in the duchy of Milan. The Florentines had eighty thousand men-at-arms, one hundred and fifty light horse, and four thousand footsoldiers, being necessarily better prepared than the others because of their fear, which they felt always, that the imperials would assault Tuscany; hence they paid their troops at the stipulated times, which was just the opposite of what the others did. But the Duke of Urbino, besides his old troubles, was greatly displeased and almost desperate, knowing that the King of France and Lautrec, both charging him with infidelity, did not speak honorably of him. Even more distressing to him was the fact that the Venetians held him in the lowest esteem; for having become suspicious of either his fidelity or constancy, they had placed his wife and son, who were in Venice, under strict guard, so that they could not leave without permission; and they openly criticized his recommendation, which was that Lautrec should march toward Rome without attempting any actions in Lombardy.

Therefore, everything was lazily asleep in that army, who held it as a sign of grace that the imperials did not draw nearer. A little later, after having received two scudi apiece from the Marquis del Guasto who came to the army, the Germans (who had gotten along badly with the Spanish) returned to Rome, and the Spaniards and Italians scattered about at Alviano, Tigliano, Castiglione della Teverina, and toward Bolsena; but the plague had so decimated the numbers of the Germans especially, that it was believed that there only remained ten thousand footsoldiers in all the Emperor's armies.

But before their departure, the captains of the League committed an act worthy of eternal shame. For when Gentile Baglioni returned to

Perugia at the wish of Orazio, who had shown signs of reconciliation, declaring that their disagreements were harmful and dangerous for everyone, Federico da Bozzole went there to get Gentile to understand that since it had been known that he was dealing secretly with the enemy, they intended to make certain of him. And although Gentile offered justifications of his actions, and promised to go to Castiglione del Lago, Federico left him under guard to Gigante Corso, a Venetian colonel; but that same evening he was slain, together with two of his nephews, by some of Orazio's henchmen, and at his orders; and on the same day, Orazio had Galeotto, brother to Braccio and also a nephew of Gentile, assassinated outside of Perugia.

The Pontiff Departs from the Castel Sant' Angelo after Signing a Humiliating Treaty

Finally, after lengthy negotiations, there was concluded in Rome on the last day of October a treaty with the General* and Serenon, in the name of Don Ugo, who ratified it afterward: that the Pope would offer no opposition to the Emperor in Milan or Naples; that he would concede to him the crusade in Spain, and one-tenth of ecclesiastical revenues in all his realms; that Ostia and Civitavecchia (which Andrea Doria had previously given up) would remain in the Emperor's hands as security for the observance of the treaty; that Civita Castellana should be consigned to him, which town had refused to admit imperial troops, after Mario Perusco, the fiscal procurator, had entered the fortress by secret orders of the Pope, although he had pretended to the contrary; that similarly, the fortress of Forlì should be delivered up to the Emperor, and Ippolito and Alessandro, the Pope's nephews, given as hostages, and until they came to Parma, the cardinals Pisano, Trivulzio and Gaddi, whom the Pope's nephews had led with them into the kingdom of Naples; that the Pope should immediately pay the Germans 67,000 ducats, and 35,000 to the Spaniards. These conditions fulfilled, the imperials would release him with all his cardinals, and they would leave the Castel Sant' Angelo and Rome, considering himself free once he had been brought safely to Orvieto, Spoleto or Perugia. And that within fifteen days after his departure from Rome, he should pay again a similar sum to the Germans, and the rest later (which together with the first payment amounted to more than

---

* Francesco Quiñones, General of the Franciscans, Cardinal of Santa Croce.

350,000 ducats) should be paid within three months to the Germans and the Spaniards, according to their portions.*

In order to be able to carry out these agreements and get out of prison, the Pontiff had recourse to those remedies which he had not wanted to adopt in order not to enter there; and so for money he created some cardinals, for the most part persons unworthy of such an honor; besides this, he conceded the tithes in the kingdom of Naples and the power to dispose of Church property. Thus those things dedicated to the cult of God were, by concession of the Vicar of Christ, put to the use and maintenance of heretics (so unfathomable is divine justice).

By these means, having settled and guaranteed the payments at the stipulated times, and having given as hostages, as security for the troops, the cardinals Cesis and Orsini, who were brought by Cardinal Colonna to Grottaferrata; and having expedited everything and fixed the ninth of December as the date when the Spaniards would accompany him to a safe place, the Pope, fearing some change of plan because of the ill will which he knew Don Ugo bore him, or for any other reason that might disrupt the agreement, secretly stole out of the Castello early the night before, in the guise of a merchant, and was accompanied up to Montefiascone by Luigi da Gonzaga, an imperial soldier, who was waiting for him at Prati with a large company of arquebusiers. At Montefiascone almost all the footsoldiers were dismissed, and Luigi himself accompanied the Pope to Orvieto, into which city he entered by night, unaccompanied by any of his cardinals. Certainly a most noteworthy example, something perhaps which has never happened since the Church became great: that a Pope, fallen from such power and reverence, is held in captivity, loses Rome, and his entire domain falls into the power of others; and that the same Pope, within the space of a few months, is restored to liberty, that which was taken from him is restored, and in a very short time, he is once more returned to his former greatness. So authoritative is the papacy among Christian princes, and the respect which all of them have for it.

. .
.

The Pope wrote a letter to Lautrec, thanking him for his efforts to obtain his freedom and for having counseled him to seek freedom under any circumstances. These efforts had been of great importance in constraining the imperials to come to a decision [to set him free]. Hence the

---

* In these last four books, Guicciardini frequently interposes the word *credo*—"I believe"—before specific figures, indicating that he intends to check further. In fact, the word is rarely found in the first sixteen books—another rebuttal to Ranke's condemnation of Guicciardini for uncritical use of sources (Gherardi, *op. cit.*, IV, 152).

Pope acknowledged himself no less bound to the King and to himself than if he had been liberated by their arms, whose progress he would have voluntarily waited for if necessity had not forced him, for the conditions proposed were continually changing for the worse, and because he had plainly understood that his liberation could not be effected by way of a treaty; and the longer this was deferred, into so much the worse a state fell the authority and domain of the Church: but above all he had been motivated by the hope of having served as an opportune instrument who would deal with his King and the other Christian princes for the common good.

Such were his words at the beginning, sincere and simple as seemed proper to the pontifical office, the words of a Pope especially who had suffered such grievous and bitter admonitions from God. Nevertheless, since his usual nature had not changed, nor had his imprisonment deprived him of his astuteness or greed, when the men sent by Lautrec and Gregory Casale, ambassador of the King of England, had arrived at the Pope's court (the year 1528 already having begun) to urge him to confederate with the others, the Pope began to give various replies: now giving them hope, now excusing himself that having neither men, money nor authority, such a declaration on his part would be useless to them, and yet might be harmful to himself, for it would give cause to the imperials to do him harm in many places; now indicating that he would like to satisfy this demand if Lautrec would advance: a thing which he greatly desired to make the Germans leave Rome. For they were destroying the relics of that miserable city and all the surrounding towns, utterly disobeying their captains, and frequently rioting among themselves, refusing to depart, and demanding new money and ransoms.

The King of France Challenges the Emperor to Single Combat. Henry VIII Seeks to Nullify His Marriage with Catherine of Aragon

Thus as preparations for war continually intensified, hatred among princes became ever more inflamed, each of them seizing upon any occasion to insult and contend with each other, no less with stratagems and rivalries than with arms. For about two years before in Granada, at the time when, in like fashion, the peace treaty between himself and the King of France was being negotiated, the Emperor had spoken to the President of Grenoble, ambassador of the King of France, certain words inferring that in order that their differences should not cause Christian peoples and so many innocent persons to suffer any longer, he would be willing to settle these disputes with him in single combat. Later he had repeated the same words to the herald, when not long ago the latter had declared war on him, adding further that the French King had behaved villainously in failing to maintain his given pledge. When the King of France had heard these speeches, he felt that he could not let them pass by in silence without ignominy (although the Emperor's challenge was perhaps more worthy to be made between knights than princes of such eminence). On the 27th of March in a very large hall of his palace in Paris, the King of France assembled all his princes, ambassadors and his entire court, then made his own appearance in very great pomp, wearing his richest garb amidst a very ornate company, and sat down upon the throne, and had the Emperor's ambassador summoned. The latter demanded that he be dispatched forthwith, inasmuch as it had been decided that when this ambassador had been brought to Bayonne he should be liberated at the same time as the ambassadors of the allies, who were being brought to Bayonne for the same purpose.

The King then spoke, justifying his actions, on the ground that the Emperor, by unheard of and inhuman examples holding the French ambassador and those of his allies, was therefore the principal cause why he also was being held; but now that he was to go to Bayonne in order that all of them would be set free at one time, he wished him to bear his letter to the Emperor, and to deliver a message from him in this wise: that when the Emperor had told the herald that the French King had failed in his pledge, he had spoken falsely, and that as many times as he repeated it that many times he was lying; and that instead of a reply, in order not to delay settlement of their quarrel, he would notify him of the field where both of them were to fight. And when the ambassador refused to bear such a letter and deliver such a message, the King then added that he would send it by the herald, which he would understand just as well; and knowing furthermore that he had impugned the honor of his brother, the King of England, yet he was not speaking of that because he knew the King was able to defend himself, but if he should be impeded in so doing by bodily indisposition, he offered to put his person to the test for him.

A few days later, the King of England issued a similar challenge, with similar solemnity and ceremony. Surely it hardly redounded to the honor of the princes of Christendom, that while waging among themselves wars of such importance and so prejudicial to all of Christendom, they should also trouble their minds with such ideas.

. .
.

And yet, amidst the great heat of war and clash of arms, the King of England was not deflected from his amatory involvements: so passionately indeed were these beginning to flood his soul that they gave rise at last to horrible and unheard of cruelty and wickedness. To his great and eternal shame, he who had acquired from Pope Leo the title of Defender of the Faith because he had shown himself most observant to the Apostolic See, and because he had had a book written in his own name against the impious and poisonous heresy of Martin Luther, now became known and was entitled an impious oppressor and persecutor of the Christian religion.

The King of England had as wife Catherine, daughter of Ferdinand and Isabella, sovereigns of Spain, a queen certainly worthy of such parents and held in the highest love and veneration in the entire realm because of her virtue and prudence. While Henry VII was alive, she had been first married to Arthur, his eldest son; but no sooner had she slept with him than she became a widow by her husband's untimely death and was by common agreement of her father and father-in-law married to Henry, the younger brother, after a dispensation from Pope Julius had been received because of the impediment of so close an alliance. Of this marriage a male child had been born, but after he had been torn from them by his untimely death, no other children were born, except a daughter [Mary Tudor]. This gave occasion for many persons in the court to murmur that they had been deprived of male issue because the marriage was illegal and not subject to the highest dispensation.

Because of this, and because he knew of the King's desire for sons, the Cardinal of York* seized this opportunity and began to persuade the King that he should repudiate his first wife who in justice was not his wife, and contract another matrimony; being moved in this not by conscience or a simple yearning that the King should have male issue, but because he was convinced that he could induce the King to take as his wife Renée, daughter of King Louis; which he desired extremely, for, knowing himself to be hated by the entire realm, he wanted to prepare himself against anything that might happen both during the King's life and after his death. He was also induced to this by the great hatred he had conceived against the Emperor, who was not satisfying his boundless pride either by outward shows or deeds: and in view of the great prestige which the King and he had with the Pope, he had no doubts that he would obtain from him the legal right to grant a divorce.

The King lent ear to this counsel, not because he was influenced by those ends which the Cardinal of York had in mind, but moved (as many said) less by his desire to have sons than by the fact that he was enamored of a maid-in-waiting to the Queen, a person of low birth, whom the King

---

* Thomas Wolsey, Cardinal, and Archbishop of York.

HENRY VIII

Portrait by Hans Holbein in Corsini Gallery, Rome (COURTESY OF FRATELLI ALINARI)

had set upon to take for wife. When this plan, which had not been known to the Cardinal of York or to the others, began to reveal itself or be conjectured about, the Cardinal of York had no means of dissuading him from the divorce, for he would have lost prestige by advising him to the contrary of that to which he had previously persuaded him. The King was already asking the opinions of theologians, lawyers, and prelates, many of whom had advised him that his marriage was not valid, either because they really believed this, or else (as men are wont to do) to satisfy their Prince.

Therefore, when the Pope was liberated from prison, the King sent ambassadors to him urging him to enter into the League, and to work for the restitution of Ravenna (according to his instructions), but principally to obtain the right of divorce; which he did not seek to have by way of a dispensation, but by a declaration that his marriage with Catherine was null and void. And the King was convinced that the Pope would easily have granted this to him because he was weak in power and reputation and not supported by the power of any other princes, and he would also be motivated by the recent benefits of great favors which he had received from the King of England with regard to his liberation, knowing especially that the Cardinal of York had great influence with the Pope since he had always favored his policies, and before that, those of Leo. And in order that the Pope could not allege any excuse of fear for the offense against the Emperor that would result from this (Charles being the son of Catherine's sister), and to entice him with a gift, he offered to stand the costs for four thousand footsoldiers appointed to guard the Pope.

The Pope hearkened to this proposal; but although he considered how important the matter was, and the great shame that might result from it, nevertheless finding himself at Orvieto and still neutral between the Emperor and the King of France, and not trusted very much by either of them, and therefore deeming it vital that he maintain his friendship with the King of England, he dared not gainsay this demand; rather, pretending to be eager to satisfy the King, but all the while procrastinating by finding difficulties in the methods proposed, he inflamed the King's hopes and importunities and those of his ministers, which were continually growing (and proved the source of many woes).

But when the Pope had heard Vaudemont and Longueville* who had been sent by the King of France, and had answered them in general terms, he sent the Bishop of Pistoia together with Longueville to the King to

---

* This paragraph, confusedly placed in the text, following as it does immediately after the matter of Henry's divorce, refers with Joycean abruptness—"Ma," "but"—to a passage long before, wherein Lautrec had sent to the Pope, Vaudemont, captain general of all the landsknechts, and Longueville, dispatched by the King of France, to solicit the Pope to declare against the Emperor.

make him realize that being without money, without forces, and without authority, his declaration would not result in any consequences for the allies; he could only benefit from a peace treaty, and that therefore he had commissioned the Bishop to go to the Emperor to urge him with rigorous words to such a treaty. But the King would not agree to this, for although he was not dissatisfied by the Pope's neutrality, he suspected that he might be sending the Bishop to make another deal altogether. Nor would the Emperor have been displeased if the Pope remained neutral.

[W]HILE THE WAR IS RESUMED IN NAPLES AND IN THE NORTH], THE PONTIFF PERSISTED IN HIS DETERMINATION NOT TO DECLARE HIMSELF FOR anyone: but because he was holding diverse negotiations, the King of France was already suspicious of him; nor was he in the Emperor's good graces either, if for no other reason than because he had sent the Cardinal Campeggio to England as his legate to discuss, on that island, the controversy delegated to him and the Cardinal of York.

For since that King was insisting on a declaration of nullity of his first marriage, the Pope, who had spoken many words about it with Henry's ministers (inasmuch as, finding that other princes did not trust him very much, the Pontiff made every effort to keep himself under the King's protection), had most secretly drawn up a decretal bull in which the marriage was declared invalid. This was told to the Cardinal Campeggio, and he was commissioned to show it to the King and the Cardinal of York, saying that he had a commission to publish it if acknowledgment of the King's case should not succeed prosperously in the court, so that they might more easily consent to have the case juridically debated, and tolerate with a more equitable soul the long drawn-out proceedings (which he had enjoined the Cardinal Campeggio to retard as much as he could); and not to promulgate the bull unless first he had received a new commission from the Pope. The Cardinal Campeggio tried to convince the King that the Pope's intention was ultimately to grant the divorce, which he felt he would have to do and which it is believable he had already in mind to do.

The ambassadors of the Emperor at Rome strongly protested about this appointment of the legate to England and the delegation of the case, but their objection was less authoritative because of the difficulties which the Emperor's affairs were then undergoing in the kingdom of Naples.

[*Typhus, plague, want of provisions, and deserting landsknechts create difficulties for the imperials besieged within Naples, yet they continue to hold fast against the French. The King of France suffers a great blow when the Admiral Andrea Doria, five years in his service, now goes over to the Emperor, and later withdraws his galleys and occupies Genoa, liberating his native city under the protection of the Emperor. Meanwhile Naples is furnished with food when the Venetian galleys withdraw, and now the plague strikes the French, whose commanding general, Lautrec, dies. The French are forced to lift their siege and disperse, and the victorious imperials issue forth from Naples. Their new commander, after the death of Don Ugo di Moncada, is Filibert de Chalons, Prince of Orange.]*

Now the Pope turned all his thoughts, although secretly, to the reacquisition of the state of Florence. Circumventing the French ambassadors, he engaged in various negotiations, holding out various hopes to them and the other allies that he would enter the league with them. Nevertheless, partly motivated by fear of the Emperor's greatness and his prosperous successes, and partly through hope of inducing him more easily than he could induce the King of France to help place his family back into power in Florence, he was more inclined to the Emperor than to the King of France. . . .

The Downfall of the Cardinal of York

THUS drawing closer every day to the Emperor's cause, and already being in very close touch with him, the Pontiff sent his chamberlain, the Bishop of Vazone, to Charles. And the divorce proceedings in England he referred to the higher court of the Sacra Rota*. Indeed, he would have done this long before, had he not been held back out of respect for the bull which was already in England in the hands of his legate Campeggio.

For the Emperor's power and interests having grown in Italy, the Pope not only did not wish to offend him any further, but also wanted to revoke the offense which he had already given him. Therefore, even before he became ill, he had decided to refer the divorce case to the higher court, and had sent Francesco Campana to England to Cardinal Campeggio, pretending to the King that he was sent for other reasons, although related to that case, but actually with a commission to Campeggio to burn the bull. And although Campeggio delayed in carrying this out because the Pope's illness intervened, after the Pontiff had recovered, he carried out his orders. Hence the Pope, freed of this fear, referred the matter to

* The ecclesiastical tribunal in Rome which ordinarily judges appeals from sentences emanating from the bishopric courts. Under the pontifical government it also passed judgment, and especially, in civic matters.

the higher court to the greatest indignation of that King, especially when demanding the bull of the Cardinal, he learned what had happened to it.

These things brought about the downfall of the Cardinal of York, for the King assumed that this Cardinal's authority was so great with the Pope, that if the marriage with Anne Boleyn had been acceptable to the Cardinal, he could have obtained everything he wanted from the Pope. And so angered was King Henry because of this, that he lent ear to the envy and calumny of the Cardinal's adversaries, stripped him of his money, his goods, his priceless furniture, and leaving him only a small part of his ecclesiastical revenues, he relegated him with a few servants to his bishopric. And not much later, either because he had intercepted letters which Wolsey had written to the King of France, or for some other reason, instigated by the same people who feared that the Cardinal might regain his former power, because of certain words spoken by the French King indicating that he favored him, he was cited to defend an accusation introduced against him in the Royal Council. But while he was being brought to the court as a prisoner, he suffered a stroke en route and died, either through fury or fear, on the second day of his illness: a noteworthy example in our times of the power of fortune and envy in the courts of princes.

New Disturbances in Florence. A Radical Succeeds as Gonfaloniere

At this time new disturbances to the great detriment of that regime occurred in Florence against Niccolò Capponi, Gonfaloniere, who was almost at the end of the second year of his government. These troubles were stirred up mainly by the envy of some of the leading citizens, who took advantage of the ignorance and vain suspicions of the multitude. During his entire period in office, Niccolò had kept in mind two main objectives: to defend against new envy those who had been honored by the Medici—indeed, he sought that the leading citizens of this group should participate in honors and public counsels with all the other citizens —and in those matters which did not affect their freedom, not to exacerbate the Pope.

Both of these aims were most useful to the Republic, for many of those persons who had been persecuted as enemies of the government, now being secure and treated well, would have been united in preserving it, especially since they knew that because of what had happened during the period of the uprising, the Pontiff took little satisfaction in their deeds.

And although the Pope ardently desired the return of the Medici, yet not being provoked anew, he had less reason to plunge into the situation and to complain (as he did continually) to other princes. But the ambition of some others opposed these aims, some of whom knew that if those who had been friends of the Medici, men undoubtedly of greater experience and value, were admitted into the government, their authority would be lessened. Therefore they thought of nothing else but keeping the multitude stirred up by suspicion of the Pope and of the friends of the Medici; calumniating the Gonfaloniere for these reasons (and in order that he should not obtain the prerogation of the magistracy for the third year), and charging that he was not as opposed to the Medici as the interest and prestige of the Republic required.

But the Gonfaloniere did not become upset by these calumnies, and considering it very important not to irritate the Pope, he kept in touch with him privately by letters and envoys. But these efforts were not initiated nor carried on without first informing several of the leading citizens and chief magistrates,* nor for any other end than to dissuade the Pope from any precipitous action.

But a letter received from Rome having by chance been intercepted, in which there were some expressions which might generate suspicions among those who did not know the origin and foundation of these matters, and having fallen into the hands of several of those holding the supreme magistracy, this aroused several young people to sedition, who seized the public palace by force of arms and kept the Gonfaloniere practically under arrest; and when the magistrates and many citizens had been summoned, they decided almost tumultuously that he should be deprived of his position. This was approved by the Grand Council, after which his case was referred to the examination of the law, and absolved by the court, he was accompanied to his house with the greatest honor by almost all the nobles; but Francesco Carducci took his place as gonfaloniere, a man unworthy of such honors if you consider his past life, his qualifications, and his depraved aims.

Treaty of Barcelona Between Pope and Emperor.
    *Treaty of Cambrai Between the Emperor and the
    King of France*

Thus arms had been laid aside almost everywhere in Italy as a result of the misfortunes of the French troops [in Lombardy as well as Naples], and the leading princes turned their thoughts toward various agreements.

* Members of the Signoria, or the Priors; the governing body of the city.

The first that was effectuated was between the Pope and the Emperor, drawn up in Barcelona, very favorable for the Pope; either because the Emperor wanted to pass into Italy and sought to remove obstacles, deeming the Pope's friendship necessary for this purpose; or else, wishing by means of very generous clauses, to give the Pope all the more reason to forget the wrongs which he had suffered from his ministers and from his army.

The agreement provided that there should be a perpetual peace and alliance between the Pope and the Emperor in mutual defense; that the Pope should concede passage through the Church domains to the imperial army if it wished to leave the kingdom of Naples; that with regard to the new matrimony, and for the tranquility of Italy, the Emperor would restore the young son of Lorenzo de' Medici* to the same position of greatness in Florence which his family had possessed before they were expelled (the expenses for the said restitution to be defrayed according to a stipulation between the Pope and Emperor); that he would endeavor as soon as possible, either by arms or some more suitable means, to restore Cervia, Ravenna, Modena, Reggio and Rubiera to the Pontiff, without prejudicing the claims of the empire and the Apostolic See; that once he had received the above-stated towns, the Pontiff would concede the investiture of the kingdom of Naples to the Emperor as remuneration for that benefit received, reducing the tribute of the last investiture to a white horse in acknowledgment of fealty, and would accord to the Emperor his ancient right of nomination of twenty-four cathedral churches then in dispute, the disposition of the churches which were not to be in patronage, and other benefices, remaining to the Pope; that when the Emperor passed into Italy, the Pontiff and he would meet to draw up a treaty to bring tranquility to Italy and universal peace in Christendom, receiving each other with the requisite and usual ceremonies and honors; that should the Pope ask the secular might of the Emperor to conquer Ferrara, as advocate, protector, and first-born son of the Apostolic See, he would assist him to the end with all his power, and they should agree regarding the expenses, manner and form to be employed, according to times and circumstances; that the Pontiff and the Emperor by common consent would consider some means whereby the case of Francesco Sforza might be examined legally, and by judges beyond suspicion, so that he might be restored if he were found innocent; and otherwise, although the Emperor

---

* The younger, nephew of Leo X, and therefore grandnephew of the Magnificent. When Lorenzo had died (May 4, 1519), however, he had left only one child, his infant daughter Catherine (later to become Queen of France). "The young son" referred to here was possibly the Pope's own bastard son, Alessandro "the Moor," whom Clement brought forward as an illegitimate son of Lorenzo in order to qualify him for ruler of Florence. Alessandro was seventeen years old at this time; the "new matrimony" was to be with the Emperor's daughter Margaret, then eight years old.

considered the disposition of the duchy of Milan as pertaining to him, he would dispose of it with the advice and consent of the Pope, and invest it in a person acceptable to the Pontiff, or any other way that seemed expedient for Italian peace. . . . That the Emperor and his brother Ferdinand, King of Hungary, would do everything possible in order to bring the heretics back into the true path, and the Pope would employ spiritual remedies; and if they remained contumacious, the Emperor and Ferdinand would force them by arms, and the Pope would see to it that the other Christian princes assisted according to their several means. . . .

And to make this treaty of friendship and alliance more stable, it was to be confirmed by a close family union: the Emperor promising to give his bastard daughter Margaret, with a dowry of 20,000 ducats a year, to Alessandro de' Medici, [bastard] son of Lorenzo, late Duke of Urbino, upon whom the Pope had decided to confer the temporal glory of his house; for when he had been at death's door, the Pope had created Ippolito, Giuliano's son, a cardinal.*

At the same time, in separate clauses they agreed: that the Pope would concede to the Emperor and his brother, to defend themselves against the Turks, one-fourth of the revenues of ecclesiastical benefices, in the way that his predecessor Adrian had done; that he would absolve all those who had sinned against the Apostolic See in Rome or other places, and all those who had given aid, counsel, or favor, or who had participated, or played some part in the things which had been done, or had tacitly or expressedly approved or lent their support; that inasmuch as the Emperor had not announced the crusade, which the Pope had conceded to him in less ample form than other crusades previously granted, this one would be revoked, and the Pontiff would grant him another in fuller and more ample form, like those conceded by popes Julius and Leo.

Before this agreement was reduced to writing, all difficulties having been resolved, the Emperor learned of the rout of Saint Pôl**; and although some suspected that in order to take advantage of his opportunity he might want to change some of the things discussed, nevertheless he promptly confirmed everything which had been negotiated, ratifying it the same day, which was the 9th of June, in front of the main altar of the cathedral church of Barcelona, full of innumerable spectators, and promising by solemn oath to observe the treaty.

. .
.

---

* Since the Pope and Cardinal Ippolito were also both illegitimate, the confluence of bastardies is indeed somewhat imposing. Ippolito had previously been destined as the ruler of Florence.

** François de Bourbon, Count of St. Pôl, one of the allied captains who had been defeated in his efforts to save the castle at Genoa; one of the most courageous generals of Francis I.

But negotiations for an agreement between Charles and the King of France proceeded no less warmly. After the commissions came, Cambrai was destined for this purpose, a place which proved to be the seat of the most important decisions.

Madame Margaret of Austria was to meet there with Madame the Regent [Louise of Savoy], mother of the King of France*; meanwhile, that King sought by every means and art not to come to any agreement with the Emperor, promising (although he had no intention of fulfilling his promise) the ambassadors of the allies in Italy that he would make no accord without their approval and satisfaction. For the French sovereign feared that, unbeknownst to him, they themselves might come to an agreement with him, in order not to remain excluded from the friendship of all. Therefore he made efforts to persuade them not to hope for peace, but rather to turn their thoughts toward preparations for war (having in all these intrigues the consent of the King of England).

In the course of continually dealing with these matters, the King of France dispatched the Bishop of Tarbes to Italy with a commission to go to Venice, to the Duke of Milan, to Ferrara, and to Florence, to arrange matters in connection with the war, and to promise that if the Emperor marched into Italy, the King of France would move in at the same time with a most powerful army; the other allies for their part contributing the necessary supplies.

And yet negotiations for an agreement were being constantly carried on; and for this purpose, on the 7th of July, both Ladies entered, by different gates and with great pomp, into Cambrai, and being lodged in two adjoining houses which had a common entrance leading from one to the other, they spoke together on that selfsame day, and through their agents began to deal with the details of the treaty. Meanwhile the Venetians, very fearful of the results of this gathering, were making the greatest offers to the King of France who, for his part, had gone to Compiegne where he could be closer at hand to resolve whatever difficulties might ensue.

Convening at Cambrai were not only the two Ladies, but also the Bishop of London and the Duke of Suffolk for the King of England, for these negotiations were being held with the consent and participation of that King. The Pope sent also the Archbishop of Capua, and there were the ambassadors of all the allies.

But the French reports to these ambassadors were very far from the truth of what was being discussed, for the King of France was pre-

---

* The treaty of Cambrai—the first great settlement of European affairs—is often referred to as the *Paix des Dames,* since it was negotiated by the Emperor's aunt, the Archduchess Margaret, Regent of the Low Countries, and Louise of Savoy, mother of the King of France.

sumptuous or else solely concerned with his own interests (which consisted entirely in recovering his sons). When the Florentines strongly urged him to follow the example of what his predecessor and father-in-law King Louis had done in the year 1512, namely, permit them to reach an agreement with Charles the Emperor for their own safety, he refused, declaring that he would never conclude any treaty of peace without including them in it, and that he was most prepared to wage war. Indeed, he was continually declaring the same thing to all the others, even amidst the most detailed negotiations.

. . .

Finally, on the 5th of August, the treaty of peace was solemnly announced in the main church of Cambrai. The first article of this agreement was: that the sons of the King of France should be freed, the King paying the Emperor for their ransom 1,200,000 ducats; and to the King of England for him 200,000; that within six weeks after ratification, he would restore to the Emperor all his possessions in the duchy of Milan; that he would depart from Asti and give up his claims to it; that as quickly as possible he would leave Barletta and his holdings in the kingdom of Naples; that he would solemnly declare to the Venetians that, according to the clauses of the capitulations at Cognac, they should render up the towns they had seized in Puglia; and in the event that they failed to do so he (the French King) would declare himself their enemy and help the Emperor for the recuperation thereof with thirty thousand scudi per month and twelve galleys, four ships, and four galleons, all paid for six months; that he would pay for that which was in his possession of the galleys captured at Portofino, or their value, deducting those which Andrea Doria or other agents of the Emperor had captured; that according to what had been previously covenanted at Madrid, he would renounce sovereignty over Flanders and Artois, and give up the regions of Tournai and Arras, the possession of Nivers, to release the Emperor of obligation to the state above Brabante; that he would cancel the trial of Bourbon and rehabilitate the honor of the deceased and return his goods and property to his successors (although Charles afterward complained that as soon as the King had recovered his sons, he seized these things again); that the goods and property of anyone which had been taken because of the war, should be restored either to those persons or to their successors (which also gave the Emperor cause for complaint, for the King did not restore the property of the Prince of Orange); that all letters of challenge should be considered null and void, even those of Robert de la Mark.

In this treaty, the Pope was included as the principal party, the Duke of Savoy was included in general, as a subject of the empire, and in particular as a deputy of the Emperor. The treaty also specified that the

King was not to involve himself any longer in Italian or German affairs in favor of any potentate to the prejudice of the Emperor, although the French King maintained afterward that this treaty did not prohibit him from recovering what the Duke of Savoy occupied in the realm of France, and what he claimed belonged to him by reason of Madame the Regent, his mother.

There was also a clause to the effect that the Venetians and Florentines would be understood as included in the treaty of peace in case, within four months, they settled their differences with the Emperor (which was like a tacit exclusion); and the same with regard to the Duke of Ferrara. But there was no mention of the Neapolitan barons and exiles.

The agreement having been drawn up, the King came immediately to Cambrai to visit Madame Margaret, and yet not being altogether without shame for so undignified an act, he avoided for several days, alleging various excuses, appearing before and holding audience with the allied ambassadors. Then finally, listening to them separately, he offered as his excuse that he could not have done otherwise, if he wished to recover his children; but that he was sending the Admiral* to the Emperor for their benefit. He also gave other vain hopes, promising to lend the Florentines forty thousand ducats to help them in their imminent danger, which turned out to be like his other promises. And claiming to do so for their satisfaction, he dismissed Stefano Colonna, whose services he no longer intended to employ, in order that he might enter the service of the Florentines.

Pope and Emperor Join in Preparations to Attack Florence

As soon as the Emperor had reached the accord with the Pontiff, he sent instructions to the Prince of Orange to attack, at the Pope's request, the Florentine state with his army; when he arrived at Aquila, the Prince mustered his forces at the frontiers of the kingdom. The Pope immediately urged him to continue his march; therefore on the last day of July, the Prince went to Rome without his men to arrange for supplies. At Rome, after various parleys, which were often near to breaking off because the Pope raised difficulties with regard to expenses, it was finally resolved that the Pontiff would give him thirty thousand ducats at present, and forty thousand more in a short while; in order that he, at the Emperor's expense, should first conquer Perugia, casting out Malatesta Baglioni, and bring that city under obedience to the Church; and should then assail the Florentines in order to restore the Medici family in that

---

* Philippe Chabot, Count of Charny, was made admiral of France in 1526, after the death of Bonnivet at Pavia in 1525.

city: a thing which the Pope considered very easy to do, since he was convinced that, abandoned by everyone, the Florentines would, according to the custom of their leading citizens, be more ready to yield than to put their country into grave and manifest peril.

Therefore the Prince mobilized his forces, which consisted of three thousand German footsoldiers, the last survivors of those who had come to Italy from Spain with the Viceroy, and from Germany with George Frundsberg, and four thousand unpaid Italian footsoldiers under various colonels: Pierluigi da Farnese, the Count of San Secondo, and Colonel di Marzio and Sciarra Colonna. And to satisfy the Prince, the Pope removed three cannon and some other artillery pieces out of the Castel Sant' Angelo. Following Orange, was to come the Marquis del Guasto with the Spanish footsoldiers who were in Puglia.

But in Florence, where the young people had already been armed for several months and drawn up in ordinances of militia, and where the people were most loyal to their government, intentions were quite otherwise; and they devoted themselves to raising forces and making various provisions. They had requested Stefano Colonna of the King of France as captain of the footsoldiers, and they were seeking to get Ercole d'Este, captain-general of all their troops, to ride to their aid (as he had always given them to understand he would do) with the hundred lances he commanded for the King of France. They were preparing to fortify the city and destroy all the outlying districts where there were great houses and most beautiful monasteries and edifices; although the Duke of Urbino said that Florence would be stronger with the *borghi*,* if they but knew how to fortify them. They were recruiting up to ten thousand footsoldiers, and obstinately preparing for defense even though they could see no aid whatever in the offing since they placed little faith in the Venetians who had promised to help them with three thousand footsoldiers.

. . .

While these matters were being prepared on every side, the Emperor left Barcelona with a great fleet of ships and galleys on which there were a thousand horsemen and nine thousand footsoldiers. Then after having sailed for fifteen days, not without travails and danger, he arrived on the 12th of August at Genoa, where he learned of the treaty drawn up at Cambrai; and at the same time in Lombardy, Captain Felix with eight thousand Germans entered his service and pay. The Emperor's arrival with such great apparatus of war terrified all of Italy, already certain of having been left as prey by the King of France. Therefore the Flor-

* Populated sections immediately outside the walls.

entines, dismayed at the news, elected four ambassadors among the leading citizens of the city to go to the Emperor and congratulate him on his arrival, and seek to settle their affairs. But afterward, steadily regaining their courage, they modified these instructions, restricting them solely to deal with the Emperor concerning their own interests and not to discuss their differences with the Pope: in the hope that because of the memory of things past, and the small confidence which usually exists between popes and emperors, Charles would consider his power threatened, and would have very little desire to augment the power of the Church by adding to it the authority and forces of the state of Florence. The Venetians were very much displeased that although the Florentines were allies of theirs, they had sent ambassadors to their common enemy, without their participation; and the Duke of Ferrara also complained about it, although following their example he also sent ambassadors immediately; and the Venetians gave their consent that the Duke of Milan do the same. A long time before, the Duke had held secret meetings with the Pope to bring him to an agreement with the Emperor, knowing even before Saint Pôl's overthrow that he could hope for very little from the French King and the Venetians.

. . .

The Florentines continued their preparations, having tried in vain to get the Emperor to halt his armies until he had heard their ambassadors. They demanded that Don Ercole d'Este, first-born of the oldest son of the Duke of Ferrara, who had contracted six months before to serve as their captain-general, come with his troops as he was bound to do. But although Ercole had accepted the money sent to him to raise one thousand foot-soldiers chosen to serve as his guard while on the march, nevertheless, because his father set considerations of state ahead of fidelity, he refused to come, and did not even return the money (although he sent his cavalry): whence the Florentines canceled the contract for the second year.

. . .

When the Florentine ambassadors presented themselves to the Emperor, in their first meeting they congratulated him on his arrival, and attempted to make him understand that the city of Florence was not ambitious but grateful for benefits received, and ready to ease the path of anyone who would take it under his protection. They also offered their excuses that the city of Florence had entered into league with the King of France, at the will of the Pope who commanded them at that time, and had continued in this league out of necessity. But they proceeded no further, because they were not commissioned to conclude any agreements but simply to give notice of their proposals, and they were under express command of the Republic not to lend ear to any negotiations with the Pope; and they could visit his other legates but not the Cardinal de' Medici.

The Grand Chancellor, newly elected cardinal, replied that it was necessary for them to satisfy the Pope; and when they complained about the injustice of such a demand, he responded that since the city had been in league with the Emperor's enemies and had dispatched forces against him, it had lost its privileges and devolved upon the empire, and that therefore the Emperor Charles could dispose of it at his own will. Finally they were told in the Emperor's name that they should procure a mandate enabling them to meet also with the Pope, and that then the differences with the Pope and themselves might be attended to. For if these differences were not first composed, the Emperor did not want to deal with them with regard to his own interests.

The Florentines sent them very broad instructions to meet with the Emperor, but not with the Pope. However, since Charles had left Genoa on the 30th of August and gone to Piacenza, the Florentine ambassadors followed him there, but they were not admitted into Piacenza, since it was understood they did not possess a mandate in the form which Charles had requested. Thus matters remained unresolved.

. .
.

Meanwhile the Pope was negotiating a peace treaty between the Emperor and the Venetians, in the hope of bringing it to a conclusion when the Emperor arrived at Bologna. For at first they had arranged to meet at Genoa, and then by common consent, had postponed their meeting for Bologna because it was a more convenient place. Not only was their common desire to confirm and better consolidate their union an inducement for them to be together, but also such a meeting was a necessity for the Emperor because he wanted to receive the imperial crown, while the Pope for his part was very eager to push ahead his Florence enterprise. Both of them were desirous of giving some shape to Italian affairs (which could not be done without settling the Venetian situation and that of the Duke of Milan); and also they wanted to make provisions against the imminent danger of the Turk, who had entered with an enormous army into Hungary and was marching toward Austria to attack Vienna.

The Prince of Orange Continues His March Toward Florence, and the Florentines Prepare to Defend Their City Against the Joint Forces of Pope and Emperor

[W<small>HILE</small> Cortona and Arezzo surrendered to the imperials] the Emperor meanwhile had explicitly declared that he would no longer give audience to the Florentine ambassadors unless they placed the Medici back in power; and Orange, although he openly and scornfully expressed to the ambassadors delegated to him how much he detested the Pope's cupidity and the injustice of this undertaking, yet he had made it clear that he could not help but carry it on unless the Medici were restored. Taking a roll of his troops, he found that he had 300 men-at-arms, 500 light horse, 2500 Germans, picked troops; 2000 Spanish infantry, 3000 Italians under Sciarra Colonna, Piermaria Rosso, Pierluigi da Farnese and Giovambattista Savello (later joined by Giovanni da Sassatello, who had fraudulently taken money from the Florentines with whom he had previously signed a contract) and also Alessandro Vitelli with 3000 foot-soldiers.

But since the Prince of Orange had few artillery pieces, he besought the Sienese to lend him some of theirs. The Sienese could not deny the Emperor's army the aid requested, but because of their hatred for the Pope, and for fear of his greatness, discontented by the change of the Florentine government, with whom they had had for many months an almost tacit peace and understanding growing out of their common hatred against the Pope, they provided the artillery but dallied as long as they could.

In the meantime, the Pope had heard the Florentine ambassadors and replied to them that his intention was not to alter the liberty of the city, but that he had been forced to embark on this course of action not so much because of the harm which that government had done him and the necessity of assuring his own state of affairs, but because of the agreement which he had reached with the Emperor. And now concerned with the interests of his honor, he was asking nothing except that the city should freely place itself back into his power, and that having done this, it would demonstrate its good intentions for the benefit of their common fatherland. And when later, the Pope understood that the Florentines were ever more fearful, especially after they had learned of the Emperor's dismissal of their ambassadors, and had elected new ambassadors to him, thinking they were disposed to yield to him, and anxious for a quick settlement to avoid destruction of the country, he dispatched the Archbishop of Capua posthaste to the army. Passing through Florence, the Archbishop found the disposition of the citizens different from that which the Pontiff had convinced himself was the case.

Meanwhile the Prince of Orange marched ahead; on the 24th of September he was at Montevarchi in Valdarno,* twenty-five miles from Florence, waiting for eight cannon from Siena, which were dispatched the following day; but since they were brought with the same delaying tactics by which they had been prepared, the Prince, who had brought his army up to Feghine and Ancisa by the 27th, had to remain in those quarters until the end of the 4th of October: from which the difficulty of that entire undertaking ensued.

For after the loss of Arezzo, the Florentines saw that all the hopes and promises which had been made to them on all sides were lacking, and that the fortifications of the city being constructed on the side of the mountain** were not yet carried far enough ahead that, in the opinion of military leaders, they could be placed in a defensible condition before eight or ten days, even though they might work on them with the greatest speed. And when they also learned that the enemy army was marching ahead, and from Bologna, Ramazzotto with three thousand footsoldiers had entered into action on orders of the Pope, and had sacked Firenzuola and marched into the Mugello, and fearing that he would go to Prato, the terrified citizens began to incline toward an agreement, especially because many of them had fled out of fear;*** so that during the consultations of the Council of the Ten,**** which deals with matters of defense, and in which leading citizens of that government participated, it was unanimously agreed that a mission with broad flexible powers be sent to

---

* Valley of the Arno.
** The southern hills of the city: on the ridge of San Miniato.

*** Among these Michelangelo Buonarroti, the artist, governor of fortifications, who later alleged that, suspecting that Malatesta, captain of the Florentines, would betray the city (which he subsequently did), he had complained in vain to the Gonfaloniere Carducci. Michelangelo also charged inadequacies and irregularities in the fortifications being built from San Miniato to San Niccolò. The artist fled shortly after the 10th of September, but returned between the 20th and 23rd of November (after the ban on him had been lifted) and gallantly fought out the rest of the siege in his post as governor of fortifications.

Guicciardini was placed under a similar ban on 17 March 1530 for plotting against the republic. The historian had already left Florence when the advent to power of Carducci and the radical party rendered his position untenable. (For the full document of the decree, see Roberto Ridolfi, *Vita di Francesco Guicciardini*, Rome, 1960, pp. 491–92.)

**** Niccolò Machiavelli, who, during the second Republic, had been the brilliant secretary of this council, had died June 22, 1527, and so was spared the glory and the horror of the siege.

Florence in the sixteenth century (FROM SEBASTIAN MÜNSTER'S COSMOGRAPHIA UNIVERSALE, 1575). *The Romanesque church of San Miniato is at the extreme right, the south side of the city from which the imperial troops attacked. The fact that Münster's map shows a permanent defensive wall running from San Miniato down to the city gate proves that this map was drawn after the siege. During the siege only earthworks were constructed at that point.*

Rome, submitting themselves to the Pope's will. But when this was reported to the supreme magistracy, without whose agreement no decision could be reached, the Gonfaloniere, who was stubbornly of the opposite opinion, opposed this decision, and with him there joined the popular magistracy of the Collegi (who shared power with the Tribunes like the Roman plebians) among whom generally, as it happened, there were many evil-minded persons, of great temerity and insolence. Hence the Gonfaloniere could greatly affect decisions (his views also being instigated by the boldness and threats of many of the youth), so that he blocked any other decision on that day. Yet it is manifest that if on the following day, the 28th of September, the Prince had moved his quarters ahead, those opposing an agreement would not have been able to resist the inclination of all the rest; on such small causes so often depend the outcome of serious events.

FORTIFICATION BY MICHELANGELO

This drawing of a bastion by Michelangelo, sketched over a group of male nudes, possibly relates to fortifications at the Porta al Prato, part of the series of defense works projected by the artist during his tenure as Governor of Fortifications during the siege of Florence (COURTESY OF FRATELLI ALINARI)

The Siege of Florence Begins

F‌OR there were those who interpreted Orange's vain delay as having been done on purpose to build up his forces, because artillery wasn't necessary for him to approach Florence. Hence many people in Florence took heart again. But what was more important was that work on the fortifications, which continued without even the slightest pause, using a very great number of men, was carried forward to such a degree that before Orange moved from that encampment, the captains judged that the outworks could be defended. Therefore any inclination toward agreement ceased, and the city stubbornly prepared to defend itself.

Also helping to reassure them was the fact that Ramazzotto, who had brought with him peasants without money and not soldiers, had come not with an intention to fight, but to steal; for when he had sacked the entire Mugello, he retreated into Bolognese territory with his booty, breaking up all his troops who had sold him most of the things they had plundered. Thus instead of an easy war, which would have ended with little harm to anyone, there resulted a most grave and pernicious war which could not be brought to an end until the entire country was laid waste, and the city brought to the brink of utter ruin.

On the 5th of October, Orange set forth from Feghine; but he marched so slowly, because he was waiting for the Sienese artillery which was approaching, that he did not lead all his forces and artillery into Piano di Ripoli, two miles from Florence, until the 20th. On the 24th, he quartered his entire army on the hills near the line of fortifications extending from the gate of San Miniato and covering the highest hills of the city up to the gate of San Giorgio; and also a wing from San Miniato descended to just above the road leading to the gate of San Niccolò.

Within Florence there were eight thousand footsoldiers, in good spirits; and their resolution was to defend Prato, Pistoia, Empoli, Pisa and Livorno, all of which towns they had sufficiently garrisoned, and to leave the remaining places to the fidelity and disposition of their people and to the strength of their position, rather than to send a great many soldiers to defend them.

But already the entire country was overflowing with adventurers and plunderers, and the Sienese were not only pillaging for everybody but even sending troops to occupy Montepulciano, hoping that the Prince would subsequently allow them to keep it; but since there were several

PANORAMA OF FLORENCE DURING THE SIEGE
OF THE PRINCE OF ORANGE

Fresco by Giorgio Vasari in the Palazzo Vecchio of Florence (COURTESY OF FRATELLI ALINARI)

Florentine footsoldiers there, the town easily defended itself; and a little later Napoleone Orsini, enlisted by the Florentines, arrived there with three hundred cavalrymen, who had not wanted to depart from Rome until the Pope had set out for Bologna.

When the Prince of Orange had encamped his army and spread it out widely atop the hills of Montici, del Gallo, and Giramonte, and had gotten sappers and some small artillery pieces from the Lucchese, he ordered a redoubt built to attack (it was believed) the bastion of San Miniato. In order to knock out the Prince's emplacement, the other side planted four cannon on an earthwork in the garden of San Miniato. The towns of Colle and San Gimigniano immediately surrendered to the Prince, important places for facilitating supplies coming from Siena.

On the 29th, the Prince of Orange planted four cannon on a bastion of Giramonte to destroy the campanile of San Miniato, because his army had suffered greatly from a falconet which was mounted there; and in a few hours two of the Prince's cannons exploded. Therefore having brought up another cannon on the following day and after having fired about one hundred fifty shots in vain and not being able to destroy the falconet, they abstained from firing any longer.

And now, since everyone concluded that attacking Florence was going to prove most difficult, especially by one army alone, the actions began to proceed slowly, rather with skirmishes than in the form of assault.

On the 2nd of November, there was a big skirmish at the bastion of San Giorgio and that of San Niccolò, and on the one above the road leading to Rome. And on the 4th of November, a culverin was planted on Giramonte aimed at the Palazzo dei Signori, but the cannon burst open at the very first shot.

And during those days the cavalry who were within the city made incursions to Valdipesa and took one hundred horse, the most useful part; and some of the Florentine arquebusiers and cavalrymen issued forth from Pontedera and captured sixty horse between Capanne and the Torre di San Romano.*

Pope and Emperor Meet at Bologna

A T that time the Pope arrived at Bologna; the Emperor, according to the tradition among great princes, came there after him; for it is a custom that when two princes must meet, the one possessing the higher dignity

---

* G.'s style in this entire passage is very reminiscent, in its day-by-day minutiae, of such diarists as Luca Landucci.

Here the aloof aristocrat descends into the streets with the *popolo minuto* and becomes a patriot.

presents himself first at the appointed place, it being adjudged a sign of reverence that he who is inferior should come to find him. The Emperor was received by the Pope with the highest honors and lodged in the same palace where they had contiguous rooms so that, from the outward signs and familiarity that appeared between them, it seemed they had always been the greatest friends and allies.

Fear of the Turkish invasion had already ceased, for their army, which had appeared together with the person of their Grand Seigneur before Vienna, wherein was a very strong garrison of German foot-soldiers, had launched several vain attacks and been repulsed with very great losses. Hence, doubting that they could capture the city, especially not having heavy artillery to batter it, and since their actions were restricted by the weather which in that region was most bitter, it being the month of October, the Turks raised their siege, not retiring to some nearby quarters, but turning toward Constantinople, a three-month march.

The Emperor was therefore relieved of this fear, which had pre-

MEETING OF POPE AND EMPEROR AT BOLOGNA

Portraits of Clement VII and Charles V from the fresco by Giorgio Vasari in the Palazzo Vecchio, Hall of Clement VII, Florence (COURTESY OF FRATELLI ALINARI)

viously induced him to come to an agreement with the Duke of Milan, despite the conquest of Pavia. The Turkish threat had also induced the Emperor to persuade the Pope to turn his thoughts in some way toward an agreement with the Florentines, so that with the stabilization of the Italian situation he could march with all his forces into Germany to help Vienna and his brother. But this fear of the Turks being gone, they began to deal with Italian affairs.

With regard to these, what was mostly of concern to the Pope was the Florentine campaign; and the Emperor was also very much inclined toward this, not only to satisfy the Pope as had been agreed according to the treaty of Barcelona, but also, since the city of Florence tended to be inclined toward devotion to the French crown, Charles took satisfaction in the idea of suppressing it. Therefore when the four Florentine ambassadors who had come to the Pope in Bologna also requested audience of the Emperor, he refused to hear them, except once, and then only when it pleased the Pontiff, from whom he also took the substance of the reply that he made to them.

Thus they determined to continue the enterprise, and because this Florentine campaign was proving to be more difficult than the Pope had expected, it was decided to summon into Tuscany those forces which were in Lombardy . . .

[*The difficult negotiations between Charles V and Pope Clement VII continue at Bologna through November and December, so that during that interval—while neighboring Florence is fighting for its life— Bologna is the capital of Europe. Charles wishes to settle all problems before departing northward to assist his brother, who is having trouble because of "Lutheran tumults" and indications that Suleiman and the Turks would soon return with greater forces to attack Vienna again. Not wanting to depart from Italy "leaving matters imperfect," Charles is disposed to come to an agreement not only with the Venetians but also to pardon Francesco Sforza of Milan. Thus, one by one the various states of Italy kneel to the Emperor as the ultimate arbiter of Italian destinies; Florence is utterly isolated; the subjugation of Italy to Spain is complete. An alliance of peace among Clement, Charles, Ferdinand (the Emperor's brother, King of Hungary and Bohemia), the Sforza, Mantua, Savoy, Monferrato, Urbino, Siena and Lucca is solemnly promulgated in the cathedral of Bologna the first of the new year 1530.*]

BOOK

20

THE AFORESAID TREATY OF PEACE AND CONFED-
ERATION HAD PUT AN END TO THE LONG AND
GRAVE WARS WHICH HAD CONTINUED FOR MORE
than eight years with so many horrible occurrences, and now Italy remained entirely free of tumults and dangers of arms, with the exception
of the city of Florence. For its war had served to maintain peace among
the others, but peace among the others aggravated its war.

For when the difficulties being discussed were to some degree digested
so that there seemed no doubt that an agreement would be reached, the
Emperor, removing his forces from the state of the Venetians, sent four
thousand German footsoldiers, twenty-five hundred Spanish footsoldiers,
eight hundred Italians and more than three hundred light horse, with
twenty-five artillery pieces to the war against the Florentines.

In this war, meanwhile, very few actions were taking place, nor
scarcely worthy of being written about, since those outside the walls
lacked courage to storm the city, and those within were not ready to
tempt fortune. For they felt they could hold out for many months, and
hoped that either for lack of money or other reasons, the enemy would
not long stay there.

. .
.

At the end of this year the Pope, at the request of Malatesta Baglioni,
who offered him hopes of an agreement, sent the Bishop of Faenza,
Ridolfo Pio, to Florence, but indirectly to him. The Bishop and Malatesta
discussed various matters, partly with the city's knowledge and for its
benefit, and partly secretly by Malatesta against the city. But these talks
had no effect. Indeed, it was believed that Malatesta, whose term of service
was drawing to a close, had cunningly arranged these conferences in order
that the Florentines would rehire him with the title of captain-general,
out of fear that he would abandon them; and he obtained his end.

. .
.

With the onset of the year 1530, the siege continued. And although Orange, beginning new earthworks and trenches, made a show of wishing to advance to batter the bastions, especially those of San Giorgio which were very sturdy, yet partly because of his lack of skill, and partly because of the innate difficulty, he did not put any of his plans into execution. On Stefano Colonna rested the responsibility of guarding all the heights.

Charles Is Crowned by the Pope at Bologna

The Pontiff and the Emperor decided to go to Siena to facilitate their war against Florence from a closer vantage, and then to transfer to Rome for the ceremony of the crowning. But just as they were about to depart (whether a true or feigned decision), letters arrived from Germany urgently requesting Charles to betake himself there, the electors and princes requesting his presence with regard to the Diet; Ferdinand, to be elected King of the Romans; the others with respect to the council.

Therefore, giving up his idea of going ahead, Charles took the imperial crown in Bologna on Saint Matthew's day, in the sight of great throngs but with very little pomp and expenditures—a day most propitious for the Emperor, for on that day he had been born, on that day he had taken the King of France prisoner, on that day he assumed the signs and ornaments of the imperial dignity.*

The Siege of Florence Continues

The imperial forces gave many indications of wanting to attack the city. Therefore the defenders worked on the trenches before the bastion of San Giorgio where, on the 21st of March, a sizeable skirmish took place, the attackers suffering rather heavy losses. On the 25th, the Prince of Orange struck the tower alongside the bastion of San Giorgio toward the Porta Romana, because his army was being heavily hit from that point, but finding it solid, he halted the attack after many cannonades. And since there were no other wars or booty in Italy, every day new forces were being added; from Siena came Captain [Fabrizio] Maramaldo** with two thousand footsoldiers, against the Pope's wishes.

* Charles was the last Emperor to be crowned by the Pope's hands.

** Greatly feared imperial captain who was infamous during the sack of Rome for exacting ransoms from the cardinals. Apparently this ally was too much even for Pope Clement.

The city of Volterra had surrendered to the Pontiff. But since the fortress held out for the Florentines, it was attacked in the name of the imperials by two cannons and three culverins which had arrived from Genoa. The Florentines, wishing to save the fortress, sent one hundred and fifty horsemen and five platoons of footsoldiers to Empoli, who issued forth by night and passed by the camp near Mount Oliveto; being discovered, cavalry was sent out after them, and overtook them, but were defeated by the arquebusiers and retired with some losses. The horsemen who had left Florence arrived safely, at the same time as the footsoldiers, at Empoli where they were received by Francesco Ferrucci, governor of that place. Ferrucci had been sent at the beginning of the war by the Florentines, with a few horsemen and very little authority, but during the progress of the war, taking advantage of that site and the frequent occa-

CONQUEST OF THE CASTLE OF EMPOLI

Fresco by school of Vasari in the Palazzo Vecchio, Florence. Note the placement of artillery behind defense works that seem like huge wicker baskets, and the typical conical tents of the period. (COURTESY OF FRATELLI ALINARI)

sions to seize booty, he had put together a good number of picked troops: who esteemed him so much for his bravery and generosity, that Ferrucci and his forces aroused no little hopes among the Florentines.

Ferrucci therefore left Empoli with two thousand footsoldiers and five hundred horsemen; and marching very swiftly, entered into the fortress of Volterra on the 26th of April at the twenty-first hour;* and after the soldiers had rested, they immediately attacked the town, guarded by Giovambattista Borghese with a small number of footsoldiers, and took two trenches before nightfall; with the result that on the following morning the city surrendered, and Ferrucci got the artillery that had come from Genoa . . .

On the 9th of May, there was a great skirmish outside the Porta Romana: the dead and wounded of those within the walls amounting to one hundred and thirty, those outside more than two hundred; amongst whom was Captain Baragnino, a Spaniard.

The Florentines were still hopeful of receiving some help from the King of France, who continued to promise them great reinforcements and help once he had recovered his children. In the meanwhile, to keep their hopes alive, he had assigned twenty thousand ducats to Florentine merchants, owed to them long before, in order that they might lend the money to the city; this money was brought to Pisa by Luigi Alammani, but at sundry times, so that it bore little fruit. Giampaolo da Ceri also came to Pisa, hired by the Florentines to guard that city.

But the conquest of Volterra generated much greater harm among the Florentines; for contrary to his commission, Ferrucci had left a small guard there in order that he might leave Volterra with more forces and be more certain of the fortress of Empoli. The result was that the imperials took courage to attack Volterra, came there into the field and captured it by force and sacked it. The loss of Volterra afflicted the Florentines more than anything that had happened in that war; for having planned to send large forces of new troops into that place, they hoped to create great difficulties for the army quartered along that part of the Arno, because of the very great importance of Volterra's strategic situation, thereby opening the supply line to the city which was already suffering very greatly from lack of food.

And now was added a new reason to deprive them even further of the hopes they had entertained. For at the beginning of June, the King of France paid the ransom to the Emperor, according to their agreement, and received his children back. And instead of the great aid which he had always said he had reserved until that time, he sent at the request of the Pontiff (who, in order to ingratiate himself entirely with the King's

---

* Three hours before nightfall.

ministers, had created a cardinal of the Bishop of Tarbes, ambassador resident in his court) Pierfrancesco da Pontriemoli, whom he greatly trusted, into Italy to work out the details of an agreement with the Florentines. For this reason the Florentines lost all hope of any help from the French King.

Furthermore, that King together with the King of England were now joined, and doing all they could to win over the Pope so that they might hope to separate him from the Emperor. And therefore the King of France was striving to play some role and participate to some degree in making Florence fall into the Pope's power.

. .
.

Meanwhile the shortage of food supplies became ever more acute in Florence, where victuals were no longer entering from anywhere. Yet the stubborn will to resist did not diminish. And Ferrucci having gone from Volterra to Pisa and gathering as many footsoldiers as he could, all hopes of the Florentines now rested on his arrival. For they had ordered him to set forth and come to them by whatever road and no matter what peril, planning, as soon as he had joined his forces with those in Florence, to sally forth to combat with the enemy. The success of this scheme turned out no more happily than the resolution was rash, if one may call rash those decisions spurred by dire necessity. For Ferrucci would have to pass through enemy country, occupied by a very powerful army, although dispersed in various places. The Prince of Orange taking part of his army, and gathering up more bands of Italian footsoldiers, went forth to encounter Ferrucci. Meanwhile, as the Florentines suspected, the Prince had the secret pledge of Malatesta Baglioni, with whom he was in very close contact, that in his absence the army would not attack. Therefore the Prince of Orange went to meet Ferrucci; and finding him near Gavinana in the mountains of Pistoia (which road he had taken passing from Pisa near Lucca, out of confidence in the Chancellor's faction which was friendly to the popular government), he attacked him with greatly superior forces. At the first charge, the Prince acting rather like a man-at-arms than a captain, foolhardily rushed ahead and was slain. Nevertheless, his soldiers won the victory, and among many others taken prisoner were Giampaolo da Ceri and Ferrucci, who was murdered while captive by Fabrizio Maramaldo, out of hatred (it was said) aroused in him when, during the siege of Volterra, Ferrucci had hanged one of Fabrizio's trumpeters who had been sent as a herald into the city with a message.

The Florentines Are Forced to Capitulate, and the Medici Return to Power

Thus the Florentines were abandoned of all help divine or human, and the famine spread without any hope whatever of further alleviation. Nevertheless the stubbornness of those opposed to an accord, grew even greater. For they were driven by ultimate desperation: unwilling that their own downfall should occur without the slaughter of their country, and no longer seeking means whereby they or other citizens might die to save their country, but that the country might perish together with them. They were also followed by many who were convinced that the miraculous help of God was bound to reveal itself, but not until matters were brought to such a pitch that almost no courage remained. And there was danger lest the war end with the utter extermination of that city, because the magistrates shared in that stubbornness, as did almost all those who held the reins of public authority in their hands. Thus no place remained for the others who felt otherwise but dared not express their opposition for fear of the magistrates and armed threats.

But Malatesta Baglioni, realizing that the situation was beyond remedy, practically forced them to come to an agreement; motivated perhaps by pity at seeing so distinguished a city totally perish because of the fury of its citizens, and the dishonor and damage that would ensue for him were he present at a scene of such ruination. But an even greater motive, it was believed, was his hope of obtaining from the Pope, through his accord, the right to return to Perugia.

Therefore, while the magistrates and other more impassioned citizens were trying to convince the troops to issue forth from the city to fight with the enemy, who were much greater in numbers and quartered at strong points, Malatesta refused, and their folly went so far that he was dismissed as captain and several of the more pertinacious citizens were sent to advise him of his dismissal and order him to leave the city with his troops. Malatesta became so agitated at this notice that he stabbed one of the messengers with a poignard, so that the bystanders scarcely managed to get him alive out of his hands. This episode frightened the others, and now the city was beginning to rise. Those who were less furibond restrained the rash Gonfaloniere, who armed himself, now saying that he wanted to attack Malatesta, now that he would issue forth to fight the enemy, until finally the extreme obstinacy of many yielded to the extreme necessity of all.

Thus, four ambassadors having been sent on the 9th of August to

Don Ferrando da Gonzaga, who after the Prince's death commanded the army (for the Marquis del Guasto had departed long before), an accord was reached on the following day. According to this treaty, besides obligating the city to pay eighty thousand ducats in a very few days in order that the army be withdrawn, the principal articles were: that the Pope and the city would give the Emperor power to declare within three months what the form of the government should be, safeguarding, however, their liberty; that all outrages and abuses committed against the Pope and his friends and servitors would be pardoned; and that until the Emperor's declaration arrived, Malatesta Baglioni was to remain in charge of the city with two thousand footsoldiers.

This agreement having been reached while they were gathering up the money to give to the army, whereof there was need for a far greater sum since the Pope was not very ready to help the city with money at a time of such danger, the Apostolic Commissioner, Bartolomeo Valori, came to an agreement with Malatesta, who was entirely intent on returning to Perugia; convoked the people in the piazza, according to the ancient tradition of the city to hold a parliament; and the magistrates and the others yielding to this out of fear, he introduced a new form of government. The parliament delegated authority to twelve citizens of the Medici faction to reorganize the city government as they saw fit; they returned it to that form which it used to have before the year 1527.

Afterward the army, having received its money, left the city; the Italian captains, in order to use the money for their own purposes and not pay the soldiers with it, to the great ignominy of the militia, withdrew with their money into Florence and dismissed the footsoldiers with very meager pay. The result was that these soldiers remaining without leaders dispersed in various parts; and the army of the Spaniards and Germans, paid in full, and having left vacant all the Florentine towns and dominion, went into the territory of Siena to reorganize the government of that city; and Malatesta Baglioni, the Pope having agreed on his return to Perugia, did not wait for the Emperor's declaration, but left the city entirely at the disposal of the Pope.

As soon as all the soldiers had departed, tortures and persecutions of citizens began in Florence; for those who had the government in their hands—partly to strengthen the state, partly because of the hatred stirred up against the authors of so many evils, and memory of abuses personally received, but principally because such was the Pope's intention (although he made it known to few)—so interpreted the matter (observing perhaps the surface meaning of the words but leaping over the sense), that the article, whereby pardon was promised to those who had harmed the Pope and his friends, did not cancel the wrongs and crimes committed by them in matters concerning the Republic.

Therefore, the examination having been put into the hands of the magistrates, six of the leaders were decapitated, others imprisoned and a very great number banished. This weakened the city even more, and those who had participated in these things were reduced to even more dire necessity, while the power of the Medici remained freer and more absolute and practically regal in that city, bereft of money as a result of so long and dreadful a war, deprived of many of its inhabitants, both within and without the walls, its houses lost, its goods and property elsewhere destroyed, and more than ever divided against itself—all this poverty made it all the more necessary to provide, for many more years, for their supplies from towns outside. For that year there had been neither harvest nor seed time, and the disorders of that year spread over the following years; with the result that more money left the city, afflicted and weakened as it was, for the purpose of buying grain in distant places and livestock outside of the dominion, than had been expended for so grave and so costly a war.

Call for a Universal Council to Correct the Abuses of the Roman Curia

MEANWHILE, in Germany the Emperor had convoked the Diet in Augsburg, and had had his brother Ferdinand elected King of the Romans. And with regard to the Lutherans, suspicious even of the power of the princes, and divided because of the great numbers and ambition of their followers, into various heresies almost contrary one to the other and to Martin Luther, author of this pestilence (whose life and authority were no longer of any importance, so widespread and rooted was this poison), there occurred no better remedy to the German princes than the convocation of a universal council. Even the Lutherans were urging that such a council be called, wishing to cast a mantle of religion over their cause. And it was believed that the authority of the decrees issued by such a council would be sufficient, if not to purge the souls of the heretical leaders of their errors, at least to bring back part of the multitude to sounder judgment. Besides, in Germany even those who were following Catholic opinions greatly desired a council in order to reform the exactions and excessive abuses committed by the Roman Curia. For what with the power of indulgences, and their liberality with dispensations, and their desire for the annual revenues of benefices conferred, and the outlays for sending those benefices heaping up in the offices endlessly multiplying in the papal court, it seemed they thought of nothing else but to extort great sums of money from all Christendom by these means; not having in the meanwhile any concern whatever for the salvation of souls, or that ecclesiastical matters should be correctly governed.

For many incompatible benefices were conferred upon one and the same person, or without any respect whatever for men's merits, benefices were distributed by favor either to persons incapacitated by age, or to men entirely lacking in theological learning or secular attainments and (what was worse) often upon persons of the very basest morals.

The Emperor wished to satisfy this request in which all Germany joined; and also because it was useful to his intentions in that province to placate the sources of agitation and contumacy among the people. Therefore he greatly insisted on it with the Pope, reminding him of their discussions at Bologna and urging that he summon the council, promising him (that he need not fear having to place his power and dignity in peril) that he (the Emperor) would be present to take particular care of the Pope's interests.

Nothing displeased the Pope more than this, but in order to maintain esteem for his good intentions, he concealed his attitude or his various objections. For one thing, he feared in effect that the council might diminish pontifical power too much in order to moderate the great abuses of the Curia and the indiscreet concessions of many popes. Or else he remembered that, although when he was promoted to the cardinalate witnesses had been brought forth to prove that his birth was legitimate, in truth it was the contrary; and although there was no written law prohibiting the papacy to those born in this condition, nevertheless it was an inveterate and commonly held opinion that whoever was not legitimate could not even be created a cardinal. Or he was aware that he had been assumed to the pontificate not without some suspicion of simony practiced in conjunction with Cardinal Colonna. Or he suspected that the great severity which he had employed against his country, amidst so many tumults of war, might not stain him with indelible shame before such a council, especially since the results proved that he had not been moved, as was at first announced, by a desire to bring back the city of Florence to a good moderate government, but rather by greed to make it return under the tyranny of his family.

Therefore, abhorring the idea of a council, nor considering the Emperor's pledge sufficient, discussing these matters with the cardinals deputized to deal with such problems, and they also suspecting the reforms such a council might introduce, the Pope replied, setting forth many reasons whereby it was not opportune to deal with this, since a stable peace among Christian princes was not yet in view, and it was to be feared lest the Turk should stir again, nor would it be useful that they find Christendom involved in the disputes and contentions of the council.

Nevertheless, pretending to leave the matter to the Emperor's judgment, he concluded that he would be content if he would promise the indication* of a council in the Diet, provided that it be held in Italy and in his presence, due time being assigned for assembling it; and that the Lutherans and other heretics should promise to abide by the decisions of the council, and meanwhile desist from their corruptions, and should live as they used to, as Christian Catholics, rendering their obedience to him in possession of the Apostolic See. This made the entire organization of the council difficult; for the Lutherans not only would not desist in their opinions and rites before the celebration of the council, but it was commonly believed that they abhorred the idea of the council, since they could not expect anything from it other than reprobation of their opinions (insofar as most of these opinions, the main ones, had been repeatedly condemned as heretical by older councils), but were demanding the convocation because, knowing that the Pope was so frightened of it, they were convinced that it would not be called, and thus they could maintain their cause among the people with even more prestige.

. . .

Amidst such agitations ended the year 1530, succeeded by the year 1531 during which there were very few actions. For although there were many indications that led one to understand that the King of France was discontented with the agreement drawn up with the Emperor, and most eager for new tumults, and that the King of England was also of a like inclination, since he was angry with Charles who, by defending his mother's sister was opposing the divorce, nevertheless, since the King of France had no funds, nor was yet recuperated from the travails of such long wars, the time was not yet opportune to arouse innovations. Meanwhile he applied himself to working out agreements with those princes in Germany opposed to the Emperor, as well as with the Pope in Italy, proposing, for the purpose of winning him over, a contract of matrimony between his second son and the Pope's niece; and (to the greater offense of God, and the horrible shame of the French crown, which had always made its principal profession in defending the Christian religion, for which merits the title of Christianissimo had been conferred upon it) holding dealings with the Prince of the Turks to stir him up against the Emperor, toward whom he [Suleiman] was usually ill-disposed, whether out of natural hatred against Christians or because of the controversy which he had with his brother, namely the questions over the kingdom of Hungary

---

* "A cycle of fifteen years, introduced by Constantine as a fiscal term, and adopted by the popes as part of their chronological system." (Funk and Wagnall's New College Standard Dictionary).

with the Vaivoda*, whom he had taken under his protection; and also because he was beginning to distrust the Emperor's power.

. .
.

At this time the Emperor set forth the form of the government of Florence, concealing that part of the authority given him which limited certain infringements on their liberty. For according to the very instructions which the Pope had sent him, he stated that the city should be governed by those magistrates, and in that manner, in which it used to be governed at the time the Medici ruled, and that Alessandro, the Pope's nephew and the Emperor's son-in-law, should be head of the government, and in the event of his death, his children and closest descendants in the same family should succeed one after the other. He restored all the privileges to the city conceded to it at other times by himself and his predecessors, but on condition that they would be void any time they attempted anything against the greatness of the Medici family; in the entire decree he inserted words which showed that he was basing himself not only on the power conceded to him by the parties, but also on his imperial authority and dignity.

. .
.

There were no other troubles this year of 1531; and this tranquility continued also the next year, which was more dangerous because of foreign wars than because of any movements in Italy. For burning with shame because they had been repulsed at Vienna, and understanding that the Emperor was in Germany, the Turks prepared a very mighty army, multiplying their provisions and giving notice that they intended to unleash war to force the Emperor to try a battle with them. The news of these preparations caused the Emperor to set his forces in as good order as he could, even ordering the Marquis del Guasto to march into Germany with Spanish troops and a great band of Italian horsemen and infantry; and the Pope promised to help him with forty thousand ducats every month, and sent the Cardinal de' Medici, his nephew, as apostolic legate to this expedition; and the princes and free towns of Germany prepared a very great army in favor of the Emperor and for the common defense of Germany.

But the results were very dissimilar than the rumors and terror. For Suleiman entered late into Hungary, not having been able to arrive sooner

---

* Properly, a leader of an army; in this case, the military commander or ruler of Moldavia and Wallachia. The Vaivoda referred to was John Zapolya, who had been elected King of Transylvania in 1526 by the anti-Hapsburg party, and hence was disposed to ally himself with the Turk.

THE AMBASSADORS

Painted by Hans Holbein the Younger in 1533 (or 1537). Various interpreta-
tions have been put to the weird foreshortened skull in the lower center. The
two persons represented have been identified as Jean de Dinteville, French
ambassador to England in 1532–33, and his friend Georges de Selve, Bishop
of Lavour, ambassador to Charles V. The variety of instruments on the shelves
—an armillary sphere, a rudimentary quadrant, a handheld globe, a lute, etc.—
bears witness to a typical wide range of Renaissance interests. (COURTESY OF
FRATELLI ALINARI)

because of his huge war machine and the great distance of the march, and
did not go directly with his army toward the Emperor but simply made
a show of war and a great incursion, after which he returned to Constantinople.

    Nor for his part had the Emperor showed any great readiness either,
for having learned of the Turks' approach, he did not sally forth to meet

them; and when he learned of their retreat he had not considered pursuing with all his forces this opportunity of capturing Hungary for his brother; but so eager was he to return to Spain that he ordered the Italian footsoldiers and a certain number of Germans to undertake the Hungarian campaign. But this plan also fell into disorder, for the Italian footsoldiers, stirred up by some of their leaders who saw other captains set ahead of them in this campaign, mutinied. And being unable to give reasons for their tumult, and the presence of the Emperor, who went in person to speak to them, not proving sufficient to placate them, they all set forth for Italy, marching with the greatest haste for fear of being followed, and burning many villages and houses on the march as enemy territory in revenge (as they said) for the burnings which the Germans had committed in Italy.

. .
.

The Turk's departure freed Italy of the danger of imminent war. For the King of France and the King of England, full of hatred and disdain toward the Emperor, had met between Calais and Boulogne; convinced that the Turk would have to pass that winter in Hungary and thus tie down the Emperor's forces, they decided that the King of France should invade the duchy of Milan; and they were prepared to employ bitter and fearful means to draw the Pope on their side, since up to then they had not been able to succeed by any other means. Therefore, they decided to withdraw their realms from obedience to the Pope should he not consent to what they wanted, which was, in the case of the King of France, the state of Milan, and in the case of the King of England, a decision in his favor with regard to the divorce. And they had already planned to dispatch the cardinals of Tournon and Tarbes, both very high in the counsels of the French King, to the Pope with these sharp instructions. But this plan was mollified, even before the two kings departed from their meeting, by the news of the Turk's retreat. This news also interrupted the King of England's plan to have Anne Boleyn cross over to Calais in order publicly, in that assembly, to celebrate his marriage with her, notwithstanding the fact that the case was still hanging in the court of Rome, and that he was forbidden by apostolic briefs, under pain of the gravest censures, to attempt anything to the prejudice of his first marriage.

And yet the French King, to demonstrate to the King of England how ill-intentioned he was toward the Roman Church, although his intention was to win the Pope over by gentle means, imposed by his own authority a tithe upon the clergy of the entire realm of France, and sent both cardinals to the Pope but with very different commissions than those originally planned.

. .
.

The Emperor came to Italy, and wishing to speak with the Pope, Bologna was once more chosen as their meeting place. The Pope most willingly accepted this in order not to afford any excuse for the Emperor Charles to go to the kingdom of Naples, as many of his counselors were advising him to do, thus remaining and thereby staying longer in Italy. But Charles was also opposed to this, since he was very eager to go to Spain for various reasons, but mainly because of his desire to procreate sons, his wife having remained there.

Therefore, Pope and Emperor met at the end of the year in Bologna where both of them observed the same outward shows of amity and familiarity which they had demonstrated the other time. But during the negotiations their minds were no longer in harmony as they had been before. For Charles was very eager for the council to satisfy the Germans, and bring about peace there. He declared that he wanted to dissolve the army which was a heavy burden both upon him and the others, but in order to do so safely, he insisted they renew their last alliance drawn up in Bologna to include everyone within it, and to tax the sums of money which everyone would have to contribute should Italy be attacked by the French. He also wanted the Pope's niece Catherine [de' Medici] to be married to Francesco Sforza, either to make it more necessary for the Pope to look after the preservation of that state, or to interrupt the marriage dealings being negotiated with the French King.

None of these things pleased the Pope: confederation was contrary to his desire to maintain himself as neutral as possible among Christian princes, fearful as he was of other dangers, and especially that the King of France would cease to pay obedience to him, goaded thereto primarily by the King of England. As for the council, he was strongly opposed to it for long-standing reasons. Nor was a family alliance with the Duke of Milan to his liking, for fear that it would create an almost open rupture with the King of France, and because he ardently desired to marry his niece to the King's second son.*

. .
.

The Emperor departed from Bologna the day after the alliance was stipulated, already rather certain that the marriage [of Catherine de' Medici with the French King's son] and the meeting with the King of France would go ahead, and suspecting furthermore some broader agreement between them. Embarking at Genoa, he sailed to Spain with the rather firm intention (so it was said) that if the family alliance with the French King

* The future Henry II. Guicciardini was one of Pope Clement's major negotiators at this second Bologna conference.

should be contracted, then that of his daughter with Alessandro de' Medici would not take place.

A few days later the Pope departed for Rome, accompanied by the two French cardinals, not at all disturbed by the new confederation; for the Pope, who was excellent in deceptions and manipulations when he was not overcome by fear, had shown them that the conclusion of the league would lead to the disbanding of the Spanish army, which would do the French King more good than the drawing up of the confederation could do him harm; especially since between the obligations of the confederation and the observances and executions thereof, many difficulties and various impediments might arise.

Thus they continued the negotiations already under way between them; and since the King, for his own honor and ambition more than for anything else, wanted the Pope to go to Nice, he promised (to draw him thither) not to drag him into war, not to attempt to deflect him from just limits with regard to the divorce of the King of England, and not to demand of him any new creations of cardinals. He was also greatly pushed on by the King of England [to make these commitments]. For having secretly made his mistress pregnant, the King had solemnly contracted marriage with her, in order to conceal the shame before it should be known; and shortly thereafter having had a daughter,* he had declared her, in prejudice to the daughter he had had by his first wife, Princess of the Realm of England, a title possessed by those first in the order of succession.

The Pope could not shut his eyes to such contempt for the Apostolic See, nor deny justice to the Emperor; and so with the votes of the consistory he had declared the King of England guilty of the crime of outrage.

For these reasons the King of England wanted the family alliance and meeting of the Pope with the King of France to take place, hoping that that King might serve as a means of healing the breach, and that inducing the Pope to deal with new matters against the Emperor, as he hoped, he would be forced to want the King of England included again, and draw him into their alliance; thus constituting almost a triumvirate to lay down the laws for Italian affairs.

Finally the Pope's going was decided, but not to Nice, for the Duke of Savoy raised difficulties in conceding the fortress to the Pope, in order not to displease the Emperor. The Pontiff therefore agreed to go to Marseilles; a thing greatly desired by the French King, since it was much more to his honor that the Pope be induced to meet with him in his kingdom; nor did the Pope object, wishing to satisfy him more by outward shows and gratifying his ambition than by tangible results. The

* The future Elizabeth I.

Pope strove to convince everyone that he was going to such an interview primarily to arrange for peace and make preparations for a campaign against the infidels, and to bring the King of England back on the good path, and finally, only for the interests of all.

But since he could not conceal his real reason, he sent his niece, even before his own departure, to Nice on the galleys which the King of France had sent with the Duke of Albania, the girl's uncle, to convey the Pope. After these galleys had brought the maiden to Nice, they returned to the port of Pisa where on the 4th of October the Pope and many cardinals embarked, and with very fair winds arrived at Marseilles in a few days. After he had made his solemn entry, the King of France, who had visited him before by night, followed after; and they lodged in the same palace and made many outward signs of their affection. And since the King was very intent on winning the Pope's favor, he besought him to have his niece come to Marseilles; which the Pope did most eagerly (although he had not made such a request, to show that he first wanted to deal with common problems), and when the girl arrived, the marriage was celebrated and almost immediately consummated to the incredible joy of the Pope.*

Death of Clement VII. Analysis of His Character. Election of Alessandro Farnese as Paul III

AFTER they had remained in Marseilles about a month, the Pope departed on the same galleys, and through stormy seas arrived at Savona, where having no confidence either in the provisions of the galleys or skill of the men in command, he sent them back, and was conveyed from there to Civitavecchia in the galleys of Andrea Doria. And having returned to Rome with the greatest reputation and marvelous happiness, especially in the eyes of those who had seen him prisoner in the Castel Sant' Angelo, he enjoyed very few months of fortune's favor; since he already had a presage in his soul of what was about to occur.

For it is manifest that almost immediately after his return from Marseilles, as if certain of imminent death, he had had the ring and all the other usual garments prepared which popes wear in burial; and he assured those closest to him, with a most calm spirit, that his death must occur in a very short time. And yet, not putting aside for this reason his usual thoughts and studies, he requested that a citadel stocked with am-

* Catherine was fourteen years old and Henry sixteen at the time. The Pope himself performed the ceremony (G. F.   Young, *The Medici,* New York, 1933, pp. 395-96).

munitions be built at Florence for the greater security of his house, as it seemed to him; uncertain how soon the happiness of his nephews might come to an end: of whom, mortal enemies to each other, Ippolito the Cardinal died not without suspicion of poison, less than a year after the Pope's death, and Alessandro the other nephew who ruled Florence was secretly slain by night in Florence by Lorenzo of the same Medici family, a most notorious and rash deed.

The Pope fell sick with stomach pains at the beginning of the summer, then taken with a fever, he was undone by that and other ailments over a long period, now appearing almost reduced to death's door, now regaining his forces so that he gave hope to others, but not to himself, that he would recover.

While this illness was dragging on, the Duke of Württemberg with the help of the Landgrave of Hesse and other princes, and helped by money from the King of France, recovered the duchy of Württemberg possessed by the King of the Romans. And fearing greater outbreaks, they convened with the King of the Romans against the will of the King of France, who had hoped that because of this action the Emperor would become involved in a long difficult war, or perhaps that with the victorious arms they would proceed further to stir up troubles in the duchy of Milan.

Also during this time, Barbarossa* who had become Pasha and Captain General of Suleiman's fleet moved to the conquest of the kingdom of Tunisia; but on the way he overran the coasts of Calabria and went on above Gaeta, where several of his men landed and sacked Fondi. This caused so much fear in the court and among the Romans that it is believed that had Barbarossa's men gone ahead, the city of Rome would have been abandoned. But the Pope knew nothing of this happening.

For finally, no longer able to struggle against his illness, Pope Clement VII departed from this present life on the 25th day of September; leaving in the Castel Sant' Angelo many jewels, and in the pontifical chamber a great many offices, but contrary to the opinion of all men, a very small amount of money.

A Pope who with marvelous good fortune had been exalted from base degree to the pontificate, but once in office had found fortune most variable; and if one were balanced against the other, his misfortune outweighed his prosperity. For what felicity could be compared with the infelicity of his imprisonment? With having seen the sack of Rome with such slaughter? With having been the cause of such destruction of his country?

He died hated by the court, suspected by princes, and with a reputa-

---

* Not to be confused with Frederick Barbarossa, the name refers to a family of Turkish admirals and sea rovers. This particular Barbarossa is Khizr (or Khair-ed-Din), captain pasha of Suleiman, dreaded by enemies for his active role against Christians.

tion which was rather heavy-handed and hateful than pleasing; being reputed avaricious, faithless, and not given naturally to benefit mankind.

However, although he created thirty-one cardinals during his pontificate, he did not create any for his own satisfaction, but almost always by necessity, except for the Cardinal de' Medici; whom he created rather at the suggestion of others than by his own spontaneous choice, when he was struck by a dangerous illness, and at a time when dying, he was leaving his family like beggars and devoid of any protection.

Nevertheless in his actions Pope Clement was very grave, very circumspect, very much in control of himself, and with the greatest capacity if his timidity had not often corrupted his power of judgment.

Clement having died, the cardinals on the same night that they met in conclave, unanimously elected as Supreme Pontiff, Alessandro of the Farnese family, a Roman by nation, the oldest cardinal in the court. Their votes conformed with the judgment and almost petition which Clement had made concerning Farnese, as a person worthy of being preferred over all others to so high a position. A man gifted with learning, and to all appearance good morals, who had exercised his office as cardinal with greater skill than that whereby he had acquired it; for it is certain that Pope Alexander VI had given that dignity not to him but to his sister, Madonna Giulia, an extremely beautiful young woman.

And the cardinals concurred most voluntarily in electing him because, since he was already almost a septuagenarian and considered to have a weak constitution and not in good health (which opinions were spread by him with considerable skill), they hoped that his reign as Pontiff was bound to be brief.

Whether his actions and deeds prove worthy of the expectations conceived of him, and of the immense joy with which the Roman people received the news of having a pope of Roman blood after 103 years and thirteen popes, those may bear witness who will write of what happened in Italy after his assumption. For most true and deserving of highest praise is that proverb which says that the office brings forth the worth of the person exercising it.

INDEX

INDEX

A

Adrian I, Pope, 107
Adrian VI, Pope, xxiii, xxviii, 141, 332–336, 338, 362, 410
  death of, 335
  election of, 329–331
Ahmed, Prince, 298
Alammani, Luigi, 428
Alarcon, Captain, 348, 366, 389, 390
Albania, Duke of, *see* Stuart, John
Albert I, King, 313
Albigi, Antonio Francesco degli, 263
Albret, Charlotte d', 139
Albret, Jean d', 139, 268–269
Alexander VI, Pope, 15–16, 21, 123–124, 141, 156–164, 174, 176, 297, 442
  alliance with Alfonso II, 33
  children of, 19, 28, 33, 124, 127
  death of, 165–166
  election of, 9–10
  excommunicates Savonarola, 127, 128
  flight to Orvieto, 92
  Neapolitan war treaty negotiations, 69–70
  Orsini's castle purchases and, 15–18, 20
  Venetian Senate alliance (1493), 19–20
  vices of, 10
Alexander the Great, 300, 351
Alfonso II, King of Naples, 90, 92, 163
  abdication, 71
  Neapolitan war, 22, 26, 27, 52–53, 55, 57, 66, 71
    alliance with Alexander VI, 33
    preparations, 38
    strategy, 38
Alfonso V, King of Aragon and Naples, 7, 17, 18, 19, 20, 21, 35, 133, 342
  alliance with Piero de' Medici, 10–15
  death of, 105
Allègre, Nivarais d', 249
Allègre, Yves d', 68, 249, 250
Allegri, Ivo d', 152, 156
Alva, Duke of, 343, 353–356

Alviano, Bartolommeo d', 122, 123, 167
Amboise, Charles d', 123–126, 224
  death of, 215–216
Amboise, Georges d', 139, 140
Anjou, house of, 34
  claims to kingdom of Naples, 21
Anjou, Jean d', 25, 30, 36
Anna, Duchess of Ferrara, 197
Anne of Beaujeu, 24, 133, 284
Anne of Brittany, 133, 137
Appiano, Iacopo d', 161
Aragon, Cardinal of, 33, 169
Archimedes, 50
Aremboddo, Bishop, 321
Arezzo, Bishop of, 14
Argenton, 99
Ariosti, Lorenzo degli, 225
Arithpert, King, 147
Arthur, Prince of Wales, 401
Artillery warfare, 49–52
  first Italian use of, 50
Ascanio, Cardinal, *see* Sforza, Cardinal Ascanio
Asti, Charles VIII at, 48, 49–50, 52
Attila, King of the Huns, xxiv, 35
Aubigny, Beraud, 34
Aubigny, Robert Stuart d', 50
Augsburg, Diet of, 432–434
Augustinian Order, 319
Avignon papacy, 147–148

B

Baglioni, Carlo, 271
Baglioni, Gentile, 323, 324, 386–387, 396–397
Baglioni, Giampaolo, 161, 168, 189
  expelled from Perugia, 323–324
Baglioni, Malatesta, 323, 413, 418, 425, 429, 430–431
Baglioni, Orazio, 389
Baglioni, Vitellozzo, 161
Bagnacavallo, Pocointesta da, 295
Baissey, Antoine de, 39

LIBRARY OF CONGRESS CATALOGING IN PUBLICATION DATA

Guicciardini, Francesco, 1483-1540.
   The history of Italy.

   Translation and abridgement of: Historia d'Italia.
   Previously published: New York : Macmillan, [1968,
c1969]
      1. Italy—History—1492-1559.   I. Alexander, Sydney,
1912-   . II. Title.
DG539.G813   1984   945'.06   83-43221
ISBN 0-691-05417-7 (alk. paper)
ISBN 0-691-00800-0 (pbk.)